# Occupational Health

# Occupational Health Psychology

Edited by Stavroula Leka and
Jonathan Houdmont

A John Wiley & Sons, Ltd., Publication

*To my family and my career mentors. They have all been incredible sources of support and inspiration. I am grateful to you all.*

Stavroula

*To all who have supported the development of my career in occupational health psychology, thank you.*

Jonathan

# Contents

About the Editors                                                                ix
Notes on Contributors                                                            xi
Preface                                                                         xvi

1   An Introduction to Occupational Health Psychology                             1
    *Jonathan Houdmont and Stavroula Leka*

2   Work-Related Stress: A Theoretical Perspective                               31
    *Tom Cox and Amanda Griffiths*

3   Work Organization and Health                                                 57
    *Michael P. O'Driscoll and Paula Brough*

4   Interventions to Promote Well-Being at Work                                  88
    *Raymond Randall and Karina Nielsen*

5   Psychosocial Risk Management at the Workplace Level                         124
    *Stavroula Leka and Tom Cox*

6   Workplace Health Promotion                                                  157
    *Andrew J. Noblet and John J. Rodwell*

7   Positive Occupational Health Psychology                                     194
    *Arnold B. Bakker and Daantje Derks*

8   The Physical Workspace: An OHP Perspective                                  225
    *Phil Leather, Tony Zarola, and Angeli Santos*

9   Corporate Culture, Health, and Well-Being                                   250
    *Gerard Zwetsloot and Stavroula Leka*

10 Research Methods in Occupational Health Psychology 269
*Toon W. Taris, Annet H. de Lange, and Michiel A. J. Kompier*

11 Future Directions in Occupational Health Psychology 298
*Jonathan Houdmont and Stavroula Leka*

*Author Index* 322
*Subject Index* 331

# About the Editors

**Stavroula Leka**
stavroula.leka@nottingham.ac.uk

**Jonathan Houdmont**
jonathan.houdmont@nottingham.ac.uk

*Institute of Work, Health & Organisations, University of Nottingham, International House, Jubilee Campus, Wollaton Road, Nottingham, NG8 1BB, United Kingdom*

**Stavroula Leka** BA MSc PhD PGCHE CPsychol FRSPH is Associate Professor in Occupational Health Psychology in the Institute of Work, Health & Organisations at the University of Nottingham (United Kingdom). She is director of the Institute's Masters in Occupational Health Psychology. Stavroula is a Chartered Psychologist, a Member of the British Psychological Society, the International Commission on Occupational Health, the European Association of Work & Organizational Psychology, and the European Academy of Occupational Health Psychology, and a Fellow of the Royal Society for the Promotion of Public Health. She studied psychology at the American College of Greece, followed by postgraduate studies in occupational health psychology at the Institute. Stavroula is the Director of the Institute's World Health Organization Programme. She is member of the Planning Committee of the WHO Network of

Collaborating Centres in Occupational Health and Director of its programme of work on 'Practical Approaches to Identify and Reduce Occupational Risks'. She is Chair of the Education Forum of the European Academy of Occupational Health Psychology and secretary of the scientific committee 'Work Organisation & Psychosocial Factors' of the International Commission on Occupational Health. Stavroula's main research interests are the translation of occupational health and safety knowledge and policy into practice and psychosocial risk management. Her research is well published and she has been a keynote speaker at a number of international conferences. She is coeditor of the biennial book series *Contemporary occupational health psychology: Global perspectives on research and practice*, also published by Wiley-Blackwell. Further information about Stavroula and her work can be found at www.nottingham.ac.uk/iwho/people/

**Jonathan Houdmont** BSc PGCE MSc PhD is a Lecturer in Occupational Health Psychology in the Institute of Work, Health & Organisations at the University of Nottingham (United Kingdom). He earned his BSc in Psychology at the University of Leeds, postgraduate certificate in further and adult education (PGCE) at the University of Keele, followed by an MSc and PhD in occupational health psychology at the University of Nottingham. He is director of the Institute's Masters in Workplace Health. His current research interests focus on legal and policy issues in occupational health, specifically in relation to work-related stress, and the discipline of occupational health psychology with particular emphasis on education and training. He is the author of several journal papers, edited books, chapters, and commissioned reports on these topics. Jonathan is Executive Officer of the European Academy of Occupational Health Psychology. He has been the Academy's conference coordinator, having led the delivery of international conferences in Berlin (2003), Oporto (2004), Dublin (2006), and Valencia (2008). He is coeditor of the biennial book series *Contemporary occupational health psychology: Global perspectives on research and practice*, also published by Wiley-Blackwell. Further information about Jonathan and his work can be found at www.nottingham.ac.uk/iwho/people/

# Notes on Contributors

**Arnold B. Bakker** is Professor of Work and Organizational Psychology at Erasmus University Rotterdam, The Netherlands. Arnold developed the Utrecht Work Engagement Scale (with Wilmar Schaufeli) that is currently used in 25 countries, and instigated the Job Demands-Resources model (with Eva Demerouti). His research interests include positive organizational behaviour, emotional labour, crossover, work engagement, burnout, and work–family interaction. Arnold publishes regularly in the major organizational and occupational health psychology journals. He is editor of the book *Work Engagement: A handbook of essential theory and research* (with Michael Leiter).

**Paula Brough** is an Associate Professor in Organizational Psychology at the School of Psychology, Griffith University (Australia), and Director of the Social and Organizational Psychology Research Unit. Her research encompasses the evaluation and enhancement of occupational psychological health, with particular interest in occupational stress, coping, and work-life balance. Specifically, Paula's research focuses on two main categories: (1) reducing experiences of occupational stress within the high-stress industries and (2) enhancing individual health and organizational performance. Paula is a member of journal editorial boards, serves as an academic reviewer, and regularly presents her work to both academic and industry audiences.

**Tom Cox** is Professor of Organisational Psychology and Director of the Institute of Work, Health & Organisations (IWHO), University of Nottingham (United Kingdom). His research and consultancy concerns the contribution of applied psychology to occupational health and safety with a special interest in the nature, management, and prevention of work stress and related legal and policy issues. Tom is a Non Executive Director of the Rail Safety & Standards Board, and Chair of its Advisory Committee. He is also Chair of the Board of Trustees of the CIRAS

Charitable Trust, a railway-related body for the confidential monitoring of safety incidents. Tom is currently President of the European Academy of Occupational Health Psychology. He is Managing Editor of the international quarterly *Work & Stress* and a member of the Editorial Boards of the *Journal of Occupational Health Psychology* and *Revista de Psicologia Aplicada Social*.

**Annet H. de Lange** is an Associate Professor at the Department of Social and Organizational Psychology at the University of Groningen, The Netherlands, and holds a PhD (*cum laude* doctorate) from the Radboud University of Nijmegen, The Netherlands. Her main research interests concern life-span perspectives on ageing at work, causality and longitudinal survey research, and the across-time development of the relationship between work and mental health. Her research has culminated in several honorary prizes (IBM Frye Stipendium, André Büssing Memorial Prize of the EAOHP, Stichting Praemium Erasmianum Prize (www.erasmusprijs.org), and the *Journal of Occupational Health Psychology*'s best paper of the decade award). She has published in, and reviewed for, many international journals, and is a consulting editor to the journal *Work & Stress*.

**Daantje Derks** is an Assistant Professor in Work and Organizational Psychology within the Institute for Psychology at the Erasmus University of Rotterdam (The Netherlands). She is a course director for the Minor in Work and Organizational Psychology. Her current research interests focus on the impact of computer-mediated communication on daily work life, specifically the effects of using a BlackBerry on recovery and work-home interference and impression formation around social networking sites.

**Amanda Griffiths** is Professor of Occupational Health Psychology in the Institute of Work, Health & Organisations at the University of Nottingham (United Kingdom). Her research concerns the design, organization and management of work, and its relationship with health and performance, and has been supported by organizations such as the National Institute for Health Research, Help the Aged, the BBC World Service, the British Association for Women in Policing, Shell International Exploration & Production, Ford of Europe, UNISON, the Royal College of Nursing, the British Occupational Health Research Foundation, the National Association for Colitis and Crohn's Disease, the British Government's Health & Safety Executive, the European Commission, and the World Health Organization. Current projects focus on the ageing workforce, the management of long-term health conditions, and the delivery of effective services for older patients in general hospitals.

**Michiel A. J. Kompier** has a full chair in Work and Organisational Psychology at the Radboud University of Nijmegen, The Netherlands. He heads the research programme 'Work, stress and health'. He has published many articles, books, and chapters on topics such as work stress, job design, intervention research, working time arrangements, and working conditions policies. He is past chairman of the Scientific Committee 'Work Organization and Psychosocial Factors' of the International Commission on Occupational Health, associate-editor of the *Scandinavian Journal of Work, Environment and Health,* and a member of the editorial boards of *Work & Stress,* the *Journal of Occupational Health Psychology,* and the *International Journal of Stress and Health.*

**Phil Leather** is a Reader in Occupational Psychology in the Institute of Work, Health & Organisations at the University of Nottingham (United Kingdom). He is director of the Institute's Masters degree in Occupational Psychology. Phil's current research interests fall in two principal areas: the management and control of work-related violence and the environmental psychology of the workplace and other organizational settings. The first concerns the causes and consequences of workplace violence as well as the design, delivery, and evaluation of measures taken to 'manage' it. The second research area concerns the way in which individual cognition, affect, well-being and behaviour is influenced by design characteristics of the physical environments in which we typically work. Phil's research is based upon a fundamental desire to use psychology, underpinned with sound theory and reliable evidence, to 'make a difference' – for example, by combating violence at work or in designing workplaces better suited to those who occupy them.

**Karina Nielsen** is a senior researcher at the National Research Centre for the Working Environment, Denmark. Her main research interests lie within the area of occupational health psychology. She is involved in intervention research investigating the factors that facilitate positive and sustainable changes in the work environment and employee health and well-being. A central aspect of this research is how to strengthen the evaluation of such projects using both quantitative and qualitative process evaluation. Another central focus of her research is work organization and design, especially group- and teamwork, and how you create a positive challenging working environment that allows employees to be innovative. Karina has published her research in a number of book chapters and articles in, among others, *Work & Stress* and the *Journal of Organizational Behavior.*

**Andrew J. Noblet** is an Associate Professor in Organizational Behaviour at Deakin Business School, Deakin University (Australia). Andrew's research interests are in the areas of occupational stress, organisational fairness, leader-member relationships, employee performance and workplace health promotion. Andrew also provides advisory services to private and public-sector organisations and regularly undertakes employee needs assessments, leadership training and other organisational development initiatives.

**Michael P. O'Driscoll** is Professor of Psychology at the University of Waikato (New Zealand), where he has taught courses in organizational psychology since 1981, and convenes the postgraduate programme in organizational psychology. His primary research interests are in the fields of job-related stress and coping, and work-life balance. More generally, he is interested in work attitudes and behaviours, and the relationship between work and health. He has served on the editorial boards of several academic journals, and was editor of the *New Zealand Journal of Psychology* (2001–2006). Finally, he has provided consulting services to numerous organizations, with particular focus on work and well-being.

**Raymond Randall** is a Lecturer in Occupational Psychology at the University of Leicester (United Kingdom) where he is director of the distance learning MSc in Occupational Psychology and MSc in Psychology of Work. He has worked with many organizations to help them identify and tackle the problem of work-related stress and improve job design. His interests focus on issues associated with the design and implementation of interventions that are used to deal with such problems. Ray's publications in this area show how various innovative approaches can be used to enhance the evaluation of stress management and job re-design interventions. He is also currently working with a team of Danish researchers to evaluate the impact of leadership on employee well-being. His other research interests focus on issues in selection and assessment.

**John J. Rodwell** is a Professor in Management in the Deakin Business School at Deakin University (Australia). He is the Associate Head of School (Research). His current research interests focus on management, human resource management and employee issues in the workplace, particularly in healthcare management. John has experience as a manager, academic and consultant working on a range of projects, such as stress or productivity projects, across many organizations.

**Angeli Santos** is Director of Studies of the Institute of Work, Health and Organisations at the University of Nottingham Malaysia Campus (UNMC). She is also course director of the MSc in Occupational Health and Safety Leadership and the BSc in Applied Psychology and Management Studies at UNMC. Angeli completed her PhD in Applied Psychology at Nottingham in the area of coping, support and the impact of work-related violence on police personnel. Her interests in the violence research arena extend to the design, delivery and evaluation of workplace violence training and the use of biological indicators in the measurement of violence and stress. Angeli has been involved in and supervised a number of projects in the area of environmental design, health and well-being, including the use of the arts in hospitals, environmental design and hospital recovery and open-plan office work. She has also presented papers in these areas at recent international conferences held by the Environmental Design Research Association and the European Academy of Occupational Health Psychology. Other research interests include the role of safety culture and risk-taking behaviours on accidents and attitudes to work; and correlates and barriers to career decision-making in students and early career employees.

**Toon W. Taris** received a PhD degree in Psychology from the Vrije Universiteit Amsterdam, The Netherlands in 1994. He is currently full professor in Work and Organizational Psychology at the Department of Social and Organizational Psychology of Utrecht University, The Netherlands. His research interests include work motivation, work stress, and intervention research. He has published widely on these topics in books and journals such as the *Journal of Vocational Behavior, Personnel Psychology,* and the *Journal of Applied Psychology.* He is currently Scientific Editor of *Work & Stress.*

**Tony Zarola** is Managing Director of ZEAL Solutions (United Kingdom), a psychological consultancy group dedicated to the enhancement of individual and organizational health and well-being. Passionate about psychology and its role in delivering individual and organizational effectiveness, when he's not working in the world of business, he spends his time managing and delivering research on how to make the world of work a better place.

**Gerard Zwetsloot** is a Senior Researcher and Consultant at TNO Work & Employment (The Netherlands) and Special Professor in Occupational Health and Safety Management at the Institute of Work, Health & Organisations, University of Nottingham (United Kingdom). From 1998 to 2006 he was special professor at the Erasmus Centre for Sustainability and Management of Erasmus University Rotterdam (The Netherlands). His main interest is the combination of health and safety management with business excellence and corporate social responsibility or corporate sustainability. The main underlying themes of his research are to foster processes of collective learning and social innovation, and the creation of meaningful work.

# Preface

In 1995 we both chanced upon an advertisement for a Masters degree in Occupational Health Psychology (OHP). The advertisement described a programme that was to be launched the following year at the University of Nottingham, United Kingdom, with a focus on the application of psychology to occupational health issues. This sounded innovative and appealing. Shortly thereafter we made the trip, from Greece and the North of England, to Nottingham in pursuit of the degree. At that time there were few postgraduate opportunities in OHP; with the exception of the University of Nottingham's Masters degree, provision was restricted to courses that operated within a handful of North American doctoral programmes. Other programmes existed that addressed issues within the OHP remit but few, if any, were explicit in their identification of OHP as a discrete domain of research and professional practice. Since that time the OHP educational landscape has developed considerably. Numerous programmes now exist across the globe that attract ever-growing numbers of students in pursuit of OHP career development opportunities.

In view of the rapid international expansion of OHP education and training provision, it was surprising that no textbooks had been written for the purpose of introducing students to the discipline. We are delighted and honoured to be able to address the need for such a volume with this, the first textbook of OHP written specifically for a student audience. The book comprises eleven chapters that, in sum, provide an overview of the discipline through an examination of key theoretical perspectives, issues of interest to researchers and practitioners, and drivers of OHP activities that have shaped and defined the discipline since its emergence. Each chapter is written by internationally-recognized experts who are united by a belief that psychological science can make a valuable contribution to the protection and promotion of workers' health.

Space restrictions necessitate that this textbook does not provide a comprehensive account of topic areas that exist under the OHP umbrella. The ever-changing content and context of work dictate that the relevant topics are many, varied, and in a constant state of evolution. Readers interested in taking their learning further with a view to keeping abreast of the 'hot issues' tasking OHP researchers and practitioners, are directed towards a partner volume, *Contemporary occupational health psychology: Global perspectives on research and practice*. Published by Wiley-Blackwell, the biennial series presents authoritative, stand-alone, reviews on OHP topics that are germane to the interests and activities of OHP researchers, practitioners, and students. The series also presents new empirical research where it can usefully advance the field in ways that are not typically possible within the confines of the traditional journal article. This applies particularly to developments in professional practice, education, and training.

It is our hope that you enjoy this book and find it useful in your studies. We eagerly anticipate your feedback; please do not hesitate to email us with suggestions for improvements. We will endeavour to introduce as many of these as possible in future editions.

At this point a few words of thanks are due. Our gratitude is extended to Andrew McAleer and Darren Reed, our editors at Wiley-Blackwell, for the opportunity to introduce OHP to a wide constituency of students; the reviewers from the international community of occupational health psychologists who considered the original proposal and provided invaluable feedback that has immeasurably improved the final product; the European Academy of Occupational Health Psychology for endorsing the book; and finally, our contributors for their excellent manuscripts.

Fifteen years ago we were introduced to a discipline that captured our imagination and set the course of our professional lives. We hope that this book similarly inspires you and sparks a flame of enthusiasm that leads to a rewarding career concerned with the application of psychological principles and practices for the protection and promotion of workers' health and safety.

*Stavroula Leka*
stavroula.leka@nottingham.ac.uk

*Jonathan Houdmont*
jonathan.houdmont@nottingham.ac.uk

# 1

# An Introduction to Occupational Health Psychology

## Jonathan Houdmont and Stavroula Leka

### CHAPTER OUTLINE

This chapter introduces occupational health psychology by defining the subject matter and exploring the features that make it distinct from other related areas. The influence of key research groups and studies, characteristics of the changing world of work, and legislative developments that have contributed to the development of the discipline, are considered. The chapter closes by introducing the bodies that represent and support research, training, and professional practice in occupational health psychology on the international stage.

## Introduction

There are numerous descriptors for subject specialties that concern the application of psychology in the workplace: industrial and organizational psychology, work and organizational psychology, work and health psychology, vocational psychology, and occupational psychology to name but a few. Each of these specialties has a distinct perspective on the dynamic relationship between work and the worker (although some overlap is inevitable), and exists as a formalized entity supported, to varying degrees, by representative bodies, academic and practitioner journals, international conferences, and professional training pathways. To this collection there is a new entrant that since the early 1990s has attracted interest, but about which little has been written for the student embarking upon study of the specialty: occupational health psychology.

In this chapter we set out the nature and definition of this specialty, and trace its emergence by selectively highlighting a series of influential research groups and studies, characteristics of the changing world of work, and legislative developments that have materialized during the twentieth century in Europe and North America. We conclude with an examination of the contemporary character of occupational health psychology in which consideration is given to structures that exist to support the research, training, and practitioner activities of an expanding international constituency.

## What is Occupational Health Psychology?

*Where did the term 'occupational health psychology' originate?*
*What is the vision of occupational health psychology?*
*Why is occupational health psychology important?*

Occupational health psychology (OHP) is a youthful discipline with much to offer the aspiring practitioner. This book is designed to facilitate the knowledge development of those who wish to develop a career in OHP: individuals with a curiosity and enthusiasm for the application of psychological theory and evidence to bring about improvements in the health of workers. The term 'occupational health psychology' was coined in 1990 at the University of Hawaii by a team of academics who observed unfulfilled potential for psychologists to support the development of healthy work environments (Raymond, Wood, & Patrick, 1990). OHP has grown at a rapid rate in the two decades that have passed since Raymond and colleagues set in motion a new specialty. This can be seen in, among other things, the ongoing rise in the submission rate of scientific articles to the discipline's dedicated academic journals (*Journal of Occupational Health Psychology* and *Work & Stress*), and the influence of these journals within the broader applied psychology field; the growth in researcher, educator, practitioner, and student attendance at international OHP conferences; the expansion of OHP training provision in Europe and North America; the growth in employment opportunities for OHP practitioners; and the expansion of outlets for practitioners to publish and share best practice.

Alongside these activities, debate on the nature and scope of OHP has crystallized and consensus has developed among academics and practitioners on its aims and objectives. This has allowed for the advancement of a shared vision whereby OHP is understood to have its focus on the creation of 'healthy workplaces in which people may produce, serve, grow, and be valued' (Quick et al., 1997, p. 3). Within this vision, healthy workplaces are understood to be ones 'where people use their talents and gifts to achieve high performance, high satisfaction, and well-being' (ibid.).

The appeal of OHP can be found in the important and unique role it plays in the management of challenges to safety and health in the organizational context. For many decades, prior to the advent of OHP, occupational safety and health professionals had at their disposal a knowledge- and skill-set that was fit for purpose in respect of the control and prevention of exposures to traditional work-related hazards such as physical, biological, or chemical agents (Sauter & Hurrell, 1999). The practitioner's professional toolkit was robust and effective in so far as it was designed to deal with the prevalent work-related hazards of the time. The adequacy of the toolkit was, however, called into question towards the end of the twentieth century as a consequence of the rise in workplace psychosocial hazards. Defined as 'those aspects of work design and the organization and management of work, and their social and organizational contexts, which have the potential for causing psychological, social or physical harm' (Cox, Griffiths, & Rial González, 2000, p. 14), psychosocial hazards, and the health-risks they pose, have in recent years entered the consciousness of employers, policy- and law-makers, and occupational safety and health practitioners due to their association with characteristics of the contemporary world of work such as internationalization and increased global competition, the continual evolution of information and communication technologies, and changes to the configuration of the workforce (Kompier, 2006).

Psychosocial hazard exposures hold the potential to cause serious harm. However, education and training provision for occupational safety and health professionals has traditionally neglected psychosocial issues; thus, it is in the management of these that the OHP practitioner can make a unique contribution to the prevention of occupational illness and injury, and promotion of occupational health and well-being. This is an important role; indeed, there is evidence to suggest that psychosocial hazards are likely to continue to pose a growing threat to worker well-being (see Research Close-Up 1.1). As such, the services of the OHP practitioner are likely to be of increasing value to organizations as the twenty-first century unfolds.

### RESEARCH CLOSE-UP 1.1 Emerging Psychosocial Risks

*Source:* EU-OSHA – European Agency for Safety and Health at Work (2007). *Expert forecast on emerging psychosocial risks related to occupational safety and health (OSH)*, Available at: http://osha.europa.eu/en/publications/reports/7807118/view

#### Introduction

The purpose of this study was to identify emerging psychosocial risks that may pose a threat to employee safety and health. Through the early anticipation of emerging (i.e., new and increasing) risks, the study sought to facilitate the planned targeting of resources, interventions, and strategies to tackle these.

#### Method

A Delphi consensus-building methodology was applied with an expert-group largely comprised of experienced psychological researchers in occupational safety, health, and psychosocial risks. The first survey round required the experts to propose and prioritize risks that they believed to be emerging (the *creation* stage). Based on the results, a second questionnaire was developed that listed all of the items generated in the previous round. Experts were required to indicate on a five-point Likert scale that ranged from 'strongly disagree'

Research Close-Up 1.1 *(Cont'd)*

to 'strongly agree', the extent to which they agreed that each of the topic areas was emerging (the *prioritization* stage). This procedure was repeated for the third round (the *consensus* stage).

## Results

The ten most important emerging psychosocial risks identified by the study are shown in the table below.

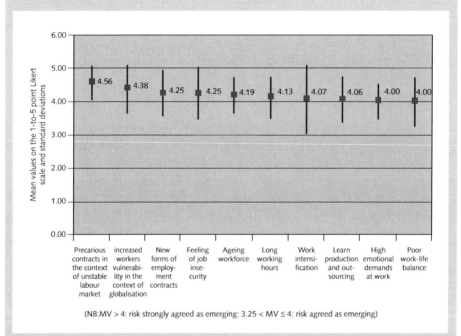

(NB:MV > 4: risk strongly agreed as emerging: 3.25 < MV ≤ 4: risk agreed as emerging)

These ten emerging psychosocial risks can be thematically grouped into five areas:

- new forms of employment contracts and job insecurity;
- the ageing workforce;
- work intensification;
- high emotional demands at work;
- poor work–life balance.

## Conclusions

The study's findings highlight that changes in the world of work over the last few decades have resulted in the rise of psychosocial risks associated with the way work is designed, organized, and managed. The results offer a basis for discussion among stakeholders to help them set priorities for future research and policy actions.

## Summary

The OHP moniker was coined in 1990, since which time the discipline has flourished in Europe and North America. Agreement can be found on the vision for OHP, and the discipline now plays an important role in the prevention of occupational illness and injury, and promotion of occupational health and well-being.

## The Definition of Occupational Health Psychology

*How is occupational health psychology defined?*
*What commonalities and differences exist between European and North*
*American definitions?*

With any youthful discipline it takes time for consensus to develop around a precise definition in respect of its key ingredients or features. OHP is no exception; although there is agreement among the discipline's protagonists on its aims and objectives, evidence of divergence can be found between North American and European perspectives on its definition (Cox, 2000). This is specifically so in relation to the specialties that inform and comprise OHP. At one level it could be argued that divergence is a mere matter of semantics because OHP protagonists the world over adhere to a universal understanding of the discipline. However, because the definitions adhered to by academics will determine, in part, the content of training programmes, divergence may have the unfortunate consequence of conspiring against the creation of programme accreditation procedures and professional training pathways that are required to sustain the discipline in the long term.

For this reason, it is imperative that international consensus is ultimately achieved on the definition of OHP. Fortunately, despite the absence of a shared heritage across the international OHP community, broad agreement on the nature of the discipline can be found in the definitions advanced by the discipline's European and North American representative bodies. In Europe, the generally accepted definition is that advanced by the European Academy of Occupational Health Psychology (EAOHP). This is based on the definition posited by Cox, Baldursson, and Rial González (2000), whereby OHP is considered 'the contribution of applied psychology to occupational health' (p. 101). This definition locates OHP at the interface between occupational health and psychology. Cox and colleagues suggest that the areas of psychology that might be applied in addressing occupational health issues include health psychology, work and organizational psychology, and social and environmental psychology. This perspective is illustrated in Figure 1.1. The contribution of these areas of psychology implies that OHP practitioners have their focus on the psychological, social, and organizational

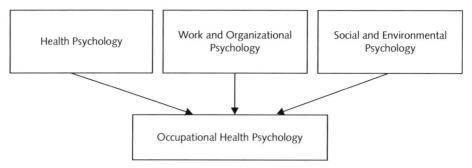

**Figure 1.1** Foundations of European occupational health psychology.

aspects of occupational health questions. The European perspective recognizes that occupational health is a multidisciplinary area and that OHP practitioners offer a focused specialization that they may usefully apply within multidisciplinary teams. In this way, it 'requires that European occupational health psychologists are aware of and recognize the contributions that can be made by others, and can appreciate their intellectual positions, knowledge and practical skills' (ibid., p. 103).

The North American perspective on OHP is in large part consistent with the European approach. Nevertheless, differences can be identified. Whereas the European tradition draws on procedures, practices, and methodologies from various fields of applied psychology, North American definitions encompass psychological perspectives alongside those from other occupational sciences such as occupational and environmental health, organizational behaviour, human factors, sociology, industrial engineering, ergonomics, and economics (Adkins, 1999; Chen, Huang, & DeArmond, 2005). This perspective gives rise to the definition advanced by the North American representative body for the discipline – the Society for Occupational Health Psychology (SOHP) – whereby OHP is viewed as involving:

> The interdisciplinary partnerships of psychological and occupational health science professionals seeking to improve the quality of working life, and enhance the safety, health and well-being of workers in all occupations. Because it exists at the intersection of behavioral science and occupational health disciplines, OHP is inclusive of knowledge and methods from psychology, public/occupational health, organizational studies, human factors, and allied fields (such as occupational sociology, industrial engineering, economics, and others). (Society for Occupational Health Psychology, 2008)

This multidisciplinary perspective, illustrated in Figure 1.2, was established at the outset of the discipline's existence in North America. In their seminal article, Raymond, Wood, and Patrick (1990) called for training in a discipline that 'would integrate and synthesize insights, frameworks and knowledge from a diverse number of specialties, principally health psychology and occupational

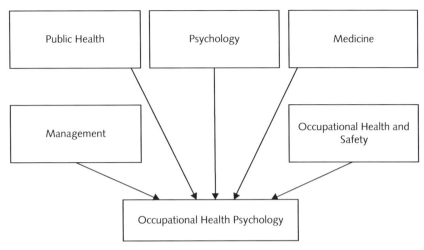

**Figure 1.2** Foundations of North American occupational health psychology (adapted from Adkins, 1999).

(public) health but also preventative medicine, occupational medicine, behavioral medicine, nursing, political science, sociology and business' (p. 1159). Interestingly, in recent times, debate in North America has resurfaced on the extent to which OHP should exist primarily as a psychological discipline (Sinclair, 2009), suggesting that opinion on its interdisciplinary status may be divided.

Despite definitional differences, there is little doubt that advocates for OHP the world over unanimously endorse the aforementioned vision for OHP delineated by Quick et al. (1997). Likewise, most would agree with the high-level characteristics posited by Cox et al. (2000) as defining the discipline. These include acknowledgement that OHP is: (a) an applied science, (b) evidence driven, (c) oriented towards problem solving, (d) multidisciplinary, (e) participatory, (f) focused on intervention, with an emphasis on primary prevention (see Definition 1.1), and (g) operational within a legal framework.

## Definition 1.1

**Primary prevention**: **Primary** interventions for the improvement of occupational health are targeted at the **source** of problems, i.e., the design, management, and organization of work. These contrast with **secondary** interventions that focus on workers' *responses* by bolstering coping resources, and tertiary interventions that centre on **effects/outcomes** through the provision of **remedial** support.

## Summary

OHP can be defined simply as 'the contribution of applied psychology to occupational health'. This 'interface' definition, adhered to in Europe, recognizes that occupational health is a multidisciplinary area and that OHP practitioners offer a focused specialization that they may usefully apply within multidisciplinary teams. The North American perspective on OHP is in large part consistent with the European approach, but differs in that it encompasses psychological perspectives alongside those from other occupational sciences.

## OHP Topic Areas

*How have OHP topic areas been identified?*
*Which topic areas fall under the OHP umbrella?*

Further evidence for the youthfulness of OHP can be found in the absence of an agreed list of topic areas that the discipline might address beyond its traditional focus on work-related stress. Although the field is yet to achieve a level of maturity whereby agreement exists in respect of the domains that ought to be encompassed within the OHP umbrella, what is clear is that irrespective of what these might be, OHP should be inclusive in so far as is reasonable (Chen, DeArmond, & Huang, 2006). Three contrasting approaches have been applied for the purpose of drawing conclusions on the topic areas that comprise the focus of OHP: scrutiny of existing educational curricula, analyses of themes as they have appeared in the discipline's academic journals, and expert surveys.

### Scrutiny of existing curricula

One approach to the identification of OHP topic areas, which has been applied in the US context, has involved the analysis of existing curricula. Scrutiny of topics addressed in 12 US doctoral OHP training programs revealed one topic taught across programs: introduction to the discipline of OHP. Work-related stress was the second most prevalent topic area, taught at seven institutions (Fullagar & Hatfield, 2005). A similar analysis of the content of 11 US doctoral curricula identified the consistent appearance of six topic areas: (a) survey (overview) of occupational safety and health, (b) job stress theory, (c) organizational risk factors for occupational stress, injury, and illness, (d) physical and psychological health implications of stressful work, (e) organizational interventions for the reduction of work-related stress, and (f) research methods and practices in public/occupational health and epidemiology (Barnes-Farrell, 2006). These curriculum areas are consistent with seven broad areas identified by Macik-Frey, Quick, and Nelson (2007) as representing the major research themes addressed in papers published in the *Journal of Occupational Health Psychology* (see below). It might be reasonable to assume that consistency between OHP curricula and published research themes has arisen owing to programme designers having relied on the latter to inform the former.

## Published research themes

Themes in the published research literature provide an indication of some important topics that ought to perhaps be included under the OHP umbrella and, specifically, within education and training curricula. Through analysis of themes addressed in papers published in the Journal of Occupational Health Psychology over an 11 year period from the journal's inception in 1996, Macik-Frey, Quick, and Nelson (2007) identified seven broad areas that represented the major themes considered by researchers. Work-related stress was identified as the single most researched area, followed by burnout; work-family issues; aggression, violence and harassment; safety; employment issues; and health issues. Within these broad areas four topics were identified as holding promise for future OHP research: positive psychology, virtual work, moods and emotions, and intervention studies.

Inness and Barling (2003) similarly reviewed the themes evident in papers published in the *Journal of Occupational Health Psychology* though not directly for the purpose of investigating those topics that might be considered within the OHP remit but, rather, to examine the extent to which OHP research reflected the objectives of the discipline, i.e., the promotion of workers' health and the improvement of organizational functioning. Nevertheless, the study provides a useful illustration of the spectrum of OHP topic areas. Among the 191 studies that comprised the sample of papers, work-related stress was examined nearly twice as frequently as the next most prevalent topic (24% of all papers). The second most frequently examined topic involved investigations into the consequences of various negative workplace experiences (such as sexual harassment, job insecurity, exhaustion, burnout, role conflict, etc.) (13%). Together, these two broad themes accounted for more than one third of all papers. Other themes, each accounting for no less than 5% of the total, included individual differences (personality traits, sense of well-being, personal control), work-family interface (work-family conflict, elder/childcare, dual earner couples), demographic characteristics (gender, ethnicity, tenure), psychosocial environment (social support, supervisor support, communication) and job characteristics (job type/industry, job design issues, organizational climate, presence of training). A further ten broad themes were identified each accounting for less than 5% of the papers. Inness and Barling concluded that the majority of the published papers had their focus on problem-oriented research questions; relatively few explicitly examined how healthy workplaces might be created. It is to this more positive perspective, one that entails treating the workplace as an arena for the protection and promotion of well-being, which they suggest future OHP research might orientate for the discipline to fulfil its potential. Positive OHP has attracted a wealth of interest in recent years; interest that is reflected in this textbook by the dedication of an entire chapter to the notion.

Some years after Inness and Barling's study, Kang, Staniford, Dollard, and Kompier (2008) reviewed the topics examined in papers published in the *Journal of Occupational Health Psychology* and extended their consideration to the discipline's other flagship journal, *Work & Stress*. In total, the analysis encompassed some 631 papers published between 1996 and 2006. Results showed that published OHP research had primarily focused on work-factors such as workload, individual influences such as motivation, and a combination of work and individual contextual factors. The authors noted the paucity of research that had accounted for factors external to organizations such as government policy, workplace-related legislation, and the effects of globalization. Adding their voice to that of Inness and Barling as well as that of Macik-Frey and colleagues, Kang et al. expressed regret at the limited number of intervention studies designed for the protection and promotion of health.

Analyses such as these offer an indication of the topics with which researchers have commonly engaged. However, beyond the intrinsic interest or importance of a topic there exists a host of factors that drive research foci and which encourage a concentration on particular topics at different points in time across social and economic contexts. Furthermore, analyses of this sort are only able to consider themes as they appear in published articles – they do not provide information on those topic areas that might have been extensively researched but which fall outside of the scope of interest, and/or the scientific publication criteria, of the discipline's flagship journals. As such, key themes evident in the published research literature provide an indication of some important topics but fall short of providing guidance on the topics that are fundamental to the discipline. Thus, an educational curriculum that reflects the key themes in published OHP research may be inadequate. Moreover, the applied nature of OHP renders it important that curricula do not merely reflect the topics that academics study but encompass issues of interest and concern to practitioners.

## Expert surveys

To ensure that education and training programmes address issues with which practitioners are tasked within the organizations that they operate, programme designers in the USA and Europe have sought to identify key topic areas from the practitioner perspective. This line of research was initiated in the USA with a survey of 1,100 human resource managers, public health professionals, and experts in disciplines allied to OHP (Schneider, Camara, Tetrick, & Sternberg, 1999). Though it revealed a need for OHP education and training, the survey stopped short of delineating a curriculum. Schneider and colleagues' study laid the groundwork for the development of OHP curricula in the US in the late 1990s, including the doctoral programme at the University of Houston. Keen to ensure that the Houston curriculum met the needs of local employers, 141 human resource managers and 27 trade union representatives were surveyed on their organization's concern about various OHP-related topics (Tetrick & Ellis, 2002). Respondents were required to indicate the degree of organizational concern associated with 31 OHP-related topics derived from the authors' knowledge of the OHP literature and human resource practices in the US. Results showed that the top ten concerns of human resource managers included: accidents, attendance, changing technology, education and training, employee commitment, physical well-being, psychological well-being, safety, teamwork, and workplace injuries. Within the list of concerns generated by trade union representatives, priority was given to issues of immediate and direct relevance to employees such as job security, occupational stress, retirement, and workload.

This line of research was further developed in the US through a survey of 67 safety and health practitioners and nine OHP academics/researchers in a study that sought to assess both the types of organizations that OHP practitioners work within and the nature of health and safety issues they are charged with addressing (Sinclair, Hammer, Oeldorf Hirsch, & Brubaker, 2006). Survey responses revealed the prioritization of 10 OHP-related issues: accidents, safety climate, personal protective equipment, compliance with US Occupational Safety and Health Administration regulations, fire safety, repetitive strain injuries, ergonomics, traumatic injuries, workers' compensation, and noise/hearing protection. Owing to the nature of the sample the results were biased towards the perceptions of practitioners, many of whom worked in safety-related occupations. Thus, the study offered a tentative indication of the topics that might be considered important to OHP from the viewpoint of a particular constituency.

In Britain, Leka, Khan, and Griffiths (2008) similarly sought to elicit the views of practitioners on these questions. The two-wave project involved a Delphi study with 30 national-level occupational safety and health experts, and a questionnaire that was administered to 1,679 occupational safety and health practitioners with a view towards the identification of (a) emerging and future occupational health priorities, and (b) occupational health (and safety) practitioner training needs in the British context. Results of the Delphi study showed that subject matter experts' top five emerging and future workplace health priorities included common mental health problems (anxiety, depression, and stress), sickness absence (monitoring, management, return to work, rehabilitation, and presenteeism), musculoskeletal disorders, engaging and advising small and medium sized enterprises, and the evaluation of workplace health interventions. Survey results revealed that practitioners identified eight priority areas in terms of emerging and future workplace health issues: common mental health problems, the use of government guidance on the management of work-related stress, the identification of emerging risks, planning for major events (e.g., pandemics), work-related driving, work-life balance, immigrant and migrant workers, and non-standard workplaces (e.g., flexiwork, telework). Together, these studies provide useful guidance on topics that might be addressed within a curriculum that seeks to prepare graduates for professional practice.

A related strand of research has involved the elicitation of subject-matter-expert opinion from OHP academics: an important constituency whose views bring considerable weight to bear in the design and implementation of university curricula. On the basis of a survey administered at two international OHP conferences, Houdmont, Leka, and Bulger (2010) sought to identify the topic areas perceived by OHP academics as central to a curriculum and assess whether European and North American differences in how the discipline is defined might present a barrier to agreement on the importance of these topic areas. The study revealed agreement between European and North American academics on the centrality of a set of topic areas to an OHP curriculum. Eleven topics were identified by both groups as 'important' and a further five as 'core'. This latter set included: interventions to promote health, organizational research methods, design of the psychosocial work environment, stress theory, and stress interventions. Considerable overlap between these five areas can be discerned. Taken as a whole, these topic areas are not inconsistent with the high level characteristics advanced by Cox, Baldursson, & Rial González (2000) as central to defining the discipline.

It might be considered surprising that definitional differences failed to give rise to contrasting perspectives among academics operating in these regions in relation to the question of which topics might be considered central to a curriculum. Given the focus in the European definition on the contribution of applied psychology to tackling occupational health issues it might be expected that European OHP academics would identify topics that have enjoyed a tradition of examination from a psychological standpoint. In contrast, individuals that adhere to the broader North American definition that encapsulates the contribution of a variety of occupational sciences alongside psychology might be expected to identify a wider list of topics. The identification of agreement between North American and European OHP academics on the 'core' topic areas might be an important factor that facilitates the development of program accreditation criteria in these regions as we enter the second decade of the twenty first century.

## Summary

A number of approaches have been taken to the systematic identification of OHP topic areas. These have included the analysis of existing educational curricula, review of published research themes, and expert surveys. The results of these studies highlight that in its short lifetime OHP has generated a wealth of scientific knowledge on work-related stress, as well as wider organizational issues as they relate to individual and organizational health, and there now appears to be broad consensus on the topic areas that are central to the discipline.

## The Work of Occupational Health Psychologists

*What do OHP practitioners do?*
*What knowledge and skills do OHP job advertisements call for?*

In his influential book, *Psychology and Industrial Efficiency* (1913), Hugo Münsterberg, a pioneer of applied psychology, observed the need for organizations:

> to appoint professionally trained psychologists who will devote their services to the psychological problems of the special industrial plant ... It is obvious that the professional consulting psychologist would satisfy these needs most directly, and if such a new group of engineers were to enter into industrial life, very soon a further specialization might be expected. Some of these psychological engineers would devote themselves to ... problems of fatigue, efficiency, and recreation; [others] the psychological demands for the arrangement of the machines; and every day would give rise to new divisions. ('The future development of economic psychology' section, para. 3)

Münsterberg's ambitions for the employment of psychologists within organizations have been realized to varying degrees across countries and industrial sectors. Almost 100 years after publication of the above tract, an ever-growing number of organizations can be seen to demonstrate awareness of the benefits to be yielded by the employment of an OHP practitioner, not only for employee health but also for the health of the organization. A much was recognized by Münsterberg who noted that the psychologist was likely to 'submit propositions which might refer exclusively to the psychological factors and yet which might be more important for the earning and the profit of the establishment than the mere buying of new machines or the mere increase in the number of laborers' ('The future development of economic psychology' section, para. 3). In fulfilment of Münsterberg's ambition, it is now possible to discern an international cohort of OHP practitioners, supported by the discipline's representative bodies, that seeks to apply psychological principles and practices within the organizational setting.

OHP practitioners work in a wide variety of organizations to promote the understanding, control and prevention of work-related illness and injury, and promotion of health and well-being. Until the dawn of the twenty-first century, job advertisements that made explicit calls for the services of an OHP practitioner were few and far between. In their employment search, OHP graduates had little choice but to attempt to match the knowledge and skills developed during their studies to the job specification given in advertisements for various occupational health, safety, or human resource roles. If called for interview, it would often be incumbent upon the interviewee to explain the discipline of OHP to the employer and convey the unique contribution offered by its practitioners. However, in recent times advertisements have begun to appear that make a direct call for the services of the OHP practitioner. For example, the real-life advertisement given in the box appeared in the British national press in 2007. Consistent with the high-level characteristics that Cox, Baldursson, & Rial González (2000) suggested appear to define the discipline, the advertisement highlights the role of the OHP practitioner working within multi-disciplinary teams on the design and delivery of interventions based on theory and evidence that are targeted at the promotion of employee well-being and organizational effectiveness.

---

### Box 1.2   Vacancy: Occupational Health Psychologist Employer: Hospital: London, England

This is an exciting opportunity to join an expanding Occupational Health Service for staff in a London teaching hospital and contribute to the psychology arm of the service. The Occupational Health Service is a multi-disciplinary team providing a service to approx 5,000 staff. You will join a Consultant Psychologist who is currently providing psychological interventions at individual, team and organizational level. We are looking for an enthusiastic and creative person with a firm commitment to staff wellbeing and organizational effectiveness. You must have the ability to adapt psychological models to occupational health contexts, with the skills to provide the usual psychological assessments and interventions and an interest in developing new brief therapy packages to meet the psychological needs of a wide variety of staff. You will assist in the development of profession-based psycho-educational programs. A key role will involve audit and evaluation of professional activities of the psychology service. We invite applications from recently qualified psychologists. There will be excellent opportunities for professional development, relevant research, and supervision.

---

One explanation for the paucity of OHP job opportunities that plagued graduates in the discipline's early years may be found in the ambiguity that initially surrounded the question of what precisely an OHP practitioner might bring to an organization in terms of knowledge and skills. Fortunately, in recent times there has been a concerted effort to clarify this matter. For example, when Fullagar and Hatfield (2005) found themselves unable to conduct an analysis of the training needs for OHP job applicants due to the apparent absence of a single advertisement in the United States that specifically called for an OHP practitioner they, instead, conducted an analysis of the knowledge, skills, and abilities required of various jobs related to OHP and to which OHP practitioners might apply. Combining the results of the analysis with information on topics taught in North American OHP curricula, Fullagar and Hatfield were able to develop a tentative OHP job description, whereby the role of the OHP practitioner is to:

Review, evaluate and analyze work environments and design programs and procedures to promote worker health and reduce occupational stress caused by psychological, organizational and social factors. Apply principles of psychology to occupational health problems. Activities may include policy planning; employee screening, training and development; and organizational development and analysis. May work with management to reorganize the work setting to improve worker health. May be employed in the public or private sector.

Elements of Fullagar and Hatfield's job description can be found in recent real-world advertisements for OHP practitioners and it is likely that job descriptions such as this will continue to be refined, and their elements increasingly permeate into employment vacancy advertisements.

## Summary

Professional practice in OHP has developed as a cohesive activity stream following the establishment of a self-sustaining scientific research base in the discipline. Year-on-year growth in opportunities for professional practice can be identified in both Europe and North America.

## The Emergence of a Discipline

*Which research traditions and legislative events gave rise to OHP?*
*Who are the key figures in the emergence of OHP in Europe and North America?*

As has been discussed, prior to the emergence of OHP in the early 1990s, occupational health practitioners were equipped to manage physical, biological, and chemical risks in the workplace. However, growing recognition of the cost to business of stress-related problems, evidence to attest to the role of psychosocial hazards in the development of work-related health problems, and radical changes to the organization of work that may foster occupational health and safety problems, triggered an acknowledgment towards the end of the 1980s that future generations of practitioners would benefit from training in psychological theory, evidence, principles, and practices (Sauter, Hurrell, Fox, Tetrick, & Barling, 1999). In essence, events conspired to highlight the need for research and training on the possible benefits to be afforded by the application of psychology to occupational health questions and, in this way, provided a foundation for the development of OHP.

Several authors have provided historical accounts of the research groups, studies, and events that led to the emergence of OHP (Barling & Griffiths, 2002; Sauter et al., 1999). These provide a useful overview of developments as they have been reported in English-language publications which, naturally enough, have focused on developments in those countries where English is the native language or commonly spoken. It is inevitable that key developments elsewhere remain unfamiliar to the English-speaking OHP community, and it is important that these are acknowledged when the comprehensive international history of the discipline is eventually written. Such an undertaking will require a book in itself. In this chapter we therefore make no attempt to present a comprehensive overview of the emergence of OHP. Rather, we selectively highlight a series of influential research groups, studies, and legislative developments that materialized during the twentieth century in Europe and North America. The list is by no means exhaustive; instead, it provides an illustration of some landmarks in the discipline's emergence.

## European developments

It is possible, if one so wishes, to trace the origins of OHP back to the philosophers of ancient Greece. However, if we skip forward several centuries to the early part of the twentieth century it is possible to discern the discipline's modern roots in Europe in the activities of a handful of psychologists.

In the British context, much of the stimulus for psychological occupational health research was to be found in the events of the First World War. Created during wartime 'to consider and advise on questions of industrial fatigue, hours of labour and other matters affecting the personal health and physical efficiency of workers in munitions factories' (Health of Munition Workers Committee, 1915, p. 864), the Health of Munition Workers Committee oversaw numerous workplace interventions that would today be considered as falling within the OHP remit. Interventions included, among others, the introduction of dining rooms separated from the factory floor that supplied food 'under restful and comfortable conditions in rooms well lighted and ventilated and properly warmed' which were concluded to be responsible for 'a marked improvement in the health and physical condition of the workers, a reduction in sickness, less absence and broken time, less tendency to alcoholism and increased efficiency and output' (ibid). Around the same time, the government also introduced so called welfare supervisors to oversee the implementation of health and welfare interventions for women and younger workers with a view towards the enhancement of productivity. In this way, the welfare supervisor can be seen as a precursor of the contemporary OHP practitioner. However, some of the interventions applied by this cohort would undoubtedly concern today's OHP practitioners: women-only rest-rooms replete with mirrors, plants, and beds (women were assumed to be more susceptible to fatigue than men), and beauty parlours to prevent women from becoming psychologically damaged by doing men's work. Others, however, such as the introduction of flexible working hours and workplace childcare facilities, are as applicable today as they were in the early part of the twentieth century. Post-war, the Committee was developed by the government of the day into the Industrial Fatigue Research Board which changed its name again in 1928 to the Industrial Health Research Board. During the interwar years the Board conducted research on a variety of topics including the impact on productivity of long working hours, sickness absence, lighting and noise, and repetitive work. The Board's research studies on workforce health took on renewed importance during the Second World War in an effort to maintain efficiency and promote productivity under wartime conditions.

Wartime imperatives were not alone among the factors that stimulated concern in Britain surrounding issues of safety and health at work in the early to middle part of the twentieth century. Trade unions formed numerous alliances in the early part of the twentieth century with groups such as the Industrial Health Education Society, formed in 1922, which fought to improve both worker health and organizational efficiency under the slogan 'health is wealth'; a banner that would not appear out of place today. Trade unions were also responsible for conducting some of the earliest national working conditions surveys of the type that are commonplace today in many countries. One early example, that of the Amalgamated Engineering Union (1944), paints a despairing and in no way unique picture of working conditions in one particular factory at that time: 'The ventilation in the sub-assembly shop is too bad for description. With the smell of rotting, rat-infested wood floors the low roofed, badly overcrowded shop is worse than the Black Hole of Calcutta' (p. 9).

After the Second World War, OHP-oriented research continued in Britain and was influential in bringing about the Health and Safety at Work Act 1974; an important piece of legislation that required employers to ensure the health, safety, and welfare of workers in so far as reasonably practicable. Although the Act has been successful in reducing the prevalence of industrial diseases and injuries, the contemporary world of work has generated a new wave of risks to workers health, namely psychosocial risks, the management of which has presented new challenges that require dedicated OHP research. This has stimulated the development of several centers of excellence in OHP research at universities across the UK including, among others, the Institute of Work, Health & Organisations at the University of Nottingham; the Institute of Work Psychology at the University of Sheffield; and the Centre for Occupational and Health Psychology at the University of Cardiff.

Elsewhere in Europe, particularly in the Northern European Nordic countries, psychosocial research gathered pace during the 1970s. Within this tradition, Swedish psychosocial researchers have played an important role in setting the stage for what was to become OHP. The interest of Swedish researchers in workplace psychosocial issues finds its roots in two factors: legislation that from as early as 1976 has recognized their importance in the determination of workers' health, and a long tradition of political democratization of work-life (Theorell, 1999). Notable landmarks in the Swedish research tradition include the studies of Bertil Gardell (1927–1987) on the importance of employee participation, and the consequences of worker alienation associated with industrialization (e.g., Gardell, 1971, 1982), Marianne Frankenhaeuser's (1925–) work on the physiological and psychological stress of working life (e.g., Frankenhaeuser & Gardell, 1976), Lennart Levi's (1930–) medically-oriented research on biological stress markers (e.g., Levi, 1972) and Töres Theorell's (1942–) studies on the relationship between working conditions and cardiovascular problems (e.g., Theorell & Floderus-Myrhed, 1977). Later, Theorell helped take psychosocial research to a wider audience through publication of the influential book *Healthy Work* in collaboration with Robert Karasek (Karasek & Theorell, 1990). A number of English-language historical accounts of Swedish psychosocial research have been written (Johnson & Johansson, 1991; Theorell, 2007). In parallel to the Swedish psychosocial research tradition, researchers in other Nordic countries conducted a series of influential psychosocial work-environment studies during the 1960s and 1970s. In Norway, for example, important advances were made in knowledge on the health benefits of autonomous work groups (Emery & Thorsrud, 1969; Thorsrud & Emery, 1970) and the psychobiology of stress (Ursin, Baade & Levine, 1978).

## North American developments

In North America, a number of events, individuals, and seminal studies paved the way for the establishment in 2004 of a regional representative body for OHP: the Society for Occupational Health Psychology (SOHP). These developments were also important to gaining the recognition of influential groups such as the American Psychological Association in respect of the discipline's distinct contribution to the management of occupational health.

It is beyond the scope of this chapter to provide a comprehensive account of the development of OHP in North America. Nevertheless, a number of important milestones can be identified. In the early to mid twentieth century a number of researchers, many of whom identified themselves as psychologists, conducted a series of seminal studies that were influential in stimulating research that might today be recognized under the OHP umbrella. Noteworthy among this group is Hugo Münsterberg (1863–1916), one of the fathers of applied psychology, who conducted a series of studies in what he referred to as economic psychology, a field that he considered ought to address 'how to find the best possible man, how to produce the best possible work, and how to secure the best possible effects' (Münsterberg, 1913, 'Means and ends' section, para. 6). Münsterberg went down in history for his far-sighted ideas about the role of psychology in the workplace and also, rather less fortuitously, for his untimely and sudden death on the lecture podium at Harvard University.

Following in the same research tradition, Arthur Kornhauser (1896–1990) is remembered for his tireless efforts to encourage psychological workplace studies that centered on the mental health of workers in preference to those concerned with productivity and organizational effectiveness. The latter he decried for the way in which 'working people are studied primarily as means to the ends of efficiency' (Kornhauser, 1962, p. 43). Through his studies involving Detroit factory workers, Kornhauser helped to locate worker health at the centre of psychological occupational research; it has been said that 'his most enduring quality was his outspoken advocacy for an industrial psychology that addressed workers' issues instead of managements' prerogatives' (Zickar, 2003, p. 363). In this way he laid the foundations for much contemporary OHP research.

Among other figures who played a pivotal role in the emergence of contemporary OHP mention must be made of Robert Kahn (1918–) who produced a number of influential books from the early 1960s onwards, among which *Work and Health* (1964) stands as one of the earliest that addressed the question of how work factors contribute to the health and well-being of employees. The work of these pioneers and their compatriots fuelled a burgeoning interest in the United States during the 1960s and 1970s on work-related psychosocial issues that was made manifest in a number of ways.

In the mid 1960s the National Advisory Environmental Health Committee, which had been established shortly beforehand by the Surgeon General of the Public Health Service, published *Protecting the health of eighty million Americans: A national goal for occupational health US Public Health Service* (US Department of Health, Education, and Welfare, 1966). The report predicted changes in the way work is conducted, many of which turned out to be true, such as a growing service economy, increased use of information and communication technologies and greater reliance on contract-workers. The report expressed anxiety about the implications of such developments for the health of workers and singled out work-related stress as a key concern. Shortly thereafter, The Occupational Safety and Health Act of 1970 came into force. This piece of legislation was groundbreaking for its acknowledgment of psychological considerations in the research that it authorized the National Institute for Occupational Safety and Health (NIOSH) to perform. For example, Section 20 mandated NIOSH to 'conduct research, experiments, and demonstrations relating to occupational safety and health, including studies of psychological factors ... motivational and behavioral factors ... job stresses on the potential for illness, disease, or loss of functional capacity in aging adults'. NIOSH subsequently embarked on an extensive programme of psychological research centred on behavioural impairment caused by chemical and physical exposures, the development of behavioural methods for detecting occupational hazards, individual differences affecting worker safety and health, work-related stress, and psychological strategies for improvements in occupational health (Cohen & Margolis, 1973). The Act was instrumental in providing opportunities for psychologists to study the relationship between work and health (Chen, Huang, & DeArmond, 2005), and triggered a wealth of research over many years.

One manifestation of this new research orientation was the integration of a suite of psychosocial questions into the nationally-representative Quality of Employment Survey series which began in 1969–70 (University of Michigan, 1970) and was followed by further surveys in 1972–3 (Quinn & Shepard, 1974) and 1977 (Quinn & Staines, 1979). Commissioned by NIOSH in collaboration with the Department of Labor and conducted by the University of Michigan, these surveys generated representative data on the organization of work which stimulated the first comprehensive US-based studies on relations between the psychosocial work environment and workers' health and safety.

A further major initiative around this time came in the form of a report produced by a task force under President Nixon: *Work in America* (1973). The report considered the available scientific evidence and concluded that preventable workplace psychosocial hazards may be responsible, along with other factors, for medical costs borne by workers and organizations. The report highlighted primary prevention as a means of decreasing medical costs and improving productivity. Interestingly, 33 years after publication of the report the authors produced a sequel; using the same methods of analysis they concluded that American workers in the twenty-first century tend to have greater job satisfaction than during the early 1970s and are more involved in decision-making at work (O'Toole & Lawler, 2006).

Any discussion on the emergence of OHP in North America must make mention of the major role played by NIOSH. One of its most important actions in this regard was the advancement at the beginning of the 1990s of an influential national strategy to combat occupational health risks and associated impairment to psychological well-being (Sauter, Murphy, & Hurrell, 1990). Within NIOSH, Steve Sauter has been a powerful advocate for OHP. In collaboration with the American Psychological Association, NIOSH was instrumental in the establishment of graduate OHP training programmes in the 1990s and the organization of a series of international conferences on work and well-being that began in 1990 and have continued periodically since that time. In addition, NIOSH was closely involved in the establishment of the *Journal of Occupational Health Psychology* in 1996.

Partly in response to initiatives led by Steve Sauter and colleagues at NIOSH that turned a national spotlight on psychosocial issues at work and highlighted 'a need for closer integration between behavioral science, medicine, and management to address

### Pioneer　　Steven Sauter (1946–)

Steven Sauter has risen to prominence in the USA as a result of his dedicated efforts to integrate the behavioural sciences into the mainstream of research and practice targeted at the control and prevention of work-related illness and injury. He is perhaps best known for being the driving force behind the development of a US research agenda on the organization of work and for promoting the application of research from the social sciences towards the improvement of occupational health. Steven has spent much of his career at the US National Institute for Occupational Safety and Health (NIOSH) where he presently assumes the position of Coordinator of the NIOSH Research Program on Work Organization and Stress-Related Disorders. In collaboration with NIOSH colleagues and the American Psychological Association (APA), he founded the *Journal of Occupational Health Psychology* in 1996, and he was instrumental in the establishment of the Society for Occupational Health Psychology in 2004. The first graduate training programmes in occupational health psychology in the US and the long-running Work, Stress, and Health conference series are also products of his work with the APA. In 2006, the European Academy of Occupational Health Psychology made Steven an Academy Fellow in recognition of his long-standing contribution and commitment to occupational health psychology. In 2007, NIOSH honoured Steven with the James P. Keogh Award for Outstanding Service in Occupational Safety and Health.

distress at work' (Quick, 1999, p. 123), the term 'occupational health psychology' was finally coined in the USA in 1990 (Raymond, Wood, & Patrick, 1990).

## Summary

The emergence of OHP as we know it today can be traced back to a series of seminal 'industrial psychology' experiments in the early part of the twentieth century. As that century progressed, a number of groups in Europe (particularly in the Northern European Nordic countries), and the USA, established themselves as world leaders in psychosocial research. The activities of these groups found encouragement in occupational health and safety legislation on both sides of the Atlantic Ocean.

# The Occupational Health Psychology Community

*Which bodies represent OHP?*
*What activities do these groups engage in?*

In response to the dramatic and sudden arrival of OHP on the world stage in the 1990s, an international band of protagonists was quick to appreciate that the discipline would benefit from the establishment of representative bodies. These would serve to shape and drive forward developments in the discipline, and consolidate its position within occupational health provision. OHP now benefits from two regional representative bodies that enjoy constructive, mutually beneficial, working relationships. These are the European Academy of Occupational Health Psychology (EAOHP), and in North America, the Society for Occupational Health Psychology (SOHP).

### European Academy of Occupational Health Psychology

The European Academy of Occupational Health Psychology has its roots in discussions that began in 1997 between a group of academics, led by Tom Cox, at what would later become the Institute of Work, Health & Organisations (IWHO) at the University of Nottingham (UK), and the departments of Occupational Medicine at Skive Syghus and Herning Syghus (Denmark). Those discussions led to the establishment of an organizing committee, empowered by an enabling document signed in 1998, dedicated to bringing about 'an institution [that is] urgently needed in Europe to bring together and support those concerned for research, teaching and practice in relation to psychological, social and organisational issues in occupational health, and to promote excellence in such activities' (European Academy of Occupational Health Psychology, 1998). The Academy was formally constituted in 1999 at the First European Workshop on Occupational Health Psychology in Lund, Sweden, organized by the Universities of Lund and Kristianstad. In the years immediately following its inception the Academy operated out of the Institute of Work, Health & Organisations in the care of a team led by Tom Cox and actively supported by a pan-European group of individuals and institutions.

In 2006 the Academy was registered as a charity under English law, a move that served to ensure its continued growth as a formal, transparent and democratic operation that exists for the benefit of its members and the advancement of the discipline. In accordance with the legal requirements of charitable status, the Academy is governed by a panel of trustees that empowers an Executive Committee with responsibility for day-to-day operations. Charitable status requires the Academy to possess a constitution that is enshrined in law, and procedures for the election of members to the Executive Committee. These innovations have provided a launch pad for efforts to decentralize the Academy's operations with a view to involving a broad range of individuals in the management of the Academy's activities. As a result, the Academy is today managed by a team that is truly European in its incorporation of individuals from numerous Member States, and this pan-European character is reflected in the Academy's activities.

The most high profile of the Academy's activities, and that which acts as a metaphorical camp fire for all to gather around, is its conference series. Conferences have been held in Lund, Sweden (1999); Nottingham, England (2000); Barcelona, Spain (2001); Vienna, Austria (2002); Berlin, Germany (2003); Porto, Portugal (2004); Dublin, Ireland (2006); Valencia, Spain (2008); and, Rome, Italy (2010). The success of these has grown year on year; attendance has grown from approximately one hundred delegates at the first conference to many times that number at more recent gatherings. Over the years the demographic makeup of delegates has changed; whereas the early conferences were almost exclusively attended by academics, recent conferences have attracted cohorts of practitioners, students, and local occupational safety and health specialists who wish to receive an introduction to the discipline.

The Academy bestows three categories of honour. These are important for encouraging research, education, and practice in the discipline, and for recognizing excellence. The first of these, Fellowships, are awarded to those who have made an exceptional contribution to OHP through research, professional practice, or educational activities over an extended period. In this way the Academy is able to recognize the outstanding input made by these individuals to advancing the discipline. The Fellowship roll of honour reads as a list of some of the leading OHP

**Pioneer**    Tom Cox CBE (1947–)

Tom Cox CBE is an applied psychologist who has dedicated his career to the advancement of research, education, and practice in occupational health psychology. In a career spanning more than 40 years at the University of Nottingham in the UK, Tom has developed an international reputation for injecting his science with an indefatigable drive to share the fruits of the discipline with as wide an audience as possible. Tom arrived at the University of Nottingham in 1966 to pursue an undergraduate degree in psychology. That was followed by a PhD which secured a lectureship in the Department of Psychology where he soon became internationally renowned on the publication of his seminal book *Stress* in 1978. The book was among the first to consider theory and practice on work-related stress and remained a bestseller for more than two decades. In 1986, Tom established the international quarterly journal *Work & Stress* which soon established itself as one of the leading journals in applied psychology, and was later to become the affiliated journal of the European Academy of Occupational Health Psychology. In the early 1990s, he initiated the programme of work for which he is perhaps best known: the development of a risk management paradigm for the control and prevention of work-related stress. His work in this area informed the design and operationalization of the British government's guidance on work-related stress. In 1997, Tom instigated discussions that led to the creation of the European Academy of Occupational Health Psychology, and he became its founding president. In 1999 he left the Department of Psychology to form a school of applied psychology: the Institute of Work, Health & Organisations (IWHO). A postgraduate research institute committed to 'healthy people, healthy work, and healthy organizations', since its inception IWHO has been at the forefront of OHP activities in Europe, hosting *Work & Stress*, the EAOHP, and providing the world's first Masters Degree in the discipline. Tom has received widespread recognition for his work. Most notably, he was awarded the Commander of the British Empire by Queen Elizabeth II in 2000 for services to occupational health. In 2008 he was awarded a lifetime achievement award by the Society for Occupational Health Psychology.

protagonists. It includes: Tage Kristensen (2000), Jose Maria Peiro (2001), André Büssing (2003) (posthumous), Johannes Siegrist (2003), Lois Tetrick (2003), Michiel Kompier (2004), Kari Lindstrom (2006), Steve Sauter (2006), Julian Barling (2008), Töres Theorell (2008), and Cary Cooper (2010).

## Pioneer    Tage S. Kristensen (1943–)

Tage is one of the pioneers of psychosocial work environment research in Denmark. He became well known for his work in the field of work and cardiovascular diseases following publication of two comprehensive reviews of the research published in 1989 in the *Scandinavian Journal of Work, Environment, and Health*. Since that time, Tage has produced some 200 publications and given more than 100 conference presentations in this field. In 1991 he was one of the founders of the Committee on Cardiology in Occupational Health under the International Commission on Occupational Health (ICOH), and he served as chairman of this committee for a number of years. In 1995 he arranged the first international conference on the topic of Work Environment and Cardiovascular Diseases. In 1994 he founded the Danish Society of Psychosocial Medicine under the aegis of the International Society of Behavioral Medicine. He was a member of the Governing Council of the International Society of Behavioral Medicine (ISBM) for many years. He is also known for being the driving force behind two psychosocial questionnaires that have been widely used in international research: The Copenhagen Psychosocial Questionnaire (COPSOQ) and the Copenhagen Burnout Inventory (CBI). In 1998 he was one of the organizers of the First International ICOH Conference on Psychosocial Factors at Work and also one of the founding fathers of the Scientific Committee on Psychosocial Factors under the ICOH. During the past 10–15 years he has been working actively on psychosocial intervention research and published numerous works in this field. Internationally he has been keynote speaker, chairman, and organizer at a large number of congresses and workshops, and he has given courses on psychosocial factors at work in many countries. He was the first professor at the National Institute of Occupational Health in Copenhagen, Denmark (2000–2008) and is now working as an independent researcher and consultant. He has received a number of national awards and was appointed fellow of the European Academy of Occupational Health Psychology in 2001.

Through its association with the journal *Work & Stress*, the Academy has awarded an annual Best Paper Prize since 2006. Decision criteria include citations as well as the interest that the paper has attracted (as indicated from download data). In addition, to encourage excellence in the next generation of OHP researchers, and in recognition of early-career distinction, the André Büssing Memorial Prize is awarded annually in the memory of the Academy's first

Vice-President. Awarded on the basis of the design, execution, relevance, and presentation of a study revealed at the Academy's conference, recipients have included:

- Annet de Lange (then at Vrije Universiteit Amsterdam, the Netherlands) (2004), for research on the relationship between work characteristics and health outcomes as a function of age;
- Nele de Cuyper (Katholieke Universiteit Leuven, Belgium) (2006), for studies on employability among insecure and temporary workers;
- Lieke ten Brummelhuis (Utrecht University, the Netherlands) (2008), for an examination of copying co-workers' sickness absence in teams.

New research of relevance to OHP is published in numerous occupational health, business management, and ergonomics journals. Among these research outlets there exist two quarterly international journals that are dedicated to serving the field. The first of these, *Work & Stress*, was established in 1996 by Tom Cox. As previously mentioned, the journal has established a reputation for publishing high quality peer-reviewed papers concerned with the psychological, social, and organizational aspects of occupational and environmental health, and stress and safety management, and is now ranked among the top ten in applied psychology. Since 2000, *Work & Stress* has been published in association with the European Academy whose members receive an individual subscription as part of their membership package.

## Society for Occupational Health Psychology

The Society for Occupational Health Psychology (SOHP) was established in 2004 under the inaugural leadership of Leslie Hammer (Portland State University), whom, along with a group of likeminded academics and practitioners, sought to develop a professional group for the discipline on the American continent. The Society fulfils its objectives:

By obtaining, and disseminating to the public factual data regarding occupational health psychology, through the promotion and encouragement of psychological research on significant theoretical and practical questions relating to occupational health, and by promoting and encouraging the application of the findings of such psychological research to the problems of the workplace. (Society for Occupational Health Psychology, 2008, p. 1)

Discussions on the creation of the Society began in 2001 with a meeting hosted by Paul Spector and Tammy Allen at the University of South Florida that was attended by representatives from the North American universities which, at that time, offered OHP programmes. A series of meetings ensued over the next 3 years that led to the establishment of the SOHP and instalment of its first officers in October 2004. From the outset, SOHP had a cooperative relationship with the American Psychological Association. In 2008, SOHP became a formal co-organizer of the Work, Stress, and Health conference series. This series began with a conference in Washington, DC (1990) that was followed by two further events in Washington (1992, 1995), after which the conference moved around North America, taking in Baltimore, MD (1999); Toronto, Canada (2003); Miami, FL (2006); Washington, DC (2008); and San Juan, Puerto Rico (2009).

In the same way that the EAOHP is affiliated to the journal *Work & Stress*, SOHP has a formal link with the *Journal of Occupational Health Psychology* (JOHP). Launched in 1996 as a result of collaboration between the NIOSH and the American Psychological Association, SOHP members receive a personal subscription to the journal. JOHP publishes research, theory, and public policy articles and has been edited by a number of pre-eminent North American occupational health psychologists.

### International Coordinating Group for Occupational Health Psychology

Both the EAOHP and the SOHP hold permanent seats on the International Coordinating Group for Occupational Health Psychology (ICG-OHP). Created in 2000, the ICG-OHP meets annually to encourage collaboration between existing and emerging representative groups in shaping the future of OHP. The Group's website featuring news on the latest international OHP developments can be found at www.icg-ohp.org.

## Summary

OHP is represented by two regional bodies: the European Academy of Occupational Health Psychology and, in North America, the Society for Occupational Health Psychology. Both groups operate activities such as conferences and the production of publications for the promotion of research, education, and practice. Each has a permanent seat on the International Coordinating Group for Occupational Health Psychology that exists to encourage fruitful collaboration among vested interest parties.

## SUMMARY AND CONCLUSIONS

- OHP is a young discipline that emerged out of the confluence of changing characteristics of work and the workforce, legislative events, and research advances in the twentieth century.
- OHP can be defined as the application of the principles and practices of psychology to occupational health issues.
- Contemporary changes to the content and context of work suggest that the prevalence of psychosocial risks is likely to increase. OHP practitioners have a unique contribution to make to the management of such risks.
- The discipline is represented by European and North American bodies that work collaboratively to support the sustainable development of the field.

This chapter has introduced the reader to the discipline of OHP, the nature of its practice, the emergence of the discipline, and the representative bodies that support research, education, and practice on the international stage. Having read this chapter, it is hoped that you will have developed an appreciation of the unique blend of knowledge and skills that the OHP practitioner brings to the management of occupational safety and health issues associated with the contemporary world of work. We hope that you, as we, are excited about the opportunities laid out for OHP practitioners to promote well-being and the quality of working life, and to achieve the development of healthy workplaces that support healthy communities.

### Suggestions for Further Reading

Barling, J., & Griffiths, A. (2002). A history of occupational health psychology, in J. C. Quick & L. Tetrick (Eds.). *Handbook of occupational health psychology* (pp. 19–34). Washington, DC: American Psychological Association.

Hammer, L., & Schonfeld, I. (2007). The historical development of the Society for Occupational Health Psychology. *Society for Occupational Health Psychology Newsletter, 1,* 2.

Münsterberg, H. (1913). *Psychology and industrial efficiency,* Boston: Houghton Mifflin. This book provides a fascinating insight into hopes and ambitions for the development of the field by one of the pioneers of research related to OHP. It is out of copyright, and it can be downloaded free of charge at www.gutenberg.org/etext/15154.

Sauter, S. L., Brightwell, W. S., Colligan, M. J., Hurrell, J. J., Jr., Katz, T. M., LeGrande, D. E., et al. (2002). *The changing organization of work and the safety and health of working people* (DHHS [NIOSH] Publication No. 2002-116). Cincinnati, OH: National Institute for Occupational Safety and Health. Available at www.cdc.gov/niosh/pdfs/02-116.pdf.

Sauter, S., Hurrell, J., Fox, H., Tetrick, L., & Barling, J. (1999). Occupational Health Psychology: An emerging discipline, *Industrial Health, 37*, 199–211.

## References

Adkins, J. A. (1999). Promoting organizational health: the evolving practice of occupational health psychology. *Professional Psychology: Research and Practice, 30*, 129–137.

Amalgamated Engineering Union (1944). *First Report on Health and Welfare Enquiry 1944 Part I.* Author.

Barling, J., & Griffiths, A. (2003). A history of occupational health psychology, in J. C. Quick & L. Tetrick (Eds.). *Handbook of occupational health psychology* (pp. 19–34). Washington, DC: American Psychological Association.

Barnes-Farrell, J. (2006). History of OHP and education of OHP professionals in the United States. In S. McIntyre, & J. Houdmont (Eds.), *Occupational health psychology: Key papers of the European Academy of Occupational Health Psychology (Vol. 7)* (pp. 425–426). Maia, Portugal: ISMAI Publishers.

Chen, P. Y., DeArmond, S., & Huang, Y. H. (2006). Occupational health psychology. In S. G. Rogelberg (Ed.). *The encyclopedia of industrial and organizational psychology.* CA: Sage Publishing.

Chen, P. Y., Huang, Y. H., & DeArmond, S. (2005). Occupational health psychology: Opportunities and challenges for psychologists in the 21st century. *Research in Applied Psychology, 27*, 43–56.

Cohen, A., & Margolis, B. (1973). Initial psychological research related to the Occupational Safety and Health Act of 1970. *American Psychologist, 7*, 600–606.

Cox, T. (1978). *Stress,* London: Macmillan.

Cox, T. (2000). Chair's address: European Academy of Occupational Health Psychology: Present and future. In T. Cox, P. Dewe, K. Nielsen, & R. Cox (Eds.), *Occupational health psychology: Europe 2000* (pp. i–ii). Nottingham: IWHO Publications.

Cox, T., Baldursson, E., & Rial González, E. (2000). Occupational health psychology. *Work & Stress, 14*, 101–104.

Cox, T., Griffiths, A., & Rial González, E. (2000). *Research on work-related stress.* Luxembourg: Office for Official Publications of the European Communities.

EU-OSHA – European Agency for Safety and Health at Work (2007). *Expert forecast on emerging psychosocial risks related to occupational safety and health (OSH),* Available at: http://osha.europa.eu/en/publications/reports/7807118/view

Emery, F., & Thorsrud, E. (1969). *Form and content in industrial democracy.* London: Tavistock.

European Academy of Occupational Health Psychology (1998). *Enabling Document.* Retrieved 1 July 2008, from www.eaohp.org.

Fullagar, C., & Hatfield, J. (2005, April). *Occupational health psychology: Charting the field,* Paper presented at the 20th annual SIOP Conference, Los Angeles, CA.

Frankenhaeuser M., & Gardell B. (1976). Underload and overload in working life: Outline of a multi-disciplinary approach. *Journal of Human Stress, 13*, 35–46.

Gardell, B. (1971). *Alienation and mental health.* Stockholm: Personaladminstrativa Radet.

Gardell, B. (1982). Worker participation and autonomy: a multilevel approach to democracy at the workplace. *International Journal of Health Services, 12*, 527–528.

Hammer, L., & Schonfeld, I. (2007). The historical development of the Society for Occupational Health Psychology. *Society for Occupational Health Psychology Newsletter, 1*, 2.

Health of Munition Workers Committee (1915). Health of Munition Workers Committee. *British Medical Journal, 2*, 863–864.

Houdmont, J., Leka, S., & Bulger, C. (2010). The definition of curriculum areas in occupational health psychology. *European Academy of Occupational Health Psychology Newsletter, 7*, 3–5 (February).

Innes, M., & Barling, J. (2003). *Putting health back into occupational health psychology.* Paper presented at the British Psychological Society Occupational Psychology Conference, Bournemouth, UK (January).

Johnson, J., & Johansson, G. (1991). *The psychosocial work environment: Work organization, democratization and health.* Amityville, NY: Baywood Publishing Company.

Kahn, R. L. (1964). *Work and Health.* New York: Wiley.

Kang, S. Y., Staniford, A. K., Dollard, M. F., & Kompier, M. (2008). Knowledge development and content in occupational health psychology: A systematic analysis of the Journal of Occupational Health Psychology and Work & Stress, 1996–2006). In J. Houdmont, & S. Leka (Eds.), *Occupational health psychology: European perspectives on research, education, and practice (Vol. III)* (pp. 27–62), Nottingham: Nottingham University Press.

Karasek, R., & Theorell, T. (1990). *Healthy work: Stress, productivity and the reconstruction of work life.* New York: Basic Books.

Kompier, M. (2006). New systems of work and workers' health. *Scandinavian Journal of Work, Environment and Health, 32*, 421–430.

Kornhauser, A. (1962). Toward an Assessment of the Mental Health of Factory Workers: A Detroit Study. *Human Organization, 21*, 43–46.

Leka, S., Khan, S., & Griffiths, A. (2008). *Exploring health and safety practitioners' training needs in workplace health issues.* Wigston, UK: Institution of Occupational Safety and Health.

Levi, L. (1972). Stress and distress in response to psychosocial stimuli: laboratory and real life studies on sympathoadrenomedullary and related reactions. *Acta Medica Scandinavica Supplementum, 528*, 1–166.

Macik-Frey, M., Quick, J., & Nelson, D. (2007). Advances in occupational health: From a stressful beginning to a positive future. *Journal of Management, 33*, 809–840.

Münsterberg, H. (1913). *Psychology and industrial efficiency,* Boston: Houghton Mifflin. This book provides a fascinating insight into hopes and ambitions for the development of the field by one of the pioneers of research related to OHP. It is out of copyright, and it can be downloaded free of charge at www.gutenberg.org/etext/15154.

O'Toole, J., & Lawler, E. (2006). *The new American workplace.* NY: Palgrave Macmillan.

Quick, J. C. (1999). Occupational health psychology: The convergence of health and clinical psychology with public health and preventive medicine in an organizational context. *Professional Psychology: Research and Practice, 50*, 123–128.

Quick, J. C., Camara, W. J., Hurrell, J. J., Jr., Johnson, J. V., Piotrkowski, C. S., Sauter, S. L., & Spielberger, C. D. (1997). Introduction and historical overview. *Journal of Occupational Health Psychology, 2*, 3–6.

Quinn, R., & Shepard, L. (1974). *The 1972–73 quality of employment survey.* Ann Arbor: Survey Research Center, Institute for Social Research, University of Michigan.

Quinn, R. & Staines, G. (1979). *The 1977 quality of employment survey.* Ann Arbor: Survey Research Center, Institute for Social Research, University of Michigan.

Raymond, J., Wood, D., & Patrick, W. (1990). Psychology training in work and health. *American Psychologist, 45,* 1159–1161.

Sauter, S., & Hurrell, J. (1999). Occupational health psychology: Origins, content and direction. *Professional Psychology: Research and Practice, 30,* 117–122.

Sauter, S., Murphy, L., & Hurrell, J. (1990). Prevention of work-related psychological disorders: A national strategy proposed by the National Institute for Occupational Safety and Health (NIOSH). *American Psychologist, 45,* 1146–1158.

Sauter, S., Hurrell, J., Fox, H., Tetrick, L., & Barling, J. (1999). Occupational Health Psychology: An emerging discipline, *Industrial Health, 37,* 199–211.

Schneider, D., Camara, W., Tetrick, T., & Sternberg, C. (1999). Training in occupational health psychology: Initial efforts and alternative models. *Professional Psychology, 30,* 138–142.

Sinclair, R. (2009). The future of OHP: The experts speak (Part I). *Society for Occupational Health Psychology Newsletter, 5,* 11–13 (January).

Sinclair, R., Hammer, L., Oeldorf Hirsch, A., & Brubaker, T. (2006). *Do academics and practitioners agree on perceived occupational health priorities?* Paper presented at the Work Stress and Health conference, Miami, FL (March).

Society for Occupational Health Psychology (2008). *Part I: Constitution and Bylaws,* Retrieved 1 July 2008, from www.sohp.psy.uconn.edu/SOHP%20Constitution%20 (January%202008).pdf.

Tetrick, L., & Ellis, B. (2002). Developing an OHP curriculum that addresses the needs of organizations and labor unions in the USA. In C. Weikert, E. Torkelson, & J. Pryce (Eds.), *Occupational health psychology: Empowerment, participation and health at work,* (pp. 158–161). Nottingham: IWHO Publications.

Theorell, T. (1999). How to deal with stress in organizations? A health perspective on theory and practice. *Scandinavian Journal of Work, Environment and Health, 6,* 616–624.

Theorell, T. (2007). Psychosocial factors in research on work conditions and health in Sweden. *Scandinavian Journal of Work, Environment and Health, 33,* suppl 1, 20–26.

Theorell, T., & Floderus-Myrhed, B. (1977). 'Workload' and risk of myocardial infarction – a prospective psychosocial analysis. *International Journal of Epidemiology, 6,* 17–21.

Thorsrud, E., & Emery, F. E. (1970). *Mot en ny bedriftsorganisasjon* [Towards a new organization of enterprises]. Oslo: Tanum.

University of Michigan (1970). *Survey on working conditions. Final report on univariate and bivariate tables.* (Contractor's Report). Washington, DC: Employment Standards Administration, Department of Labor.

US Department of Health, Education, and Welfare (1966). *Protecting the health of eighty million Americans: A national goal for occupational health.* Washington, DC: US Government Printing Office.

Ursin, H., Baade, E., & Levine, S. (1978). *Psychobiology of stress: A study of coping men.* New York: Academic Press.

*Work in America:* Report of a special task force to the Secretary of Health, Education and Welfare (1973). Cambridge, MA: MIT Press.

Zickar, M. (2003). Remembering Arthur Kornhauser: Industrial psychology's advocate for worker well-being. *Journal of Applied Psychology, 88,* 363–369.

# 2

# Work-Related Stress
## A Theoretical Perspective

## Tom Cox and Amanda Griffiths

### CHAPTER OUTLINE

This chapter offers a theoretical perspective on work-related stress. It considers the theories and models that frame our current understanding and offers an architecture for organizing these theories. It distinguishes between the earlier theories and the more contemporary ones, offering a critique that allows us to understand both the arguments and the paradigms driving the development of those theories and their respective strengths and weaknesses. It also considers the relationship between theory and practice and the value of theory in driving practical and feasible interventions and evaluation. Finally, it suggests what the future development of theory in this area should offer.

## Introduction

Over 30 years ago, one of the first structured and holistic approaches to the topic of stress was published (Cox, 1978). The tract contributed to the development of a theoretically focused discussion of the nature of stress. Among other things, it offered an architecture for structuring our knowledge of stress theory. This was based on the idea that there were essentially three types of models in use which together provided the framework for a rapidly developing 'industry' of research and practice. Over the following years, other such accounts have been published, including an influential review on work-related stress published by the European Agency for Safety and Health at Work (Cox, Griffiths, & Rial González, 2000). Considering the developing landscape created by this progression of reviews and related publications, it is interesting that little seems to have changed in relation to theories of work-related stress over those 20 or so years. Arguably, there have only been four developments of note.

The first development has been the adoption of Karasek's (1979) job Demand–Control (DC) theory of stress at the national and international policy levels. The second development has been the rise in importance of Siegrist's (1996) Effort–Reward Imbalance (ERI) theory and the now frequent comparison of this theory with that of Karasek's in terms of how well they account for the available research data. The third development has been the translation of theories of work-related stress into a practical method for reducing the associated risks to worker health and safety at the organizational level: psychosocial risk management (see Chapter 5). The key here has been the development of a holistic model of work-related stress describing the bigger picture in terms of stressors as hazards, exposures, and pathways to harm. This model is underpinned by the adoption of the language of 'risk' by many applied researchers and practitioners working within occupational health psychology. Finally, there now appears to be recognition that our theories no longer have an adequate conceptual and methodological framework for either research or practice, and that the next major developments have to be in this area. There is particular concern for the way in which we evaluate our interventions to reduce the risks associated with stress at work at both the organizational and individual levels (Cox, Karanika-Murray, Griffiths, & Houdmont, 2007; Griffiths, 1999).

Against this background, this chapter attempts two things: first to provide an overview of contemporary theories of stress in relation to work and, second, to discuss recent advances in theory and identify possible future developments. It begins by considering the importance of theory to occupational health psychology.

## There Is Nothing So Practical As A Good Theory

*Why is theory important?*
*What do theories allow us to do?*

For many reading this book, the idea of being excited by a chapter focused on theory may feel slightly strange. Occupational health psychologists are committed to making a difference and therefore are preoccupied with hands on research and practice. Translating the former into the latter or, more straightforwardly, practicing occupational health psychology, is their main aim. Thinking about theory may seem too abstract and unworldly and of no direct relevance to what they do or want to do. They are wrong as the somewhat clichéd quotation from Kurt Lewin (1952), the father of social psychology, would suggest: 'there is nothing more practical than a good theory' (p. 169).

Theory is important. Theories are our way of making sense of the world and making explicit how we think the world operates. Good theories are testable and by testing them we can make better sense of the world. Scientific theories are built on evidence and are, in common parlance, both 'tried and tested'. However, theories provide not only an explanation of how things work but, through such explanation, an ability to predict what might happen next and a vehicle for intervening and controlling those events. Their value, for applied scientists, lies in what they add to our ability to intervene in and control events (hopefully and morally for the better). It is the combination of the two underlying philosophies of empiricism and pragmatism in occupational health psychology that characterizes its development and use of theory.

In providing our understanding of the world, and our explanation of the way it works, theory also provides us with definitions of key concepts and events. Here our theories of work-related stress give us the definitions that we need to answer the simple but critical question: 'what is stress?'

Of course, there are many different theories of work-related stress and thus many different definitions. Occupational health psychology is no different to any other discipline in the social and health sciences in this respect. Often these theories are offered as alternatives and in competition; a good example is the previously mentioned current fascination with comparing the theories of Karasek (1979) and Siegrist (1996). In one respect this is healthy and stimulates research but in another it is less so as it focuses us on the differences between theories rather than on what they have in common.

The authors' approach here is to discuss what contemporary theories have in common by suggesting a taxonomy, or architecture, for these theories. In doing so, the most striking conclusion to be drawn is that the main theories share a common framework in describing a system of events and a process which involves both environmental components and individual psychological, physiological, and behavioural ones. At the heart of this system of events are interactions among the various components involved while the whole system sits in the wider context of the relevant social, organizational, and societal environments. Much of our involvement in work-related stress is positioned within occupational health and safety, and, as such, legal and economic concerns form an important part of its wider context. This system can be conceptualized in terms of hazards, exposures, and pathways to harm. This chapter is framed by this global model of work-related stress.

## Summary

Theories are important because they are our way of making sense of the world and making explicit how we think the world operates. Good theories are testable and by testing them we can make better sense of the world. Good theories of work-related stress ought to help us to manage the challenge presented by the phenomenon.

# A Taxonomy of Theories of Stress
· · · · · · · · · · · · · · · · · · · · · · · · · · · · · · · · · · · · · · · · · · · · · · · · · · · · ·

*What are the differences between early theories of work-related stress and
contemporary ones?*
*What are the early theories, who was responsible for developing them, and what
do they say about work-related stress?*
*Why were the early theories judged inadequate and how are contemporary
theories an improvement on what preceded them?*
*What are the main contemporary theories and how do they differ from one another?*
*Which are the more adequate theories in terms of their ability to account for the
empirical evidence, conceptual validity, and application?*

This section, which represents the body of the chapter, presents a conceptual architecture for understanding the development of our main theories of stress and their
relationship to one to another. The content is effectively a taxonomy of theories of
work-related stress. Taxonomies are useful devices for simplifying and organizing our
thinking about issues and events. They help us make sense of complexity. A taxonomy
provides us with an intellectual architecture for imposing structure and meaning on
complexity. In doing so, taxonomies should simplify things only as far as is needed
and no further, and they should remain open to review and modification.

In 1978, the first author suggested a simple taxonomy of theories of stress based
on two simple distinctions (Cox, 1978): first, between early and (then) more recent
or contemporary theories, and second, within these two groups, between stimulus
and response based theories (early theories) and interactional (structural based)
and transactional (process based) theories (contemporary theories). This taxonomy is represented in Figure 2.1.

### Early stimulus based theories ('engineering' models)

The conceptual model underpinning the early stimulus based theories of stress was
simple, mechanistic, linear, and largely derived from the discipline of engineering.
The essential argument was that events in the external environment could cause a
behavioural and physiological reaction in the individual exposed to them. The
reaction was understood to be reversible unless a threshold was reached. Events
were seen as aversive (threatening) if not noxious (damaging or harmful). Thus,
stress was conceptualized as a characteristic of the external environment to be
treated as an independent variable, i.e., the environmental cause of ill-health. This
perspective was succinctly expressed by Sir Charles Symonds (1947) (cited in Cox
(1978)) in a report that discussed psychological disorders in Royal Air Force flying
personnel: 'Stress is that which happens to the man, not that which happens in
him; it is a set of causes, not a set of symptoms.' This approach to the understanding of stress led to the development of the concept of a 'stress threshold' and
research on individual differences in respect of this threshold.

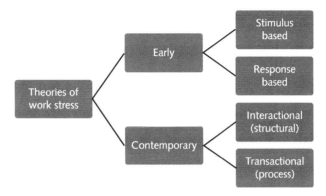

**Figure 2.1**   Taxonomy of theories of work-related stress.

## Early response based theories ('physiological' models)

Early response based theories, deriving from medicine, used a different termin-ology to describe what was essentially the same conceptual system. Aversive or noxious characteristics of the environment were seen as the stressors and stress was identified as the reaction of the individual to those stressors. In this way, stress is understood to be the dependent variable, i.e., a physiological response to a threatening environment. Perhaps best known, over the years, for his elucidation of the response based approach was Selye (1950, 1956), who defined stress as 'a state manifested by a specific syndrome which consists of all the non-specific changes within the biologic system'.

Selye described in some detail the possible neuro-endocrine mechanisms involved in the physiological and behavioural response to being exposed to environmental stressors. His research focused on the role of the adrenal glands (medulla and cortex) and he described a non-specific and general pattern of stress response which appeared to unfold over time across the life of a species and be a characteristic of most if not all mammalian species. Selye (1956) proposed a three-stage pattern of response to stress which he termed the General Adaptation Syndrome (GAS). When the animal first encounters acute stress in the form of threat or actual harm, it responds with an *alarm* or *emergency reaction*. This is followed by a *recovery* or *resistance* stage during which the animal repairs itself and stores energy. If the stress-causing events continue, *exhaustion* sets in. This third stage is what became known popularly as burnout. Classic symptoms of burnout include loss of drive and energy, emotional flatness, and (in humans) dulling of responsiveness to the needs of others. Interestingly, there appears to be much overlap between the symptoms of burnout and those of depression and of chronic fatigue syndrome. In the extreme of Selye's GAS model, *exhaustion* can precede *death* mediated by a final reoccurrence of the *emergency response:* a last throw of the dice.

Selye (1956) provided an explanation of how the activation of the GAS could translate into physical ill-health and the conditions which he thought were affected by the stress response he termed 'diseases of adaptation'. The theory stimulated a research focus during the 1980s on a range of physiological mechanisms including the anterior pituitary-adrenal cortical system and the sympathetic-adrenal medullary system (e.g., Cox & Cox, 1985; Cox, Thirlaway, Gotts, & Cox, 1983) and conditions recognized as being affected by work-related stress, such as cancer (e.g., Cox & Mackay, 1982).

The work of Selye was consistent with that of Cannon (1929) who first described the so-called fight-or-flight response to threat. This response has also been called the acute stress response. Cannon's theory (1929) states that animals react to threats with a general discharge of the sympathetic nervous system, priming them for fight (defensive aggression) or flight (escape). This pattern of response was later recognized as the first stage of the GAS.

The response based theory of stress, as a synthesis of the work of Selye, Cannon, and related researchers, became dominant in the 1960s and remains well supported despite contemporary advances in our thinking. Such advances became necessary as the early theories became less able to account for the research data without continual modification and as the dominant conceptual frameworks in psychology and physiology changed. Crucially, the response based perspective fails to take into account individual differences; it assumes all individuals will respond to a stressful situation in exactly the same way and neglects to take into account variance between and within individuals in respect of the interpretation of the threatening nature of a stimulus.

Furthermore, the focus on stress being 'within' the individual has resulted in some of Selye's ideas having been misinterpreted and misapplied. Le Fevre, Matheny, and Kolt (2003), for example, have noted that misinterpretation of Selye's ideas has led some to suggest that there can be positive stress (eustress) or, at least, an optimal level of stress. The former idea derives from confusion between stress and challenge, whereby a reasonable level of challenge is required as a characteristic of living things. Sometimes this sort of notion becomes muddled with the Yerkes and Dodson inverted U concept (see Chapter 3, Figure 3.1). Yerkes and Dodson (1908) described an inverted U-shaped relationship between strength of electric shock and task performance in mice and some may have overgeneralized what proved to be a fragile finding to people and to work-related stress. This has resulted in some managers believing that a certain level of work-related stress may actually be good for their employees; a perspective which may encourage interventions that concentrate on individuals and their responses to stress independent of the organizational context within which the problem occurs.

## Contemporary theories

A new genre of theory came to the fore during the 1970s. These contemporary theories were characterized by two things: first, they more obviously allowed for an interaction between the individual and their environment and, second, they ascribed a more active role for the person in that interaction introducing a new raft of psychological concepts to explain the interaction. Contemporary stress theory is psychological in that it either explicitly or implicitly recognizes the part played by psychological processes, such as perception, cognition, and emotion. These appear to determine how the individual recognizes, experiences, and responds to stressful situations, how they attempt to cope with that experience and how it might affect their physical, psychological, and social health. Such an approach allows for individual differences and that, in turn, has generated an interest both in the assessment of individuals' perception and experience of stress and in the relationships among experience, personality, behavioural style, and health. At the same time, a major area of concern has developed in relation to coping with stress and the ways in which coping can moderate, if not mediate, the effects of stress on health (Cox & Ferguson, 1991; Dewe, 1991; Dewe, Cox, & Ferguson, 1993; Dewe, Leiter, & Cox, 2000; Lazarus & Folkman, 1984).

Contemporary theories of stress treat it as a negative (unpleasant) emotional experience which occurs when individuals perceive themselves to be subject to excessive demands, or demands with which they cannot cope. The behavioural and physiological correlates of the experience of stress change the way the individual sees and thinks about the world, the way in which they behave, and their pattern of physiological activity. These changes, under certain circumstances, can increase the risk of psychological, physical, and social ill-health, and inappropriate behaviour.

The two types of theory identified herein, interactional (structural) and transactional (process), vary in where they place their emphasis in this unfolding situation and how active they see the individual in determining the overall situation and its outcomes. The interactional theories are focused on the architecture of the situations that give rise to the experience of stress and place less emphasis on the processes involved and the individual's attempts to cope following that experience. The transactional theories, by comparison, are concerned with processes such as cognitive appraisal and coping and therefore ascribe a more active role to the individual in determining outcomes. Arguably reflecting a greater input from clinical and social psychology, the interplay between the individual and their environment has been described as 'a transaction' with all the implications of such a terminology. The interactional or structural theories take a stronger input from social epidemiology as evidenced in the sort of studies that supported the development of those theories and the backgrounds of some of their main proponents.

A host of theories, and variants thereof, have developed within both the interactional and transactional families. It is neither possible nor advisable to attempt to survey them all. Here the strategy will be to identify and briefly discuss the main contributions and recent important developments.

### Contemporary interactional theories: Person–Environment Fit theory

Much contemporary stress theory finds a point of origin in the work of the Social Science Research Group at the University of Michigan and, in particular, that of Kahn (see Chapter 1), French, Caplan, and van Harrison. Together, they developed the seminal Person–Environment Fit (P–E Fit) model (Caplan, 1983; Edwards, Caplan, & van Harrison, 2000; French & Caplan, 1972; van Harrison, 1978). The P–E Fit model makes explicit not only the importance of the interaction between the individual and their environment in shaping their response to work situations and events but also the importance of the individual's perception of the environment, themselves, and the interaction between them. The P–E Fit model makes a clear distinction between the objective P–E Fit and the subjective one. The notion of 'fit' suggests a balancing or matching mechanism between, on the one hand, environment demands and individual needs and, on the other, what the environment supplies and the individual's ability (to cope). In organizational terms, there are two aspects of fit that the model considers: the degree to which an employee's attitudes and abilities meet the demands of the job and the extent to which the job environment meets the workers' needs (in particular, the extent to which the individual is permitted and encouraged to use their knowledge and skills in the job setting).

P–E Fit theory argues that stress can arise as a result of a lack of fit. Logically, this can take one of three forms (Edwards, Caplan, & van Harrison, 1998) where:

- The demands of the work environment exceed the employee's exceed ability.
- The employee's needs consistently fail to be met by the work environment.
- A combination of these two situations exists, i.e., where an employee's needs are not being met while at the same time their abilities are overstretched.

Consistent with the available evidence and with most other contemporary theories, P–E Fit theory suggests that lack of fit may give rise to both psychological symptoms (e.g., sleep disturbances, anxiety, panic attacks, dysphoria, restlessness) and physical symptoms (e.g., raised blood pressure, raised serum cholesterol, lowered immunity of stress) (Edwards, Caplan, & van Harrison, 1998).

Such mechanisms of fit, balance, or match have proved popular in all areas of psychology. The notion of fit also recognizes that there is an important role for the individual's perception in that process. However, at the same time, there have been criticisms of such an approach (Edwards and Cooper, 1990; Le Fevre et al., 2003). The main criticisms have been in relation to the assumption that the concept of 'demand' being too broad, the concept of fit being ill-defined and difficult to measure and the assumption that lack of fit is necessarily undesirable. In answer to these criticisms, the theory, like others, offers a framework for approaching the study and management of work-related stress. The concepts that it draws on are general but valid within psychology and there is no prohibition of their refinement in particular contexts and for particular purposes. Similarly, the central notion of fit is also an established explanatory concept within psychology and, again, there is no prohibition of its refinement.

The question of the most appropriate operationalization of fit and the answer to the question 'how do we best measure fit?' is partly an empirical one. The answer to the question 'is a lack of fit necessarily undesirable?' is also an empirical one.

It can be argued that different aspects of the P–E Fit model were developed and gave rise to Karasek's (1979) Demand–Control theory and Siegrist's (1996) Effort–Reward Imbalance theory, each of which is discussed below. In both cases, the notion of interaction is present and, in the case of Siegrist's theory, that of fit or imbalance. The concepts used by Karasek have resonance with those of the Michigan School while those employed by Siegrist owe more to equity theory in social psychology. Interestingly, both of these more recent theories have stimulated more empirical research than the P–E Fit model (or any other contemporary theory). Currently, they are dominant in occupational health psychology research.

## Contemporary interactional theories: Job Demand–Control theory

Karasek started his academic career as a sociologist. He formulated his job Demand–Control theory as part of his doctoral work in the mid 1970s and published the theory in a seminal article in 1979. The theory combines epidemiological views on the relationship between work demands and health complaints, on the one hand, with studies on job satisfaction and motivation on the other. Central in the model is the interaction between a particular set of work characteristics: job demands and job control. The model is usually presented diagrammatically as a $2 \times 2$ matrix of 'low and high demand' against 'high and low control' (Figure 2.2).

Simplistically, this allows for four different types of job (Karasek & Theorell, 1990; Stansfeld & Candy, 2006):

- 'High strain jobs': high demands with low control (the most risky to health).
- 'Active jobs': high demands with high control (less risky to health, average levels of job strain).
- 'Low strain jobs': low demands with high control (below average levels of job strain).
- 'Passive jobs': low demands with low control (the demotivating nature of this job type might induce average levels of job strain).

DC theory is expressed in terms of two testable notions: (1) the combination of high job demands with low job control is associated with psychological and physical strain (high strain jobs), and (2) jobs in which both demands and control are high lead to well-being, learning, and personal growth (active jobs). The early evidence suggested that this might be true (Karasek & Theorell, 1990) especially where the data were drawn from large scale studies and focussed on cardiovascular health outcomes. Some more recent data also support the basic notion of the strain hypothesis that there is an interaction between demands and control in producing

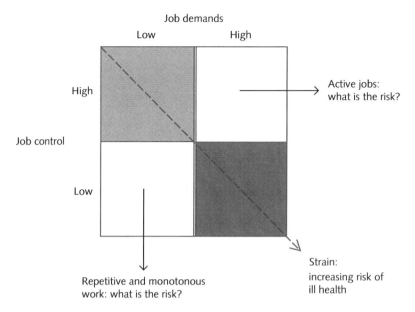

**Figure 2.2**  Job Demand–Control theory of stress (after Karasek, 1979).

health effects. Oeji, Dhondt, and Wiezer (2006) reported on a secondary analysis of data from the Third European Working Conditions Survey (the data were collected in 2000) and showed that high strain jobs, compared to the three other types, were associated with the highest levels of musculoskeletal disorders and stress-related health problems and the lowest satisfaction with working conditions. However, the evidence for the strain hypothesis is not overwhelming.

Stansfeld and Marmot (2002) reviewed many of the studies published on the DC model in relation to coronary heart disease. Although they found consistent results with regards to the effects of control on health outcomes, they concluded that there were only mixed results with regards to the full model and the critical interaction between demands and control (the strain hypothesis). Similarly, van Der Deof & Maes (1999) found that only 15 out of 31 studies reviewed supported the inter-action hypothesis in respect of psychological outcomes. De Lange et al. (2003) asked whether the failure of many studies to support the strain hypothesis could be largely due to their poor design. They therefore selected and examined what they judged to be the best 19 longitudinal studies available to them. They concluded, as did Stansfield and Marmot (2002), that overall these studies provided only modest support for the strain hypothesis with only 8 of the 19 studies showing evidence of the critical interaction between demands and control in producing the measured effects. In 2006, Taris re-analysed the results of an earlier review of 64 studies that incorporated the strain hypothesis. Of these, 33 made no comment on any interaction effects. The remaining 31 reported on 90 separate tests of the hypoth-esis and, of these, only 9 produced evidence to support the notion of an interaction between demands and control.

More recently, research has emerged which suggests that the model might better account for psychological health outcomes if coping resources are taken into account; in other words, through the incorporation of a key dimension of the transactional perspective on stress. For example, Noblet, Rodwell, and McWilliams (2006) found that internal resources, in the form of problem- and emotion-based coping, improved the model's ability to predict psychological health. Similarly, Kjaerheim, Haldorsen, and Andersen (1997) found that in isolation the Demand–Control model failed to predict heavy drinking in 3,204 Norwegian waiters and chefs. However, the model's ability to predict heavy drinking increased when individual coping resources (measured as frequency of difficulty in relaxing after work) were factored in.

An overview of the criticisms of the job Demand–Control theory suggests a number of issues that, together, might account for its modest performance. The key criticisms are: variance and uncertainty concerning the operationalization of the two key constructs, i.e., job demands and control (decision latitude); the model's focus on just two of a wide range of job characteristics gives undue weight to the strain hypothesis; and the model's assumed applicability to all health-related outcomes.

Three things can be concluded from the ongoing critique of the job Demand–Control model. First, both demand and control are important determinants of health-related outcomes but may act independently rather than interactively; second, the effects of the interaction between demand and control are modest and may be strongest in relation to cardiovascular health and; third, such effects may be easier to demonstrate at the population level than at the organizational or individual levels. Despite these caveats, many researchers persist in using Karasek's (1979) theory, sometimes uncritically, and it has had major impact at the policy level.

## Contemporary interactional theories: The Iso-Strain model

An attempt to broaden the scope of the job Demand–Control model has been made by Johnson and Hall (1988) who introduced a third factor: social support. This extension of the model has become known as the Demand–Control–Support model (DCS) or Iso-Strain model (see Research Close-Up 2.1).

The development of the Iso-Strain model reflected the growing interest in research in social support in its own right and how it might moderate or mediate effects on health. Essentially, the three factor derivative of the Demand–Control model postulated that lack of social support would strengthen the effects of the risky interaction. The high risk situation then became characterized by high demands, low control, and low social support. This formulation finds resonance in other contemporary theories of work stress and is remarkably similar to the transactional models described some time before by Lazarus (1966).

The data suggest that while the interactional effects referred to above can exist, social support also acts directly in the determination of health related outcomes.

Despite or because of this, the interest in social support has continued to grow and questions are now being asked about the relationship between social support and demand. Do particular types of support (informational, emotional, and practical) interact differently with the various types of demand? The idea that only specific types of social support can buffer the negative effects of exposure to particular demands has been referred to as the 'matching hypothesis' (Beeher, 1995; Cohen and Willis, 1985). Peeters and Le Blanc (2001), among others, have found support for this hypothesis in the context of staff burnout in oncology care in the Netherlands. Interestingly, support available from within the organization was not more effective than that from other sources, such as family members, in buffering the effects of workplace stressors. Social support from family members was more effective in moderating the relationship between workload demands and *depersonalization* while that from colleagues was more effective in relation to emotional demands and *depersonalization*. This finding, however, contradicts those of earlier studies which have found that social support from within the organization is more effective in buffering the effects of workplace stressors than that from outside the organization (Leather, Lawrence, Beale, & Cox, 1998; Rosen & Moghadam, 1990). This may be a fruitful area for further research.

---

### RESEARCH CLOSE-UP          2.1   The Iso-Strain model

*Source:* Johnson, J. V., & Hall, E. M. (1988). Job strain, workplace social support and cardiovascular disease: A cross sectional study of a random sample of the Swedish working population. *American Journal of Public Health, 78,* 1336–1342.

Johnson and Hall reported a study which incorporated consideration of social support within Karasek's job Demand–Control model. The study involved 13,779 working adults in Sweden. Their jobs were characterized in terms of the DC model but, in addition, measures of social support from supervisors and colleagues were taken. The outcome measures related to cardiovascular health.

On the basis of the results, Johnson and Hall proposed an extension of the DC model with the incorporation of social support, resulting in the description of a Demand–Control–Support (DCS) model which also came to be known as the 'Iso-Strain' model. The predictions made by the DCS model strongly resemble those of the DC model but assume that the strain hypothesis of the DC model will especially apply under conditions of low social support.

## Contemporary interactional theories:
## Effort–Reward Imbalance (ERI) model

The common interactional origins of Siegrist's Effort–Reward Imbalance (ERI) theory and Karasek's Demand–Control theory have been argued above but the theories differ in the way they conceptualize the key elements of the interaction. While the influence of social epidemiology can be detected in the nature of both the theories and their associated research methods, Karasek draws on the concepts used by the Michigan School while Siegrist delves elsewhere in social psychology. ERI theory derives from equity theory and focuses on the effort expended in work and the rewards offered for that effort. It is possible that the two theories are simply different ways of cutting the same cake. To this extent, they may reflect different perspectives on the same system much like our explanation of the difference between the stimulus and response based models (early theories).

Siegrist (1996) argues that where the individual's perceptions of the rewards of working do not match their perceptions of the effort involved, then this imbalance can carry a risk to health and associated behaviours (Figure 2.3).

Siegrist suggests that stress related to an imbalance between effort and reward can arise under three conditions, where an employee:

- has a poorly defined work contract or where that employee has little choice concerning alternative employment opportunities;
- accepts that imbalance for strategic reasons such as the prospect of improved future working conditions;
- copes with the demands of work through over commitment.

The theory is rooted in the notion of distributive justice and assumes that effort at work is spent as part of an essentially psychological contract based on the norm of social reciprocity where rewards are provided in terms of money, esteem, and career opportunities including job security. A lack of reciprocity between effort and reward, in what are for the employee high cost and low gain situations, causes emotional distress associated with stress responses. The recurrent violation of the

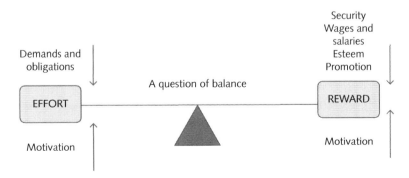

**Figure 2.3**   The Effort–Reward Imbalance theory of work-related stress.

norm of reciprocity may elicit a sense of being treated unfairly and suffering injustice which can damage not only the psychological contract between the employee and their organization but also negatively affect their self-esteem.

In a growing number of reviews (e.g., Kivimaki et al., 2006; Schnall, Belkic, Landsbergis, & Baker, 2000; Stansfeld & Candy, 2006; Stansfield & Marmot, 2002; Tsutsumi & Kawakami, 2004; van Vegchel, de Jonge, Bosma, & Schaufeli, 2005), the ERI model has been shown to account for an appreciable amount of the data variance in relation to health-related outcomes. A number of large-scale epidemiological studies have likewise found strong support for the model. Kouvonen et al. (2005) found that high ERI was associated with high body mass index in a sample of 45,810 male and female employees, and Kouvonen et al. (2006) demonstrated that women and men with high ERI were 40 per cent more likely to have simultaneously $\geq 3$ lifestyle risk factors (e.g., smoking, drinking, physically inactive, high BMI) compared with their counterparts with low ERI.

When compared to Karasek's model, the ERI model appears to do slightly but significantly better. However, the best prediction of health-related outcomes comes from combining the two models. This was demonstrated clearly by Peter, Siegrist, Hallqvist, Reuterwall, and Theorell (2002) who showed that it was possible to improve the estimation of risk of myocardial infarction by combining information from the two models; an outcome they attributed to the Demand–Control model's focus on situational (extrinsic) characteristics and the Effort–Reward Imbalance model's concentration of person (intrinsic) characteristics in addition to situational ones.

It can be concluded that interactional models offer an appealing theoretical framework which attracts some evidential support. On balance, the more recent of the two dominant models, the ERI model, has attracted the least criticism and appears to better account for the available data. Together, these two interactional theories offer a straightforward and robust theoretical anchor point from which to develop refinements to the models in order to better account for the experience of work-related stress (Uhmann, 2007; van Veldhoven, Taris, de Jonge & Broersen, 2005). The conceptual development of interactional models has proceeded with examples such as the Demand-Induced Strain Compensation (DISC) model (de Jonge & Dormann, 2003) that seeks to integrate the DC and ERI models into a single framework; the Job Demands–Resources (JDR) model (Bakker, Demerouti, Taris, & Schreurs, 2003) and the Demand–Skill–Support model (van Veldhoven et al., 2005). These models share two characteristics: a firm theoretical underpinning and recognition that personality, personal agency, and personal resources all play a role (Schaufeli, 2004).

## Contemporary transactional stress theory

Transactional theories of stress encompass much of what has been shown likely through the development, testing, and application of the structural interactional theories. In particular, the concepts of demand, control, and social support have proved common and useful cornerstones. In a sense, transactional theories attempt to describe the processes by which exposure to the work environment, say in terms the person's experience of demands, control, and social support drive the experience of stress, the individual's reactions to it, their attempts at coping, and the effects on their health and behaviour. The perceptual and cognitive processes involved have been named by Lazarus (1966) as 'cognitive appraisal'.

The notion of 'transaction' implies that work-related stress is neither resident in the employee's work environment nor an expression of their reaction to that environment (Cox, 1978). Rather, 'stress ... reflects the conjunction of a person with certain motives and beliefs with an environment whose characteristics pose harm, threats or challenges depending on these personal characteristics' (Lazarus, 1990, p. 3). The integration of the *structural* aspects of the interactional approach with a *process* oriented approach allows for a *stress process* to be described (Cox & Griffiths, 1995) in terms of five basic components:

- Antecedent factors: exposure to both the classical hazards of work and those inherent in the design and management of work and work organizations (psychosocial hazards).
- Cognitive processes that give rise to the emotional experience of stress deriving from the employee's perceptions of the demands placed on them, their ability to cope with those demands, their needs, and the support that they receive both at work and outside of work.
- The psychological, behavioural, physiological correlates of the emotional experience of stress some of which represents attempts at coping.
- The wider or secondary effects of stress which may be expressed in terms of ill-health, poor social and organizational behaviour and which, in turn, have implications for the employee's organization, family, and social situation.
- Feedback from the wider environment partly reflecting the success or otherwise of coping. This, in a sense, completes a cycle of activity which establishes the stress process as something which is ongoing.

Cognitive appraisal can be associated with the (negative) emotional experience of stress, with attempts to cope, and with other psychological, behavioural and physiological changes. The processes involved demonstrate, in systems terms, both feedforward and feedback and the interactions are multiple and cross-level as well as being time based. This system is complex and unstable and a long way away from the simple 'blackbox' linear mechanistic system that was described by the early theories. It has its origins with Lazarus and Folkman (1984) in clinical psychology and, for them, was focused at the individual level.

The original model of Lazarus and Folkman (1984) has been developed by Cox and his colleagues at the University of Nottingham, UK (Cox, 1978; Cox, Griffiths, & Leka, 2003; Leka, Griffiths, & Cox, 2002). The developments of the original theory by Cox initially focused on five things. The first development was a strengthened emphasis on the individual's perception of situations and events and of themselves and the relative dismissal of objective data as *the* determinant, in this context of work-related stress, of health outcomes. This has led, in later research on psychosocial risk management, to a participative methodology based on the education of the workers involved (to allow them to participate) and the valuing of their input as *knowledgeable experts* with regards their own work.

The second development was the introduction into the appraisal process of the concept of the individual's ability to meet the demands made of them and the recognition that this ability might change (naturally) with tiredness, illness, or age. Work situations may become 'stressful' because the person is tired due to long working hours or due to the home situation. They may become stressful because the person is ill and their capacity is reduced or because they are becoming older and the profile of their skills is changing. Making explicit the role played by 'individual ability' in the appraisal process opens up the possibility of linking stress concerns to organizational functions such as selection, training, and employee support. Furthermore, the concern for issues of 'individual ability' has acted as a Trojan horse for introducing related concepts such as emotional intelligence, stress resistance, and resilience into our consideration of work-related stress.

The third development was the recognition that if demands and abilities had somehow to be balanced, then under-demand as well as over-demand might give rise to the experience of stress. The first author's research on repetitive and monotonous work practices and their effects on health shaped this possibility (Cox, 1980; Cox, Thirlaway, & Cox, 1982). While it was clear that such practices did detrimentally effect workers' health, most previous stress-based explanations had argued in a contorted fashion that somehow these practices were high or excessively demanding. Clearly they are not.

The fourth development was to argue for important functional nuances in relation to cognitive appraisal and, in particular, the impact of internal demands deriving from the individual's needs and the requirement for demands to be seen to be important to the individual to have any effect. These particular caveats already existed in the stress research literature but had been largely ignored and needed restating.

Finally, the conceptualization of the stress appraisal process was developed into the basis for a practical risk management approach at the organizational level. This required three things. First, it was necessary to position the work-related stress process within a traditional health and safety framework and, second, it was necessary to develop a psychosocial taxonomy of stressors to facilitate risk assessment. It was necessary to draw out from the research on work-related stress and the conceptualization of stress, a set of process principles for applying psychosocial risk management. All three things have been accomplished and the methodology developed has informed the taxonomy of psychosocial stressors adopted by the European Agency for Safety and Health at Work (Cox, Griffiths, & Rial González, 2000), the British Health & Safety Executive's Management Standards initiative (Cox, 1993; Mackay, Cousins, Kelly, Lee, & McCaig, 2004), the development of the Work Organisation Assessment Questionnaire (WOAQ: Griffiths, Cox, Karanika, Khan, & Tomas, 2006), and has contributed to the development of the European Framework for Psychosocial Risk Management: PRIMA-EF (Leka & Cox, 2008).

Whereas Cox and colleagues' perspective has largely been on the organizational level of the theory, Philip Dewe and colleagues at Birkbeck College, University of London (UK), has concentrated on individual stress appraisal and coping dimensions of the model (e.g., Dewe, 2001, 2003, 2004; Dewe & Trenberth, 2004; Trenberth & Dewe, 2005; Troup & Dewe, 2002). For a review of Dewe's contribution to this area of scholarship, see Dewe and Cooper (2007). Dewe has tackled the question of 'how do people appraise and cope with stress at work?' by trying to find a methodology that is 'fit for purpose'. Here 'fit for purpose' means that the answer has to be sufficiently global to generalize across groups and situations but sufficiently contextual to allow meaningful explanation and prediction. The original taxonomy of coping strategies suggested by Lazarus and Folkman (1984) has proved attractive in its simplicity but too global to allow either detailed explanation or useful prediction. However, idiopathic descriptions of coping, largely captured using qualitative research techniques, while offering a rich understanding of one or several individual's cope with their problems, usually do not generalize sufficiently to allow any prediction of how others or other groups might react to the problems that they face.

*Limitations of the transactional perspective*
The single most significant drawback of the transactional stress process is that it is difficult to operationalize (i.e., measure) its various elements. This leads to a situation whereby 'though avowedly espousing the transactional framework, much job stress research can in fact be depicted as reflecting an interactional model of stress, where the various components (stressors, strains, and coping) are treated as static constructs and as having uni dimensional effects' (Cooper, Dewe, & O'Driscoll, 2001).

The challenge in measuring work-related stress in accordance with a transactional perspective could be seen in the attempt of the authors to 'define a case of work-related stress' (Cox, Griffiths, & Houdmont, 2006). Commissioned by the British Health & Safety Executive, the study aimed to identify the structure of a case definition for work-related stress for use in large-scale nationally representative workforce surveys. Of central importance to the study's objectives was the assimilation of the views of national-level experts from eight broadly defined stakeholder groups that hold a vested interest in policy and research developments as they relate to work-related stress. These include employers' representative bodies, trade unions, occupational health practitioners, occupational health psychologists, clinical and counselling psychologists, insurers, legal professionals and workplace health and safety regulatory and enforcement bodies. Through the use of a template analysis approach, a set of themes relating to elements of a transactional case definition was identified. These included (a) the declared experience of work-related stress, (b) evidence of unreasonable exposure to psychosocial hazards associated with work, (c) evidence of psychological ill-health (anxiety and depression) of equivalence to clinical morbidity, (d) changes in work behaviour (absence) or presentation to a health professional for stress-related symptoms, and (e) the absence of negative affectivity. It was concluded that the case definition adequately reflected the transactional nature of the stress process and was suitable for translation into an assessment tool for use in future large-scale surveys of work-related stress. However, the fact that it involved five separate elements highlighted, yet again, the difficulty in measuring work-related stress in an efficient and expedient manner while remaining consistent with the transactional perspective.

## Summary

Theories of work-related stress can be divided into the early stimulus and response based models and contemporary psychological models. Within the contemporary family of models can, in turn, be identified two categories: interactional (structural) and transactional (process) theories. Transactional models appear to account most fully for the experience of work-related stress, but present a challenge in terms of the measurement of the construct.

## Observations on Theories

*What attributes do the various contemporary theories share?*
*Does common ground between theories provide any consensus in answering*
*the question: 'what is stress?'*

The authors have attempted to present contemporary theories of stress in a way that makes clear their origins and the common ground that they share and, in doing so, edges us towards a shared understanding of what stress is. This is critical for the advancement of research in this area and also our ability to translate research into policy and practice. Part of the challenge is to be able to answer the question 'what is stress?' in a way that is easily understood by the lay person and those that govern us but which also conveys the depth of scientific understanding on which that answer is built. Consensus in this task is important.

The theories discussed herein share several qualities. First and foremost, these theories are all built on the interaction between the individual and their work environment and, to varying extents, all recognize the importance of the individual's perception of that interaction. Second, most theories share a conceptual framework built around notions of demand, control, and support with variations including ability, needs, effort, coping, and reward. These, it can be argued form a natural family of concepts vested in both social psychology and in work and organizational psychology. Third, they all treat the individual as active in the interaction between the key person and environment factors and, in particular, see their attempts at coping as being an important moderator or mediator of health-related outcomes. Finally, they all treat stress as a system or process with a complex set of internal mechanisms including feedforward, feedback, and multiple level interactions. Some make this explicit, whereas others imply it or, at least, do not detract from it. Possibly reflecting the complexity of the system, most also talk about the linkages between the experience of stress and health outcomes in terms of a probabilistic model.

Stress is treated as an emotional state triggered by the person's appraisal of their situation at work. It is experienced as unpleasant and occurs when people realize that they cannot cope with the demands made on them when those demands are important or when their efforts are not adequately rewarded. The experience of stress may be made more likely if the person feels that they have insufficient control over their situation or receive too little support from others. This type of definition is consistent with all of the contemporary psychological models considered herein. Stress is a cognitive-emotional state which is unpleasant and which can be associated with significant changes in an individual's way of thinking about and behaving in the world and their associated physiological function. The person attempts to cope in a way that ultimately reduces the unpleasant experience of stress. Successful coping may reduce the threat that stress carries for individual health. In this sense, the European Commission's definition of work-related stress offers a 'catch all' definition:

> A pattern of emotional, cognitive, behavioural and physiological reactions to adverse and noxious aspects of work content, work organisation and work environment ... Stress is caused by poor match between us and our work, by conflicts between our roles at work and outside it, and by not having a reasonable degree of control over our own work and our own life. (Levi & Levi, 2000)

## Summary

The various contemporary psychological theories of work-related stress share a number of attributes. These allow for the identification of a 'catch all' definition of work-related stress, as presented by the Levi and Levi (2000) to the European Commission.

## Future Developments

*How might the research agenda push forward theoretical developments?*
*How might societal needs advance theory?*

### Developing the research agenda

There are two different ways of answering the 'what next?' question, reflecting whether the answer is pushed by extending the current research agenda or whether it is pulled by future societal needs. Very little that is truly new and significant has happened in the past 20 or so years. That observation is how this chapter began. Many involved in stress research appear to be bent on repeating earlier and arguably well-established findings with new groups of workers or in new countries or with new stressors. Being unkind, such activity is effectively fiddling at the margins of knowledge.

Stress research has reached something of a plateau and the 'what next?' question must be focused here on taking research to the next level. What the authors believe is required is not more of the same by way of research studies but a paradigmatic shift in focus, theory, and methodology. We need new ways of thinking about work-related stress and new ways of exploring this new conceptual world to build a new generation of theories. The authors, from their personal perspectives, see two areas that might lead this revolution.

The first is a strengthened focus on organizational level interventions and the testing of theories through practice. To quote from Lewin (1935), 'if you want to truly understand something, try to change it'. Perhaps a different type of theory is needed to account for organizational interventions; one that can embrace not only the content of the intervention but also the processes of intervention and its management. Such theories do not yet exist in a coherent and unified form. Possibly there is much to be learned here from work and organizational psychology, social psychology, management science, and the sociology of work.

The second, which is not unrelated, is consistency in how we think about the systems that represent people at work in their organizations in relation to their experience of stress. At one level, many talk about these systems being very complex, having non linear components and being unstable and changeable. This is the level of *intellectualized* description. At the level of research and the evaluation of organizational interventions, those same systems are generally treated as being relatively simple, linear, and stable. This reality is arguably shaped both by our formal models and theories and by the research and evaluation designs we use and the statistics that we apply to the data collected. The disjunction is obvious and is significant and damaging and needs to be resolved.

It will take many years for these changes to take place, during which time the topic of work-related stress risks being abandoned in favour of less-developed and seemingly more innovative concepts. There are signs that this is already happening with fast-growing interest in more positive concepts such as well-being and resilience. However, change has occurred in the past and brought with it new advances in understanding. Those mentioned here relate to the change in theoretical perspective that occurred during the 1960s and 1970s to great effect, moving us from the early theories to contemporary theory.

## Societal Needs

There are, at least, two levels at which we can consider societal needs in relation to work-related stress and stress theory. The first level is that which is proximal to our applied science of occupational health psychology and which reflects what it believes are the important societal questions that it is addressing or can address now. These needs tend to reflect smaller questions, are more focused and specific, with an immediate scientific base, and established methodologies. Most imply an obvious translation of research into policy or practice. Examples might be the effectiveness of different types of social support in relation to the impact of different work demands on workers' psychological health or the effectiveness of increasing worker control over their work processes on job satisfaction or absenteeism. Most of these 'needs' can be deduced from knowledge of current research activity and an ability to see the applications of that research and prioritize them in the societal context.

The second level is driven by society, rather than our applied science, and often challenges our thinking and ability to solve the questions that it poses. If the first level builds upwards from our discipline, the second level is much more top down. These needs tend to reflect 'the big questions' of the age and do not necessarily have immediate links into what we currently do by way of research and practice or the theories which characterize our discipline. The 'big questions' are by definition large, often ill defined, not completely understood and usually requiring new theories, approaches, and methodologies. At the moment, the 'big questions' include, among others: the management of the global economy and the strengths and weakness of an unregulated free market in relation to occupational and public health; the impact of organizational restructuring on health and safety; the relationships among unemployment, poverty, crime, and health; the effects of terrorism on safety and health; the relationship between work and domestic life.

There is no immediate answer to the questions that this second level of societal need poses for occupational health psychology. However, in the medium term they will necessarily shape our thinking and the research landscape of our discipline if only through the effects of changes in funding priorities. This is not new and, in part, describes the evolution of our (and any other applied) discipline. With the changes in thinking and research will come new theories and their emergence will take our knowledge of work-related stress to a new level. It might even be argued that since the end of the 1980s there has been a greater degree of stability in most aspects of the lives of the majority of citizens in Europe and North America. This has meant that the second-level needs of society have not been so pressing and occupational health psychology and stress research have focused on the first-level needs. This focus on first level needs does not create such a pressing environment for change in relation to theory and research. This might explain the current plateau in thinking. The virtue in the necessity of addressing second-level societal needs is that we move forward in our thinking.

## Summary

This section has considered the 'future' question for the development of stress theory and, more widely, for stress research. What may be required now is a conceptual and methodological breakthrough that will lift both our thinking about work-related stress and our research and practice to the next level. It can be argued that the area is on a plateau. Much has been achieved in terms of our understanding of stress, its effects at work, and how it can be best prevented and managed. However, something new is now required to add significantly to that knowledge and take us off the plateau.

## SUMMARY AND CONCLUSIONS

The chapter closes as it began with an overview of the broad developments in work-related stress theory that have occurred over the past 30 years. They are:

- the application of Karasek's (1979) Demand–Control theory of stress at national and international policy levels and, in some countries, to national legislation in health and safety;
- the rise in importance in research of Siegrist's (1996) Effort–Reward Imbalance theory and the now frequent comparison of this theory with that of Karasek's in terms of how well they account of the available research data;
- the translation of theories of work-related stress into a practical method for reducing the associated risks to worker health and safety at the organizational level: psychosocial risk management;
- the recognition that our theories do not have an adequate conceptual and methodological framework in either research or practice and that the next major developments have to be in this area;
- recognition of the value of these advances, that they might not be enough, and that something more radical is needed. A revolution in our thinking is required which sees a shift in our theoretical and methodological positions. This requires:
  - a strengthened focus on organizational level interventions and the testing of new theories of intervention processes;
  - innovation and consistency in how we describe and research the systems that represent people at work in their organizations and interventions to reduce the risk to health associated with the experience of stress related to work. What is needed, among other things, are new ways of analysing data that describe the hazard–harm relationship which underpins contemporary stress theory.

## Suggestions for Further Reading

Cooper, C. L., & Dewe, P. (2004) *Stress: A brief history.* Oxford: Blackwell Publishing.

Cooper, C. L., Dewe, P., and O'Driscoll, M. (2001) *Organisational stress: A review and critique of theory, research, and applications.* Thousand Oaks, California: Sage.

Cox, T., Griffiths, A. J., & Rial González, E (2000) *Research on work-related stress.* Luxembourg: Office of the Official Publications of the European Communities.

Dewe, P., Leiter, M., & Cox, T. (2000) *Coping, health, and organizations.* London: Taylor & Francis.

## References

Bakker, A. B., Demerouti, E., De Boer, E., & Schaufeli, W. B. (2003). Job demands and job resources as predictors of absence duration and absence frequency. *Journal of Vocational Behaviour, 2*, 341–356.

Beeher, T. A. (1995). *Psychological stress in the workplace.* London: Routledge.

Cannon, W. B. (1929). *Bodily changes in pain, hunger, fear and rage: An account of recent research into the function of emotional excitement.* New York: Appleton-Century-Crofts.

Caplan, R. D. (1983). Person-environment fit: Past, present and future. In C. L. Cooper (Ed.), *Stress research: Issues for the eighties.* Chichester: John Wiley & Sons.

Cohen, S., & Wills, T. A. (1985). Stress, social support, and the buffering hypothesis. *Psychological Bulletin, 98*, 310–357.

Cooper, C. L., Dewe, P., and O'Driscoll, M. (2001) *Organisational stress: A review and critique of theory, research, and applications.* Thousand Oaks, California: Sage.

Cox, T. (1978). *Stress.* London: Macmillan.

Cox, T. (1980). Repetitive work. In C. L. Cooper, & R. Payne (Eds.), *Current concerns in occupational stress.* Chichester: John Wiley & Sons.

Cox, T. (1993). *Stress research and stress management: Putting theory to work.* Sudbury: HSE Books.

Cox, T., & Cox, S. (1985). The role of the adrenals in the psychophysiology of stress. In E. Karas (Ed.), *Current issues in clinical psychology,* London: Plenum Press.

Cox, T., & Ferguson, E. (1991) Individual differences, stress and coping. In C. L. Cooper, & R. Payne (Eds.), *Personality and stress: Individual differences in the stress process.* Chichester: John Wiley & Sons.

Cox, T., & Griffiths, A. (1995). The nature and measurement of work stress: Theory and practice In J. R. Wilson, & E. N. Corlett (Eds.), *Evaluation of human work: A practical ergonomics methodology.* London: Taylor & Francis.

Cox, T., Griffiths, A. J., and Rial González, E (2000) *Research on work-related stress.* Luxembourg: Office of the Official Publications of the European Communities.

Cox, T., Griffiths, A., & Houdmont, J. (2006). *Defining a case of work-related stress.* Sudbury: HSE Books.

Cox, T., Griffiths, A., & Leka S. (2003). Work organization and work-related stress. In K. Gardiner & M. Harrington (Eds.), *Occupational hygiene.* London: Blackwell Science.

Cox, T., Karanika-Murray, M., Griffiths, A. J., & Houdmont, J. (2007). Evaluating organisational-level work stress interventions: Beyond traditional methods. *Work & Stress, 21*, 348–362.

Cox, T., & Mackay, C. J. (1982) Psychological factors and psychophysiological mechanisms in the aetiology and development of cancers. *Journal of Social Science and Medicine, 16,* 381–396.

Cox, T., Thirlaway, M., & Cox, S. J. (1982). Repetitive work, well-being and arousal. In H. Ursin & R. Murison (Eds.), *Biological and psychological bases of psychosomatic disease.* Oxford: Pergamon Press.

Cox, T., Thirlaway, M., Gotts, C., & Cox, S. (1983). The nature and assessment of general well-being. *Journal of Psychosomatic Research, 27,* 353–359.

de Jonge, J., & Dormann, C. (2003). The DISC model: Demand-Induced Strain Compensation mechanisms in job stress. In M. F. Dollard, A. H. Winefield, & H. R. Winefield (Eds.), *Occupational stress in the service organizations* (pp. 75–102). London: Taylor & Francis.

Dewe, P. (1991) Primary appraisal, secondary appraisal and coping: Their role in stressful work encounters. *Journal of Occupational Psychology, 64,* 331–351.

Dewe, P. (2001). Determinants of coping: Some alternative explanations and measurement issues, *Psychological Reports, 88,* 832–834.

Dewe, P. (2003) A closer examination of the patterns when coping with work related stress: Implications for measurement. *Journal of Occupational and Organizational Psychology 76,* 517–524.

Dewe, P. (2004). Work stress and coping: Theory, research and practice. *British Journal of Guidance and Counselling, 32,* 139–142.

Dewe, P., & Cooper, C. L. (2007). Coping research and measurement in the context of work related stress. In G. P. Hodgkinson, & J. K. Ford (Eds.), *International Review of Industrial and Organizational Psychology, 22,* Chichester: John Wiley & Sons.

Dewe, P., Cox, T., & Ferguson, E. (1993). Individual strategies for coping with stress at work: A review. *Work & Stress, 7,* 5–15.

Dewe, P., Leiter, M., & Cox, T. (2000) *Coping, health, and organizations.* London: Taylor & Francis.

Dewe, P., & Trenberth, L. (2004) Work stress and coping: Drawing together research and practice. *British Journal of Guidance and Counselling, 32,* 143–156.

Edwards, J. R., & Cooper, C. L. (1990). The person-environment fit approach to stress: Recurring problems and some suggested solutions. *Journal of Organizational Behaviour, 11,* 293–307.

Edwards, J. R., Caplan, R. D., & van Harrison, R. (1998). Person-environment fit theory: conceptual foundations, empirical evidence, and directions for future research. In C. Cooper (Ed.), *Theories of organisational stress,* New York, NY: Oxford University Press.

French, J. R. P. Jr., & Caplan, R. D. (1972). Occupational stress and individual strain. In A. J. Marrow (Ed.). *The failure of success.* New York: Amacon.

Griffiths, A. J. (1999). Organisational interventions: Facing the limitations of the natural science paradigm. *Scandinavian Journal of Work Environment & Health, 25,* 589–596.

Griffiths, A. J., Cox, T., Karanika, M., Khan, S., & Tomas, J. (2006). Work design and management in the manufacturing sector: Development and validation of the Work Organisation Assessment Questionnaire. *Occupational and Environmental Medicine, 63,* 669–675.

Johnson, J. V., & Hall, E. M. (1988). Job strain, workplace social support & cardiovascular disease: A cross sectional study of a random sample of the Swedish working population. *American Journal of Public Health, 78,* 1336–1342.

Karasek, R. (1979). Job demands, job decision latitude and mental strain: Implications for job design. *Administrative Science Quarterly, 24*, 285–306.

Karasek, R., & Theorell, T. (1990). *Healthy work: Stress, productivity and the reconstruction of working life.* New York: Basic Books.

Kivimaki, M., Virtanen, M., Elovainio, M., Kouvonen, A., Vaananen, A., & Vahtera, J. (2006). Work stress in the etiology of coronary heart disease: A meta analysis. *Scandinavian Journal of Work, Environment and Health, 32*, 431–442.

Kjaerheim, K., Haldorsen, T., & Andersen, A. (1997). Work-related stress, coping resources, and heavy drinking in the restaurant business. *Work & Stress, 11*, 6–16.

Kouvonen, A., Kivimaki, M., Cox, S., Cox, T., & Vahtera, J. (2005). Relationship between work stress and body mass index among 45,810 female and male employees. *Psychosomatic Medicine, 67*, 577–583.

Kouvonen, A., Kivimäki, M., Virtanen, M., Heponiemi, T., Elovainio, M., Pentti, J., Linna, A., & Vahtera, J. (2006). Effort–reward imbalance at work and the co-occurrence of lifestyle risk factors: cross-sectional survey in a sample of 36,127 public sector employees. *BMC Public Health, 6*, 24.

Lazarus, R. S. (1966). *Psychological stress and the coping process.* New York: McGraw-Hill Book Company.

Lazarus, R. S. (1990). Theory-based stress measurement. *Psychological Inquiry, 1*, 3–13.

Lazarus, R. S., & Folkman, S. (1984). *Stress, appraisal and coping.* New York: Springer.

Le Fevre, M., Matheny, J., & Kolt, G. S. (2003). Eustress, distress and interpretation in occupational stress. *Journal of Managerial Psychology, 18*, 726–744.

Leather, P. J., Lawrence, C., Beale, D., & Cox, T. (1998). Exposure to occupational violence and the effects of intra-organisational support. *Work & Stress, 12*, 161–178.

Leka, S., & Cox, T. (2008). *PRIMA-EF: Guidance on the European Framework for Psychosocial Risk Management.* Geneva: World Health Organization.

Leka, S., Griffiths, A., & Cox, T. (2002). *Guidelines on work organisation & stress.* Geneva: World Health Organization.

Levi, L., & Levi, I. (2000). Guidance on work-related stress. Spice of life, or kiss of death? Luxembourg: Office for Official Publications of the European Communities.

Lewin, K. (1935) *A dynamic theory of personality.* New York: McGraw Hill Custom Publishing.

Lewin, K. (1952). *Field theory in social science: Selected theoretical papers by Kurt Lewin.* London: Tavistock.

Mackay, C. J., Cousins, R., Kelly, P. J., Lee, S., & McCaig, R. H. (2004). Management Standards and work-related stress in the UK: Policy background and science. *Work & Stress, 18*, 91–112.

Noblet, A., Rodwell, J., & McWilliams, J. (2006). Organisational change in the public sector: Augmenting the demand–control model to predict employee outcomes under New Public Management. *Work & Stress, 20*, 335–352.

Oeij, P., Dhondt, S., & Wiezer, N. (2006). Conditions for low stress-risk jobs: Europe's case. *European Journal of Social Quality, 6*, 81–108.

Peeters, M. C., & Le Blanc, P. M. (2001). Matching the support between job demands and sources of social support: A study among oncology care providers. *European Journal of Work & Organisational Psychology, 10*, 53–72.

Peter, R., Siegrist, J., Hallqvist, J., Reuterwall, C., & Theorell, T., (2002). Psychosocial work environment and myocardial infarction: Improving risk estimation by combining two alternative job stress models in the SHEEP Study. *Journal of Epidemiology and Community Health, 56*, 294–300.

Rosen, L. N., & Moghadam, L. Z. (1990). Matching the support to the stressor: Implications for the buffering hypothesis. *Military Psychology, 2*, 193–204.

Schaufeli, M. (2004). The future of occupational health psychology. *Applied Psychology: An International Review, 53*, 502–517.

Schnall, P. L., Belkic, K., Landsbergis, P., & Baker, D. (Eds.) (2000). The workplace and cardiovascular disease. *Occupational Medicine: State of the Art Reviews, 15*, 1–334.

Selye, H. (1950). *Stress*, Montreal: Acta Incorporated.

Selye, H. (1956). *Stress of life*. New York: McGraw-Hill.

Siegrist, J. (1996). Adverse health effects of high effort – low reward conditions at work. *Journal of Occupational Health Psychology, 1*, 27–43.

Stansfeld, S., & Candy, B. (2006). Psychosocial work environment and mental health: A meta-analytical review. *Scandinavian Journal of Work Environment and Health, 32*, 443–462.

Stansfeld, S., & Marmot, M. (Eds.) (2002). *Stress and the heart. Psychosocial pathways to coronary heart disease*. London: BMJ Books.

Taris, T. (2006). Bricks without clay: On urban myths in occupational health psychology. *Work & Stress, 20*, 99–104.

Trenberth, L., & Dewe, P. (2005). An exploration of the role of leisure in coping with work related stress using sequential tree analysis. *British Journal of Guidance and Counselling 33*, 101–116.

Troup, C., & Dewe, P. (2002). Exploring the nature of control and its role in the appraisal of workplace stress. *Work & Stress, 16*, 335–355.

Tsutsumi, A., & Kawakami, N. (2004). A review of empirical studies on the model of effort–reward imbalance at work: Reducing occupational stress by implementing a new theory. *Social Science and Medicine, 59*, 2335–2359.

Uhmann, S. (2007). On the beaten track: What are promising variations on and extensions to the job demands–control model? *Paper presented at the 13th European Congress of Work and Organisational Psychology*, Stockholm, Sweden, May 9–12.

van Harrison, R. (1978). Person-environment fit and job stress. In C. L. Cooper & R. Payne (Eds.), *Stress at work*. Chichester: John Wiley & Sons.

van Vegchel, N., de Jonge, J., Bosma, H., & Schaufeli, W. (2005). Reviewing the effort–reward imbalance model: Drawing up the balance of 45 empirical studies. *Social Science and Medicine, 60*, 1117–1131.

van Veldhoven, M., Taris, T., de Jonge, J., & Broersen, S. (2005). The relationship between work characteristics and employee health and well-being: How much complexity do we really need? *International Journal of Stress Management, 12*, 3–28.

Yerkes, R. M., & Dodson, J. D. (1908). The relation of strength of stimulus to rapidity of habit-formation. Journal *of Comparative Neurology and Psychology, 18*, 459–482.

# 3

# Work Organization and Health

Michael P. O'Driscoll and Paula Brough

## CHAPTER OUTLINE

The previous chapter in this volume (by Cox and Griffiths) has provided a valuable review of various theoretical accounts of work-related stress and well-being. The present chapter builds upon their conceptual overview by describing some of the key relationships among work/organization factors and workers' health and well-being outcomes. The chapter specifically examines psychosocial hazards or stressors which have been demonstrated by research to have a bearing on either individual well-being or organizational productivity-related variables (such as job satisfaction, organizational commitment, job performance, absenteeism, and turnover). Our aim is not to present an exhaustive review of the vast literature on these topics, but rather to provide representative evidence and discussion of relationships between workplace hazards and health, along with suggestions for future research developments in this field.

## Introduction

The potential impact of work-related factors on the psychological and physical health and well-being of workers has been clearly established in research spanning more than 50 years, along with the notion that individuals and organizations share a responsibility to optimize well-being. To achieve this optimization, it is essential to examine the range of factors which may significantly contribute to physical health and psychological well-being, to determine the influence which these exert and, most importantly, to ascertain how work-related factors may be manipulated to ensure that at the very least they are not harmful to individual workers, and ideally that they make a positive contribution to their health and well-being. The aim of the present chapter is to provide an overview of some of the more common work-related predictors of physical health and psychological well-being and to summarize conclusions which have been drawn from research on these variables.

Above we introduced the concepts of 'hazards' and 'stressors', both of which have been used in the stress and well-being literature. These terms refer to occurrences or events which individuals are exposed to which may threaten their health or well-being. The concept of *hazard* derives from the literature on risks and risk management, whereas the term *stressor* is more closely aligned with theoretical models of stress and stress management (including coping). For present purposes, however, they are functionally equivalent and (for simplicity) we will use the expression 'stressors' when describing stimuli which have the potential to generate negative outcomes for individuals.

The chapter focuses on two major issues: types of stressors and types of people who are likely to experience these stressors. First we discuss research on a selection of stressors which have figured prominently in the literature on work-related health and well-being. Specifically, we describe seven types of stressor which have been frequently researched. As noted above, our intention is not to offer an exhaustive review of research, but rather to summarize the major findings and their implications. Following this overview, we examine specific groups of workers who are more likely to have exposure to these stressors, in particular high-risk occupations (such as police officers and corrections employees), female workers, and employees with dependants (who are more prone to experience work-to-family conflict). The chapter concludes with some general observations about the impact of work stressors or hazards, along with suggestions for future research and practice.

## Workplace Psychosocial Stressors
· · · · · · · · · · · · · · · · · · · · · · · · · · · · · · · · · · · · · · · · · · · · · · · · · ·

*What are the major types of work-related stressors?*
*How do psychosocial stressors at work affect health and well-being?*
*What is the role of personal control in reducing stress and enhancing well-being?*
*Does social support alleviate psychological strain and improve well-being?*

There have been several efforts to develop taxonomies of work-related stressors (or hazards). These taxonomies are valuable in that they provide a set of categories of different types of stressor which may have a substantial impact on health and well-being at work. Cooper and Marshall (1976) made an early attempt to categorize job stressors, which was updated by Cartwright and Cooper (1997).

These researchers focused on both job-specific and organizational sources of strain, suggesting that there are six primary stressors:

- intrinsic characteristics of the job itself;
- the person's role(s) in the organization;
- their relationships with other people at work;
- career prospects and progression;
- organizational factors, including the structure, culture and climate of the organization; and
- the home-to-work interface.

An extension of the Cooper et al. typology has been provided by Johnson and her colleagues (Johnson et al., 2005), who added three further categories to the above list: job security, pay and benefits, and resources and communication. The first five categories incorporate hazards within the workplace, whereas the sixth reflects the spill-over between experiences at work and those off the job. Some stressors are predominantly physical in nature (e.g., the temperature of the work environment) and others pertain mainly to physical safety (e.g., the design of equipment). In the present chapter, however, we focus on *psychosocial* stressors rather than those which are solely physical. Specifically, we target seven factors that have been found to exert considerable influence on workers' levels of health and well-being: work demands, working hours and patterns, job control, social support, work–family conflict, role changes, and anti-social behaviours. Although we will discuss each of these separately, it is important to realize that stressors do not operate in isolation from each other, and that their interactive effects on health and well-being may be cumulative. For example, Wellens and Smith (2006) observed that exposure to a combination of physical stressors and time pressure was linked with higher levels of salivary cortisol and blood pressure (which are both indicators of strain). Nevertheless, exposure to a single stressor can also be damaging to well-being, especially if that stressor is intense or very pronounced.

Before discussing the specific stressors, we should note that other typologies (in addition to that presented above) have also been constructed. De Jonge and Dormann (2006), for instance, differentiated between cognitive, emotional, and physical stressors. In their research on health-care employees, intellectual demands and complex tasks were regarded as cognitive stressors, dealing with illness and death were examples of emotional stressors, and tasks such as lifting patients were classified as physical stressors. Although this differentiation is useful, in practice it is likely that some stressors will contain more than one element and that some will span all three kinds of stressor. Hence defining a particular stressor as cognitive, emotional, or physical may not always be possible.

Another interesting (and potentially important) distinction has been explored by LePine, Podsakoff, and LePine (2005) between *challenge* stressors and *hindrance* stressors. A challenge stressor is one that imposes demands (challenges) on the person, but the individual perceives that they can meet these demands and master the situation. Confronting this kind of stressor is likely, therefore, to yield positive rather than negative outcomes for the person's well-being. To a large extent, viewing stressors as challenging hinges around the degree of control that the person feels they can exert – see our later discussion of this variable. A hindrance stressor, on the other hand, is one that the individual perceives as a 'threat' to their health or well-being and one that they may not be able to control. Overlaying the hindrance-challenge stressor differentiation onto the Cooper et al. typology, factors such as work demands and workload are viewed as challenge stressors, whereas role ambiguity and conflict, inter-personal conflict, and organizational politics were regarded by LePine et al. as hindrance stressors. From a meta-analysis of research on work-related stressors, LePine and colleagues concluded that challenge stressors were positively associated with motivation and performance, whereas hindrance stressors were linked negatively with these outcomes.

## Work demands

A considerable amount of research has been conducted to investigate the impact which demands from work have on health and well-being, and there is consistent evidence that excessive work demands are deleterious, in terms of both personal and organizational outcomes. Of course, work demands can take a number of forms, including physical, cognitive, and emotional demands, and all three of these demand types have been shown to influence well-being. Early thinking was that the relationship between work demands and well-being (or stress) was curvilinear (see Figure 3.1), that is that both very low and very high demand levels would be damaging, whereas a 'moderate' level of work demands would actually enhance well-being and job performance. However, the prediction of an inverted U-shaped relationship between demands, well-being and performance has not been universally supported and evidence typically supports a linear association between these variables (Jamal, 2007).

Much of the research carried out on the effects of work demands has built upon the job Demand–Control (DC) model originally proposed by Karasek (1979), and

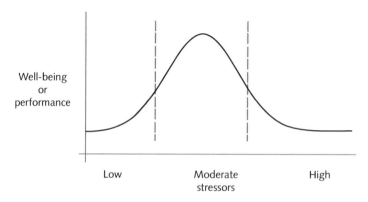

**Figure 3.1**  Curvilinear relationship between stressor level and well-being or performance.

later expanded by Johnson and Hall (1988) to the job Demand–Control–Support (DCS) model, which incorporates social support as a key variable along with control over work stressors as predictors of psychological (and perhaps physical) strain. We will discuss this model in more detail later. Suffice to say at this point that this perspective proposes moderating (buffering) effects of control and social support on the relationship of work demands with well-being and performance variables.

Other studies, however, have investigated the *direct* impact of work demands, irrespective of levels of control and/or social support. This line of research differentiates between quantitative and qualitative workload. Quantitative demands include the amount of work required of an individual and the timeframe for task completion, whereas qualitative overload occurs when the person feels that they do not have the required skills or resources to adequately fulfil their job requirements. Numerous studies have illustrated that both quantitative and qualitative demands are important predictors of health and well-being. For instance, Westman and Eden (1992) observed that time pressure (to complete tasks) was related to high levels of strain, anxiety, and depression, and Melamed and colleagues (Melamed, Ben-Avi, Luz, & Green, 1995) found that performing repetitive work and work underload were associated with the experience of monotony, which was linked with reduced job satisfaction and higher distress.

More recent studies have also confirmed the influence of work demands (both quantitative and qualitative) on well-being related variables. For example, Mikkelsen, Øgaard, and Landsbergis (2005) demonstrated direct positive associations between quantitative demands, emotional demands, and risk-taking demands with subjective health complaints (both physical and psychological). In a longitudinal (six-wave) investigation among US soldiers, Tucker and her colleagues (Tucker et al., 2008) also obtained evidence of the direct effect of work demands on affective strain, although they noted that the time-lag for causal effects of workload and other demand variables has not been clearly established. Specifically, they suggested that 'the time span may be different for different stressors such that high mental load may begin to affect one's health in a matter of days, whereas the health effects of shiftwork may not be realized for several years' (p. 90). Unfortunately, we have only a very rudimentary understanding of the time needed for various work demands to exert a substantial impact on health and well-being (as well as performance), but Tucker et al.'s longitudinal research goes some way to addressing this crucial issue. Clearly, more longitudinal research (which controls for existing levels of well-being) is needed to explore this issue.

Another long-standing tradition of research on work demands effects builds upon the notion of *role stressors*, articulated originally by Kahn and his colleagues in the 1960s (Kahn, Wolfe, Quinn, & Snoek, 1964). The literature on this topic is extensive and will therefore not be reviewed in detail here. Suffice to say that there is very consistent evidence that three role stressors are important to consider: role *ambiguity*, role *conflict*, and role *overload*. Ambiguity refers to uncertainty about how to perform one's role, including lack of information and unpredictability of the consequences of one's behaviour. Role conflict reflects incompatible demands being confronted by the person, such as when a supervisor or manager requires the individual to undertake two complex tasks simultaneously, or when incompatible expectations are communicated to the individual by different people. Finally, role overload (conceptually similar to the notion of work demands discussed above) relates to the number of different roles a person has to fulfil at the same time. Overload can lead to excessive demands and also create uncertainty within the person about his/her ability to perform roles.

There has been ongoing debate in the literature over which of these role stressors contributes most to detrimental health and well-being, and to date there has been no resolution of this issue. Narayanan, Menon, and Spector (1999) found that role overload was mentioned more frequently as a source of psychological strain than either role ambiguity or conflict, but other researchers have reported greater contributions to strain or well-being from either role ambiguity (O'Driscoll & Beehr, 1994) or role conflict (Jex & Elacqua, 1999). For relatively new workers on a job, role ambiguity may be a more prominent stressor, until at least they 'learn the ropes'. Role conflict may become a more salient stressor among more experienced

---

**RESEARCH CLOSE-UP       3.1   Implications of Exposure to Stressors**

*Source:* Glazer, S., & Beehr, T. A. (2005). Consistency of implications of three role stressors across four countries. *Journal of Organizational Behavior, 26*(5), 467–487.

Glazer and Beehr conducted a cross-cultural examination of the effects of role stressors on organizational commitment, anxiety, and intention to leave among nurses in four countries (Italy, Hungary, the UK, and the USA). Two types of hypotheses were proposed: (1) direct effects, that is that role stressors (conflict, ambiguity, and overload) would be directly related with the three criterion variables, and (2) indirect effects, that anxiety would mediate the relationships between role stressors and intention to leave. As predicted, all three role stressors correlated positively with anxiety, continuance commitment, and intention to leave, and correlated negatively with affective commitment. Furthermore, the strongest pathway across the four countries was between role stressors and anxiety. Although there were some between-country differences in the significance of various pathways, overall the mediation effects of anxiety were confirmed. Additionally, anxiety and organizational commitment played key mediating roles in the effects of work stressors on intention to leave. The study provides evidence to support the assertion that the stress process can be generalized across cultures.

personnel, especially if they are required to take on additional competing responsibilities. There is no doubt, however, that all three of these role stressors may be salient predictors of well-being, even though their relative impact may vary across jobs and organizational settings.

## Working hours

Research on the effects of the number of working hours on individuals' health and well-being has yielded quite mixed results. Intuitively it would appear logical to assume that longer hours on their job would be correlated with a variety of outcomes, including work–family conflict and psychological strain. A meta-analysis by Sparks, Cooper, Fried, and Shirom (1997) illustrated relatively low, but nevertheless significant, correlations between hours of work and both psychological and physiological health symptoms. However, these authors noted that there may be a non-linear relationship, with people who work more than 48 hours per week being most susceptible to health problems. A more recent meta-analysis by Ng and Feldman (2008) also obtained a negative association, and they too noted that the relationship may be non-linear. In addition, it is likely that other variables function as moderators of the relationship between working hours and well-being. For example, the type of work being performed, the level of responsibility the person has in their role, along with psychosocial factors such as the quality of relationships with other people at work, may all influence the link between work hours and health and well-being. Non-work factors, such as level of support from one's family, may also play a role by either reducing or increasing home pressures, which can also contribute to strain.

Another factor which has a marked influence on the impact of work hours is the extent to which the individual has control (autonomy) in terms of the hours they work. Time control is one form of job control (discussed below) which has been closely linked with well-being and other experiences. For instance, Hughes and Parkes (2007) observed that work time control moderated the relationship between number of hours worked and work-to-family conflict, which may play a critical role in the reduction of family satisfaction and happiness, which are salient indicators of overall well-being. Their study illustrated that work–family conflict mediated the relationship between working hours and family satisfaction, thus the impact of work hours on well-being is not necessarily direct.

Finally, a few studies have obtained gender differences in the impact of working hours on well-being variables. In a test of the iso-strain hypothesis derived from Karasek's DC model, Jones and her colleagues (Jones, O'Connor, Conner, McMillan, & Ferguson, 2007) observed that the negative association between long work hours and self-reported health behaviours was evident only among women. One potential explanation for this gender moderation is that women's family lives and responsibilities may be more disrupted by having to spend long hours at work, whereas for men the link between work hours and work-to-family conflict or interference is less pronounced.

Overall, cumulated research findings suggest that excessive work hours may be detrimental to health and well-being, but the link between working hours and well-being is neither simple nor uniform across different individuals and occupations. Nor is there definitive evidence concerning the optimal number of work hours per week, and it is apparent that this may vary considerably across individuals and settings. Hence, although efforts to improve work-life balance frequently target a reduction in the total number of hours people engage in their job, by itself this may be insufficient to significantly enhance overall well-being.

| RESEARCH CLOSE-UP | 3.2 Work-Related Stress and Negative Affectivity |
|---|---|

*Source:* Spector, P. E., Chen, P., & O'Connell, B. (2000). A longitudinal study of relationships between job stressors and job strains while controlling for negative affectivity and strains. *Journal of Applied Psychology, 85*(2), 211–218.

Spector and colleagues conducted a longitudinal study of graduate students in the USA, with the first data collection occurring during their final semester at university and the second after they had obtained employment. The major aim of the research was to examine the effects of the dispositional factor *negative affectivity* on the relationship between six job-related stressors (autonomy, inter-personal conflict, organizational constraints, role ambiguity, role conflict, and workload) and a range of occupational strain variables. Negative affectivity is defined as a tendency to experience negative emotional reactions, such as anxiety or depression, irrespective of the situation and context. Other investigators have hypothesized that negative affectivity has a major influence on this relationship, and that it is therefore important to partial out its effects when examining the association between stressors and strains. Their results supported the direct link between the six stressors and the strain variables. However, partialling out negative affectivity had no appreciable impact on stressor-strain relationships, at least in the time 1 data (at time 2 there were some effects of partialling negative affectivity). Spector and his colleagues concluded that job stressors do not always lead to strain and that attention should be paid to how specific stressors relate to specific strains. Additionally, the study provides evidence to suggest that there is little influence of third variables (such as negative affectivity) on job stressor-strain relationships. Furthermore, the results indicate that the impact of negative affectivity may fluctuate over time and situations. In conclusion, the study illustrates the job stressor-strain relationship is not purely due to by-products of negative affectivity or prior levels of strain.

## Job control

One issue which has been explored extensively in connection with job-related strain (in particular) is the amount of control which people can exert over various aspects of their job, including their overall work hours, their start/finish times, how they go about completing tasks, and the order of task completion. Some researchers have examined these various types of control individually, although for the most part they are examined collectively (Cooper, Dewe, & O'Driscoll, 2001). The importance of control (or at least *perceived* control) is emphasized in Karasek's (1979) DC model referred to earlier. Karasek posited that control serves a critical moderating function in reducing the negative impact of high work demands, and his framework has provided a platform for most research on the possible stress-moderating effects of control. Figure 3.2 illustrates the elements of this model. According to Karasek, jobs which contain very high work demands are not necessarily stressful or deleterious to well-being, if they also permit a high level of personal control on the part of the individual. Karasek referred to this condition as an 'active job'. However, if the person has little or no control over their work or the factors surrounding their job performance, they will experience high levels of psychological strain.

The basic logic underlying the above model was clearly described by Fox, Dwyer, and Ganster (1993). Excessive work demand induces anxiety in the person about their job performance and the consequences of not completing work in a specific timeframe. This anxiety can be ameliorated if workers (a) are able to make their own decisions concerning their work (decision authority) and (b) can use a variety of skills in their work (skill discretion). These two factors are normally combined by researchers into a global decision latitude or control construct. A second reason for the importance of control, although not directly specified by Karasek, is that the ability to exert control over one's environment is viewed by some theorists (e.g., Maslow, 1943) as a fundamental element of human functioning, required if the person is to feel that they are moving toward self-fulfilment or (in Maslow's terms) self-actualization. Lack of control impedes the person's ability to develop mastery over their environment, which in turn will create feelings of incompetence and

|  | Low<br>job demands | High<br>job demands |
|---|---|---|
| Low control | Passive job | High-strain job |
| High control | Low-strain job | Active job |

**Figure 3.2**  Karasek's job Demand–Control model.

hence a reduction in subjective well-being. Similarly, Warr's (2009) *vitamin model* of mental health proposes that control enables the individual to make adjustments to the environment that can offset the aversive consequences of work stressors.

Over the past 30 years a considerable number of studies have tested the Demand–Control model, especially the notion that control operates as a moderating (or buffering) variable. There is general agreement that an appropriate level of control over the environment is an important contributor to individual well-being and even physical health (e.g., Jones et al., 2007; Meier, Semmer, Elfering, & Jacobshagen, 2008), but there is disagreement over the way in which control operates. From a review of research based on the Karasek formulation, de Lange, Taris, Kompier, Houtman, and Bongers (2003) observed that previous reviews (both narrative and meta-analytic) have not been able to reach definitive conclusions about the role played by control. Specifically, although most studies have obtained direct relationships between control levels and either reduced strain or heightened well-being (cf., Meier et al., 2008), there is weak evidence for the moderating effects of control. It is argued that job control may operate as a buffer only when there is a close match with personal attributes, such as the person's level of self-efficacy and their (dispositional) locus of control. For example, in a study of service employees, Meier et al. demonstrated a three-way interaction (stressors × control × locus of control). Among workers with high *internal* locus of control, control over the job attenuated the negative impact of work stressors on psychological strain and musculo-skeletal pain; among those high on *external* locus of control, the opposite effect was obtained: high job control predicted poorer subjective well-being and physical health. Self-efficacy demonstrated similar relationships, although in this case the three-way interaction was significant only for psychological strain.

The findings of the above study are important in that they illustrate some possible limits on the positive benefits of control. Under certain conditions having more control may actually be detrimental to a person's well-being. This can occur if the level of control exceeds their desired amount or the level which they feel comfortable with. Increased control can bring with it greater expectations (from supervisors and co-workers) of responsibility and accountability for outcomes, which may not be congruent with the individual's preferences. Similarly, having high control but low mastery may also create anxiety for the person, as they may feel that they are responsible for their performance when in reality they believe they lack the skills and competencies needed to perform the task efficiently and effectively.

It was noted by de Lange et al. (2003) that most research on the DC model has been cross-sectional in design, which limits conclusions that can be drawn about cause-effect relationships. Their search yielded 45 studies which had a longitudinal design with at least two data-collection points, but only 19 of these studies met all the criteria which de Lange et al. had established for inclusion in their analyses. Only very modest support was obtained for the Karasek DC model; few significant demands × control interactions were obtained.

An expansion of the DC model is represented in Bakker and Demerouti's (2007) Demands–Resources model. These investigators view control as one (among many) resources that an individual may have at their disposal. Having autonomy or control can be beneficial in that it enables the person to decide how best they might deal with work demands, and therefore develop effective coping strategies. However, as noted above, evidence for the buffering effects of control is inconclusive, and Bakker and Demerouti suggested that control 'is only partly able to buffer the impact of job demands on employee well-being' (p. 310). In addition to personal control, physical, psychological, social, and organizational resources are also needed for managing work-related stressors.

The differentiation between hindrance and challenge stressors, which we discussed earlier, is pertinent in this context. As noted, hindrance stressors potentially impede a person's work performance and overall functioning, and are perceived by the person as a threat to their health and well-being. In contrast, challenge stressors are demands that may potentially be stressful, but are perceived by the individual as being associated with positive outcomes or resource gains. Boswell, Olson-Buchanan, and LePine (2004) found that personal control over stressors was only effective as a buffer when the person perceived demands or circumstances as hindrance stressors. When demands were perceived as a challenge, control did not moderate the relationship between stressors and psychological strain (anxiety and emotional exhaustion). Intuitively this finding makes sense – if the person does not perceive a threat to their well-being, whether or not they can exert some control over the stressor may be less relevant. One limitation in the Boswell et al. study, however, is that whether the stressors were hindering or challenging was defined in an a priori manner by the researchers themselves, rather than the research participants making this decision. In keeping with one of the basic tenets of the transactional model of stress (Lazarus & Folkman, 1984) that the individual needs to perceive a threat to their well-being in order for any stress response to be engaged in, a more comprehensive test would incorporate individuals' perceptions of the level of threat versus challenge of work-related stressors.

A final issue which we will discuss is the importance of ensuring that research captures the level of 'matching' between the stressor(s) being encountered and the types of control available to the person. This issue is not new (see Wall, Jackson, Mullarkey, & Parker, 1996), but frequently has been ignored in research on the moderating effects of control. In simple terms, there needs to be a degree of correspondence (or congruence) between the demands or stressors the person is confronted with and the type of control they can exert. For instance, if the relevant stressor is pressure to perform work to a certain standard, having control over start/finish times may not be salient, whereas control over the pace of work may well be a critical factor. Unfortunately, as we noted earlier, frequently researchers have combined different types or forms of control into a combined (overall) index of generic control, which masks the differential effects of the various types of control. Wall et al. observed that when the type of control was closely linked to specific work demands, the moderating (buffering) influence of control on anxiety and depression, as well as job satisfaction, was more likely to occur. More recently, Mikkelsen et al. (2005) distinguished between horizontal and vertical control. Horizontal control refers to influence over the specific work or tasks that the person performs, whereas vertical control relates to influence over broader organizational decisions and processes (vertical control may therefore be viewed as parallel to Karasek's notion of decision authority). Mikkelsen et al. found only relatively weak demand by control interactions, suggesting that further differentiation of types of control and their putative relationships with work demands is required.

In summary, although the concept of personal control has intuitive appeal and is soundly based in theoretical models of stress-coping and well-being (e.g., Spector, 1998; Warr, 2009), extant research has not fully supported the buffering effects of personal control. There is no doubt that control is important, and frequently has been observed to have direct relationships with reduced strain and improved well-being (Tucker et al., 2008). However, its buffering role (as hypothesized by the Demands–Control model) has not always been confirmed. As noted above, one possible reason for the lack of significant moderating effects may be inappropriate conceptualization of the control variable in much research. In addition, there may be interactive effects between perceptions of control over the environment, which is essentially a situational variable, and dispositional variables such as locus of control (de Lange et al., 2003) and self-efficacy (Schaubroeck & Merritt, 1997). Similarly, the Demand–Control model may be more applicable to some groups of workers than to others, although to date there has been little systematic investigation of its differential salience to different categories of worker.

## Social support

Another situational factor which has received substantial attention in research on stress and well-being is the extent of support which individuals receive from other people in their environment. Common sources of social support are (at work) supervisors, managers, and work colleagues, and (outside of work) family and friends. Various kinds or types of support may also be provided, including practical help (instrumental support), emotional support, advice and guidance (informational support), and appraisal support (feedback on one's behavior). Empirical research on the effects of social support has been extensive; here we summarize some of the major trends from this line of investigation rather than attempting to offer an exhaustive overview of all the findings.

Although there is incontrovertible evidence that social support makes significant contributions to psychological health and well-being (see Brough, O'Driscoll, Kalliath, Cooper, & Poelmans, 2009, Chapter 4), there has been ongoing debate about the nature of this contribution. Generally, three alternative 'pathways' have been suggested (cf. Cooper et al., 2001). The first path reflects a direct relationship between support and well-being; that is, high levels of support will have direct positive effects on reduced stress and increased well-being. Several studies have obtained empirical confirmation of this direct effect. An extension of this notion

**Figure 3.3** Social support as a mediator (intervening variable) between stressors and strain.

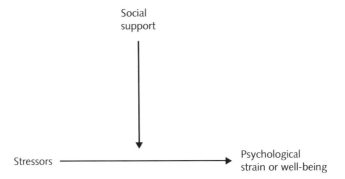

**Figure 3.4** Social support as a moderator of relationships between stressors and strain or well-being.

is a mediating effect of social support (see Figure 3.3), that is that social support functions as an intervening variable between stressors and strain or well-being outcomes. Finally, the expanded version of the job Demand–Control model proposed by Johnson and Hall (1988) proposed that, like job control, social support from colleagues, supervisors or other people can operate as a moderating (buffering) variable in the relationship between stressors and strain or well-being (see Figure 3.4). This mechanism is known as the *stress-buffering hypothesis.*

A direct effect of social support is indicated simply by a significant correlation between social support and well-being variables, which has been obtained in numerous studies (Brough et al., 2009). One explanation for this effect is that support from other people increases the individual's self-esteem, hence making them less susceptible to the deleterious effects of stressors in their environment (Cohen & Wills, 1985). The mediating model extends this logic to suggest that when people confront challenges or stressors at work (such as role ambiguity, role conflict, or role overload) they endeavour to mobilize the resources available to them, including support from other people, in the belief that these resources will help to reduce strain. Practical support and emotional support may figure especially as mediators of the relationship between work stressors and psychological health and well-being (Scheck, Kinicki, & Davy, 1997). Generally speaking, high levels of social support have been associated with improved functioning and well-being.

The moderating effect of social support, as proposed by the stress-buffering hypothesis, has also been examined frequently in empirical research. As commented above, this line of research has typically been based on the job Demand–Control–Support (DCS) model developed by Johnson and Hall (1988), which is an extension of the Karasek DC model, although not too many studies have simultaneously examined both control and support as moderator variables. The logic underlying the stress-buffering hypothesis is that people who receive social support when they are confronting stressors will experience less strain and greater well-being than their counterparts who are not able to avail themselves of such support. In other words, social support shields or protects individuals from the potentially harmful effects of aversive circumstances. This may be due to the source providing practical help (e.g., assisting the individual with a heavy work-load) or emotional support (e.g., helping the individual to modify their perception that the stressor is harmful to their well-being). Social support is viewed, therefore, as an important resource for the alleviation of strain and the promotion of well-being at work.

Unfortunately, despite its intuitive appeal and sound theoretical logic, evidence relating to the stress-buffering hypothesis is inconsistent. Some researchers have obtained supporting evidence. For instance, Moyle and Parkes (1999) observed that support from the manager reduced the amount of strain experienced by supermarket employees following forced relocation to another store, and Green-glass, Fiksenbaum, and Burke (1996) found that support from both supervisors and work colleagues exerted a positive buffering influence on teacher burnout. Other studies, however, have found no evidence for buffering. A relatively recent study by Jones et al. (2007), which we outlined earlier, examined the link between daily events at work and UK government employees' changes in mood and physical health. A strength of their investigation is that they were able to assess within-person fluctuations in mood and health on a daily basis. Jones et al. found that daily variations in mood and work hours more strongly predicted health behavi-ours than did distal variables such as job demands, control, and support. Although their results do not necessarily contradict the stress-buffering hypothesis, they do highlight the need to examine the role of support in context, and to consider the person's need for different forms of support, rather than simply assessing whether or not support is available. In other words, the role played by social support may be more complex than initially postulated by the stress-buffering hypothesis, and may depend on a variety of personal and situational factors, such as the type of situation and stressors being confronted.

Findings from other studies also suggest that assessing only the overall amount of support available to (or used by) the person is too simplistic. Rather, it is critical to examine (a) the types of support being provided, (b) the source(s) of support, and (c) importantly, what kind and level of support does the person need and desire at the time. A good illustration of the importance of these factors is offered by research carried out over 20 years ago by Kaufmann and Beehr (1986), who observed that in some situations social support may *exacerbate* rather than ame-liorate the negative impact of work stressors. They suggested that this can occur especially when the type of support offered confirms the aversive nature of the work environment (for example, where people focus on the negative aspects of their work). Kaufmann and Beehr referred to this phenomenon as *reverse buffering*. In a follow-up investigation, Fenlason and Beehr (1994) noted that where communication serves to reinforce the difficulties and problems a person is confronting at work, this type of social support is likely to *increase* rather than reduce the level of strain reported.

A limitation of many studies is that they have typically assessed only the frequency or amount of support provided, rather than other important aspects of social support. In Fenlason and Beehr's (1994) study, for instance, although positive communications from supervisors and work colleagues exhibited a negative correlation with psychological strain, and negative communications were linked with higher strain, the exact content of the communication and its source played an important role. Similarly, Chen, Popovich, and Kogan (1999) suggested that the buffering effects of social support may depend on several other factors, including the source of support (for example, supervisor versus colleague), the target of support, and the types of well-being outcomes. In other words, some forms and sources of support may be beneficial in respect of certain outcomes, but not necessarily others.

The above discussion illustrates that the impact of social support on psychological health and well-being is neither simple nor necessarily linear, and that several factors may affect the link between support and important outcomes. In addition to those mentioned above, research sometimes confounds support available to the person, the amount of support actually used, and its effectiveness. Furthermore, the match between the type of support provided, the stressors, and the person's needs has not always been ascertained. Instead, research often appears to assume that certain kinds of support (e.g., practical assistance, emotional support) are both appropriate and desired. In reality, the impact of social support can be complex and variable across situations. Clearly, more extensive exploration is needed of this important variable, in particular the mechanisms by which it affects individual health and well-being.

## Work–family conflict

The recognition that the boundary between work and non-work roles is permeable and that work performance is influenced by home/family demands (and vice versa) has generated a considerable amount of research within the last decade or so. A number of recent reviews have identified the common antecedents, moderators, and consequences of work–family conflict (e.g., Brough, O'Driscoll, & Kalliath, 2007; Eby, Casper, Lockwood, Bordeaux, & Brinley, 2005). A useful summary is to consider the consequences of work–family conflict in three main groups: (1) *work-related outcomes* (such as job satisfaction, commitment, absenteeism, and job performance), (2) *non-work-related outcomes* (including marital, family and life satisfaction, and leisure), and (3) *stress-related outcomes* (such as psychological strain, physical health, depression, burnout, and substance abuse (Allen, Herst, Bruck, & Sutton, 2000). Here, we briefly discuss one consequence from each of these three groups.

Research has demonstrated that the experience of high levels of work–family conflict can negatively influence worker's attitudes to their job. The inability to perform optimally at either work or home (due to high levels of work and/or family demands) can directly reduce worker's job satisfaction (which in turn, is associated with job commitment, work performance, and turnover intentions). For example, in tests with 1,550 managers from five countries (the US, Canada, Australia, Finland, and New Zealand), Lapierre et al. (2008) demonstrated that job satisfaction was directly influenced by work–family conflict, resulting in a reduction in the managers ratings of their overall life satisfaction. Managers employed by organizations that made little or no acknowledgment as to how work performance is influenced by family demands, recorded the highest levels of work–family conflict. This last point illustrates that organizations which actively support employees experiencing a critical life experience (such as the birth of a child, or an illness of a family member) tend to foster higher levels of satisfaction and commitment within their workers (e.g., Brough, O'Driscoll, & Biggs, 2009b).

Crossover theory (Westman, 2001) considers how strain experienced by an individual results in strain experienced by the individual's spouse, family members, or work colleagues. Westman and colleagues define crossover as 'a bi-directional transmission of positive and negative emotions, mood, and dispositions between intimately connected individuals such as spouses or organisational team members' (Westman, Brough, & Kalliath, 2009, p. 589). Crossover theory describes how work–family conflict can affect the worker's spouse and children, primarily by a decrease in levels of martial satisfaction, family satisfaction, or child behaviours. Westman, Etzion, and Chen (2009), for example, demonstrated that engagement (specifically, vigour) perceived by business travellers directly affected levels of strain experienced by their spouses. It is important to note that while crossover can occur from and to both genders, the strongest affect has been found from husbands to their spouses, although this distinction may become more blurred as investigations include *both* male and female workers and their respective spouses. Recently, for example, Bakker and Demerouti (2009) demonstrated that positive work experiences (work engagement) were transferred from working women to their male spouses. The inclusion of both crossover and work–family conflict/balance theories is recognized as a pertinent research avenue for future work–family investigations.

Finally, the direct contribution of work–family conflict to psychological strain has been widely established. For example, O'Driscoll, Brough, and Kalliath (2004) demonstrated in a longitudinal investigation of New Zealand workers that high levels of family demands were directly associated with psychological strain. It is important to note that work–family conflict may be the *cause* and/or the *consequence* of psychological strain. Conflict may be experienced due to strain caused by previous work or family stressors. Kelloway, Gottlieb, and Barham (1999) examined this point in a longitudinal investigation testing these multiple causal pathways. Kelloway et al. found that psychological strain predicted *subsequent* levels of work–family conflict. Strain and work–family conflict therefore appear to have a *reciprocal* relationship, which is plausible given the long-term nature of many work/family demands (such as dependent children).

## Role changes

Some of the early measures of stress, such as the Holmes and Rahe (1967) 'Life Events' instrument, assessed the experience of common life changes. The underlying theory was that experiencing a significant change such as a house move, bereavement, or a divorce directly influenced psychological well-being and strain (in either positive or negative directions). In a similar manner, change or uncertainty at work caused by organizational restructures, promotions, transfers, or threats of redundancies are also antecedents of work-related stress. Probst (2005) defined job insecurity, unemployment, and underemployment as *economic stressors*, caused by organizational downsizing, mergers, restructures, and technological changes. Probst described how these economic stressors are directly associated with individual health outcomes (physical health and psychological strain), organizational outcomes (e.g., job attitudes, withdrawal, and turnover), and non-work outcomes (e.g., family strain, marital problems). Probst and colleagues later developed these ideas into a multi-level model of the relationship between economic stress and well-being (Sinclair, Sears, Probst, & Zajack, 2010).

Research exploring the consequences of role changes such as redundancy and job insecurity is especially prevalent during economic hardships. Thus a burst of such research occurred in the 1970s and 1980s due to high levels of organizational restructures, mergers, and closures. This research was especially valuable in demonstrating the impact on the health of affected workers. Thus the *threat* of redundancy has been associated with physical ill-health symptoms such as high blood pressure, increased cholesterol levels, and increased stress hormone production (Pollard, 2001). Job insecurity has also been associated with mental ill-health problems such as depression, anxiety, and psychological strain (for a review, see Probst, 2005). Interestingly, some research suggests that once workers have been made redundant they are likely to experience redundancy again in the future (Leana, Feldman, & Tan, 1998), indicating that these workers are justified in feeling anxious about pending organizational changes. A recent comprehensive investigation by Vanroelen, Levecque, Moors, Gadeyne, and Louckx (2009), demonstrated associations between job insecurity, musculo-skeletal complaints, persistent fatigue, and well-being. Similarly, in a recent meta-review of the consequences of job insecurity, Cheng and Chan (2008) remarked on the strong associations between job insecurity and individual and organizational outcomes of job performance, turnover intentions, and health. Specifically, Cheng and Chan found that levels of job insecurity were highest among younger employees and employees with a short tenure, while adverse health outcomes were more pronounced in older workers.

We discussed above how work–family conflict can adversely affect the worker's spouse and children via the process of crossover, and this also applies to the threat of role changes. Research has identified the negative consequences for the affected worker's family members caused primarily by the increased strain experienced by the worker. Thus reports of marital problems, family conflict, domestic abuse and violence, spousal depression, and adverse child behaviors, well-being, and school performance have all been associated with the worker's experience of economic stressors (Hanisch, 1999; Stroem, 2002). In an investigation of the consequences of organizational downsizing, Westman, Etzion, and Danon (2001) found a direct relationship between job insecurity and psychological burnout experienced by both the worker and their spouse (via crossover). Similarly, Mauno and Kinnunen (2002) demonstrated that strain caused by job insecurity (assessed via job uncertainty, the worry over job continuity, and the probability of job-related changes) was transferred between spouses regardless of who (male or female) was the affected worker. This resulted in the spouse then also worrying about their *own* job security.

A recurring theme in organizational restructures is the *outsourcing* of jobs, which has increased with the growth of cheap labour markets in India, China and Asia. The growth of *manufacturing* industry relocations from Europe, the US, and other countries to these cheap labour markets which occurred in the 1980s and 1990s is currently being experienced again with *service* industry relocations. The stability of such service jobs for workers within western countries is therefore of concern and we predict this will produce another burst of occupational health psychology research in this area.

## Anti-social behaviours

Some recent attention has been paid to the experience of anti-social behaviours at work such as workplace violence, bullying, and harassment and the impact this has on both individual and organization outcomes. While such experiences obviously cause considerable distress for the affected workers, anti-social behaviours may also have an impact on colleagues, family members, and organizational performance. Recent reviews by authors such as Griffin and O'Learly-Kelly (2004) and Brough et al. (2009a) provide detailed examinations of the definitions, causes, and consequences of this 'dark side' of organizational behaviour. In this final description of specific psychosocial stressors we briefly describe four of the key components of these anti-social behaviours: workplace violence, aggression, bullying, and harassment.

Recent reports have observed a marked increase in the amount of violence and aggression experienced by workers. The growth of employment within the service industries (e.g., retail, tourism, hospitality, health, education, and social work) characterized by frequent customer interactions accounts for a significant proportion of this increase in workplace violence. LeBlanc and Kelloway (2002), for example, estimated that an average of twenty US employees are murdered and 18,000 workers are assaulted *each week* whilst at work. Neuman and Baron (1998) described workplace aggression as consisting of three factors: (1) *expression of hostility* (ridicule of a co-worker, rumour spreading, and verbal sexual harassment); (2) *obstructionism* (intentionally ignoring telephone calls or emails from a co-worker, sabotaging their work, and being late for their meetings); and (3) *overt aggression* (physical attacks and assaults, theft or destruction of a co-workers personal property, and destroying a co-worker's mail or messages). Neuman and

Baron reported that expressions of hostility occur most frequently and are experienced by between 30% to 70% of workers.

Consequences of aggression include individual reactions such as anxiety, fear, depression, and avoidance behaviours, and organizational consequences such as reduced performance and turnover. As well as the obvious physical ill-health and medical costs experienced by victims of workplace violence and aggression, another significant consequence is the experience of occupational stress (specifically, inter-personal conflict at work). Stress experiences typically enhance the consequences of workplace violence and aggression; resulting in work withdrawal behaviours (absenteeism and sick leave), poor psychological health (anxiety, depression, and victimization) and poor physical health (sleep problems, fatigue, and colds) (Brough et al., 2009a).

Workplace bullying and harassment is also reported at a fairly constant rate, despite the presence of harassment, discrimination, and bullying policies formally adopted by most organizations. Indeed, the organizational culture and human resource systems are considered to be at least partially responsible for workplace harassment via the maintenance of a harassment-tolerant workplace environment (for example, by not adequately punishing harassers). Recently, Willness, Steel, and Lee (2007) provided a meta-analysis of sexual harassment and noted that organizational climate was the strongest indicator of sexual harassment occurrences. Rospenda and Richman (2005) also provided a detailed review of workplace harassment and noted the significant associations between harassment and physical violence, indicating the often simultaneous multiple experiences of workplace aggression.

The majority of workplace harassment research has focused on the psychological and behavioural impact of harassment on individual victims (commonly, occupational stress, physical ill-health, and psychological burnout). However recent multi-level research has demonstrated that harassment can also negatively affect team productivity and performance. Raver and Gelfand (2005) for example, reported that sexual harassment was positively related to team conflict, such that teams who reported higher levels of harassment also experienced more conflict, reduced cohesion, and reduced performance. Willness et al. (2007) also found that harassment adversely influences workgroup productivity via worker absenteeism, withdrawal, and inhibited performance. That is, workers who observed harassment (but were not the victims or perpetrators) also reported a decrease in their own performance levels.

An interesting development in this field is the recognition that as well as the traditional downwards direction of bullying perpetrated by a manager against his/her employee, *horizontal bullying* may also occur (staff against staff) as well as *upwards bullying* (perpetrated by an employee against a manager (Branch, Ramsay, & Barker, 2007). Branch et al. reported, for example, that the 'bullied boss' is becoming an increasingly common phenomenon, with other research estimating up to 30% of managers are bullied by their subordinates (Zapf, Einarsen, Hoel, & Vartia, 2003). While bullied managers may be male or female, there are reports that female managers are especially susceptible to bullying by their male subordinates; this situation commonly occurs in male dominated occupations such as the military, correctional services, and academia (Branch et al., 2007).

## Summary

In the above section we have described some of the major factors which contribute to increased psychological strain at work and diminished subjective well-being. Although we have focused on each of these factors separately, it is important to recognize that they typically operate together and that their combined outcomes can outweigh their individual effects. Similarly, the occurrence of some factors (such as high control and social support) can offset the detrimental effects of work-related stressors.

## Special Groups of Workers

*Are some occupational groups more likely to experience work-related*
*stress and reduced well-being?*
*Why is police work stressful?*
*Are there gender differences in the experience of stress at work?*

While workers employed in any occupation may experience the psychosocial stressors identified above, a number of specific occupations have been identified as being of particularly 'high risk' for the occurrence of these stressors. Occupations which involve regular contact with other people (as patients, students, clients, etc.), high workloads, tight deadlines, and threat of physical attacks, tend to occur at the top of these lists, as do occupations within the public sector as opposed to private industry (Kalliath, Brough, O'Driscoll, Manimala, & Siu, 2009). Examples of these high-risk occupations are listed below. It is obviously important for workers within these occupations to be aware of these increased risks and for their managers to ensure that these stressors are managed appropriately.

teachers, nurses
police officers, prison officers
military, doctors
hotel managers, public administration (e.g., hospital managers)
scientific researchers, retail
fire fighters, social welfare workers
ambulance officers and paramedics, drivers of public transport (e.g., train and
    bus drivers)
bank workers.

## Police work

One occupation which has been widely recognized as a high-risk job is that of policing. As well as the risk of experiencing the psychosocial stressors identified above policing also commonly entails other experiences recognized as 'traumatic operational stressors' which can be experienced over numerous years, including: encountering major incidents involving death, violence, personal attacks, and harassment (Brough & Biggs, in press). As well as operational stressors, the impact of frequently occurring minor *job stressors* or *hassles* also contributes to the experience of occupational stress for police workers (and other workers within high stress occupations). Thus job stressors such as inter-personal conflict with colleagues and supervisors; inadequate pay, training, or career advancement; missing or faulty equipment; and bureaucracy, paperwork, and red tape have all been associated with stress outcomes. Brough (2004), for example, demonstrated that items such as excessive paperwork and inadequate job recognition were associated with psychological strain in New Zealand police, fire, and ambulance officers to a similar extent as traumatic operational stressors.

The 'emotional labour' of police work has also been identified as an occupational stressor. Emotional labour describes the requirement to behave in a manner contradictory to one's actual feelings, such as being polite to hostile members of the public. The emotional labour of police work has been associated with experiences of psychological burnout by officers (Amaranto, Steinberg, Castellano, & Mitchell, 2003). Finally, the experience of work-related stress can also be exacerbated by organizational systems that are overly bureaucratic, punitive of staff, and strictly managed. Police services recognize the influence of occupational culture to varying extents, and have made attempts to 'soften' the culture by increasing the diversity of staff, expanding training and promotion programmes, and flattening the hierarchical structure by reducing some levels of management (Brough & Biggs, in press; Chan, 2007).

## Female workers

We described above some of the common psychosocial stressors experienced by female workers namely, harassment, bullying, and work–family conflict. While such stressors are also experienced by male workers, it is still the case that these stressors tend to be experienced more often by females. In this section we therefore acknowledge specifically the additional difficulties experienced by some female workers. Some reports have identified recent increases in the incidents of workplace physical violence reported by female employees, such that more assaults are now experienced by females as compared to male workers (Heiskanen, 2007). This increase appears to be due to the growth of service occupations especially, resulting in more female workers having contact with members of the public. Workplace bullying also appears to be experienced more often by female workers. In one investigation of 7,000 French workers, Niedhammer, David, and Degioanni (2007) found that considerably more female employees than males reported being bullied at work in the previous 12 months.

Working in male-dominated occupations such as the military, police, fire, or correctional services can also entail additional stressors for some female workers. These additional stressors range from direct harassment and assault of female workers to more insidious behaviours such as exclusion and ostracism (from specific working parties, meetings, work social events, etc.). Liao, Arvey, Butler, and Nutting (2001) for example, assessed injuries reported by firefighters over a 12-year period and found that female firefighters experienced more injuries than their male colleagues. Brown and Campbell have conducted considerable research of UK female police officers and have observed that gender discrimination is a significant *additional* occupational stressor experienced by many female officers (e.g., Brown, 2007; Brown, Campbell, & Fife-Schaw, 1995). Similarly, Brough and Frame (2004) demonstrated that the experience of sexual harassment by female New Zealand police officers influenced their levels of both job satisfaction and turnover intentions. However, Brough and Frame also noted that officers with supportive supervisors reported less harassment. This observation reflects the point noted above that the organizational culture has a strong influence on the occurrence of discriminatory behaviours.

Finally, we described above the associations between work–family conflict and various individual and organizational outcomes. Work–family conflict can obviously be experienced by both male and female workers; however, the caring for dependants and the management of home demands is still conducted more often by females; consequently females tend to access organizational family-friendly polices significantly more than men do (O'Driscoll, Brough, & Biggs, 2007). Female workers tend to reduce their employment hours and conditions to accommodate family demands, more so than males, for example, by changing from full-time to part-time hours, or changing to a less demanding job role. The negative impact of these employment changes on salary earnings and benefits, superannuation (pension) entitlements, and promotion opportunities have been acknowledged (e.g., Brough et al., 2009b). Indeed it is reported that some male workers pointedly avoid accessing policies such as paternal leave, for fear of appearing 'uncommitted' to their work (Butler & Skattebo, 2004).

## Summary

Above we have discussed some potential differences between occupational groups in their experience of work-related stress. We focused specifically on police officers, an occupation known to encounter major work-related stressors, and female workers, who often confront different types of stressors than do their male counterparts. A main conclusion from this brief overview is that it cannot be assumed that all workers are faced with the same kinds of work stress, and that between-group differences are important to take into account, especially when designing interventions to combat the deleterious impact of work stress.

## RESEARCH CLOSE-UP   3.3   Economic Factors and Well-Being

*Source:* Diener, E., & Seligman, M. E. P. (2004). Beyond money. Towards an economy of well-being. *Psychological science in the Public Interest,* 5(1), 1–31.

This article reviews research surrounding well-being and economic indicators, arguing that well-being ought to be the ultimate focus of economic, health, and social policies. The article acknowledges the limitations of economic indicators, namely that income increases well-being only to a certain extent, beyond which non-monetary factors such as social connections are important. The article reviews the findings related to well-being in six specific areas: (1) Societal conditions such as democratic and stable governments, high social capital, low unemployment and low inflation are associated with higher levels of well-being. (2) The relationship between financial income and well-being is not simple and the direction of influence is not clear. (3) Associations between well-being and work performance have been clearly demonstrated. (4) Research has signified the occurrence of a reciprocal relationship between physical health and well-being. (5) Rates of mental health have not improved as nations become wealthier; instead, mental health rates have either remained constant or decreased. (6) Social relationships with others that are supportive, positive, and fill the need for social belonging are crucial to well-being. Overall, this article provides an interesting account of the limits to which money can influence happiness.

## SUMMARY AND CONCLUSIONS

In this chapter we have considered a range of important work-related stressors (or hazards) and their potential impact on the occupational health and well-being of individuals in their workplaces. As we noted early in the chapter, the effects of these stressors have been well documented in research and as a result there is substantial knowledge of their relevance to variables such as psychological strain, subjective well-being, and physical health. We should comment that, while we have examined a wide range of psychosocial stressors which are pertinent to experiences at work, our overview has not been exhaustive and there are other factors which may also be relevant for particular occupational groups or in specific settings. Nevertheless, we have covered stressors which have received most attention in empirical research on health and well-being. Below are some key points to be drawn from this chapter.

- The typologies presented early in the chapter, for example, that developed by Cartwright and Cooper (1997), provide a valuable framework for examining the impact of both work and 'non-work' factors which can impinge a person's well-being.

- Our focus has been especially on psychosocial factors, rather than aspects of the physical environment which may affect well-being. This is not to undermine the importance of the latter, however, as physical stressors (such as noise, temperature, and space) can also have a significant influence on health and well-being.

- Major stressors discussed here have been: work demands (including role stressors), excessive working hours, lack of job control, lack of social support at work, work–family conflict, role changes which lead to uncertainty and job insecurity, and anti-social behaviours in the workplace (such as aggression, harassment, and bullying). We have attempted to summarize key research on the impact of each of these types of stressor.

- It needs to be acknowledged that while each of the stressors covered in this chapter has an impact in its own right, in reality it is critical to assess combined and interactive effects of stressors rather than looking at each in isolation. Numerous studies have found that the accumulated effects of stressors can be much more detrimental than might be expected from each of them separately. This recognition raises important issues for both research and practical intervention.

- We have also examined the impact of stressors on specific groups of workers who are likely to be severely affected by stress and related occupational health problems. To illustrate the importance of sub-group investigations, we selected two groups for consideration (police officers, and women), as these groups may be exposed to specific stressors which are not experienced by others.

- Among women, the experience of work–family conflict has been demonstrated to be especially salient and to be a strong predictor of health and well-being variables. Although males may also experience stress from work–family conflict, it is evident that for women the consequences may be more detrimental.

- Similarly, it has been demonstrated that police officers have to contend with unique stressors that other occupational groups are not exposed to, therefore it is vital to examine the effects of these specific stressors and how they might be alleviated. Clearly other occupational groups also have to deal with stressors which may be relatively specific to their line of work, hence it is important to examine the impact of both generic and occupation-specific stressors.

The present chapter complements others in this volume, especially those on stress theory, risk management, interventions, and health promotion. In particular, the identification of stressors or hazards, which is sometimes referred to as a *stress audit*, underpins interventions which are designed to reduce stress and enhance well-being. A stress audit can be conducted via self-report questionnaires such as ASSET (see, for example, Johnson, 2009), coupled with observations from others (e.g., supervisors, managers) and perhaps even 'hard' data on performance, absenteeism, and other indicators of psychological engagement or withdrawal. This process also has substantial implications for the practical management of worker well-being, in that it can assist managers, occupational health and safety offices, and others in the organization to obtain valuable information on the likely antecedents of occupational health and well-being, as well as determining effective strategies for reducing stress and enhancing well-being among workers.

## RESEARCH CLOSE-UP    3.4   The Changing Nature of Work

*Source:* Sparks, K., Faragher, B., & Cooper, C. L. (2001). Well-being and occupational health in the 21st century workplace. *Journal of Occupational and Organizational Psychology, 74*(4), 489–509.

This article reviews the changing nature of the workforce in relation to well-being. The authors highlight four major areas that are of concern for well-being: (1) As we have discussed in this chapter, job insecurity can have negative outcomes for both individuals (e.g., health and medication) and organisations (e.g., absenteeism, sickness, low commitment and moral). (2) Employees working long hours are at increased risk of fatigue, sleepiness, ill health, heart problems, poor lifestyle habits (smoking, poor diet and exercise), high blood pressure, and chronic headaches. (3) Some research suggests high levels of control are related to decreased anxiety, depression and psychosomatic health complaints, and increases in life satisfaction and job performance. Other research however suggests that high levels of control positively influence productivity but do not raise levels of well-being. (4) Also as we discussed in this chapter, it is clear that a negative managerial style adversely influences employee well-being. Sparks et al. review research demonstrating that managerial behaviours such as bullying result in employee ill-health, psychosomatic stress symptoms, musculo-skeletal symptoms, anxiety, and depression. Poor managerial support such as lack of effective communication and feedback is also related to higher employee stress levels and symptoms of depression. Sparks et al. emphasise the requirement for the effective management of employee well-being and discuss why this is an increasing concern for both managers and employees.

## Suggestions for Further Reading

Brough, P., O'Driscoll, M. P., Kalliath, T. J., Cooper, C. L., & Poelmans, S.A.Y. (2009). *Workplace psychological health: Current research and practice.* Cheltenham: Edward Elgar.

Brown, J. (2007). From cult of masculinity to smart macho: Gender perspectives on police occupational culture. In M. O'Neill, M. Marks & A. M. Singh (Eds.), *Police occupational culture: New debates and discussion* (pp. 189–210). Oxford: Elsevier.

Cartwright, S., & Cooper, C. L. (2009). *The Oxford handbook of organizational well-being.* Oxford: Oxford University Press.

Gilboa, S., Shirom, A., Fried, Y., & Cooper, C. L. (2008). A meta-analysis of work demand stressors and job performance: Examining main and moderating effects. *Personnel Psychology, 61*(2), 227–271.

Grebner, S., Semmer, N. K., & Elfering, A. (2005). Working conditions and three types of well-being: A longitudinal study with self-report and rating data. *Journal of Occupational Health Psychology, 10*(1), 31–43.

Griffin, R. W., & O'Learly-Kelly, A. M. (Eds.). (2004). *The dark side of organisational behavior.* San Francisco: Jossey-Bass.

Wellens, B. T., & Smith, A. P. (2006). Combined workplace stressors and their relationship with mood, physiology, and performance. *Work & Stress, 20*(3), 245–258.

Westman, M. (2001). Stress and strain crossover. *Human Relations, 54,* 557–591.

Willness, C. R., Steel, P., & Lee, K. (2007). A meta-analysis of the antecendents and consequences of workplace sexual harassment. *Personnel Psychology, 60*(1), 127–162.

## References

Allen, T. D., Herst, D. E. L., Bruck, C. S., & Sutton, M. (2000). Consequences associated with work-to-family conflict: A review and agenda for future research. *Journal of Occupational Health Psychology, 5,* 278–308.

Amaranto, E., Steinberg, J., Castellano, C., & Mitchell, R. (2003). Police stress interventions. *Brief Treatment and Crisis Interventions, 3*(1), 47–53.

Bakker, A. B., & Demerouti, E. (2007). The Job Demands-Resources model: State of the art. *Journal of Managerial Psychology, 22*(3), 309–328.

Bakker, A., & Demerouti, E. (2009). The crossover of work engagement between working couples: A closer look at the role of empathy. *Journal of Managerial Psychology, 24,* 220–236.

Boswell, W. R., Olson-Buchanan, J. B., & LePine, M. A. (2004). Relations between stress and work outcomes: The role of felt challenge, job control, and psychological strain. *Journal of Vocational Behavior, 64*(1), 165–181.

Branch, S., Ramsay, S., & Barker, M. (2007). The bullied boss: A conceptual exploration of upwards bullying. In I. A. Glendon, B. M. Thompson, & B. Myors (Eds.), *Advances in organisational psychology* (pp. 93–112). Sydney: Australian Academic Press.

Brough, P. (2004). Comparing the influence of traumatic and organisational stressors upon the psychological health of police, fire and ambulance officers. *International Journal of Stress Management, 11*(3), 227–244.

Brough, P., & Biggs, A. (2010). Occupational stress in police and prison staff. In J. Brown, & E. Campbell (Eds.), *The Cambridge handbook of forensic psychology.* London: Cambridge University Press.

Brough, P., & Frame, R. (2004). Predicting police job satisfaction, work well-being and turnover intentions: The role of social support and police organisational variables. *New Zealand Journal of Psychology, 33*(1), 8–16.

Brough, P., O'Driscoll, M. P., & Biggs, A. (2009b). Parental leave and work–family balance among employed parents following childbirth: An exploratory investigation in Australia and New Zealand. *Kotuitui: New Zealand Journal of Social Sciences Online, 4,* 71–87.

Brough, P., O'Driscoll, M., & Kalliath, T. (2007). Work–family conflict and facilitation: Achieving work–family balance. In I. Glendon, B. Myors & B. Thompson (Eds.), *Advances in organisational psychology: An Asia-Pacific perspective* (pp. 73–92). Sydney: Australian Academic Press.

Brough, P., O'Driscoll, M. P., Kalliath, T. J., Cooper, C. L., & Poelmans, S. A. (2009a). *Workplace psychological health: Current research and practice.* Cheltenham: Edward Elgar.

Brown, J. (2007). From cult of masculinity to smart macho: Gender perspectives on police occupational culture. In M. O'Neill, M. Marks & A. M. Singh (Eds.), *Police occupational culture: New debates and discussion* (pp. 189–210). Oxford: Elsevier.

Brown, J. M., Campbell, E. A., & Fife-Schaw, C. (1995). Adverse impacts experienced by police officers following exposure to sex discrimination and sexual harassment. *Stress Medicine, 11,* 221–228.

Butler, A. B., & Skattebo, A. (2004). What is acceptable for women may not be for men: The effect of family conflicts with work on job-performance ratings. *Journal of Occupational and Organisational Psychology, 77,* 553–564.

Cartwright, S., & Cooper, C. L. (1997). *Managing workplace stress.* Thousand Oaks, CA: Sage.

Chan, J. (2007). Police stress and occupational culture. In M. O'Neill, M. Marks & A. M. Singh (Eds.), *Police occupational culture: New debates and discussion* (pp. 113–135). Oxford: Elsevier.

Chen, P., Popovich, M., & Kogan, M. (1999). Let's talk: Patterns and correlates of social support among temporary employees. *Journal of Occupational Health Psychology, 4,* 1–8.

Cheng, G. H., & Chan, D. K. (2008). Who suffers more from job insecurity? A meta-analytic review. *Applied Psychology: An International Review, 57*(2), 272–303.

Cohen, S., & Wills, T. (1985). Stress, social support and the buffering hypothesis. *Psychological Bulletin, 92,* 257–310.

Cooper, C. L., Dewe, P. J., & O'Driscoll, M. P. (2001). *Organisational stress: A review and critique of theory, research and applications.* Thousand Oaks, CA: Sage Publications.

Cooper, C. L., & Marshall, J. (1976). Occupational sources of stress: A review of the literature relating to coronary heart disease and mental ill-health. *Journal of Occupational Psychology, 49,* 11–28.

de Jonge, J., & Dormann, C. (2006). Stressors, resources, and strain at work: A longitudinal test of the triple-match principle. *Journal of Applied Psychology, 91*(6), 1359–1374.

de Lange, A. H., Taris, T. W., Kompier, M. A. J., Houtman, I. L. D., & Bongers, P. M. (2003). 'The very best of the millennium': Longitudinal research and the demand-control-(support) model. *Journal of Occupational Health Psychology, 8*(4), 282–305.

Diener, E., & Seligman, M. E. P. (2004). Beyond money. Towards an economy of well-being. *Psychological science in the Public Interest, 5*(1), 1–31.

Eby, L. T., Casper, W. J., Lockwood, A., Bordeaux, C., & Brinley, A. (2005). Work and family research in io/ob: Content analysis and review of the literature (1980–2002). *Journal of Vocational Behavior, 66,* 124–197.

Fenlason, K., & Beehr, T. A. (1994). Social support and occupational stress: Effects of talking to others. *Journal of Organisational Behavior, 15*(2), 157–175.

Fox, M., Dwyer, D., & Ganster, D. (1993). Effects of stressful job demands and control on physiological and attitudinal outcomes in a hospital setting. *Academy of Management Journal, 36*(2), 289–318.

Glazer, S., & Beehr, T. A. (2005). Consistency of implications of three role stressors across four countries. *Journal of Organizational Behavior, 26*(5), 467–487.

Greenglass, E., Fiksenbaum, L., & Burke, R. (1996). Components of social support, buffering effects and burnout: Implications for psychological functioning. *Anxiety, Stress & Coping, 9,* 185–197.

Griffin, R. W., & O'Learly-Kelly, A. M. (Eds.) (2004). *The dark side of organisational behavior.* San Francisco: Jossey-Bass.

Hanisch, K. (1999). Job loss and unemployment research from 1994 to 1998: A review and recommendations for research and intervention. *Journal of Vocational Behavior, 55,* 188–220.

Heiskanen, M. (2007). Violence at work in Finland: Trends, contents and prevention. *Journal of Scandinavian Studies in Criminology and Crime Prevention, 8,* 22–40.

Holmes, T. H., & Rahe, R. H. (1967). The social readjustment rating scale. *Journal of Psychosomatic Research, 11,* 213–218.

Hughes, E. L., & Parkes, K. R. (2007). Work hours and well-being: The roles of work-time control and work–family interference. *Work & Stress, 21*(3), 264–278.

Jamal, M. (2007). Job stress and job performance controversy revisited: An empirical examination in two countries. *International Journal of Stress Management, 14*(2), 175–187.

Jex, S. M., & Elacqua, T. C. (1999). Time management as a moderator of relations between stressors and employee strain. *Work & Stress, 13*(2), 182–191.

Johnson, J., & Hall, E. (1988). Job strain, work place social support and cardiovascular disease: A cross-sectional study of a random sample of the working population. *American Journal of Public Health, 78,* 1336–1342.

Johnson, S. (2009). Organizational screening: The ASSET model. In S. Cartwright & C. L. Cooper (Eds.), *The Oxford handbook of organizational well-being* (pp. 133–155). Oxford: Oxford University Press.

Johnson, S., Cooper, C. L., Cartwright, S., Donald, I., Taylor, P., & Millet, C. (2005). The experience of work-related stress across occupations. *Journal of Managerial Psychology, 20*(2), 178–187.

Jones, F., O'Connor, D. B., Conner, M., McMillan, B., & Ferguson, E. (2007). Impact of daily mood, work hours, and iso-strain variables on self-reported health behaviors. *Journal of Applied Psychology, 92*(6), 1731–1740.

Kahn, R., Wolfe, D., Quinn, R., & Snoek, J. (1964). *Organisational stress: Studies in role conflict and ambiguity.* New York: Wiley.

Kalliath, T., Brough, P., O'Driscoll, M., Manimala, M., & Siu, O. L. (2009). *Organisational behaviour: An organisational psychology perspective.* Melbourne: McGraw-Hill.

Kelloway, E. K., Gottlieb, B. H., & Barham, L. (1999). The source, nature, and direction of work and family conflict: A longitudinal investigation. *Journal of Occupational Health Psychology, 4,* 337–346.

Karasek, R. (1979). Job demands, job decision latitude and mental strain: Implications for job redesign. *Administrative Science Quarterly, 24,* 285–308.

Kaufmann, G., & Beehr, T. A. (1986). Interactions between job stressors and social support: Some counterintuitive results. *Journal of Applied Psychology, 71*, 522–526.

Lapierre, L. M., Spector, P. E., Allen, T. D., Poelmans, S., Cooper, C. L., O'Driscoll, M., et al. (2008). Family-supportive organization perceptions, multiple dimensions of work–family conflict, and employee satisfaction: A test of model across five samples. *Journal of Vocational Behavior, 73*, 92–106.

Lazarus, R. S., & Folkman, S. (1984). *Stress, appraisal and coping.* New York: Springer.

Leana, C. R., Feldman, D. C., & Tan, G. Y. (1998). Research predictors of coping behavior after a layoff. *Journal of Organisational Behavior, 19*, 85–97.

LeBlanc, M. M., & Kelloway, E. K. (2002). Predictors and outcomes of workplace violence and aggression. *Journal of Applied Psychology, 87*(3), 444–453.

LePine, J. A., Podsakoff, N. P., & LePine, M. A. (2005). A meta-analytic test of the challenge stressor-hindrance stressor framework: An explanation of inconsistent relationships among stressors and performance. *Academy of Management Journal, 48*(5), 764–775.

Liao, H., Arvey, R. D., Butler, R. J., & Nutting, S. M. (2001). Correlates of work injury frequency and duration among firefighters. *Journal of Occupational Health Psychology, 6*(3), 229–242.

Mauno, S., & Kinnunen, U. (2002). Perceived job insecurity among dual-earner couples: Do its antecedents vary according to gender, economic sector and the measure used? *Journal of Occupational and Organisational Psychology, 75*(3), 295–314.

Maslow, A. H. (1943). A theory of motivation. *Psychological Review, 50*, 370–396.

Meier, L. L., Semmer, N. K., Elfering, A., & Jacobshagen, N. (2008). The double meaning of control: Three-way interactions between internal resources, job control, and stressors at work. *Journal of Occupational Health Psychology, 13*(3), 244–258.

Melamed, S., Ben-Avi, I., Luz, J., & Green, M. (1995). Objective and subjective work monotony: Effects on job satisfaction, psychological distress and absenteeism in blue-collar workers. *Journal of Applied Psychology, 80*(1), 29–42.

Mikkelsen, A., Øgaard, T., & Landsbergis, P. (2005). The effects of new dimensions of psychological job demands and job control on active learning and occupational health. *Work & Stress, 19*(2), 153–175.

Moyle, P., & Parkes, K. (1999). The effects of transition stress: A relocation study. *Journal of Organisational Behavior, 20*, 625–646.

Narayanan, L., Menon, S., & Spector, P. E. (1999). Stress in the workplace: A comparison of gender and occupations. *Journal of Organisational Behavior, 20*, 63–73.

Neuman, J. H., & Baron, R. A. (1998). Workplace violence and workplace aggression: Evidence concerning specific forms, potential causes, and preferred targets. *Journal of Management, 24*(3), 391–419.

Ng, T. W., & Feldman, D. C. (2008). Long work hours: A social identity perspective on meta-analysis data. *Journal of Organisational Behavior, 29*(7), 853–880.

Niedhammer, I., David, S., & Degioanni, S. (2007). Economic activities and occupations at high risk for workplace bullying: Results from a large-scale cross-sectional survey in the general working population in france. *International Archives of Occupational and Environmental Health, 80*(4), 346–353.

O'Driscoll, M. P., & Beehr, T. A. (1994). Supervisor behaviors, role stressors and uncertainty as predictors of personal outcomes for subordinates. *Journal of Organisational Behavior, 15*(2), 141–155.

O'Driscoll, M. P., Brough, P., & Kalliath, T. (2004). Work–family conflict, psychological well-being, satisfaction and social support: A longitudinal study in New Zealand. *Equal Opportunities International, 23*(1/2), 36–56.

O'Driscoll, M., Brough, P., & Biggs, A. (2007). Work–family balance: Concepts, implications and interventions. In J. Houdmont, & S. McIntyre (Eds.), *Occupational health psychology: European perspectives on research, education and practice, Vol. 2* (pp. 193–217). Maia, Portugal: ISMAI Publishers.

Pollard, T. M. (2001). Changes in mental well-being, blood pressure and total cholesterol levels during workplace reorganization: The impact of uncertainity. *Work & Stress, 15*, 14–28.

Probst, T. M. (2005). Economic stressors. In J. Barling, E. K. Kelloway, & M. R. Frone (Eds.), *Handbook of work stress* (pp. 267–297). London: Sage.

Raver, J. L., & Gelfand, M. J. (2005). Beyond the individual victim: Linking sexual harassment, team processes, and team performance. *Academy of Management Journal, 48*(3), 387–400.

Rospenda, K. M., & Richman, J. A. (2005). Harassement and discrimination. In J. Barling, E. K. Kelloway, & M. R. Frone (Eds.), *Handbook of work stress*. London: Sage.

Schaubroeck, J., & Merritt, D. (1997). Divergent effects of job control on coping with work stressors: The key role of self-efficacy. *Academy of Management Journal, 40*(3), 738–754.

Scheck, C., Kinicki, A., & Davy, J. (1997). Testing the mediating processes between work stressors and subjective well-being. *Journal of Vocational Behavior, 50*(1), 96–123.

Sinclair, R. R., Sears, L. E., Probst, T., & Zajack, M. (2010). A multilevel model of economic stress and employee well-being. In J. Houdmont, & S. Leka (Eds.), *Contemporary occupational health psychology: Vol. 1: Global perspectives on research and practice (2010/2011)*, Chichester: Wiley-Blackwell.

Sparks, K., Cooper, C. L., Fried, Y., & Shirom, A. (1997). The effects of work hours on health: A meta-analytic review. *Journal of Occupational and Organisational Psychology, 70*, 391–408.

Sparks, K., Faragher, B., & Cooper, C.L. (2001). Well-being and occupational health in the 21st century workplace. *Journal of Occupational and Organizational Psychology, 74*(4), 489–509.

Spector, P. E. (1998). A control theory of the job stress process. In C. L. Cooper (Ed.), *Theories of organisational stress*. Oxford: Oxford University Press.

Spector, P. E., Chen, P., & O'Connell, B. (2000). A longitudinal study of relationships between job stressors and job strains while controlling for negative affectivity and strains. *Journal of Applied Psychology, 85*(2), 211–218.

Stroem, S. (2002). Keep out of the reach of children: Parental unemployment and children's accident risks in Sweden 1991–1993. *International Journal of Social Welfare, 11*, 40–52.

Tucker, J. S., Sinclair, R. R., Mohr, C. D., Adler, A. B., Thomas, J. L., & Salvi, A. D. (2008). A temporal investigation of the direct, interactive, and reverse relations between demand and control and affective strain. *Work & Stress, 22*(2), 81–95.

Vanroelen, C., Levecque, K., Moors, G., Gadeyne, S., & Louckx, F. (2009). The structuring of occupational stressors in a post-Fordist work environment. Moving beyond traditional accounts of demand, control and support. *Social Science & Medicine, 68*(6), 1082–1090.

Wall, T., Jackson, P., Mullarkey, S., & Parker, S. (1996). The demands–control model of job strain: A more specific test. *Journal of Occupational and Organisational Psychology, 69*, 153–166.

Warr, P. B. (2009). Environmental 'vitamins', personal judgments, work values and happiness. In S. Cartwright, & C. L. Cooper (Eds.), *The Oxford handbook of organisational well-being* (pp. 57–85). Oxford: Oxford University Press.

Wellens, B. T., & Smith, A. P. (2006). Combined workplace stressors and their relationship with mood, physiology, and performance. *Work & Stress, 20*(3), 245–258.

Westman, M. (2001). Stress and strain crossover. *Human Relations, 54,* 557–591.

Westman, M., Brough, P., & Kalliath, T. (2009). Expert commentary on work-life balance and crossover of emotions and experiences: Theoretical and practice advancements. *Journal of Organisational Behavior, 30*(5), 587–595.

Westman, M., & Eden, D. (1992). Excessive role demand and subsequent performance. *Journal of Organisational Behavior, 13*(5), 519–529.

Westman, M., Etzion, D., & Chen, S. (2009). The crossover of exhaustion and vigor between international business travelers and their spouses. *Journal of Managerial Psychology* (24), 269–284.

Westman, M., Etzion, D., & Danon, E. (2001). Job insecurity and crossover of burnout in married couples. *Journal of Organisational Behavior, 22*(5), 467–481.

Willness, C. R., Steel, P., & Lee, K. (2007). A meta-analysis of the antecendents and consequences of workplace sexual harassment. *Personnel Psychology, 60*(1), 127–162.

Zapf, D., Einarsen, S., Hoel, H., & Vartia, M. (2003). Empirical findings on bullying in the workplace. In S. Einarsen, H. Hoel, D. Zapf, & C. L. Cooper (Eds.), *Bullying and emotional abuse in the workplace: International perspectives in research and practice* (pp. 103–126). London: Taylor & Francis.

# 4

# Interventions to Promote Well-Being at Work

## Raymond Randall and Karina Nielsen

### CHAPTER OUTLINE

This chapter describes a variety of interventions that can be used by occupational health psychologists in their attempts to improve the health of employees and organizations. There is a wide variety of interventions available, many of which are based on strong theories that explain the links between work and well-being. Interventions can be classified according to their objectives into primary, secondary, and tertiary interventions. Examples of each type of intervention are presented in order to give the reader a flavour of intervention practices within organizational settings. This chapter also contains a critical analysis of intervention effectiveness including a detailed discussion of research design, evaluation criteria, and the practical challenges of evaluation research. Both process evaluation and effect evaluation are examined in detail. In closing the chapter the conclusions that can be drawn about intervention effectiveness, and the priorities for the future in research and practice, are presented.

## Intervention Design, Implementation, and Evaluation in Occupational Health Psychology

............................................................

*What is the role of theory as the basis for intervention?*
*What intervention strategies are available for use in organizations?*
*Why are intervention studies relatively rare in the scientific literature?*

Many parts of this textbook provide detailed reviews of theory in occupational health psychology (OHP). Such theories help us to understand the links between work and health, and the mechanisms that underpin these links. A goal of most researchers and practitioners in OHP is to use these theories to develop effective interventions that improve well-being, health, satisfaction, and performance at work. In this chapter the design, implementation, and evaluation of these interventions is discussed.

In most of the research examined in this chapter, sound theory has been used to guide the development and implementation of interventions. Fortunately, reading this textbook should make you aware that there is no shortage of good theory from which interventions can be developed. The negative emotional experience of stress is important in many of the theories that describe the links between work and well-being. Therefore, stress management interventions are the focus of this chapter. Because there are many different theories that explain the links between work and health, it follows that many different intervention options have emerged from this theoretical literature.

It is worth noting that interventions also allow us to test theory. If an intervention built upon a theory is shown to be effective, this helps to validate that theory. For example, a recent review of stress management interventions has examined the effectiveness of a range of different cognitive interventions in a variety of organizations (Richardson & Rothstein, 2008). These findings lend support to contemporary theories of work-related stress that emphasize the importance of appraisal and cognition.

Setting aside these scientific considerations, perhaps the most important reason for studying intervention research is that it helps researchers and practitioners to develop their knowledge of what needs to be done to tackle problems in organizations. Unfortunately, for some types of intervention, there is still relatively little research available. This is because applied intervention research is not easy to carry out: the organizational setting presents many challenges for even the most skilled researchers and practitioners. For example, many intervention studies do not include control groups because denying employees an intervention may be seen as unethical by researchers or as undesirable by key stakeholders within the organization (Randall, Griffths, & Cox, 2005). These challenges, and how occupational health psychologists have responded to them, will be analysed during this chapter.

The sustained growth of intervention research is vital for the growth of OHP as a discipline. Intervention research is needed now more than ever as government guidance and legislation in many countries requires organizations to assess and manage risks to psychological well-being (Cox, Griffiths, & Rial González, 2000). While assessment methods are now becoming quite mature, intervention research is relatively new. In recent years there has been a noticeable shift in emphasis from interventions targeted at the individual (e.g., counselling) to interventions targeted at the organization (e.g., changing working conditions or job design). LaMonatgne, Keegel, Louie, Ostrey, and Landsbergis (2007) found that between 2001 and 2005 over two thirds of published stress management intervention studies included interventions targeted at tackling the sources of work-related stress (compared to just over one-third in the period 1990–1995). This is encouraging because there is increasing pressure from various government bodies for practitioners to focus their efforts more on prevention than cure.

There are many controversies within intervention research that make it a lively and vibrant topic for the student of OHP. The general consensus is that the small body of research into the effectiveness of interventions has produced many inconsistent findings and there is much uncertainty about which interventions work best (Briner & Reynolds, 1999; Murphy & Sauter, 2003). There has been a tendency for researchers to focus on examining only the effects of interventions and, as a result, the reasons for intervention success and failure are often poorly understood. The interventions discussed in this chapter are often complex changes occurring in complex social settings. It is difficult to make the argument that they closely resemble simple experimental manipulations that many psychologists learn about in their research training. This means that the implementation and evaluation of the interventions is not straightforward. For example, the way that an intervention is designed, implemented, and perceived appears to be related to its effectiveness (Bunce, 1997; Murphy & Sauter, 2003; Randall, Nielsen, & Tvedt, 2009). This chapter also contains a discussion of how implementation processes and intervention context have been examined in order to understand better how and why interventions work.

As occupational health psychologists our clients are likely to ask the question 'what will work?' when intervention is discussed. Even for those familiar with the diverse and complex intervention literature it is not always easy to give a clear and unequivocal answer. A key objective of this chapter is to gather up the many threads in intervention research and practice in order to present a clear summary of what is known, what is not yet known, and what is uncertain about a variety of interventions.

## Summary

The role of theory as the basis for action is a thread that runs throughout this textbook; good theory can inform the selection and design of interventions to protect and promote occupational health. Intervention research as it relates to work-related stress remains a relatively young topic area for a variety of reasons, not least the difficulty of conducting 'scientific' interventions and evaluations thereof, though considerable advances are currently being made in these areas.

## Levels of Intervention

*What are the levels of intervention?*
*What is the focus of primary, secondary, and tertiary interventions?*

Anyone wanting to intervene in a way that has a positive impact on occupational health must be aware of the mechanisms that link work and health. For example, if we know *factor A* (a work characteristic) is linked to employee health – and the evidence for that linkage is good – we might want to intervene to ensure that *factor A* is well managed. If for some reason this is not possible then we might look to protect employees against the effects that *factor A* might have on them. If we know that we cannot achieve either of these things we might then look to see how the damage caused by *factor A* can be repaired.

Therefore, to intervene is to disrupt (in a *positive* way) the mechanisms that link problems at work to problems with individual and organizational health. Interventions attempt to break damaging linkages between work and employee health, repair the damage caused, or capitalize on those linkages by making positive changes in the work environment.

As you may have seen elsewhere in this textbook, the mechanisms linking work and health differ from one theory to another. For example, using the Demand-Control-Support model (Karasek & Theorell 1990) to guide intervention design could lead to an intervention that enhanced employees' opportunities to use their skills in the workplace. The theory would also predict that such an intervention may well lead to improvements in employee health. Siegrist's (1996) Effort-Reward Imbalance model would indicate that interventions should focus on improving the perceived fairness between effort and rewards such as money, esteem, and career opportunities. This might be achieved by changing job design or by training employees to cope better with perceived unfairness. Many models of work-related stress emphasize the importance of employee cognition in the links between work and well-being. Some interventions (e.g., cognitive behavioural techniques) are designed to help employees develop more positive psychological responses to situations they encounter in the working environment. Such an intervention is thought to work because by influencing cognitions the intervention breaks or weakens the link between exposure to poor working conditions and poor employee health.

A student of occupational health psychology can be faced by a bewildering array of interventions. This is, perhaps, an encouraging sign that organizations and researchers are taking a tailored approach to intervention design and delivery as recommended by Leka and Cox in Chapter 5 of this text. The downside to this is that it can make it difficult to identify the similarities and differences in approaches to intervention. In reading about interventions you will see that similar interventions (e.g., interventions to increase control at work) are implemented in many different ways (Bond, Flaxman, & Loivette, 2006).

A useful way to makes sense of this disparate literature is to think in terms of the *level of intervention*. This means setting aside the specific details of an intervention, and instead focusing on the *objectives of the change* that is being attempted. More specifically, this taxonomy is based on how the intervention disrupts the stress process. Different researchers have different ways of categorizing interventions, but within these different approaches a taxonomy consisting of three levels of intervention (primary, secondary, and tertiary) can often be identified.

## Primary interventions

The objective of these interventions is to target the problem at source. Most often they are designed to deal with aspects of work design, organization, and management that are perceived to be problems by a significant proportion of employees (e.g., the psychosocial risks, or *stressors*, identified in Chapter 3). These interventions are sometimes referred to as *organizational-level interventions, job re-design intervention, psychosocial interventions, or work environment interventions.* In some studies these are called primary prevention because the objective is to remove, or to manage better, the source of the problem. The logic is that this then prevents employee health being damaged by the problem, because the problem no longer exists.

Strictly speaking, these are not preventative measures, because they usually deal with a problem that already exists. For example, a group of employees who report low levels of support at work may receive an intervention that gives them more frequent contact with their colleagues. However, this intervention might not have happened if the problem had not existed and been identified. True prevention would need to occur in the initial design of the working environment before a job role became active (not surprisingly there is very little published research on this issue, although perhaps there should be). A proper risk assessment (see Chapter 5), or problem analysis, is arguably a more crucial precursor to this type of intervention than it is to other types of intervention. Without this assessment a suitable intervention for tackling a problem cannot be designed (Elo, Ervasti, & Mattila, 2008).

## Secondary interventions

These interventions are designed to disrupt in the psychological mechanisms through which problems at work are linked to employee well-being. This involves breaking (or weakening) the links between exposure to sources of stress and their negative outcomes. The objective of secondary intervention is to reduce or eliminate the harm that employees might experience, but not to reduce directly their exposure to problems at work.

Secondary intervention aims to give employees the skills they need to respond to stressors in a way that reduces the impact that work-related problems have on them. Most of these interventions focus on training employees to respond in a positive way to difficult working conditions (by thinking and/or behaving differently).

## Tertiary interventions

These interventions are aimed at employees who are already experiencing significant problems with their well-being. Such interventions are designed to help employees who have already been harmed in some way by their working conditions. In many organizations there is often a referral route to allow employees to access specialist help for their condition.

Nowadays, tertiary interventions tend to be used for helping individuals for whom efforts at the primary and secondary intervention level are not possible or do not prove effective (though both situations should be relatively rare).

## Summary

Interventions can be categorized as primary, secondary, and tertiary. Primary interventions are targeted at tackling the (occupational) source of the problem, secondary interventions largely involve 'bolstering' employees' ability to cope with occupational psychosocial hazard exposures, and tertiary interventions offer remedial support for manifested problems.

## Designing and Implementing Interventions

*What issues need to be considered in intervention design?*
*How are interventions implemented?*

### Implementing primary interventions

Primary interventions require changes to working practices. These interventions are designed to tackle problems being experienced by a group of employees and are designed to work in the same way for all employees exposed to that problem. This means that they are targeted at the *group-level* rather than the individual employee. For relatively simple interventions (e.g., increasing the number of staff meetings to tackle problems with low social support at work) the change process can be straightforward. The design of primary interventions can take time, effort, and some resources. Managers may think that primary interventions are difficult to implement, disruptive, and expensive. However, reviews focusing on primary interventions show that this is rarely the case (e.g., Bond, Flaxman, & Loivette, 2006). Most primary interventions are not expensive and the change process, if handled correctly, need not be disruptive.

In many examples, the process of involving employees in the design and implementation of primary interventions can lead to positive outcomes in itself (Elo et al., 2008). As a result of such findings it is rare to find primary interventions that do not involve employees in intervention design. However, it is noticeable that in comparison to other types of intervention there are relatively few published studies of primary interventions. This is because primary intervention may not be seen as the strategy of choice: managers may think that sources of stress are resident in the individual (i.e., the result of an individual weakness, or lack of resilience). Before primary interventions are chosen, managers and senior managers may need persuading that some occupational health problems can have their root cause in the design, organization, and management of work. This can be uncomfortable for managers because it may be seen as shifting the responsibility for the problems across to them and away from individual employees (Murphy & Sauter, 2003).

Because they work by reducing exposure to chronic work stressors, primary interventions often take time to work and evaluation periods tend to be lengthy (an evaluation period of 6 months or more is not uncommon). Kompier, Geurts, Grundemann, Vink, and Smulders (1998) showed that primary interventions take time to work because these interventions take time 'bed in' within an organization as employees become accustomed to new working practices. Murphy and Sauter (2003) point out that employees may also need training and support to adapt to new working practices. This requires a degree of patience and commitment from those delivering and receiving the intervention.

In the face of these challenges to implementation and evaluation, the potential benefits of primary interventions need to be significant. Well-validated stress theory indicates that primary intervention should be the most effective in the medium- to long-term because it removes the need for employees to deal with problems that can place their health at risk (Semmer, 2003, 2006). Effective primary intervention means that individual differences in coping skills, coping ability, and personality are rendered relatively unimportant because the source of the problem has been removed. There is also increasing pressure from governments for organizations to tackle occupational health problems at their source. This means that as part of an overall strategy for promoting occupational health, primary interventions needs to be implemented whenever it is practicable to do so. The case for primary intervention reflects the adage 'prevention is better than cure'.

Parkes and Sparks (1998) distinguish between two different types of primary intervention: *sociotechnical* intervention and *psychosocial* intervention. Sociotechnical interventions are those designed to change objective aspects of work (e.g., reduce number of tasks, improve work equipment, increase the number of staff meetings, etc.). Intervention choice tends be driven by theory or research linking the objective working conditions to poor employee and/or organizational health. Sociotechnical interventions often also bring about change in perceptions of work: this is important because perception, appraisal, and cognition play a key role in most theories of occupational health.

Psychosocial interventions are those designed to cause change that is perceived by employees (e.g., enhance job control, improve perceived social support, reduce perceived role ambiguity, etc.). Psychosocial interventions tend to involve employees in the intervention design process because their perceptions are hypothesized to be important to making the change appropriate and effective. This type of intervention is often a context-specific response to the identification of a context-specific problem. This approach is in contrast to 'off the shelf' secondary and tertiary interventions which are usually delivered by experts from outside the group targeted for intervention. Participative action research (PAR) often results in primary interventions being designed and implemented (see Definition 4.1).

A further classification of primary interventions is used by van der Hek and Plomp (1997). This splits primary interventions into those that are at the 'interface' between the individual and the organization (e.g., relationships at work,

---

## Definition 4.1

'Participative action research … involves researchers, management and union representatives, and 'shop floor' employees in a joint problem-solving process whereby diverse points of view can be aired and different interests can be accommodated. Since such an approach necessitates labour and management working together to jointly define problems and develop solutions, it is likely to overcome differences in union and management conceptions of stress … and to lead to mutually satisfactory intervention.' Heaney et al. (1993, p. 499).

---

participation, role conflict, role ambiguity, and autonomy) and those that are organizational (e.g., job re-design/re-structuring, training, changes to organizational structures, etc.).

It is not possible to describe all primary interventions within this chapter. Instead a small sample of different interventions is summarized in Box 4.1. Descriptions of many other primary interventions can be found in reviews of intervention research such as Cooper, Dewe, and O'Driscoll (2001); Egan, Bambra, Petticrew, and Whitehead (2008); Parkes and Sparkes (1998); Richardson and Rothstein (2008); and Giga, Noblet, Faragher, and Cooper (2003).

---

## Box 4.1

### Presenting problem: Poor job design

*Terra (1995).* This intervention took place in a manufacturing firm where employees did monotonous work. Through discussions between consultants, managers, and employees it was decided to introduce a degree of self-management into production teams to give employees more opportunities to communicate and collaborate with colleagues, more variety in their work, and more autonomy. There was a significant decrease in absence levels after the intervention, but the research did not collect data on perceived changes in working conditions (nor did it have a control group).

### Presenting problem: Role ambiguity

*Schaubroeck, Ganster, Sime, and Ditman (1993).* This intervention was carried out in a US university over a 2-year period and used a series of meetings and reviews to help managers clarify the aims and objectives of their roles. This process was designed to identify gaps in managerial accountability and areas of roles that might overlap with others' roles and thus create conflict. The intervention had some success in increasing role

## Box 4.1    *(Cont.)*

clarity but had no significant effect on employee health. (See also Research Close-up 4.2.)

### Presenting problem: Work–non-work interface

*Kim and Campagna (1981).* This intervention tested the effects of the introduction of flexible working hours (i.e., flexible start and finish times around 'core' working hours). Short–term absences were found to decrease and there was some evidence of increases in performance for those given flexible working hours. Short-term absence levels increased among a comparable group of employees not given flexible working hours.

### Participative Action Research Studies (many such interventions address problems with control at work)

*Elo, Ervasti, and Mattila (2008).* Employees participated in 'work conferences' designed to allow them time to identify and find solutions for tackling problems with work. These conferences led to the design and implementation of other interventions including: ergonomic interventions; the introduction of regular staff meetings; systems being put in place for communicating information about management decisions; and flexible working schedules to help employees balance work and non-work demands. The intervention led to some changes in perceived working conditions (but not employee health) with the biggest changes being observed for those who had participated most in the work conferences.

*Bond, Flaxman, and Bunce (2008).* This intervention involved employee representatives (both managers and colleagues) meeting in 'steering groups' that were facilitated by the research team. In the steering groups, work problems were identified and solutions discussed and decided upon. In-between steering group meetings, steering group members consulted with their colleagues about the issues discussed in the group. The meetings resulted in several interventions being implemented including: greater control being given to teams to decide the allocation of workload and work schedules; employees being given more discretion on the timing, ordering, and scheduling of work tasks; team members participating in the work planning process; more flexibility over breaks and lunch and when particular tasks were completed (brought about changing short work cycles to longer ones); and monthly one-to-one meetings between team members and team leader to discuss ideas for problem solving and personal development. The intervention appeared to bring about a significant reduction in psychological distress and absence: these changes were linked to increases in job control associated with the intervention.

## Implementing secondary interventions

Secondary interventions usually involve making employees aware of the impact their work is having on them before delivering training interventions to equip them with flexible coping strategies. These interventions often require organizations to 'buy-in' expertise (in the form of well-qualified trainers or therapists). This can be costly, but interventions are usually completed in a few months (and many in a few weeks) with employees attending a number of short training sessions during that time. These interventions have the advantage that they can be used when primary prevention is not a viable option. For example, many people working in the medical profession will be required to deal with distressing situations (such as the death of a patient). These situations cannot be 'designed out' of the job with primary interventions.

The most common form of secondary intervention is stress management training (SMT). SMT is a group of worker-oriented techniques that seek to make employees more aware of sources of stress and the impact these have on them. In this sense the training is tailored to allow employees to consider the specific stressors they face. However, this awareness is then used as a basis for the teaching of generic 'off the shelf' stress reduction skills that are shaped by theory rather than by an assessment of the work situation. SMT is designed to break the link between work and poor employee health: it focuses on modifying employees' cognitive appraisals or coping styles. Because it provides generic skills it has been argued that SMT provides employees with strategies that will help them to respond in a more healthy way to a range of different stressors they may encounter in the workplace (Murphy & Sauter, 2003).

The various secondary interventions work in different ways. *Cognitive behavioural interventions* are designed to help employees think differently about their work situation. These are *active interventions*: the training encourages employees to put problems in a more appropriate perspective by recognizing negative thoughts and replacing them with positive ones, or to act in a way to reduce their exposure to the problem (such as re-organizing their workload). Deploying this *different thinking and behaviour* requires skill and effort on the part of the employee. These interventions may overlap with more practical individual problem-solving interventions such as time management or assertiveness training which provide employees with a wider a range of skills that allow them to respond positively to challenges or problems.

Other more *passive secondary interventions* focus directly on minimizing the adverse consequences of employees' reactions to stress. Interventions such as meditation and relaxation are designed to reduce tension and anxiety by placing the employee in a state that precludes tension and anxiety (e.g., by focusing their mind on something that stops them thinking about the source of stress). A brief description of the main types of secondary intervention is given below.

*Cognitive behavioural therapy training*
Cognitive Behavioural Therapies (CBTs) are based on the concept that human behaviour and stress-related emotions (such as anger, sadness, guilt, helplessness, etc.) can be influenced by changes in cognition. CBT aims to change the way that

an individual perceives sources of stress in their work environment. For example, this can be done by re-labelling sources of stress (e.g., an employee seeing a situation as 'stressful' could re-label it as 'challenging'). Techniques from Ellis's Rational Emotive Behavioural Therapy can be used to help employees re-construct their views of what is going on around them (Dryden & Neenan, 2003). For example, employees can be trained in techniques that they use to evaluate problems and their reactions to them as temporary and controllable (rather than as fixed and being out of their control). This method is sometimes used in Stress Inoculation Training (SIT: Miechenbaum, 1977). In SIT, employees practice using their newly developed strategies placed in increasingly stressful situations during training to give them the opportunity to practice thinking differently about the problems they are facing. Cecil and Forman (1990) show how SIT has been used to help teachers manage their responses to stressful classroom situations.

CBT interventions are based on established theory-based therapeutic techniques. Beck's cognitive therapy (Beck, 1995) uses the theory that our emotions and judgments come from fixed patterns of thinking (schemas) that are based on previous experiences. When employees are faced with difficult situations these schemas can be triggered causing over-reactions and unpleasant emotions. For example, employees might over-generalize (the schema triggering the automatic thought 'this always happens to me …'), use mental filtering (only perceiving negatives) or put themselves under excessive pressure ('I should feel this …'). What Beck's CBT aims to do is enable participants to become aware of these negative thoughts. The training then aims to allow people to challenge those errors by assessing evidence for and against them. Box 4.2 gives an overview of how changes in these schemas might be achieved during CBT.

Acceptance and Commitment Therapy (e.g., Bond & Bunce, 2000) is also now being used in stress management interventions. This involves training individuals to accept their emotions as natural reactions to difficult events and, rather than dwell on these emotions, to focus instead on contingencies (i.e., actions that will help them to complete tasks).

*Relaxation based stress management training*
Relaxation training is designed to train the mind to recognize when the body is becoming tense and seek ways to combat/avoid this: it is a method designed to teach people how to cope better with the consequences of stress. This is different to CBT which challenges people to tackle their thinking 'head on'. Physical based relaxation training techniques are designed to enable deep muscle relaxation (e.g., by using stretching or deep breathing exercises). For example, Toivanen et al. (1993) describes a three-step progressive relaxation process; first, participants practise gaining deep diaphragm breathing; secondly, they practice relaxation of the abdominal muscles; and thirdly, they practise focusing the mind on breathing. Cognitively-based relaxation techniques use imagery and meditation (clearing the mind of external thoughts and focusing on inner stillness). An example is cue

---

### Box 4.2 An example of a CBT-based training technique

*Source:* adapted from Randall, R., & Lewis, R. (2007). Stress management interventions. In E. Donaldson-Feilder (Ed.), *Well-being and Performance*. London: CIPD.

In this example, the training has three parts:

1. Participants are asked to monitor their negative thoughts, by writing down all the automatic thoughts that pop into their minds. For example:

*'Think of something, it might be an object or a person or a situation, that makes you feel stressed. Take 30 seconds to both monitor and write down all the automatic thoughts that come into your head over this period'.*

2. Participants are trained to recognize the connection between those automatic 'pop up' thoughts and their subsequent actions or behaviour. Once this is done, participants are asked to analyse those automatic thoughts, looking for evidence for and against their validity. For example:

*'Try to do this based on the previous exercise. Which of these automatic thoughts were realistic? Which were based on fact and which were just interpretations of your thinking? What are the facts around this person/object/situation?'*

3. Participants are trained to substitute the automatic thoughts with more realistic interpretations and to practice doing this. The idea is that after doing this 20–50 times, this becomes an automatic process and therefore a skill that can be used outside of the training environment.

---

controlled relaxation (Paul & Shannon, 1966) which trains participants to become relaxed by repeating a cue word (e.g., 'calm') at times of stress.

*Biofeedback*

This technique allows people to be made aware of their physiological responses to stress so that they can use techniques to manage those same responses. Participants are shown measurements from devices such as a finger thermometer, a galvanic skin resistance monitor, or a heart rate monitor. This is often used when participants are being trained to use relaxation techniques and biofeedback enables them to see if they are using relaxation methods effectively enough. Several different sources of data might be fed back including blood pressure (to show if peripheral blood vessels are being dilated), galvanic skin response (to show decreasing sweat gland activity), or heart rate activity. Feedback enables participants to renew or re-double their efforts at relaxation to exert a greater influence on their physiological state. The aim is that through the use of biofeedback, participants are able to learn to use relaxation techniques effectively enough to manage their physiological responses to stress without the need to be attached to equipment that gives them biofeedback (e.g., when they are faced with stressful situations in the work environment).

### Job-related skills training

These interventions include courses in time management, assertiveness, and training to help with carrying out core components of the job. For example, Sharp and Forman (1985) provided teachers with training in classroom management skills as a stress management intervention. In a sense, these are not secondary interventions, as their *modus operandi* has much in common with primary interventions. These interventions are designed to improve the 'fit' between the worker's perception of their own skills and their perceptions of the demands being placed on them by the work environment (see the discussion on Person-Environment Fit theory in Chapter 2).

A hypothetical example may help you to understand the mechanism through which job-related skills training works. Imagine you were asked to leave your home this minute and fly an aeroplane, fully loaded with passengers, without any additional training. This is likely to be quite a stressful experience. If, however, you were given many months of training, studied for, and passed exams and various tests of your skills and competence, before being asked to fly the aeroplane, then the experience is likely to be somewhat less stressful. These interventions receive relatively little coverage in the research literature, and are often over-looked by organizations in their intervention planning (Cox, Randall, & Griffiths, 2002) but appear to be relatively effective (Richardson & Rothstein, 2008). This evidence also suggests that good employee selection processes that match employees' knowledge, skills, abilities, and attitudes to the demand of the job may help to improve occupational health.

### Multimodal stress management training

The 'packaging up' of several secondary interventions is quite common in stress management training. Different techniques and methods are used concurrently after an initial awareness phase where participants learn about the causes and consequences of occupational stress. This is often followed by the development of a range of skills including both coping skills and job-related skills to help employees organize and manage their work in a different way. The assumption is that a combination of techniques will work better than any single technique in isolation. The accuracy of this assumption is examined later in this chapter.

## Implementing Tertiary Interventions

With the information we now have about the effectiveness of primary and secondary interventions, organizations are usually advised to use tertiary interventions as a 'safety net' when primary or secondary intervention is not possible or effective. Tertiary interventions also have wider objectives than primary and secondary intervention. Many organizations use Employee Assistance Programmes (EAPs) to provide employees with access to support when they are experiencing problems with both work-related and non-work-related issues (e.g., a legal advice helpline). Employees may refer themselves for help, but in many organizations line managers have some responsibility for identifying individual employees who might benefit from tertiary intervention. The term EAP has now become synonymous with tertiary intervention.

EAPs now provide individual consultations, counselling resources, skills training, health promotion advice, and access to preventative healthcare. EAPs are often used as referral route for primary or secondary interventions. Job re-design can be used at an individual level to help employees return to work after a period of absence. Employees experiencing significant health problems may often be offered secondary interventions. Workplace health promotion (see Chapter 6) may also be integrated with tertiary intervention.

For some organizations tertiary interventions remain the focal point of their efforts to manage occupational health. Of course, tertiary interventions only become effective once the employee is experiencing significant problems and repair damage rather than prevent it. Just as with other primary and secondary interventions there are numerous factors that seem to be associated with the success of EAPs (Randall & Lewis, 2007). These include:

- commitment and support from senior management, and the co-operation with unions (if applicable);
- clear and written agreement on the purpose, policies and procedures of the EAP (including client confidentiality);
- training of managers to help them identify problems and refer employees appropriately to the EAP;
- frequent communication concerning EAP services to employees;
- a continuous care programme, including follow-up of individual cases;
- continual work to foster employee trust and confidence in confidentiality of programme;
- maintenance of records to allow for programme evaluation.

Because tertiary interventions often prompt the delivery of primary or secondary interventions, they will not be discussed at length in this chapter. This is not to down-play the importance of tertiary intervention. However, the space within this chapter does not allow a comprehensive review of the complex implementation and evaluation processes associated with their provision within EAPs. For an excellent comprehensive review of EAPs see Cooper, Dewe, and O'Driscoll (2003).

## Summary

A host of interventions exist at each level. It is important that the intervention chosen is appropriate for the problem identified. This 'matching' of problem to intervention can be established through a tailored risk assessment.

## Evaluating Interventions (I): Effect Evaluation

*What criteria can be used to evaluate interventions?*
*How can quasi-experimental procedures be used to evaluate interventions?*
*What challenges does intervention evaluation present?*

### Criteria for intervention effectiveness

An examination of published intervention studies reveals that a vast array of outcome variables has been used in the research. This is an important issue for students of OHP because it adds complexity to the question 'which interventions are effective?' Some interventions are designed to improve individual well-being; others are a response to organizational-level problems such as high levels of absence. Therefore, judgments about the effectiveness of an intervention can depend on the criteria used to evaluate it. For example, an intervention designed to reduce levels of absence, which results in no change in absence levels but significantly improves levels of job satisfaction, might well be judged to have failed. Perhaps more significantly in the research literature, the theoretical basis for intervention usually informs the choice of measures. For example, if an intervention was designed to address problems with control at work, a measure of employees' perceptions of control at work would be included in the intervention study.

Measures of intervention effectiveness need to have reliability, validity, and sensitivity. Reliability refers to the extent to which the measure is free from error. In organizations, employee absence data are only reliable if absence behaviour is properly recorded and this may not always be the case (Darr & Johns, 2008). Validity refers to the extent to which a measure is measuring what it is intended to measure. For example, a measure of psychological well-being might not have good validity if healthy employees' responses on the questionnaire are influenced by dissatisfaction with their level of pay. Sensitivity refers to the extent to which the measure will reflect significant changes in the variable being measured. For example, a measure of employee well-being that asks employees to report on their health over the preceding 6 months might not be sensitive enough to detect changes 1 month into an intervention programme.

For students and practitioners of OHP it is important to be aware of the strengths and limitations of different outcome measures when evaluating published research. At present it appears that using a range of outcome variables is desirable, but not always possible. Students should not be too quick to dismiss the value of well-designed studies that use a limited range of outcome measures. It is rather naïve to assume that researchers are ignorant of the qualities of various outcome measures: instead it is likely that practical and ethical constraints limit the choice of outcome measures in intervention research. Practitioners will often be working within significant organizational constraints that prevent them from using the strongest available research methods and designs.

The measures most frequently used to measure intervention outcomes can be grouped into five categories: psychological measures; measures of disease/physical health; physiological (and physical health) measures; behavioural measures; and organizational measures. You will also notice that the majority of these measures are designed to detect problems rather than to measure positive aspects of well-being: this could be seen as a weakness in published intervention research. Positive intervention research is a new phenomenon; some of the first results to emerge from the fledgling positive OHP intervention literature are reviewed by Arnold Bakker and Daantje Derks in Chapter 7.

Psychological outcomes are usually measured with self-report questionnaires. The use of such measures is common in intervention research. Psychological outcome variables include various measures of individual psychological health such as burnout, anxiety, and depression. These measure also include measures of affect (mood) and attitudes particularly relevant to the work setting such as self-efficacy, motivation, intention to leave the organization, and job satisfaction. Many interventions also take measures of perceived work characteristics: these measures are especially important for primary interventions as they are thought to work by bringing about changes in perceived working conditions. Often measures of work characteristics are used twice: once to identify problems and then later to evaluate the effectiveness of an intervention. Cognitive performance has only been used in a small number of studies (Parkes & Sparkes, 1998). Cognitive performance is often classed an objective measure because good performance is difficult to fake (i.e., employees cannot present an impression of their performance that they see as desirable).

There has been considerable criticism of the use of self-report measures in intervention research. Parkes and Sparkes (1998) argue that such measures are a poor substitute for the measurement of important organizational outcomes (such as absence), or changes in behaviour. This argument is based on the view that self-report data often has low reliability and validity and that ease of use does not off-set these problems. However, some psychological measures are important to measure the *immediate effects* of change (e.g., changes in self-efficacy are thought to precede changes in behaviour). Such measures are relatively uncontaminated by a range of organizational factors that impact on organizational-level measures (Kompier & Kristensen, 2001). Well-designed and well-researched self-report measures can therefore provide crucial data when evaluating interventions.

Physiological measures include blood pressure (the physiological measure most frequently used in intervention research), galvanic skin responses, blood hormone levels, and muscular tension. These measures are less common in intervention research in organizations. This is because the practicalities of gathering such data and the ethical complications that come with them often prevent their use. Parkes and Sparkes (1998) criticized the under-utilization of these measures and little has changed since (Richardson & Rothstein, 2008). This is probably an indication of the difficulty of gathering such data rather than an indicator of researchers' ignorance of the existence of these data collection methods. Physical health data (e.g., somatic symptoms) is often collected using a questionnaire survey (and could therefore be argued to have both psychological and physiological components). Physical disease (morbidity), such as rates of coronary heart disease, is rarely used in intervention research because it requires research to be carried out over long periods. Such variables are more commonly used in theory development research (e.g., Karasek & Theorell, 1990).

Behavioural outcome measures include sleeping patterns, exercise levels, and other maladaptive coping behaviours such as smoking and alcohol use. These measures are often used to examine the impact of tertiary interventions: problems in these areas indicate that employees have already been 'damaged' in some way by their work.

Organizational outcome measures include various measures of job performance, absence levels, accidents or 'near miss' incidents, and actual staff turnover. From the client perspective these are the most important outcomes, and it is always encouraging to see such measures used in intervention research (see Research Close-Ups 4.1 & 4.2). Often such measures are thought to be better because the data is 'objective' and is of great value to the organization. For example, if absence rates are reduced cost savings can be calculated. However, absence records are often kept in a rather haphazard way by organizations and the links between perceived working conditions and absence are not always clear (Darr & Johns, 2008). In addition, employee absence behaviour is influenced by a huge range of factors and self-reported health may have only a modest impact on absence levels. There are a host of problems with the reliability, validity, and sensitivity of measures of employee performance (Arnold et al., 2004). In addition, the relationship between exposure to stressful working conditions and performance is complex and can vary from one situation to another (Sullivan & Bhagat, 1992). The properties of organizational measures should be subject to as much scrutiny as psychological measures. The quality and suitability of organizational data needs to be established before it can be used as a marker of intervention effectiveness.

In describing the various criteria for effectiveness it is important to point out that not all measures of intervention outcomes correlate with one other. For example, intervention work in the health care sector has shown that high levels of job satisfaction and low levels of absence are frequently found among groups of employees who report poor well-being (Cox, Randall, & Griffiths, 2002). This indicates that employees can find their job satisfying and be reluctant to take time off, while still finding the job to be wearing them out. Job satisfaction can be seen to occupy the 'middle ground' between individual-level and organizational-level outcomes. But the relationship between individual well-being and organizational-level variables is a complex one: a satisfied worker is not always a productive worker (Sullivan & Bhagat, 1992). High absences levels can be associated with good psychological health because being away from work allows the employee to escape the problems that have an adverse effect on their psychological well-being.

What is clear from the literature is that the choice of outcome measures generally reflects the nature of the intervention. Most primary intervention studies include psychological measures of work characteristics and employee health. Recent reviews indicate that the use of organizational-level outcomes is more common in primary interventions that it is in other types of intervention research (e.g., Giga, Noblet, Faragher, & Cooper, 2003).

Secondary interventions often use self-report measures of psychological outcomes. This seems appropriate since the interventions are designed to target directly employees' reactions to potentially stressful situations. However, this leaves some uncertainly about the impact of these interventions on organizational outcomes such as absence, turnover, and job performance.

The variety of outcome measures highlights another reason why risk assessment is a crucial precursor to intervention. Unless it can be established that a problem is linked to an undesirable outcome, it is difficult to predict how tackling the problem with impact on any given outcome. The impact that the various intervention strategies have on organizational and individual health is discussed in more detail later in this chapter (see under the heading 'The Effectiveness of Interventions').

## Research Designs for Evaluating Interventions

For those new to OHP it would seem that finding out whether interventions make a difference should be a simple process. We might gather data before the intervention and repeat the process after the intervention. After an intervention we can ask questions such as: do employees think their job is better designed and managed than it was before the intervention? Are aspects of their work that were once a problem no longer a problem for them (or at least less of a problem)? Has employee well-being improved? Have absence levels decreased? Are fewer people leaving the organization? And so on. At the same time alternative explanations for any observed changes would need to be examined and ruled out. The priority for intervention researchers in OHP is to test whether interventions are effective for employees in functioning organizations.

Quite reasonably, most students of OHP begin their studies with the notion that intervention effectiveness needs to focus on the outcomes of change (*effect evaluation*). This might lead to the question: did the group that received the intervention change more than a similar group that did not receive the intervention? Unfortunately, things are not quite as simple as this. One of the aims of this chapter is to describe the challenges of evaluation and how these challenges can be met.

Most intervention research uses the *natural science paradigm* as a basis for evaluation (Cox, Karanika, Griffiths, & Houdmont, 2007). This approach draws heavily upon the methodology used in experimental studies (e.g., laboratory-based psychology experiments or medical research) that use controlled manipulation of exposure to interventions to test their effects. The natural science paradigm focuses on effect evaluation (i.e., it is designed to answer the question: 'what changes?'). A classic example of the use of this paradigm is the randomized control trials (RCTs) that are often used to evaluate the effectiveness of medicines. This involves at least two groups of participants: a control group and an intervention (treatment) group. The control group may be given a placebo treatment and participants will be randomly allocated to the control group or the intervention group. The idea is that the only differences between the control and the intervention group are the active ingredients of the intervention. Therefore, changes observed in the control group can be attributed to the effect of the intervention. The influence of this paradigm is very obvious in the research designs that have been most often used to evaluate interventions.

However, organizations are not laboratories, so in most cases 'perfect' research designs cannot be used. Quasi-experiments do not use random allocation of individual participants to control and intervention groups since this is rarely possible (and potentially unethical) in organizational settings. Instead, employees from one department might be assigned (sometimes at random) to an intervention group, while employees from another department are assigned to a control group. The control group might then get the intervention at some later (a 'waiting list' group) to avoid ethical problems associated with denying employees access to an intervention. In these designs the researcher retains a degree of control over employees' exposure to interventions. If there are links between exposure to the intervention and changes in measures of occupational health, then it may be that the intervention is driving those changes.

Having a control group is seen as essential because it helps to rule out *threats to the validity* of the findings. These threats are the alternative explanations for change (or lack of change). These might be other concurrent changes in the organization such as a merger or down-sizing (see Murta, Sanderson, & Oldenburg, 2007) or changes that would have happened without the influence of the intervention. For example, there may be seasonal effects on absence levels such that absence may drop after winter, regardless of the effect of the intervention. To retain the power of these designs, exposure to the intervention must be carefully monitored (often referred to as a *manipulation check*) and steps taken to ensure that it remains the only substantial difference between the two groups. In practice, often researchers cannot ensure that the control and intervention groups are equivalent in every respect apart from intervention exposure. Therefore other data is usually gathered during the intervention (e.g., participants' age, gender, length of service, previous year's absence, the department they work in, etc.) in order to examine whether these factors are also linked to intervention outcomes.

There are various quasi-experimental designs that can be used during evaluation, too many to examine in this chapter. The interested reader is referred to

Cook and Campbell (1979) for a thorough (if sometimes complex) description of the designs available. Beehr and O'Hara (1987) provide a more accessible discussion of how these designs can be used to evaluate stress interventions.

Establishing and maintaining research designs can be very challenging in organizational settings. This is especially true for primary interventions. From a management perspective, it is often important to expose as many people as possible and as quickly as possible to an effective intervention: this mitigates against establishing control groups. The simple pre-post design without a control group (Box 4.4a) is what many practitioners implement. Unfortunately, the lack of a control group means that it is not possible to rule out alternative explanations for change through the design of the study alone (Cook & Campbell, 1979). Studies of primary interventions that use a single control group (Box 4.4b) are, in many cases, the most complex that can be achieved. Fortunately, such studies can be extremely informative since sophisticated data analysis techniques and the measurement of a range of variables allow for reliable and valid conclusions to be drawn. Research Close-up 4.1 shows an example of this type of evaluation study.

A very strong design for organizational interventions is known as the *Solomon four-group design* as shown in Box 4.4c. This design is the 'gold standard' in quasi-experimental research. It is well known that the process of being observed (e.g., being asked to complete a questionnaire) can have a positive impact on research participants (they may feel better because someone is paying attention to them and their problems, regardless of whether anything is done to deal with those problems). This is known as the *Hawthorne effect* and the Solomon four-group design can identify whether this is occurring.

Box 4.4c shows how this design works. If there are changes that occurs independent of the impact of the intervention repeated tests without intervention (Group 2) will show significant change over time. If measuring before the intervention was having an effect then the post-test scores for Group 2 would be different to the post-test scores for Group 4 (no pre-intervention measure). By the same logic, pre-testing would also be having an impact if the post-test scores for Group 3 were different to the post-test scores for Group 1 (i.e., the change was biggest in an intervention group that had been measured before the intervention). Clearly, establishing such a design requires a considerable degree of goodwill and flexibility on the part of the client organization and an organizational context (in terms of organizational structures and the number of participants) that can support the research design. The rarity of this design in intervention research shows how infrequently such opportunities present themselves to researchers. Research Close-up 4.2 shows a very rare example of this design. Students of OHP should not be too quick to dismiss research that does not follow this design!

Indeed, because of organizational constraints on research design there are still relatively few intervention studies that use control groups. Most researchers have focused their energies on looking at how pre-post designs (both with and without a control group) can be strengthened. Murphy (1996) has published a 'star rating' system that can be used to evaluate the quality of study designs used in effect evaluation research (the more stars, the stronger the design) (see Box 4.5).

These constraints are less severe for secondary interventions. This is because these interventions are usually training courses delivered by well-qualified experts, away from the work environment. As a result those implementing the intervention have a much greater degree of control over its design and delivery.

## RESEARCH CLOSE-UP    4.1   PAR Intervention

*Source:* Bond, F. W., & Bunce, D. (2001). Job control mediates change in a work reorganization intervention for stress reduction. *Journal of Occupational Health Psychology, 6,* 290–302.

This intervention study shows the powerful effects that PAR can have on important indicators of organizational and individual health. It also shows how a simpler study design than that used by Jackson (1983) of two groups (a control group and an intervention group with pre- and post- intervention measures) can be used to identify the mechanism through which an intervention exerts its effects. The study was carried out in a UK government department and 97 employees participated. The PAR intervention involved a series of problem-solving committee meetings with volunteers from the intervention group being helped by the researchers. The committees were tasked with identifying interventions that would increase job control: the interventions they implemented included discussion of the allocation of administrative tasks (so that the team as a whole would have some input into and control over their workload), and systems for getting quick advice (via email) from managers if employees were unsure about how to complete a task. The results of the study were striking: compared to the control group, employees from the group implementing PAR reported less mental ill-health, lower sickness absence, and higher job performance. What was also clear from the study was the mechanism of change: the data showed that the increases in job control brought about by PAR were driving many of the improvements found in the PAR group. This is important because if the mechanisms of change can be identified there is a good chance that in other settings, with different groups of employees, the mechanism of change can be replicated and similar positive results achieved. A subsequent review of the literature by Bond, Flaxman, and Loivette (2006) has found that improving job control appears to have a consistent and significant impact on employee health across a variety of intervention settings. In extending this work, Bond, Flaxman, & Bunce (2008) have found that an individual difference (psychological flexibility) appears to be related to the extent to which job control is affected by a primary intervention. This is interesting because it is one of very studies that show how individual differences interact with exposure to a primary intervention to determine intervention effectiveness.

## Box 4.4   Research Designs for the Valuation of Interventions

### a.  Pre-post single intervention group, no control group design

|  | Measure before intervention? | Intervention delivered? | Measure after intervention? |
| --- | --- | --- | --- |
| Group 1 | Yes | Yes | Yes |

### b.  Pre-post single control group intervention design (see Research Close-Up 4.1)

|  | Measure before intervention? | Intervention delivered? | Measure after intervention? |
| --- | --- | --- | --- |
| Group 1 | Yes | Yes | Yes |
| Group 2 | Yes | No | Yes |

### c.  Solomon four-group design (see Research Close-Up 4.2)

|  | Measure before intervention? | Intervention delivered? | Measure after intervention? |
| --- | --- | --- | --- |
| Group 1 | Yes | Yes | Yes |
| Group 2 | Yes | No | Yes |
| Group 3 | No | Yes | Yes |
| Group 4 | No | No | Yes |

Bunce and Stephenson (2000) point out that intervention studies need to have good-sized samples in order to identify reliable effects. However, many employees work in small or medium sized enterprises and alternative evaluation methods may be needed in such organizations (Randall, Cox, & Griffiths, 2007). The use of long-term follow-up measures can identify when the effect (if any) of the intervention becomes apparent, and if that effect is maintained. Interventions can also be taken away from groups to examine whether improvements are lost (although this may pose ethical challenges). Several authors have also argued that in analysing data more efforts should be made to examine which groups of employees benefit most from the intervention (Murphy & Sauter, 2003). For example, Kompier and Kristensen (2001) contend that interventions can only be effective for employees who are experiencing a problem before the intervention. Van der Hek and Plomp (1997) noted that voluntary participation in interventions does not necessarily attract the workers who are at risk. Therefore analysis of the effects of the

| RESEARCH CLOSE-UP | 4.2  The 'Perfect' Design |

*Source:* Jackson, S. E. (1983). Participation in decision-making as a strategy for reducing job-related strain. *Journal of Applied Psychology, 68,* 3–19.

Susan's Jackson's study is a very rare example of a sophisticated quasi-experimental study being used to evaluate the impact of a primary intervention. Jackson tested whether allowing hospital employees to have more input into decision making (through the introduction of staff meetings within hospital units) led to improvements in various aspects of their working conditions, well-being, and factors such as absence that are important to organizational performance. The study used the Solomon Four-Group Design, random allocation of groups within the hospital to intervention and control groups, and it included long-term follow-up evaluation. There was also a strong manipulation check that examined whether the intervention had been delivered as planned (e.g., by inspecting records of what had been discussed at staff meetings). It is very difficult to identify any significant problems with the research design and methodology used in this study. Employee perceptions of several different working conditions were measured including influence, social support, role ambiguity, and role conflict. The analysis required to track the impact of the intervention was very complex (structural equation modelling was used) and showed that the intervention worked through a multi-stage mechanism. Increased participation reduced problems with work roles (e.g., role conflict and ambiguity). Reduced problems with work roles led to less emotional strain and higher job satisfaction. Lower emotional strain was linked to lower levels of absence and lower turnover intention. Importantly, the study also showed that the results of the intervention took some time to materialize: there was no significant effect after 3 months, but a significant effect at 6 months when the employees in the intervention groups had held many more meetings. The study also shows that even in carefully designed and controlled intervention research it can be difficult to predict the mechanisms through which primary interventions exert their effects. Susan Jackson had hypothesized that changes in communication and social support would be important drivers of the impact of the intervention on employee well-being. In fact it was the reduction in role conflict and role ambiguity, and the increase in perceived influence, brought about by the intervention, that were the most important.

intervention on all employees might be misleading. Finally, many researchers agree that intervention studies should more often include organizational outcome data.

In response to criticisms of intervention research design, two possible ways of improving the evaluation of interventions have been presented. The first is that

---

### Box 4.5    Study Design Star Ratings

\* Research that is descriptive or anecdotal

\*\* Research without intervention but with results that can be useful in future intervention research

\*\*\* Research not involving a control group or randomization but with an evaluation

\*\*\*\* Research involving a systematic study with control groups but without randomization

\*\*\*\*\* Research involving a systematic study with a randomized control group

---

### Pioneer    Michael Kompier

Michiel Kompier is head of the Department of Work and Organizational Psychology of the Radboud University Nijmegen (The Netherlands). His research covers a range of important topics in occupational health psychology. These include work-related stress, the psychosocial work environment, work motivation, job design, mental work load, sickness absenteeism, work disability, work and health, productivity, overtime work, work-home interaction, and working conditions policies. His research portfolio includes a number of influential and important prevention and intervention studies in organizations. It is very rare to find within a researcher's portfolio so many examples of good research being carried out within real-life settings. What is particularly striking about his work is the use of a number of different methodologies to investigate the effects of interventions in functioning organizations. This has led to a number of significant advances in our understanding of the effectiveness of interventions. In this chapter you will see that his work has yielded many important insights into intervention change mechanisms. He has also encouraged researchers to think carefully about the choice of evaluation measures and analysis strategies so that research reflects the reality of the organizational setting. As a consequence, his research has proved to be of immense value to academics and practitioners alike.

---

researchers must continue to strive to find ways of implementing more complex designs in the face of substantial difficulties in organizational settings. The second way forward contends that such complex designs are likely to remain difficult to establish and maintain, and therefore researchers need to find ways of learning more from imperfect study designs (Semmer, 2006). Semmer's view is that it is rather naïve to assume that researchers are ignorant of good research design, but rather that the organizational environment usually places significant constraints on research design and this means that more attention needs to be paid to discovering why interventions work (or fail). The implications of this argument are examined in more detail later in this chapter (see under the heading below, 'Evaluating Interventions (II): Process Evaluation').

## The Effectiveness of Interventions

There are two approaches that can be taken when commenting on the effectiveness of interventions. The first is to critically evaluate each published study to determine whether the intervention described is effective or ineffective. This strategy would quickly highlight the inconsistencies in the findings of intervention research. Sometimes similar interventions work well in one setting, but the effects fail to transfer to other settings. Van der Hek and Plomp (1997) noted that when looking at a range of interventions is was difficult to compare them because there was such variety in respect of the group targeted for intervention and the outcome measures used.

An alternative approach is to combine the results of good-quality research and analyse the data from them to identify the common findings across similar interventions (while seeking explanations for inconsistent findings). This second approach is called *meta-analysis* and there are several such studies that reveal much about the effectiveness of interventions. However, the body of intervention research is still relatively small and it is important to note that even meta-analyses leave some important questions still to be answered.

Meta-analyses are useful for OHP students and practitioners because findings that are common tend to have a better chance of being repeated in new research settings. Meta-analysis also helps to identity any factors that, aside from the intervention itself, may impact upon its effectiveness (e.g., the outcome measures used). The logic is that the results of a meta-analysis of intervention research can be used to guide the choice of interventions in the future.

The most recent large-scale rigorous meta-analysis of primary and secondary intervention is that reported by Richardson and Rothstein (2008). Their review of 36 studies (only five of which were primary interventions) yielded some important findings. As you may expect from reading this chapter they found that strong research designs were more common in the evaluation of secondary interventions than they were in the evaluation of primary interventions. The criteria for including studies in this meta-analysis were very rigorous and the review may have excluded several studies that contain interesting and important findings.[1] However, setting these concerns aside for a moment, this meta-analysis found the largest effects for cognitive-behavioural secondary interventions delivered *without* other interventions. According to this review, relaxation interventions were the second most effective intervention. The authors argue that cognitive-behavioural secondary interventions are more effective than relaxation because they require more active involvement on the part of the employee (in contrast to the passive process of relaxation). This puts employees in a better position to use the techniques in the work environment. However, this is a good example of frequency of use not being highly correlated with effectiveness: because relaxation techniques are cheap they are popular.

Richardson & Rothstein (2008) note the majority of research into secondary interventions uses psychological outcome measures of individual health and rarely consider organizational outcomes: this may explain the relatively large average effects. In their review, van der Klink, Blonk, Schene, and van Dijk (2001) found that secondary interventions have little impact on levels of job satisfaction. Murphy and Sauter (2003) argue that stress management training significantly reduces self-reported somatic complaints, arousal, and distress but that these changes rarely lead to changes in organizational-level outcomes.

In contrast, primary interventions are often evaluated using organizational outcome measures. This may go some way to explaining why average effect sizes for primary interventions appear to be small. Absence and turnover can be affected by a whole range of different factors within the organizational context (as such they are quite distant from the effects of the intervention, whereas measures of depression are quite 'close' to a CBT intervention). It is perhaps to be expected that the impact of an intervention on organizational outcomes tends to be modest, but nonetheless is significant. Parkes and Sparkes (1998) commented that changes in self-report measures (in particular working conditions) are larger than changes in organizational-level outcomes for the majority of primary intervention studies. Perhaps the lack of corresponding large effects on employee well-being is to be expected. Zapf, Dormann, and Frese (1996) argued that working conditions have a relatively modest impact on well-being because they are only one of many factors that influence individual health. As a consequence, any change in working conditions might have a modest but significant impact when health is used as an evaluation criterion. Darr and Johns (2008) showed that the links between perceived stress and absence are not always strong. As Kompier and Kristensen (2001) have argued, it is only reasonable to expect interventions to have an impact on the variables they target directly. Additional, indirect effects on other outcome measures are much more difficult to predict and explain. Changes in perceived working conditions appear to be a necessary, but not sufficient, condition for change in individual health and organizational outcome measures.

There appears to be one important caveat to these findings for primary interventions. Some working conditions have a particularly strong link to organizational outcomes, and by changing these working conditions it is possible to have a significant impact on problems such as high absence and poor performance. Bond, Flaxman, and Loivette (2006) found that several modest primary interventions had a significant impact on organizational outcomes, especially work performance. The authors argue that when intervening to enhance control, 'a little goes a long way' (p. 10). In addition, the authors demonstrated that the cost savings and benefits of these outcomes were often very significant for the organizations involved: small statistical effects sizes can be linked to 'meaningful financial savings' (p. 11). The review showed that the business case for other working conditions was less convincing (although for factors such as support it was still good) but this conclusion was mainly due to the small number of research studies available for the research team to review. One other important conclusion form this work is that different working conditions may be related to different organizational outcomes (e.g., support at work is linked to performance, while problems with work roles are more closely linked to turnover intention). Much more research is needed to examine whether primary interventions do indeed exert such specific effects in terms of organizational outcomes.

Richardson and Rothstein's (2008) analysis also revealed that secondary interventions were more effective singly than in combination. This is a surprising result because different approaches to interventions address different parts of the stress process. It may be that organizations attempting to implement many interventions at once spread their resources too thinly and the quality of implementation suffers as a result. At present there is a lack of intervention research that has *combined* primary and secondary interventions. Research by Bond, Flaxman, and Bunce (2008) indicates that this could be a very fruitful avenue for future intervention research: they found that employees with well-developed psychological flexibility benefited the most from a primary intervention.

All of this analysis on intervention effectiveness should be viewed with caution. Reviewers are still working with a very small (albeit increasing) number of intervention studies. Even within this small pool of research there is a great deal of variety that makes it even more difficult to draw conclusions that have a good chance of generalizing across to new interventions studies. As discussed earlier in this chapter, the quality of intervention research also varies greatly. This means that there are still many uncertainties and debates about the effectiveness of interventions.

## Summary

Interventions should be designed so as to permit their evaluation. As such, great care should be taken at the design stage, within the parameters that bound research in real-world organizations. However, imperfect design does not necessarily preclude sound rigorous evaluation.

## Evaluating Interventions (II): Process Evaluation

*What is process evaluation and how can it help us to understand why interventions succeed or fail?*
*Why is process evaluation needed?*
*What benefits might be generated by the integration of process evaluation and outcome evaluation?*

The current situation regarding primary interventions might be troubling for students of OHP. Primary interventions based on a valid theory that explains the links between work and well-being are unlikely to be inherently ineffective (Semmer, 2003, 2006). Secondary interventions seem to have an impact on individual level outcomes, but evidence of their impact on organizational outcomes is lacking.

It has been suggested that one way of increasing both the quality and quantity of published intervention research is to make more use of intervention *process evaluation* (Griffiths, 1999; Randall, Griffiths, & Cox, 2005; Semmer, 2006). Process evaluation focuses more on evaluating the mechanisms of change than it does on evaluating the outcomes of change. Such a development is important because there are significant inconsistencies in the outcomes of interventions that need to be explained. Process evaluation can help to answer questions such as 'if the intervention was successful elsewhere, why has it failed here?' Process evaluation involves collecting data about intervention activities and the context within which it was conducted. This data can come from various sources including organizational records, the perceptions of the recipients of the intervention and the accounts of those delivering the intervention. By combining process evaluation with effect evaluation the validity of intervention research findings can be significantly strengthened (Cook & Shadish, 1994).

The evaluation of secondary interventions can also benefit from process evaluation. Bunce (1997) identified a number of factors aside from the intervention itself that can impact upon the outcomes of secondary interventions (see Research Close-Up 4.3). Van der Hek and Plomp (1997) highlight that the qualifications of the trainer are important in determining the outcomes of stress management training interventions.

The increasing interest in process evaluation has been stimulated by a growing realization that intervening in organizations is very different to manipulating variables in an experimental environment (Griffiths, 1999). Intervening in organizations is usually a complex procedure that is carried out in a complex, uncontrolled, and unpredictable environment (Randall, Nielsen, & Tvedt, 2009). The impact that this context has on organizational research can be very significant and is often under-measured and under-analysed (Johns, 2006).

Primary interventions have been the focus of recent developments in process evaluation research. This is because there are greater inconsistencies in studies of the effectiveness of these interventions, and because they are more complex in their design and delivery than secondary interventions The researcher usually has only a modest level of control over the way an intervention is delivered (i.e., they are more at the mercy of the organizational context). This is because the intervention is complex, has many active ingredients, and is delivered in complex and uncontrolled contexts (Cox et al., 2007). Problems with the processes of intervention planning and/or implementation, or a hostile intervention context may help to explain the inconsistent effects of primary interventions (Nielsen, Fredslund, Christensen, & Albertsen, 2006). What participants experience and perceive during

**RESEARCH CLOSE-UP      4.3    Processes Factors**

*Source:* Bunce, D. (1997). What factors are associated with the outcome of individual-focused worksite stress management interventions? *Journal of Occupational and Organizational Psychology, 70,* 1–17.

This paper takes a close look at how a variety of factors appear to influence the outcomes of individual interventions. It is one of very few to discuss the links between intervention processes and intervention outcomes in relation to secondary interventions. In reviewing a large number of studies, David Bunce examines the various 'active ingredients' of interventions, some of which are more to do with the way the intervention is delivered than the intervention itself. For example there is evidence that 'session processes' are significantly related to intervention success. Often secondary interventions are delivered to groups of employees, and it appears that the sense of safety, comfort, and belonging that employees develop during the training can have a direct influence on intervention outcomes. Other 'active ingredients' include the employees' perceptions of the credibility of the trainer, the strength of the bond that the trainee develops with them, and the employees' expectations of the training course. In addition, Bunce identifies a number of individual differences (such as self-efficacy) that can dilute or enhance the potency of an intervention for each individual employee. Of course, all of this does not mean that the intervention itself is ineffective or simply having a placebo effect. However, this review does show that intervention impact can be reduced or increased by participants' individual differences and their perceptions of the intervention process. This review highlights how important process evaluation is when attempting to make sense of the outcomes of any intervention study. Process evaluation is now becoming recognized as a very important element of intervention research for all levels of intervention.

the intervention is not always the same as what had been planned for them (Elo, Ervasti, & Mattila, 2008; Randall, Cox, & Griffiths, 2007). As a result, without process evaluation, Type III errors can be made when interventions are evaluated. A Type III error occurs when the conclusion is made that an intervention is ineffective when it is the faulty implementation that leads to failure (Dobson & Cook, 1980). This error could be made in some intervention studies which conclude that an intervention yields disappointing effects.

Another benefit of process evaluation is that it strengthens studies that do not have a control group. Process evaluation identifies differences in intervention exposure within an intervention group that can be used to shape the analysis of intervention outcomes (Randall, Griffiths, & Cox, 2005). Therefore process evaluation may facilitate valid evaluation in situations where controlled quasi-experimentation is not possible, or when carefully-planned study designs are disrupted (Semmer, 2006).

When reading intervention studies you will doubtless encounter many anecdotal accounts of how problems with implementing the intervention, or disruptive events occurring in the organization diluted the impact of the intervention. Much of this analysis is relatively weak and is often poorly integrated with outcome evaluation (Egan, Bambra, Petticrew, & Whitehead, 2008). This raises the chance that Type III errors are being made in previous intervention research. However, the situation is changing and there have been many recent advances in process evaluation.

Much of the early work on process evaluation used qualitative methods to explore the previously uncharted territory of intervention processes. Several important qualitative studies of primary interventions carried out by Norwegian researchers revealed numerous implementation and contextual factors that could be related to intervention outcomes (e.g., Nytrø, Saksvik, Mikkelsen, Bohle, & Quinlan, 2000; Saksvik, Nytrø, Dahl-Jørgensen, & Mikkelsen, 2002). Kompier et al. (1998) examined the intervention processes followed by a number of well-designed interventions to identify the factors that were critical to the success of a range of different stress management interventions. Sometimes it is possible to use organizational records and observations as manipulation checks in intervention research as a means of ensuring the intervention is being delivered (see Research Close-Up 4.2 for an example).

There is also a body of research that has found considerable variability in how a group of employees exposed to an intervention appraise their experiences of that intervention (Lipsey & Cordray, 2000; Mikkelsen & Saksvik, 1999; Mikkelsen, Saksvik, & Landsbergis, 2000; Vedung, 2006). It also appears that these appraisals of the intervention itself, and the way it is implemented, explain variance in intervention outcomes above and beyond that explained by objective measures of intervention exposure (Nielsen, Randall, & Albertsen, 2007). Since perception plays such a central role in the experience of work stress is also appears likely that it plays a key role in how employees respond to interventions (Randall, Nielsen, & Tvedt, 2009).

To date research has identified a number of factors that appear to be important in the implementation of interventions. These include:

• Worker involvement in the intervention process, senior management commitment to stressor reduction over the long-term, and an organizational culture that is supportive of the intervention process (e.g., Kompier et al., 1998; Murphy & Sauter, 2003).
• Organizational and individual capability and motivation to change i.e., whether employees have the skills, resources, and support needed to help them make the most of the intervention (Nytrø et al., 2000; Saksvik, Nytrø, Dahl-Jørgensen, & Mikkelsen, 2002).

- Employees' readiness for change, line management support for the intervention, employee perceptions of their participation in intervention design and of the active ingredients of the intervention i.e., whether they notice the key components of the change process (Randall, Nielsen & Tvedt, 2009).
- Employees' perceptions of intervention quality and the amount of information they are given about the intervention (Nielsen, Randall & Albertsen, 2007).

Some studies of intervention processes have now begun to test whether employee perceptions of intervention processes for primary interventions are linked to intervention outcomes (Randall, Nielsen, & Tvedt, 2009). The results of this type of research will allow OHP practitioners to advise their clients on how to implement interventions in a way that maximises the chances of success. Process evaluation can also be used by organizations to identify problems with implementation before they result in irrecoverable damage to intervention effectiveness.

## Summary

Process evaluation is a new strand of investigation within intervention research. It focuses on evaluating the mechanisms of change rather than evaluating the outcomes of change. Initial process evaluation studies suggest that research in this area will help to explain why interventions that work well in one organizational context may not do so in another. In this way they will help researchers and practitioners to identify the 'ingredients' for successful intervention implementation.

## SUMMARY AND CONCLUSIONS

This chapter shows that intervention is a complex topic for both students and practitioners of OHP. We argue that this also makes it an interesting and vibrant area of research and practice. The conclusion often found in research papers that 'more research is needed' is an extremely appropriate summary of the current state of intervention research. As the volume of research grows it will become easier to identify consistent trends and patterns in the findings that can be used to design, implement and evaluate future interventions.

That said, some findings do seem to be relatively secure. Primary interventions that are based on a good analysis of the problem, designed with the involvement of organizational stakeholders, and implemented carefully have a good chance of success. This appears to be particularly true for interventions that enhance control at work (an issue that has been the subject of a good amount of intervention research) and it may be the case for other work stressors once more evaluation research becomes available. Secondary interventions appear to have a consistent impact on individual-level outcomes, but their impact on organizational outcomes (e.g., absence and performance) is less certain. Indeed, there is a need for greater research that looks at the links between intervention and changes in organizational outcomes. It would also be useful to see researchers take a more detailed look at the reliability, validity, and sensitivity of so-called 'objective' organizational-level measures of intervention effectiveness.

For all types of interventions, the way they are implemented goes some way towards determining effectiveness. The influence of intervention processes and intervention context on intervention outcomes is likely to be an area of focus for much future research.

It appears likely that no single approach to intervention provides a 'silver bullet' for dealing with occupational health problems. Given the current body of research, organizations are best advised to adopt an integrated approach to intervention that is based around the results of rigorous risk assessment. Tailoring the selection of intervention strategies and the design of intervention delivery to the presenting problem and the organizational context offers the best chance of success.

Secondary and tertiary interventions are particularly suitable when some task(s) that is inherent to good job performance is likely to be stressful (e.g., dealing with angry members of the public, witnessing traumatic events, handling a very unpredictable or intense workload, etc.). These interventions also help individuals to deal with a range of problems at work. However, an important part of the role of the OHP practitioner is to make organizations aware that there is much that can be achieved with primary interventions.

## Note

1. This is a common problem with meta-analysis. Large portions of the research literature were excluded. Other researchers (e.g., Bond, Flaxman, & Loivette, 2006) have analysed a larger number of primary interventions and found different results.

## Suggestions for Further Reading

Bond, F. W., Flaxman, P. E., & Loivette, S. (2006). A business case for the Management Standards for stress. Sudbury: HSE Books. Available online at www.hse.gov.uk/research/rrpdf/rr431.pdf.

Cox, T., Karanika, M., Griffiths, A., & Houdmont, J. (2007). Evaluating organizational-level work stress interventions: Beyond traditional methods. *Work and Stress, 21,* 348–362.

Murphy, L. R., & Sauter, S. L. (2003). The USA perspective: Current issues and trends in the management of work stress. *Australian Psychologist, 38,* 151–157.

Randall, R., Nielsen, N., & Tvedt, S. (2009). The development of five scales to measure participants' appraisals of organizational-level stress management interventions. *Work and Stress, 23,* 1–23.

Richardson, K. M., & Rothstein, H. R. (2008). Effects of occupational stress management programs: A meta-analysis. *Journal of Occupational Health Psychology, 13,* 69–93.

## References

Arnold, J., Silvester, J., Patterson, F., Robertson, I., Cooper, C., & Burnes, B. (2004). *Work Psychology: Understanding human behaviour in the workplace* (4th ed.). Harlow: Prentice Hall.

Beck, J. S. (1995). *Cognitive therapies: Basics and beyond.* New York: Guilford.

Beehr, T. A., & O'Hara, K. (1987). Methodological designs for the evaluation of occupational stress interventions. In S. V. Kasl, & C. L. Cooper (Eds.), *Stress and health: Issues in research methodology* (pp. 79–112). Chichester: Wiley.

Bond, F. W., & Bunce, D. (2000). Mediators of change in emotion-focused and problem-focused worksite stress management interventions. *Journal of Occupational Health Psychology, 5,* 156–163.

Bond, F. W., & Bunce, D. (2001). Job control mediates change in a work reorganization intervention for stress reduction. *Journal of Occupational Health Psychology, 6,* 290–302.

Bond, F. W., Flaxman, P. E., & Bunce, D. (2008). The influence of psychological flexibility on work redesign: Mediated moderation of a work reorganization intervention. *Journal of Applied Psychology, 93,* 645–654.

Bond, F. W., Flaxman, P. E., & Loivette, S. (2006). *A business case for the Management Standards for Stress.* Norwich: Her Majesty's Stationery Office, Research Reports.

Briner, R., & Reynolds, S. (1999). The costs, benefits, and limitations of organizational level stress interventions. *Journal of Organizational Behavior, 20,* 647–664.

Bunce, D. (1997). What factors are associated with the outcome of individual-focused worksite stress management interventions? *Journal of Occupational and Organizational Psychology, 70,* 1–17.

Bunce, D., & Stephenson, K. (2000). Statistical considerations in the interpretation of research on occupational stress management interventions. *Work & Stress, 14,* 197–212.

Cecil, M. A. & Forman, S. G. (1990). Effects of stress inoculation training and co-worker support groups on teachers' stress. *Journal of School Psychology, 28,* 105–118.

Cook, T. D., & Campbell, D. T. (1979). *Quasi-experimentation: Design and analysis issues for field settings.* Chicago: Rand McNally.

Cook, T. D., & Shadish, W. R. (1994). Social experiments: Some developments over the past fifteen years. *Annual Review of Psychology, 45,* 545–579. Palo Alto, CA: Annual Reviews.

Cooper, C., Dewe, P., & O'Driscoll, M. (2001). Organizational interventions. In C. Cooper, P. Dewe, & M. O'Driscoll (Eds.), *Organizational stress: A review and critique of theory, research, and applications* (pp. 187–232). Thousand Oaks: Sage Publications.

Cooper, C. L., Dewe, P., & O'Driscoll, M. (2003). Employee assistance programs. In J. C. Quick, & L. Tetrick (Eds.), *Handbook of occupational health psychology* (pp. 289–304). Washington, DC: American Psychological Association.

Cox, T., Griffiths, A., & Rial González, E. (2000). *Research on work-related stress.* Luxembourg: Office for Official Publications of the European Communities.

Cox, T., Karanika, M., Griffiths, A., & Houdmont, J. (2007). Evaluating organisational-level work stress interventions: Beyond traditional methods. *Work & Stress*, 21, 348–368.

Cox, T., Randall, R., & Griffiths, A. (2002). *Interventions to control stress at work in hospital staff.* Sudbury: HSE Books.

Dahl-Jørgensen, C., & Saksvik, P. Ø. (2005). The impact of two organizational interventions on the health of service sector workers. *International Journal of Health Services*, 35, 529–549.

Darr, W., & Johns, G. (2008). Work strain, health, and absenteeism. *Journal of Occupational Health Psychology, 13,* 293–318.

Dobson, L. D., & Cook, T. J. (1980). Avoiding Type III error in program evaluation: Results from a field experiment. *Evaluation and Program Planning, 3,* 269–376.

Dryden W., & Neenan M. (2003). *Essential rational emotive behaviour therapy.* Chichester: Wiley.

Egan, M., Bambra, C., Petticrew, M., & Whitehead, M. (2008). Reviewing evidence on complex social interventions: appraising implementation in systemic reviews of the health effects of organisational-level workplace interventions. *Journal of Epidemiology & Community Health.* Published online 21 August 2008 (doi:10.1136/jech.2007.07.1233).

Elo, A.-L., Ervasti, J., & Mattila, P. (2008). Evaluation of an organizational stress management program in a municipal public works organization. *Journal of Occupational Health Psychology, 13,* 10–23.

Giga, S. I., Noblet, A. J., Faragher, B., & Cooper, C. L. (2003). The UK perspective: A review of research on organisational stress management interventions. *Australian Psychologist, 38,* 158–164.

Griffiths, A. (1999). Organizational interventions: Facing the limits of the natural science paradigm. *Scandinavian Journal of Work, Environment and Health, 25,* 589–596.

Heaney, C., Israel, B., Schurman, S., Barker, E., House, J., & Hugentobler, M. (1993). Industrial relations, work stress reduction, and employee well-being: A participatory action research investigation. *Journal of Organizational Behavior, 14,* 495–510.

Jackson, S. E. (1983). Participation in decision-making as a strategy for reducing job-related strain. *Journal of Applied Psychology, 68,* 3–19.

Johns, G. (2006). The essential impact of context on organizational behavior. *Academy of Management Review, 31,* 386–408.

Karasek, R. A., & Theorell, T. (1990). *Healthy work: Stress, productivity, and the reconstruction of working life.* New York: Basic Books.

Kim, J. S., & Campagna, A. F. (1981). Effects of flexitime on employee attendance and performance: A field experiment. *Academy of Management Journal, 24,* 729–741.

Kompier, M., Geurts, S., Grundemann, R., Vink, P., & Smulders, P. (1998). Cases in stress prevention: The success of a participative and stepwise approach. *Stress Medicine, 14,* 155–168.

Kompier, M. A. J., & Kristensen, T. S. (2001). Organizational work stress interventions in a theoretical, methodological and practical context. In J. Dunham (Ed.), *Stress in the workplace: Past, present and future* (pp. 164–190). London: Whurr.

LaMonatgne, A. D., Keegel, T., Louie, A. M., Ostrey, A., & Landsbergis, P. A. (2007). A systematic review of the job-stress intervention evaluation literature, 1990–2005. *International Journal of Occupational and Environmental Health, 13,* 268–280.

Lipsey, M., & Cordray, D. (2000). Evaluation methods for social intervention. *Annual Review of Psychology, 51,* 345–375.

Meichenbaum, D. (1977). *Cognitive behavior modification.* New York: Plenum.

Mikkelsen, A., Saksvik, P. Ø., & Landsbergis, P. (2000). The impact of a participatory organizational intervention on job stress in community health care institutions. *Work & Stress, 14,* 156–170.

Mikkelsen, A., & Saksvik, P. Ø. (1999). Impact of a participatory organizational intervention on job characteristics and job stress. *International Journal of Health Services, 29,* 871–893.

Murphy, L. R. (1996). Stress management in working settings: A critical review of the health effects. *American Journal of Health Promotion, 11,* 112–135.

Murphy, L. R., & Sauter, S. L. (2003). The USA perspective: current issues and trends in the management of work stress. *Australian Psychologist, 38,* 151–157.

Murta, S. G., Sanderson, K., & Oldenburg, B. (2007). Process evaluation in occupational stress management programs: A systematic review. *American Journal of Health Promotion, 21,* 248–254.

Nielsen, K., Fredslund, H., Christensen, K. B., & Albertsen, K. (2006). Success or failure? Interpreting and understanding the impact of interventions in four similar worksites. *Work & Stress, 20,* 272–287.

Nielsen, K., Randall, R., & Albertsen, K. (2007). Participants' appraisals of process issues and the effects of stress management interventions. *Journal of Organizational Behavior, 28,* 793–810.

Nytrø, K., Saksvik, P. Ø., Mikkelsen, A., Bohle, P., & Quinlan, M. (2000). An appraisal of key factors in the implementation of occupational stress interventions. *Work & Stress, 14,* 213–225.

Paul, G., & Shannon, D. (1966). The treatment of anxiety through systematic desensitization in therapy groups. *Journal of Abnormal Psychology, 71,* 124–135.

Parkes, K. R. & Sparkes, T. J. (1998). *Organizational interventions to reduce work stress: Are they effective? A review of the literature.* Sudbury: HSE Books.

Randall, R., Cox, T., & Griffiths, A. (2007). Participants' accounts of a stress management intervention. *Human Relations, 60,* 1181–1209.

Randall, R., Griffiths, A., & Cox, T. (2005). Evaluating organizational stress-management interventions using adapted study designs. *European Journal of Work and Organizational Psychology, 14,* 23–41.

Randall, R., & Lewis, R. (2007). Stress management interventions. In E. Donaldson-Feilder (Ed.), *Well-being and Performance.* London: CIPD.

Randall, R., Nielsen, N., & Tvedt, S. (2009). The development of five scales to measure participants' appraisals of organizational-level stress management interventions. *Work & Stress, 23,* 1–23.

Richardson, K. M., & Rothstein, H. R. (2008). Effects of occupational stress management programs: A meta-analysis. *Journal of Occupational Health Psychology, 13,* 69–93.

Saksvik, P. Ø., Nytrø, K., Dahl-Jørgensen, C., & Mikkelsen, A. (2002). A process evaluation of individual and organizational occupational stress and health interventions. *Work & Stress, 16,* 37–57.

Saksvik, P. Ø., Tvedt, S. D., Nytrø, K., Andersen, G. R., Andersen, T. K., Buvik, M. P., & Torvatn, H. (2007). Developing criteria for healthy organizational change. *Work & Stress, 21,* 243–263.

Schaubroeck, J. Ganster, D. C., Sime, W. E., & Ditman, D. (1993). A field experiment testing supervisory role clarification. *Personnel Psychology, 46,* 1–25.

Siegrist, J. (1996). Adverse health effects of high-effort/low reward conditions. *Journal of Occupational Health Psychology, 1,* 27–41.

Semmer, N. (2003). Job stress interventions and organization of work. In L. Tetrick & J. C. Quick (Eds.), *Handbook of occupational health psychology* (pp. 325–353). Washington, DC: American Psychological Association.

Semmer, N. K. (2006). Job stress interventions and the organization of work. *Scandinavian Journal of Work and Environmental Health, 32,* 515–527.

Sharp, J. J., & Forman, S. G. (1985). A comparison of two approaches to anxiety management for teachers. *Behavior Therapy, 16,* 370–383.

Sullivan, S. E., & Bhagat, R. S. (1992). Organizational stress, job satisfaction and performance: Where do we go from here? *Journal of Management, 18,* 353–374.

Terra, N. (1995). The prevention of job stress by redesigning jobs and implementing self-regulating teams. In L. Murphy, J. Hurrell, S. Sauter, & G. Keita (Eds.), *Job stress interventions* (pp. 265–281). Washington, DC: American Psychological Association.

Toivanen, H., Länsimies, E, Jokela, V., & Hänninen, O. (1993). Impact of regular relaxation training on the cardiac autonomic nervous system of hospital cleaners and bank employees. *Scandinavian Journal of Work Environment and Health, 19,* 319–325.

Van der Hek, H., & Plomp, H. N. (1997). Occupational stress management programmes: A practical overview of published effect studies. *Occupational Medicine, 47,* 133–141.

Van der Klink, J. J. L., Blonk, R. W. B., Schene, A. H., & van Dijk, F. J. H. (2001). The benefits of interventions for work-related stress. *American Journal of Public Health, 91,* 270–276.

Vedung, E. (2006). Process evaluation and implementation theory. In E. Vedung (Ed.), *Public policy and program evaluation* (pp. 209–245). Piscataway, NJ: Transaction Publishers.

Zapf, D., Dormann, C., & Frese, M. (1996). Longitudinal studies in organizational stress research. A review of the literature with reference to methodological issues. *Journal of Occupational Health Psychology, 1,* 145–169.

# 5

# Psychosocial Risk Management at the Workplace Level

## Stavroula Leka and Tom Cox

### CHAPTER OUTLINE

This chapter builds on the previous ones by focusing on a specific type of bespoke approach that has grown in popularity in recent years in occupational health psychology research and practice: psychosocial risk management. The chapter describes the approach and its application to the management of work-related psychosocial risks. Several international examples of psychosocial risk management are considered with a particular focus on the European framework for psychosocial risk management (PRIMA-EF). Grounded in policy and representing a legal requirement for employers in many countries, psychosocial risk management is central in the occupational health psychologist's research and professional practice.

## Introduction

As discussed in Chapter 1, in recent decades significant changes have taken place in the world of work that have resulted in emerging risks and new challenges in the field of occupational health and safety (EU-OSHA, 2007). The significant changes observed in the organization and management of work have resulted in emerging occupational safety and health risks: namely, risks identified as new and observed to be increasing. The most salient issue in relation to the consequences of the changing world of work relates to the increased exposure to recognized psychosocial hazards (ibid.).

The term 'psychosocial hazards' relates to that of psychosocial factors that have been defined by the International Labor Office (ILO, 1986) in terms of the interactions among job content, work organization, and management, and other environmental and organizational conditions, on the one hand, and the employees' competencies and needs on the other. Psychosocial hazards are relevant to imbalances in the psychosocial arena and refer to those interactions that prove to have a hazardous influence over employees' health through their perceptions and experience (ILO, 1986). A simpler definition of psychosocial hazards might be those aspects of the design and management of work, and its social and organizational contexts, that have the potential for causing psychological or physical harm (Cox & Griffiths, 2005).

There is a reasonable consensus in the literature on the nature of psychosocial hazards (see Box 5.1) but it should be noted that new forms of work give rise to

---

### Box 5.1   Psychosocial Hazards

*Source:* adapted from Leka, Griffiths, & Cox (2003) *Work organization and stress.* Geneva: World Health Organization.

| | |
|---|---|
| Job content | Lack of variety or short work cycles, fragmented or meaningless work, under use of skills, high uncertainty, continuous exposure to people through work |
| Workload and work pace | Work overload or underload, machine pacing, high levels of time pressure, continually subject to deadlines |
| Work schedule | Shift working, night shifts, inflexible work schedules, unpredictable hours, long or unsociable hours |
| Control | Low participation in decision making, lack of control over workload, pacing, shift working, etc. |
| Environment and equipment | Inadequate equipment availability, suitability or maintenance; poor environmental conditions such as lack of space, poor lighting, excessive noise |
| Organizational culture and function | Poor communication, low levels of support for problem solving and personal development, lack of definition of, or agreement on, organizational objectives |
| Interpersonal relationships at work | Social or physical isolation, poor relationships with superiors, interpersonal conflict, lack of social support |
| Role in organization | Role ambiguity, role conflict, responsibility for people |
| Career development | Career stagnation and uncertainty, under promotion or over promotion, poor pay, job insecurity, low social value to work |
| Home–work interface | Conflicting demands of work and home, low support at home, dual career problems |

new hazards – not all of which are yet represented in scientific publications. Factors such as poor feedback, inadequate appraisal, communication processes, job insecurity, excessive working hours, and a bullying managerial style have been suggested as imminent concerns for many employees. A number of models exist in Europe and elsewhere for the assessment and management of risks associated with psychosocial hazards (termed psychosocial risks) and their impacts on the health and safety of employees and the healthiness of organizations (in terms of, among other things, productivity, quality of products and services, and general organizational climate).

The scientific evidence suggests that the experience of work-related stress provides an important link between employees' exposure to psychosocial hazards at work and subsequent and related ill effects to their health (harm) (Cox, 1993; Cox, Griffiths, & Rial-González, 2000). As such it can be dealt with either at the organizational level at source, by reducing exposure to hazards that are experienced as stressful, or at the individual level, by treating the experience of stress itself and its health effects. The risk management approach primarily focuses on the former strategy although most attempts to reduce the risk to health associated with exposure to psychosocial hazards necessarily involve both organizational and individually focused interventions (Cox, Griffiths, Barlow, Randall, Thomson, & Rial-González, 2000).

## The Risk Management Approach
## in Occupational Health and Safety

The use of risk management in occupational safety and health (OSH) has a substantive history, and there are many texts that present and discuss its general principles and variants (e.g., Cox & Tait, 1998; Hurst, 1998; Stanks, 1996) and its scientific and socio-political contexts (e.g., Bate, 1997). The risk management approach to dealing with health and safety problems is clearly advocated by European legislation and is described in some detail in supporting guidance. It is, for example referred to in the European Council's Framework Directive 89/391/ EEC (European Council, 1989), and in the national legislation of European Union (EU) member states such as in the UK's Management of Health and Safety at Work Regulations 1999 and its accompanying Approved Code of Practice. It is also implicit in official European, national, and international guidance on health and safety management (e.g., Leka, Griffiths, & Cox, 2003; Cox et al., 2000).

Risk management in OSH is a systematic, evidence-based, problem solving strategy. It starts with the identification of problems and an assessment of the risk that they pose; it then uses that information to suggest ways of reducing that risk at source. Once completed, the risk management actions are evaluated. Evaluation informs the whole process and should lead to a reassessment of the original problem and to broader organizational learning (Cox, Griffiths, & Leka, 2005).

Risk management is often based on two distinct but intimately related cycles of activity: risk assessment and risk reduction. This is made clear in the European Commission's *Guidance on risk assessment at work* (European Commission, 1996). Risk management is essentially organizational problem solving applied to the reduction or containment of risk, with the emphasis on risk reduction. Various models of risk management exist in the OSH literature; most are structured and operate through a prescribed and rational sequence of actions.

Decision-making is a critical feature of organizational problem solving in general and of risk management in particular. Einhorn and Hogarth (1981) have argued that such decision making can be broadly considered in terms of four interacting sub-processes: information acquisition, evaluation, action, and feedback. The presence of feedback in the models of problem solving and risk management implies that these processes are cyclical in nature and should be treated as activities that are ongoing. It is in this sense that risk management is sometimes described as a vehicle for continuous improvement in OSH.

A typical model of risk management includes seven steps (Cox et al., 2000):

1. identification of hazards;
2. assessment of associated risk;
3. design of reasonably practicable control strategies (interventions);
4. implementation of control strategies;
5. monitoring and evaluation of effectiveness of control strategies;
6. feedback and reassessment of risk;
7. review of information needs, and training needs of employees.

Various staged models of risk management exist in the OSH literature; for example, Cox and Tait (1998), and van der Heijden and Stern (1992). These models vary in the emphasis that they place on the type of problem that they address (e.g., mechanical hazard or microbiological hazard), on the focus of the likely control intervention (e.g., the person working with the hazard, their work system or the culture of their organization), or on the control strategy to be used (prevention at the organizational level, enhanced training or improved occupational health support). Of course, in any real situation, these three factors are likely to be inter-related. Often a mixture of foci and strategies must be used to deal effectively with a hazardous situation in which there are many challenges to health and safety.

## Policy and Risk Management

According to EU legislation and the International Labor Office, occupational safety and health, including compliance with the OSH requirements pursuant to national laws and regulations, are the responsibility and duty of the employer. The employer should show strong leadership and commitment to OSH activities in the organization, and make appropriate arrangements for the establishment of an OSH

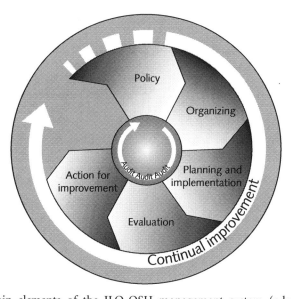

**Figure 5.1** Main elements of the ILO-OSH management system (adapted from ILO, 2001).

management system (ILO, 2001). The system should contain the main elements of policy, organizing, planning and implementation, evaluation, and action for improvement, as shown in Figure 5.1.

Risk assessment is a central element of the risk management process. It has been defined by the European Commission in its *Guidance on risk assessment at work* as 'a systematic examination of the work undertaken to consider what could cause injury or harm, whether the hazards could be eliminated, and if not what preventive or protective measures are, or should be, in place to control the risks' (European Commission, 1996). In this context, it is important to understand the concepts of hazard, risk, and harm. *Hazard* refers to the capability of a certain element at work (materials, work environment, work organization, and practices, etc.) to cause damage or harm. In some contexts, particularly outside health and safety research, they are also called risk factors. *Harm* refers to the damage, injury or disease caused to a person through work. It includes both physical and psychological outcomes. *Risk* refers to the association between hazards and harm, in other words, to the likelihood that a certain hazard can cause harm.

Once hazards and their associated risks have been identified, the control cycle for risk management would continue with the design and implementation of interventions. These interventions are evaluated through a second risk assessment process and thus the cycle continues. The basic health and safety equation of hazard-risk-harm has been offered as a conceptual framework (see Figure 5.2).

A number of significant developments towards the management of psychosocial risks have been achieved at the policy level. In the EU, the major one has been the introduction of the 1989 European Council Framework Directive 89/391/EEC on

**Figure 5.2** Hazard, risk, and harm.

Safety and Health of Workers at Work on which a new EU risk prevention culture has since been established. Important documents in this context include: the European Commission's Guidance on Work-Related Stress (2002), the European Commission's Green Paper on Promoting a European Framework for Corporate Social Responsibility (2001), the European *Framework Agreement on Work-Related Stress* (European Social Partners, 2004), and the European *Framework Agreement on Harassment and Violence at Work* (European Social Partners, 2007).

At the international level, significant developments have been the declaration of the Global Plan of Action for Workers' Health at the recent WHO World Health Assembly (WHO, 2007); WHO guidance on psychosocial risks, work-related stress, and psychological harassment (e.g., WHO, 2003a; 2003b; 2007); ILO initiatives to promote social dialogue on health and safety issues; and various ILO conventions on workers' health. Examples of these policy-level developments can also be found at the national level: the Management Standards approach (HSE, 2005) to dealing with work-related stress in the UK; Health Covenants in the Netherlands; the 'victimization at work' ordinance in Sweden; and specific anti-bullying legislation recently introduced in some countries, for example in France, Finland, Belgium, and the Netherlands. We will now turn to look at how risk management has been applied to psychosocial factors at work.

## Risk Management and Psychosocial Factors at Work

The first model using the risk management paradigm to prevent and manage psychosocial risks and work-related stress was proposed in the UK in the early 1990s (Cox, 1993), and was based on a general summary of systematic problem-solving processes as used both in applied psychology and in management science. The premise was that the risk management paradigm was already understood by managers and had been widely in operation in many countries for some years with respect to the management of chemicals and other substances known to be hazardous to health (Cox, Griffiths, & Randall, 2003).

The starting point for the development of the risk management approach for psychosocial risks was based on the changing nature of work and of work problems and work-related ill-health (Cox, 1993). The interpretative framework implicit in the analysis of this data, relevant to the question of psychosocial risk management and the management of work-related stress, was clearly that of the traditional health and safety equation of *hazard–harm–risk*. However, there was the additional suggestion that work stress might be a mediating factor in the relationship between hazard exposure and subsequent harm (Cox, Griffiths, & Rial-González, 2000). However, Cox, Griffiths, and Rial-González (2000) suggested prudence when establishing expectations of what was achievable when adapting a general model of psychosocial risk management. They highlighted two issues as important; first, there cannot be an exact point-by-point translation of models developed for more tangible and physical risks to situations involving psychosocial hazards and work stress. There is a need to think logically and creatively when adapting such models. The issues that arise should be decided in the light of (local) legal requirements and practical constraints, informed by our knowledge of applied science and should be part of an overall process. Second, a psychosocial risk management approach must not be 'complicated or technical' in terms of its specifications, as the goal is not absolute accuracy and specificity of its measures or the mechanisms underpinning its decision making. Instead it simply needs to be 'good enough' to enable employers and employees to move forward in solving the associated problems and comply with their legal duty of care (Griffiths, 1999). In finding a practical method for managers, the objective is not to seek an exhaustive, precisely measured account of all possible stressors for all individuals; instead it is to produce a reasonable account, with sound scientific basis, of the major likely stressors for any given working group. In other words, it is not an activity carried out for the benefit of researchers, but one pursued with the aim of making a difference to employees' working conditions within organizations (Cox, Griffiths, & Randall, 2003; Leka, Griffiths, & Cox, 2005).

## The Psychosocial Risk Management Model

The model underpinning risk management for psychosocial hazards is relatively simple. Before a problem can be addressed, it must be analysed and understood, and an assessment made of the risk that it presents. Much harm can be done, and resources squandered, if precipitous action is taken on the assumption that the problem is obvious and well enough understood. Most problems, even those that present simply, are complex and not always what they seem. Some form of analysis and risk assessment is required. Figure 5.3 illustrates a general model of risk management for psychosocial hazards.

The *risk assessment* provides information on the nature of the problem, the psychosocial hazards and the way they might affect the health of those exposed to them, and the healthiness of the organization. Adequately completed, the risk assessment allows the key features of the problem (risk factors) to be identified and some priority given to them in terms of the nature and size of their possible effects or the number of people exposed. These data can be used to inform the development of an action plan to address the problems at source (Cox, Griffiths, & Randall, 2003; Satzer, 2009).

The information from the risk assessment is discussed, explored and used to develop an action plan: the *translation* of the risk assessment information into

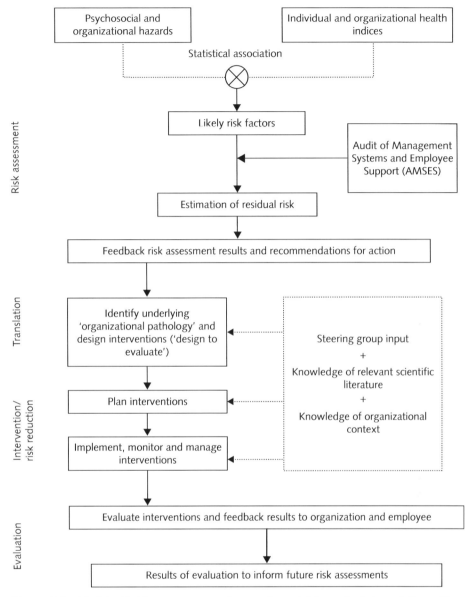

**Figure 5.3** Model of risk management for psychosocial hazards (adapted from Cox, Griffiths, & Randall, 2003).

a reasonable and practical plan to reduce risk. Usually, the discussion and exploration of the problems and likely risk facilitates the discovery of any underlying organizational pathology – major problems that may be hidden but give rise to the problems and likely risk factors. This often makes *intervention* easier as the underlying organizational pathology can be targeted instead of, or as well as, its symptoms (the problems and likely risk factors) (Cox, Griffiths, & Leka, 2005).

The development of the action plan, based on the evidence from the risk assessment, involves deciding on: what is being targeted, how and by whom, who else needs to be involved, what the time schedule will be, what resources will be required and how the action plan will be evaluated. If properly handled, planning to reduce risk in relation to psychosocial hazards is no different from any other management activity. The action plan is then implemented and its progress monitored and reviewed, and the processes involved and their outcomes eventually evaluated.

The *evaluation* of action plans is an important step, but one that is often overlooked or avoided. Not only does it tell the organization how well something has worked in reducing psychosocial hazards and the associated harm but it allows the re-assessment of the whole situation, providing a basis for organizational learning. Essentially it establishes a continuous process for improvement.

# Key Aspects and Stages in Psychosocial Risk Management

Managing psychosocial hazards is *not* a one-off activity but part of the ongoing cycle of good management of work and the effective management of health and safety. As such it demands a long-term orientation and commitment on the part of the management of an organization. As with the management of many other occupational risks, psychosocial risk management should be conducted often, ideally on a yearly basis.

## Risk assessment

Analysing possibly hazardous situations and assessing the risk that they might pose to the health of individuals or the healthiness of their organizations is not rocket-science (Cox, 1993). Such an assessment only has to be good enough to provide sufficient and appropriate evidence to initiate discussions of psychosocial hazards at work and provide an informed basis for managing those problems through a risk reduction action plan.

Risk assessment can be operationalized through a six-step process (Cox, Griffiths, & Rial-Gonzalez, 2000):

1. hazard identification;
2. assessment of harm;
3. identification of likely risk factors;
4. description of underlying mechanisms;
5. audit of existing management systems and employee support;
6. draw conclusions about residual risk and priorities.

The risk assessment brings together two elements to allow the identification of likely risk factors. First, it requires the identification of psychosocial hazards.

Psychosocial hazards are usually situation specific; what is present in one type of work or affects a particular type of worker may not be present in another job or affect a different type of worker. The risk assessment has to consider particular defined work situations (e.g., by examining the workplace, type of worker, work process, etc.). It is not an organization-wide approach.

The identification of psychosocial hazards relies on the expert judgment of groups of relevant working people about the adequacy of the design and management of their work. The knowledge and expertise of working people in relation to their jobs is recognized and treated as valuable evidence. This information is treated at the group level and consensus is measured in those expert judgments on working conditions. The method does not seek to catalogue individual views about work.

Second, information about the possible harm associated with psychosocial hazards is collected both from the risk assessment and from otherwise available organizational records, such as absence data and occupational health referrals. This information is used to determine which of the psychosocial hazards actually affects the health of those exposed to them or the healthiness of their organization. This exercise, relating psychosocial hazards to their possible effects on health, can be an exercise of logic or can be more formally investigated using simple statistical techniques. Most organizations will use the former approach.

A baseline should be established through risk assessment. Surveys can be part of this process, and they are an important element in some of the available tools for the management of psychosocial risk factors. However, other qualitative and observation methods can also be used, especially in smaller enterprises, provided the scope is the same and there is a clear intention of taking timely action on the results. The risk assessment should take into consideration diversity issues and should not ignore the wider context, such as the occupational sector characteristics or socioeconomic and cultural variations across countries.

The exercise of logic is straightforward and involves comparing groups or areas that differ in terms of their exposure to, or report of, the psychosocial hazards in terms of the data on possible health outcomes. What is required here is that the exercise of logic is described and that decisions based on it are justified in terms of the available evidence so that they can be audited at a later stage if necessary.

Bringing together the information on psychosocial hazards and their possible health effects allows the identification of likely risk factors. These risk factors can be prioritized in terms of the nature of the hazard or the harm it causes, the strength of the relationship between hazard and harm, or the size of the group affected.

However, before action can be sensibly planned, it is necessary to analyse what is already in place to deal with psychosocial hazards and its effects on the individual or their organization. This analysis requires an audit (review, analysis, and critical evaluation) of existing management practices and employee support. This is an examination of initiatives for handling psychosocial hazards, work-related stress, and other associated health outcomes. The support available to employees to help them cope or look after them if they are affected is also examined (Leka, Griffiths, & Cox, 2005).

This information from the audit together with the risk assessment information allows a notion of the residual risk to be formulated (i.e., the risk associated to psychosocial hazards that is not currently being managed by the organization). All this information feeds forward to the process of translation: discussing and exploring the risk assessment data to allow the development of an action plan for risk reduction.

## Translation

One of the necessary developments from the traditional risk management model is the translation phase, where identified risk factors are discussed, prioritized and targeted by means of specifically designed actions (Cox, Griffiths, & Randall, 2003). The risk assessment information is used as evidence on which to base the planning of the risk reduction activities. In practice, those involved in action planning discuss and explore the results of the risk assessment (the likely risk factors and the problems identified by the majority of staff), developing their understanding of the problems identified. This often leads to the discovery of any underlying problems and this can add to the power of the translation exercise. It helps the planning of risk reduction to know if there are deep problems that are driving the likely risk factors.

The development of the action plan, based on the evidence from the risk assessment, involves a number of decisions as discussed before. If properly handled, planning to reduce risk in relation to psychosocial hazards is no different from any other management activity.

## Intervention and risk reduction

Interventions can help prevent health complaints through the design of work and the reduction of hazards; they can provide tools to manage hazards so that risks are reduced; or they can provide treatment and rehabilitation for those who have already been harmed by the exposure to hazards. The emphasis here, and in European legislation on health and safety, is on primary risk reduction targeted on the organization as the generator of the risk. However, in practice, it is often also necessary to consider how support and rehabilitation for those already affected can be improved or provided. Commonly three levels of interventions have been used to address psychosocial risks in the workplace: primary, secondary and tertiary level interventions (see Chapter 4 for a description of the levels of interventions). The management of psychosocial risks should prioritize interventions that reduce risks at source. There are a number of arguments for giving them precedence. Legislation prioritizes such measures within organizations and the need to target problems at source. They also can be significantly cost-effective as the focus of interventions is put on the causes and areas within the organization where change is required. Moreover, they promote organizational healthiness as they address issues relating to organizational culture and development.

Besides psychosocial factors, and the understanding of underlying organizational factors, priority setting in psychosocial risk management is always influenced by other factors. In everyday practice, prioritization is also influenced by:

- the capabilities in the organization (including risk awareness and understanding);
- the costs of investments needed and their expected business benefits;
- the feasibility of the measures or interventions (including whether they fit the company culture);
- anticipation of future changes in work and work organization.

Tackling those factors is also an option that needs to be considered in the priority setting process. However, the implementation of the action plan for risk reduction needs to be carefully and thoughtfully managed. It is effectively a change process and, like all change processes, has to be planned and managed to be effective. Ownership and participation play an essential role in the implementation process. The more ownership by managers and workers is developed, the more likely it is that the action plan will be realized and risk reductions achieved. The progress of the action plan must be systematically monitored and discussed, as well as provision made for its evaluation.

## Evaluation

Evaluation is a thread that runs through the entire risk management process. It is essential for any action plan to be evaluated to determine how well and in what respects it has worked. The process of implementation as well as the outcomes of the action plan must be evaluated. Evaluation must consider a wide variety of different types of information and draw it from a number of different but relevant perspectives (e.g., staff, management, stakeholders, etc.).

The results of the evaluation should allow the strengths and weaknesses of both the action plan and the implementation process to be assessed. This information must not be treated as an issue of success or failure, praise or blame, but treated more dispassionately. It should inform a reassessment of the original problem and of the overall risk management process, as well as providing feedback on the outcomes. The organization should use the evaluation to establish a vehicle for continuous improvement and also as the basis for drawing out learning points that may be of use in future risk management projects. However, the evaluation of organizational interventions is not always straightforward. Qualitative approaches such as stakeholder interviews are often found to be a cost-effective and satisfactory technique. In addition, because organizational interventions are not an 'all-or-nothing' event, it is useful to explore how far any planned action was actually implemented, and whether or not it reached its intended audience. Exploring subtle variations in implementation (evaluating process as well as outcome) can provide a useful technique for evaluation (see Chapter 4).

The organization should use the evaluation to establish a vehicle for continuous improvement and also as the basis for sharing (discussing and communicating) learning points that may be of use in future risk management projects, but also in the (re)design of work organization and workplaces as part of the normal organizational development process. Again, a long-term orientation is essential and should be adopted by organizations. Lessons learned should be discussed and, if necessary redefined, in the existing work meetings and in the social dialogue within the firm. Lessons learned should be communicated to a wider company audience. Finally they should be used as input for the 'next cycle' of the psychosocial risk management process.

### Outcomes of the risk management process

Knowledge on the outcomes of the risk management process is an important input for the continuous risk assessment process. In essence, psychosocial risk management is synonymous with best business practice. A healthy organization is defined as one with values and practices facilitating good employee health and well-being as well as improved organizational productivity and performance (Cox et al., 2000). Managing psychosocial risks and workplace health relates to managing the corporate image of organizations (Frick & Zwetsloot, 2007). It can lead to a reduction of the cost of absence or mistakes and accidents and hence associated production. In addition, it can reduce the cost of medical treatment and associated insurance premiums and liabilities. It can contribute to the attractiveness of the organization as being a good employer and one that is highly valued by its staff and its customers. It can lead to improvements of work processes and communication and promote work effectiveness and efficiency. It can also contribute to the promotion of health in the wider community setting. And it can contribute to the development of an innovative, responsible, future-orientated corporate culture.

## Best Practice in Psychosocial Risk Management

A number of psychosocial risk management models have been developed in different countries. Some examples are presented in the next section. However, before examining them in more detail, it is important to identify aspects of best practice that underpin these models.

### Relevance for broader policy agendas

Psychosocial risk management is relevant not only to occupational health and safety policy and practice but also to broader agendas that aim to promote workers' health, quality of working life, and innovation and competitiveness. It can contribute to the creation of positive work environments where commitment, motivation, learning, and development play an important role and sustain organizational development.

## Good psychosocial risk management is good business

In essence, psychosocial risk management is synonymous with best business practice. As such, best practice in relation to psychosocial risk management essentially reflects best practice in terms of organizational management, learning and development, social responsibility and the promotion of quality of working life and good work.

## Evidence-informed practice

Risk management in health and safety is a systematic, evidence-informed practical problem solving strategy. As stressed before, the overriding objective is to produce a reasoned account of the most important work organization factors associated with ill-health (broadly defined) for a specific working group and one grounded in evidence.

## Ownership

Psychosocial risk management is an activity that is closely related to how work is organized and carried out. As a consequence, the main actors are always managers and workers that are responsible for the work to be done. They can, of course, be supported by internal or external experts or by external service providers. However, in the management process it is very important that managers and workers feel that they 'own' the psychosocial risk management process. Outsourcing ownership to service providers is a failure factor, even when, e.g., in the case of a rehabilitation programme, most of the activities can be done by external agents. In relation to ownership by managers it is very important to emphasize the link with good business, e.g., by assessing business benefits besides health benefits, or by developing business cases.

## Contextualization and tailoring

Contextualization, tailoring the approach to its situation, facilitates practical impact. Because national and workplace contexts differ, contextualization is always needed to optimize the design of the risk management activities, to guide the process and maximize the validity and benefit of the outcome. In order for comprehensive strategies to be effective, it is suggested that psychosocial risk prevention and management programmes should be developed and modified to meet the needs of the organization and tailored to the context of the organization's occupational sector (Giga, Cooper, & Faragher, 2003). Tailoring aims to improve the focus, reliability, and validity of the risk management process. It also improves the utilization of the results of the risk assessment. It improves the feasibility of the results and helps in planning the assessment process in such a way that scientific evidence is also taken into account. Areas that should be considered in the tailoring process include: what the process covers (in terms of hazards, target, and data collection), who implements the project, and the specific aims of the process. Some options in this respect are presented in Box 5.2.

---

### Box 5.2   Tailoring the Psychosocial Risk Management Process

*Source:* adapted from Leka et al. (2008). *Towards the development of a European framework for psychosocial risk management at the workplace.* Nottingham, UK: I-WHO publications.

Coverage of the risk management process

*Hazards:*
  – only psychological factors
  – both psychological factors and social interaction

*Target:*
  – task
  – individual
  – group

*Data collection techniques:*
  – observation
  – interview
  – questionnaire
  – a combination of various methods

Who implements the management project
  – OHS personnel, occupational safety personnel
  – employer and employees together
  – psychologist or a person specialized in psychosocial matters

Specific aims of the management process
  – general risk management based on safety and health regulations
  – focused psychosocial risk assessment of work processes, or work groups
  – assessment of an individual's psychosocial risk
  – assessment of possible harmful effects

---

### Participative approach and social dialogue

Inclusion of all parties in prevention efforts can reduce barriers to change and increase their effectiveness. Including all actors can also help increase participation and provide the first steps for prevention. Access to required information is also facilitated with a participative approach. It is clear that each member of an organization, and other social actors which surround it, have expert knowledge of their environment (needed for successful tailoring) and the best way to access this is through inclusion. In good risk management models, the validity of the expertise that working people have in relation to their jobs is recognized. A successful risk management programme will always be led and managed by the workers themselves (Cox, Griffiths, & Randall, 2003).

## Multi-causality and identification of key factors

In everyday practice, psychosocial risks have many causes. Typically, factors like characteristics of work organization, work processes, work-life balance, team and organizational culture, and societal arrangements (e.g., the provision of occupational health services and social security arrangements) all play a role. Some of these may be very apparent; others may require analysis to identify them as underlying causal factors. As a consequence there are usually no quick fix solutions at hand; a continuous management process is required. To be effective it is important to understand the most important underlying causal factors before solutions are selected.

## Solutions that are fit for purpose

Scientific evidence is important to inform the psychosocial risk management process. However, in its purest form (scientific evidence from randomized clinical trials) it requires research on standardized items, in controlled situations, and involvement of large populations. Knowledge from this kind of research is usually not very practical, especially not for small and medium-sized enterprises (SMEs). Risk management for psychosocial hazards is not a research exercise: it is focused clearly on intervening to reduce harm caused by exposure to these risks. It is therefore more important to make the problems in SME practice, for example, the starting point for research, and to develop knowledge and solutions that are 'fit for purpose'.

## Different levels of interventions with focus on measures at source

As already discussed, the emphasis is on primary risk prevention targeted at the organization as the generator of risk. However, specific actions targeted at the individual level (secondary and tertiary interventions) can also play an important role depending on the magnitude and severity of the problem within organizations and its effect on employee health. Developing continuous and sustainable initiatives to promote employee and organizational health and well-being through psychosocial risk prevention and management involves the development of strategies that comprehensively address psychosocial risks and their associated health effects (Giga, Cooper, & Faragher, 2003). This requires practitioners and organizations to move beyond uni-model interventions (either individual or organizational approaches; or primary, secondary, or tertiary-level programmes) to multi-model interventions (using a combination of such approaches; Sutherland & Cooper, 2000; LaMontagne, Keegel, Louie, Ostry, & Landsbergis, 2007).

## Ethics

The management of psychosocial risks is about people, their (mental) health status, and business and societal interests. Protecting the psychosocial health of people is not only a legal obligation, but also an ethical issue. As interests between various agents involved differ, their sphere of influence is not always clear. Shifting of consequences from enterprises to individuals or society at large may occur (externalization). Frequently there are ethical dilemmas that are easily overlooked or that (often implicitly) underlie a seemingly fully rational discussion.

## Capabilities required

Policies for psychosocial risk management require capabilities, respectively at the macro level and at company level. The capabilities required comprise:

- adequate knowledge of the key agents (management and workers, policy makers),
- relevant and reliable information to support decision-making,
- availability of effective and user friendly methods and tools,
- availability of competent supportive structures (experts, consultants, services and institutions, research and development).

Across countries, there are great differences in existing capabilities. In those countries where only minor capabilities are available, this is a major limiting factor for successful psychosocial risk management practice. It is also linked to inadequate inspection of company practices in relation to these issues. It is important here to refer to the role and influence of cultural aspects such as risk sensitivity and risk tolerance (both at the company and societal levels). These aspects are important and need to be considered as they can facilitate or hinder the effectiveness of psychosocial risk management. These are often relevant to awareness, education and training, and availability of expertise and appropriate infrastructures at the organizational and national levels.

# Psychosocial Risk Management: International Examples

A number of approaches based on the risk management paradigm have been developed and implemented. This section focuses on reviewing some current best practice approaches, and identifying their key features. These models have been developed and implemented in different countries and in different sectors or organizations (in terms of nature and size).

## Health Circles – Federal Association of Company
## Health Insurance Funds (BKK) – Germany

Health circles were designed in Germany to facilitate health promotion at the workplace with an emphasis on organizational and psychosocial factors (Aust, 2002) (see Figure 5.4). Although they were not specifically developed to tackle work-related psychosocial factors, their nature makes them an appropriate tool for this objective. Health circles are participative actions where employees identify the major health-related problems in the workplace and implement appropriate solutions. The areas which are assessed include lifestyle changes and changes to the work environment and organization. It is a flexible approach where the general method can be tailored to various situations and companies. Assessed outcomes vary according to the requirements of the organization. Typical outcomes include reducing absenteeism, increasing job satisfaction, reducing turnover rates, reducing early retirement, and higher motivation (Brandenburg & Slesina, 1994).

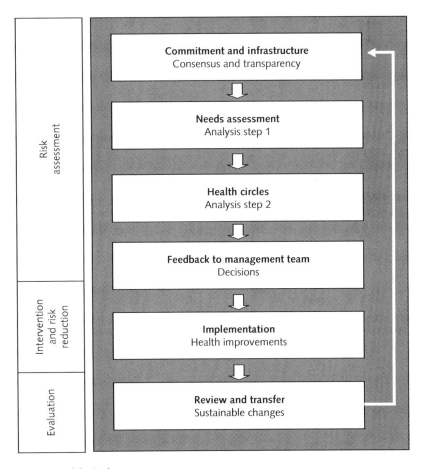

**Figure 5.4**  Health circles.

*Development process*
Health circles were developed in the 1980s. They responded to changes in legislation, which required companies to place more emphasis in prevention activities. They were designed following other participative problem-solving approaches, such as quality circles. Because of this, they are based on the assumption that employees are experts in their work and the management of the work environment.

*Implementation*
Health circles are generally implemented in departments which have specific problems related to absenteeism or dissatisfaction. They are formed by a group of employees, who evaluate psychosocial risk factors and define solutions to tackle the identified problems, and a trained professional, who acts as a moderator. Meetings are generally held during work hours and last for about one hour and a half. In most cases, the process includes between six and ten meetings.

The process has six steps:

1. Commitment and infrastructure: A contract is signed between employees and management. This guarantees commitment of all parties with the project goals. It also allows a focus on consensus and transparency.
2. Needs assessment: A health surveillance report is produced from company or insurance data. The report focuses on overall absenteeism rates, absenteeism length and diseases reported as the causes for absenteeism. It can be used to identify departments where absenteeism is particularly problematic and allows the identification of possible psychosocial hazards. This report is often followed by an employee survey, where both hazards (physical and psychosocial) and employee health and well-being are assessed.
3. Health circles: A steering committee is formed by those responsible for safety and health, who oversee the process. About 10 to 15 participants are invited to each health circle. These include representatives from employees, company and unions, and a moderator. The health circle develops health improvement suggestions. Participants are asked to propose solutions to the problems identified through the surveillance report and employee survey. In this way, the meetings focus on those problems which are identified by a larger number of employees. During this process, meetings are recorded and their results are reported to all employees in the affected department.
4. Feedback to management team: The management team is informed of the progress and suggestions produced by the health circle. They make decisions regarding which suggestions to implement and the order in which these are implemented.
5. Implementation of solutions: Proposed solutions are implemented throughout the process. These provide the basis for health improvements.
6. Review and transfer: In the last health circle meeting, all participants are asked to evaluate what has been achieved. It is also common that a follow up meeting is conducted with the participants in the health circle to complete the evaluation of the process. In some cases, the employee survey is repeated in the

department where changes were implemented. This allows the assessment of changes in outcomes.

The completion of the process, including the six steps outlined above, takes around 15 months.

*Practical applications and evaluation*

Health circles have been applied in hundreds of companies over the years. Overall, participants report high satisfaction with the approach. Aust and Ducki (2004) reviewed eleven studies, which included 81 health circles. They concluded that health circles are an effective tool for the improvement of physical and psychosocial working conditions. Health circles also have a positive effect on outcomes including enhanced employee health and well-being and reduced sickness absence.

Overall, health circle participants report high satisfaction with the composition of the group, number of meetings and the process of identifying problems and developing suggestions. In most cases, companies implement a good percentage of the solutions proposed by the health circle (between 45% and 86%). These changes improve working conditions and the health status of workers, and reduce absenteeism. An evaluation of the satisfaction with the process (using surveys) and an evaluation meeting to look at results are included in the process. Outcome evaluations are mentioned in the approach, so tangible changes in the work environment are not necessarily assessed. Health circles can be particularly useful in a culture used to participative strategies (Beermann, Kuhn, & Kompier, 1999).

## Istas21 (CoPsoQ) Method – Trade Unions' Institute of Work, Environment and Health (ISTAS) – Spain

Istas21 (see Figure 5.5) is a psychosocial risk management method, adapted from the Copenhagen Psychosocial Questionnaire (CoPsoQ). Although the main focus of this method is the evaluation of risks, a manual is included with descriptions of the risk management process. Its aim is to provide a method for the assessment of psychosocial risk factors which is valid for the Spanish population. It also aims to be used as a basis for the development of prevention actions using the risk management paradigm. The method is provided free of charge, with the conditions that: it is used as a tool for prevention strategies through the risk management approach, employees take active part in the process, results are confidential and questionnaires anonymous, and that the instrument is not modified. The focus of the assessment is on the association between psychosocial risks and a series of outcomes, which include: job satisfaction, general health, mental health, vitality, behavioural stress symptoms, physical stress symptoms and cognitive stress symptoms. The interventions which can be developed through the use of the approach are tailored to the needs of each company (Moncada, Llorens, & Kristensen, 2002).

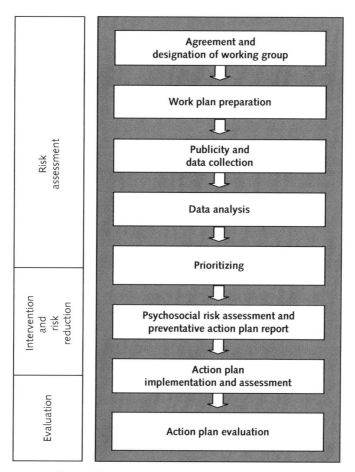

**Figure 5.5**   Istas21 (CoPsoQ) method.

*Development process*

The Istas21 method was adapted in 2002 by Moncada, Llorens, and Kristensen for the Spanish Trade Unions' Institute of Work, Environment and Health (ISTAS). The development process is clearly based on stress theories, particularly Karasek's job demands-job control model, because of which the evaluation of risks in this approach includes only those psychosocial factors for which there is strong evidence of risk to health: psychological demands, active work and skills development, social support and quality of leadership, and compensation (insecurity and esteem).

The questionnaire has been validated both in its original Danish version and in its Spanish adaptation. It is available in three versions: a long version for research, a medium length version for companies with more than 30 employees, and a short version for small enterprises and self-assessment. There is not much scope for tailoring, although some questions can be adapted to suit specific situations, and clear guidance is provided in this respect.

The terms of the licence agreement which appear in the Istas21 method are not part of the CoPsoQ. These provide the means to place the emphasis on risk reduction and not only the assessment of risks. This is a clear advantage as it makes the basic assumptions of the risk management process clear and known to any users.

*Implementation*

The method consists of a validated questionnaire. The licence for the use of the instrument is dependent on agreement of the conditions of use, which include its use for prevention purposes, participation, anonymity, and confidentiality, and no tailoring over what is stated in the manual. The action process includes the following activities:

1.  Agreement and designation of a working group: The method is presented to the management team and employees representatives. Agreement is sought and a document signed, which includes the consent to take part in the process and agreement with the licence conditions outlined above. Once an agreement is signed, a work group is designated. This group must include representatives of management, health and safety (prevention), and employees. It is also recommended to include company directors not directly associated with health and safety management. This work group is responsible for the completion of the action process.
2.  Work plan preparation: The reach of the programme and units of analysis (such as departments, roles, etc.) are defined, the questionnaire is generated, including the adaptation of some clearly defined items, and a plan is developed for the provision of information to stakeholders. This information-sensitization plan may include formal documents, meetings with workers and/or supervisors, and other techniques which are deemed appropriate.
3.  Publicity and data collection: At this stage, information is provided to employees, the questionnaires are distributed and data is gathered.
4.  Data analysis: Data is analysed to produce six kinds of results: standardized coefficients for all psychosocial risk factors; proportion of employees in each level of exposure; proportion of employees in each level of exposure for each risk factor; satisfaction and stress symptoms results; general health, mental health and vitality; and frequencies of all answers to the questionnaire. Results are interpreted and a report produced. Feedback is provided to management, employee representatives, employees and supervisors.
5.  Prioritizing: The relative importance of exposures is defined by the work group. They then propose and prioritize prevention interventions, although this can also be done by prevention circles formed by affected employees and experts (health and safety and production). Information on these proposals is then provided to management, employee representatives, employees, and supervisors.
6.  Psychosocial risk assessment and preventative action plan report: This report summarizes the work done. It should be treated as work in progress and amended if new prevention strategies are deemed adequate.

7. Action plan implementation and assessment.
8. Action plan evaluation.

Activities 1 to 6 are detailed in the manual; the last two are just mentioned.

## SME-vital – Health
## Promotion Switzerland – Switzerland

SME-vital was developed between 2001 and 2004 by the Institute of Social and Preventive Medicine, University of Zurich, and Institute of Occupational Medicine, Baden. The project was funded by the public foundation 'Health Promotion Switzerland'. It consists of a web-based workplace health promotion (WHP) toolbox for small and medium-sized enterprises (SMEs). The toolbox has been available on the internet in German and French since July 2004. Although the focus of this tool is on health promotion, the approach is broad and includes the management of psychosocial risk factors. Primary outcomes are defined by the

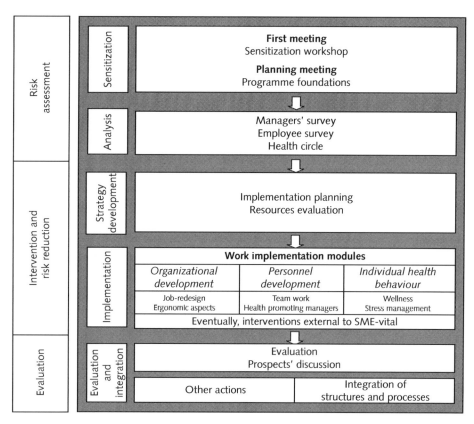

**Figure 5.6** SME-vital.

dimensions of the employee questionnaire: job task, work organization, participation, leadership, working climate, commitment, physical and psychological well-being, etc. Additional outcomes vary by interest of the organization, e.g., absenteeism, company image, organizational processes, customer satisfaction (Bauer & Gutzwiller, 2006; Bauer, Schmid, Lehmann, Kuendig, & Kissling, 2004).

The toolbox contains ten modules which follow the risk management paradigm (see Figure 5.6). After a starter-workshop with the top management, three modules help to analyse the situation in the company (two surveys and a health circle) and six modules enable dealing with the problems identified by the analysis. An overall WHP project management guide shows how to structure the overall WHP process. Although the tool was originally developed for SMEs, in practice it has also been used by large organizations. The quantitative analysis tools provided are only suitable for companies with at least 30 employees.

*Development process*

The comprehensive WHP model of the European Network of Workplace Health Promotion constitutes the theoretical basis of the toolbox. This model covers the following four principles (Luxembourg Declaration, 1997): participation of all staff, integration into all areas of the organization, project management following a problem-solving cycle, comprehensiveness with equal consideration of individual- and environment-directed measures. Because work-related physical determinants of health are relatively well covered by legally required health and safety systems, the WHP toolbox particularly emphasizes psychosocial determinants of health in the working environment.

*Implementation*

The implementation of SME-vital in companies follows the following process:

1. Initiate WHP: Information brochure and 'starter workshop' with top-management for initial motivation for WHP, for organizational analysis of the potential and general aims of WHP in the specific company and for setting up an implementation plan for the following modules.
2. WHP analysis: Employee and management surveys for detailed bottom up and top down analysis of health promoting working conditions. The management survey analyses current work organization, personnel management practices and employee benefits from the managers' perspective. The employee survey analyses strengths and weaknesses regarding job task, work organization, participation, leadership, working climate, and commitment from an employee perspective. The survey instrument can be filled out online and aggregated results are automatically generated for the participating companies.
3. Develop WHP strategy: Module 'health circle' is a joint employee-management approach for analyzing the above survey results, conducting a problem analysis, setting company specific targets for the WHP process and developing a joint action plan.

4.  Implement the plan: Depending on the company-specific needs, companies
    can choose from the following six readily available implementation modules
    grouped into three levels of intervention:
    *   Organizational development: how-to guide for improving workplace
        ergonomics, practical guideline on how to go through a participatory job
        redesign process.
    *   Personnel development: training for team development (communication,
        collaboration, external partners), management training for health promot-
        ing leadership style.
    *   Individual health behaviour: how-to guide for wellness-related activities in
        a company (physical activity – relaxation – nutrition); stress management
        training.
5.  Evaluate the results: monitoring changes based on a repeated application of
    employee and management surveys; controlling of achievement of company-
    specific targets.
6.  Consolidate and institutionalize WHP: establish 'health circles' as sustainable
    structure (joint employee-management committee) for WHP.

The general approach and generic instruments can be adapted to the specific
company context and needs. It has been implemented in various organizations
and industrial sectors.

*Practical applications and evaluation*
SME-vital was implemented in ten pilot-companies. This process showed that the
modules support a WHP process corresponding to the underlying comprehensive
WHP model of the European Network for WHP. The toolbox was well received
by the pilot SMEs. All ten companies actively participated during the entire
programme and most continue WHP activities. The modules proved flexible
enough to fit the context and interests of very diverse SMEs. During a final
assessment conducted by an external, independent evaluator, participating
companies reported the following main benefits of the programme:

*   Better communication between employees and management; improved work-
    ing climate.
*   Increased motivation and performance of employees.
*   Increased competency in coping with demands and ongoing organizational change.
*   For broader dissemination, linkage of the WHP toolbox to established manage-
    ment systems such as total quality management needs to be improved.

The programme's implementation and impact were assessed using a one-group pre-
post test design. Baseline assessment was conducted at the beginning of the programme
and a follow-up survey was carried out 18 months later. The pilot SMEs were
heterogeneous in size, economic sector and organizational structure. Seven SMEs,
consisting of 50 to 350 employees, took part in both the baseline and follow-up survey

(67% average response rate, n = 572 and 56% average response rate, n = 479, respectively). The questionnaire covered 8 dimensions of the working environment and contained items addressing the health status of the employees. In the follow-up survey, a set of items was added to assess awareness of the programme, participation, accessibility, personal competency building and profit from the programme and its impact on the working environment and health from an employee perspective.

Overall, monitoring of the working environment and health status in the SMEs revealed only minimal differences between the two measurement points. Yet, employees were affirmative of the programme's impact, especially concerning working issues that are more accessible to change, e.g. employee participation and teamwork. Awareness of and participation in the programme varied considerably, depending, among other factors, on employee turnover. In general, the programme was rated as satisfactory and its continuation was desired. Employees participating closely in the programme thought they had accessibility, had built their personal competency and profited from the programme more than workers who did not take part.

All users of SME-vital have to register. Registration data include company characteristics, state of WHP, attitudes towards WHP, and modules downloaded. All employee survey data across companies are aggregated and are available as a benchmark. Over 500 companies have registered and downloaded material. Over 120 companies have conducted the employee survey online (Kohlbacher, Bauer, Lehmann, & Kündig, 2005).

## Work Positive pack with HSE's Management Standards – Health and Safety Authority, Health and Safety Executive, and National Health Service – Ireland, Scotland, England, and Wales

The 'Work Positive pack with HSE's Management Standards' is an update of the 'Work Positive' stress management approach for SMEs. It incorporates the new British Health and Safety Executive's Management Standards for stress at work as well as the findings of the evaluation of Work Positive. It was commissioned to a private consultant by the Health and Safety Authority in Ireland (HSA), the Health and Safety Executive in the UK (HSE), and Health Scotland (HEBS).

Work Positive consists of a resource pack that assists organizations through a comprehensive process of identifying and reducing the potential causes of stress in organizations. The resource pack is primarily targeted at small to medium-sized enterprises (SMEs) but is appropriate for larger corporations that are geographically spread or split into divisions (O'Connor, 2002) (see Figure 5.7).

*Development process*
In 1996, Health Scotland commissioned the Institute of Occupational Medicine (IOM) to develop a risk management approach for workplace stress. This approach was called the organizational stress health audit or OSHA. The five step Work Positive approach was developed as an effort to build on the strengths of OSHA while at the same time addressing its weaknesses. Work Positive was developed in

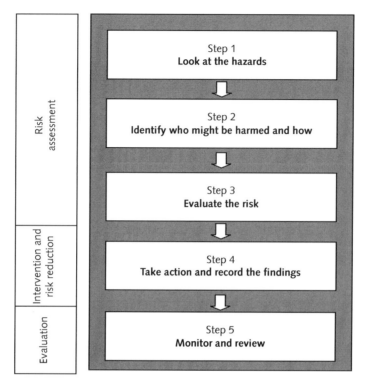

**Figure 5.7**  Work Positive.

two phases. In the first stage a questionnaire and benchmarking tool were designed. The questionnaire was based on the structure of the OSHA interviews (and known causes of work-related stress). The benchmarking tool was developed following the business excellence model. The second stage involved the piloting of these tools in fourteen organizations. The Work Positive pack was then sent to ten organizations throughout a range of different sectors. The experience within these companies was analysed and is provided as case study materials. In this way, industry specific examples for the use of a generic approach are provided.

Work Positive, in its original form, was operational widely throughout Scotland, England, Wales and Ireland. A further redevelopment was completed in line with the introduction of the HSE Management Standards. In 2004–2005 the HAS, HSE and HEBS commissioned work to revise the existing Work Positive – Prioritizing Organizational Stress Resource to incorporate the new HSE Management Standards for stress at work as well as the findings of the past evaluation of Work Positive. The new Work Positive pack incorporates the six Management Standards developed by the HSE and includes normative data from the UK.

*Implementation*
Work Positive is a step by step process that assists in the identification and management of potential causes of stress. It has been adapted to include the six

Management Standard headings (Demands, Control, Support, Relationships, Role, and Change). The complete process includes five steps:

- Step 1 – Look at the hazards: This step includes planning and assessment of risks. Important elements for planning include the provision of information to senior management, setting up a steering group with representatives across the organization, the identification of a coordinator, the provision of information to participants and ensuring that employees are aware of available support if they are already suffering from stress or a stress-related illness. Once this is completed, the steering group uses the HSE Management Standards to review the organizations' policies, systems and procedures using a benchmark exercise. They also gather organizational information regarding outcomes which have been associated to stress (e.g., absence, turnover, performance, etc.).
- Step 2 – Identify who might be harmed and how: The steering group should identify who is to be included in the risk assessment. Issues which are considered at this stage include the definition of high risk groups, the maintenance of anonymity of results and how to establish an environment of openness, trust and honesty.
- Step 3 – Evaluate the risk: At this stage, a risk assessment questionnaire is distributed among the staff and the data analysed. The survey based tool incorporates the HSE Management Standards. The questionnaire, an analysis tool, a tutorial and a manual are available free of charge.
- Step 4 – Take action and record the findings: Focus groups are organized with representatives from the employees. The issues identified in the risk assessment are discussed here and solutions are developed. Emphasis is placed in providing an environment were employees feel free to raise their concerns and give opinions regarding possible actions. An action plan is developed as a result of this stage, based on a template.
- Step 5 – Monitor and review: The steering group meets regularly to review the action plan and ensure its completion. Progress is assessed in relation to the benchmarking exercise conducted in step 1. It is important at this stage that employees and management receive feedback on progress and can still contact the steering group with any concerns. It is recommended that the questionnaire is applied at regular intervals, both to check for progress and to assess any emerging risks.

Work Positive is available online. The user can host it and send it to participants through email.

*Practical applications and evaluation*
To date, Work Positive has been used on approximately 25,000 employees. The original tool was piloted in four organizations. The questionnaire was completed by employees while a coordinator from the organization completed the benchmarking exercise. Both the employees and the coordinator also completed an evaluation questionnaire. In addition, interviews were conducted with a random sample of employees. The general response to the questionnaire and benchmarking

exercise was positive. Minor changes to the questionnaire were made taking into consideration the results of the pilot study. Case studies for eleven companies are presented in the Work Positive website, which provide examples of how organizations have tackled the five steps outlined above.

---

### Case Study 5.1:   PRIMA-EF

PRIMA-EF refers to the European framework for psychosocial risk management. The framework was developed on the recognition that throughout Europe, researchers, practitioners, government bodies, social partners, and organizations differ in awareness and understanding of psychosocial risks (Leka & Cox, 2008a; 2008b). Although in some EU member states there appears to be widespread awareness of the nature and impact of these issues as well as agreement among stakeholders on their prioritization for the promotion of health, productivity, and quality of working life, this situation is not reflected across the enlarged EU. Even though in some EU member states systems and methods have been developed to deal with these challenges at different levels, a unifying framework that recognizes their commonalities and principles of best practice that can be used across the EU had been lacking.

In addition, it was recognized that particular challenges in relation to psychosocial risks and their management exist both at the enterprise level and at the macro level. On the enterprise level there is a need for systematic and effective policies to prevent and control the various psychosocial risks at work, clearly linked to companies' management practices. On the national and the EU level, the main challenge is to translate existing policies into effective practice through the provision of tools that will stimulate and support organizations to undertake that challenge, thereby preventing and controlling psychosocial risks in our workplaces and societies alike. At both levels, these challenges require a comprehensive framework to address psychosocial risks.

PRIMA-EF was developed through funding of the European Commission's 6th Framework Programme. The PRIMA-EF consortium is led by the Institute of Work, Health & Organizations (I-WHO) at the University of Nottingham and involves the German Federal Institute for Occupational Safety & Health (BAuA), the Italian National Institute for Occupational Safety and Prevention (ISPESL), TNO Quality of Working Life – Work & Employment (Netherlands), the Polish Central Institute for Labor Protection (CIOP-PIB), and the Finnish Institute of Occupational Health (FIOH). The Consortium is also supported by an Advisory Board including key organizations such as the World Health Organization, the International Labor Organization, DG Employment, Equal Opportunities & Social Affairs, DG Health & Consumers, the International Commission on Occupational Health, the European Agency for Safety & Health at Work, the European Foundation for the Improvement of Living & Working Conditions, and the main social partner (employer and trade union) organizations in Europe (BUSINESSEUROPE, ETUC, ETUI, ETUI-REHS, UEAPME, CEEP, and UNIZO).

PRIMA-EF provides a framework to promote policy and practice at national and enterprise level within the European Union. It is meant to accommodate all existing (major) psychosocial risk management approaches across the EU. The framework is built from a theoretical analysis of the risk management process, identifying its key elements in logic and philosophy, strategy and procedures, areas and types of measurement, and from a subsequent analysis of typical risk management approaches as used within the EU.

The model developed is relevant to both the enterprise level and the wider macro policy level. The developed framework was used to examine key issues of relevance to the management of psychosocial risks at work, such as policies, stakeholder perceptions, social dialogue, corporate social responsibility, monitoring and indicators, standards and best practice interventions at different levels. In doing so, the project aimed at identifying the current state of the art in these areas and to suggest priorities and avenues for improvement on the basis of the key aspects of the framework.

To achieve its aim and objectives experts, researchers, social partners, and a number of key European and international organizations were involved throughout the project activities. A number of methods were used to explore the above issues, including literature and policy reviews, interviews, surveys, focus groups and workshops. The scientific findings of the PRIMA-EF project have also been used to develop user friendly tools for use at the enterprise and policy levels such as indicators, guidance sheets, inventories and web-based tools. All outputs are available through www.prima-ef.org.

## SUMMARY AND CONCLUSIONS

Dealing with psychosocial risks is an increasingly important part of the challenge of safety and health at work. Many of the effects of such issues appear to be mediated by the experience of stress and the available evidence indicates that work-related stress is a major source of ill-health among the working population. The complex aetiology of work-related stress provides us with an interesting challenge and its mechanisms and causes may never be completely understood in their finest detail. However, there is a moral, as well as a scientific and legal imperative to act in order to reduce the harm associated with psychosocial risks and work-related stress. The risk management paradigm provides a framework for positive action – focused on prevention and on work organization.

## Suggestions for Further Reading

Elo, A. L., Leppaenen, A., & Silanpaa, P. (1998). Applicability of survey feedback for an occupational health method in stress management. *Occupational Medicine, 48*, 181–188.

Leka, S., & Cox, T. (2008a). *The European Framework for Psychosocial Risk Management: PRIMA-EF.* Nottingham, UK: I-WHO Publications. ISBN 978-0-9554365-2-9. Available online at: www.prima-ef.org.

Leka, S., & Cox, T. (2008b). PRIMA-EF: Guidance on the European framework for psychosocial risk management – A resource for employers and worker representatives. Geneva: World Health Organization. ISBN 978-92-4-1597104. Available online at: www.prima-ef.org.

Leka, S., Hassard, J., Jain, A., Makrinov, N., Cox, T., Kortum, E., Ertel, M., Hallsten, L., Iavicoli, S., Lindstrom, K., & Zwetsloot, G. (2008). *Towards the development of a European framework for psychosocial risk management at the workplace.* Nottingham, UK: I-WHO publications. ISBN 978-0-9554365-3-6.

Malchaire, J., Piette, A., D'Horre, W., & Stordeur, S. (2004). The SOBANE strategy applied to the management of psychosocial aspects. Louvain: Catholic University of Louvain. Available online at: www.deparisnet.be/PSY/Eng/Sobane_guide_psychosocial_aspects.pdf.

Peiró, J. M. (2000). Assessment of psychosocial risks and prevention strategies: The AMIGO model as the basis of prevenlab-psicosocial methodology. *Psychology in Spain, 4(1)*, 139–166.

Satzer, R. (2009). Stress – Mind – Health. The START procedure for the risk assessment and risk management of work-related stress. Dusseldorf: Hans-Böckler-Stiftung.

## References

Aust, B. (2002). Health circles – a participative approach to improve health-related working conditions – Germany. In European Agency for Safety and Health at Work, *How to tackle psychosocial issues and reduce work related stress* (pp. 40–45). Luxembourg: Office for Official Publications of the European Communities.

Aust, B., & Ducki, A. (2004). Comprehensive health promotion interventions at the workplace: experiences with health circles in Germany. *Journal of Occupational Health Psychology, 9*(3), 258–270.

Bauer, G., & Gutzwiller, F. (2006). *Arbeits- und sozialmedizin: Betriebliche gesundheitsförderung.* In J. Haisch, K. Hurrelmann & T. Klotz (Eds.), *Medizinische Prävention und Gesundheitsförderung.* Bern. Herbst: Verlag Hans Huber.

Bauer, G., Schmid, M., Lehmann, K., Kuendig, S., & Kissling, D. (2004). *Entwicklung und evaluation eines nationalen programms für betriebliche gesundheitsförderung in KMU. In Gesellschaft für Arbeitswissenschaft e. V. (Hrsg.): Tagungsbericht Arbeit und Gesundheit in Effizienten Arbeitssystemen.* Dortmund: GfA-Press.

Bate, R. (1997). *What risk?* Oxford: Butterworth-Heinemann.

Beermann, B., Kuhn, K., & Kompier, M. (1999). Germany: Reduction of stress by health circles. In M. Kompier & C. Cooper (Eds.), *Preventing stress, improving productivity: European case studies in the workplace* (pp. 222–241). London: Routledge.

Brandenburg, U., & Slesina, W. (1994). Health promotion circles: A new approach to health promotion at worksite. *Homeostasis in Health and Disease, 35*(1–2), 43–48.

Cox, T. (1993). *Stress research and stress management: Putting theory to work.* Sudbury: HSE Books.

Cox. T., & Griffiths, A. (2005). Monitoring the changing organization of work: A commentary. *Sozial- und Präventivmedizin, 47*, 354–355.

Cox, T., Griffiths, A., Barlow, C., Randall, R., Thomson, L., & Rial-González, E. (2000). *Organizational interventions for work stress: A risk management approach.* Sudbury: HSE Books.

Cox, T., Griffiths, A., & Leka, S. (2005). Work organization and work-related stress. In K. Gardiner & J. M. Harrington (Eds.), *Occupational hygiene* (3rd ed., pp. 421–423). Oxford: Blackwell Publishing.

Cox, T., Griffiths, A., & Randall, R. (2003). A risk management approach to the prevention of work stress. In M. J. Schabracq, J. A. M. Winnubst & C. L. Cooper (Eds.), *Handbook of work & health psychology* (2nd ed., pp. 191–206). Chichester: John Wiley & Sons.

Cox, T., Griffiths, A., & Rial-González, E. (2000). *Research on work-related stress.* European Agency for Safety & Health at Work. Luxembourg: Office for Official Publications of the European Communities.

Cox, S., & Tait, R. (1998). *Safety, reliability and risk management.* Oxford: Butterworth-Heinemann.

Einhorn, H. J., & Hogarth, R. M. (1981). Behavioral decision theory: Processes of judgment and choice. *Annual Review of Psychology, 32*, 53–88.

EU-OSHA – European Agency for Health and Safety at Work (2007). *Expert forecast on emerging psychosocial risks related to occupational safety and health.* Luxembourg: Office for Official Publications of the European Communities.

European Council (1989). Council Directive 89/391/EEC of 12 June 1989 on the introduction of measures to encourage improvements in the safety and health of workers at work. Official Journal of the European Communities. Luxembourg: Office for Official Publications of the European Communities.

European Commission (1996). *Guidance on risk assessment at work.* Brussels: European Commission.

European Commission (2001). *Promoting a European framework for CSR, Green Paper.* Luxembourg: Office for Official Publications of the European Communities.

European Commission (2002). *Guidance on work-related stress – Spice of life or kiss of death?* Luxembourg: Office for Official Publications of the European Communities.

European Social Partners (2004). *Framework Agreement on Work-Related Stress.* Brussels: European Social Partners – ETUC, UNICE (BUSINESSEUROPE), UEAPME and CEEP. Available at: www.ec.europa.eu/employment_social/news/2004/oct/stress_agreement_en.pdf

European Social Partners (2007). *Framework Agreement on Harassment and Violence at Work.* Brussels: European Social Partners – ETUC, BUSINESSEUROPE, UEAPME and CEEP. Available at: www.ec.europa.eu/employment_social/news/2007/apr/harassment_violence_at_work_en.pdf

Frick, K., & Zwetsloot, G. (2007). *From safety management to corporate citizenship: An overview of approached to managing health.* In U. Johanson, G. Ahonen, & R. Roslender (Eds.), *Health and management control.* Stockholm: Thomson International.

Giga, S. I., Cooper, C. L., & Faragher, B. (2003). The development of a framework for a comprehensive approach to stress management interventions at work. *International Journal of Stress Management, 10*(4), 280–296.

Griffiths, A. J. (1999). Organizational interventions: Facing the limits of the natural science paradigm. *Scandinavian Journal of Work, Environment and Health, 25*(6), 589–596.

HSE (Health and Safety Executive) (2005). *Promoting health and safety as a key goal of the Corporate Social Responsibility agenda.* Research Report 339.

Hurst, N. W. (1998). *Risk assessment: The human dimension.* Cambridge: Royal Society of Chemistry.

ILO (International Labor Office) (2001). *ILO Guidelines on Occupational Safety and Health Management Systems (OHS-MS).* Geneva: International Labor Office.

ILO (International Labor Office) (1986). *Psychosocial factors at work: Recognition and control.* Occupational Safety and Health Series No: 56. International Labor Office, Geneva.

Kohlbacher, M., Bauer, G., Lehmann, K., & Kündig, S. (2005). KMU-vital – das betriebliche gesundheitsförderungsprogramm von gesundheitsförderung schweiz. In O. Meggender, K. Pelster & R. Sochert (Hrsg), *Betriebliche Gesundheitsförderung in kleinen und mittleren Unternehmen – Modelle und Erfahrungen aus Deutschland, Österreich und der Schweiz.* Bern: Verlag Huber.

LaMontagne, A. D., Keegel, T., Louie, A. M. L., Ostry, A., & Landsbergis, P. A. (2007). A systematic review of the job-stress intervention evaluation literature, 1995–2005. *International Journal of Occupational Environmental Health, 13,* 268–280.

Leka, S., & Cox, T. (2008a). *The European Framework for Psychosocial Risk Management: PRIMA-EF.* Nottingham, UK: I-WHO Publications. Available online at: www.prima-ef.org.

Leka, S., & Cox, T. (2008b). *PRIMA-EF: Guidance on the European Framework for Psychosocial Risk Management – A resource for employers and worker representatives.* Geneva: World Health Organization. Available online at: www.prima-ef.org.

Leka, S., Griffiths, A., & Cox, T. (2003). *Work organization and stress.* Geneva: World Health Organization.

Leka, S., Griffiths, A., & Cox, T. (2005). Work-related stress: The risk management paradigm. In A. S. G. Antoniou & C. L. Cooper (Eds.), *A research companion to organizational health psychology.* Chichester: Wiley.

Leka, S., Hassard, J., Jain, A., Makrinov, N., Cox, T., Kortum, E., Ertel, M., Hallsten, L., Iavicoli, S., Lindstrom, K., & Zwetsloot, G. (2008). *Towards the development of a European framework for psychosocial risk management at the workplace.* Nottingham, UK: I-WHO publications. ISBN 978-0-9554365-3-6.

Moncada, S., Llorens, C., & Kristensen, T. S. (2002). *Metodo Istas21 (CoPsoQ): Manual para la evaluación de riesgos psicosociales en el trabajo.* Instituto Sindical de Trabajo, Ambiente y Salud (ISTAS).

O'Connor, M. (2002). 'Work positive' – a stress management approach for SMEs – HEBX and HSA joint commission – Scotland and Ireland. In European Agency for Safety and Health at Work, *How to tackle psychosocial issues and reduce work related stress.* Luxembourg: Office for Official Publications of the European Communities.

Satzer, R. (2009). Stress – Mind – Health. The START procedure for the risk assessment and risk management of work-related stress. Dusseldorf: Hans-Böckler-Stiftung.

Stanks, J. (1996). *The law and practice of risk assessment.* London: Pitman.

Sutherland, V. J., & Cooper, C. L. (2000). *Strategic stress management: An organizational approach.* New York: Palgrave.

van der Heijden, K. A., & Stern, R. M. (1992). The role of risk assessment in the work of the World Health Organization in Europe. Proceedings of the International Conference on Risk Assessment. UK Health and Safety Commission, London, 78–87.

WHO (2003a). *Work organization and stress.* Geneva: World Health Organization.

WHO (2003b). *Raising awareness to psychological harassment at work.* Geneva: World Health Organization.

WHO (2007). *Workers' health: Global plan of action.* Geneva: World Health Organization.

# 6

# Workplace Health Promotion

## Andrew J. Noblet and John J. Rodwell

### CHAPTER OUTLINE

This chapter focuses on the concept of workplace health promotion (WHP). Much of the current thinking on what it means to promote health at work is based on contemporary definitions of 'health' and 'health promotion'; hence this chapter will begin with a discussion of these background concepts. We will then examine the two dominant approaches to promoting health at work – the individually-oriented lifestyle approach and the more holistic settings-based approach – and will use the literature to emphasize the need for practitioners to make a shift from the former to the latter. The extent to which WHP initiatives actually protect and promote health rests heavily on how programmes are planned, implemented, and evaluated. The final section will therefore focus on a programme-planning framework that can be used to guide the development of comprehensive WHP programmes that respond to the needs of both employees and employers. As workplace health professionals, organizations will expect that occupational health psychologists (OHPs) will play leading roles in the development of comprehensive, settings-based WHP initiatives. With this in mind, it is critical that OHPs have a sound understanding of the processes, methods, and resources involved in developing settings-based programmes.

## Introduction

A friend of one of the authors recently recounted his first experience as a participant in a company-sponsored 'workplace health promotion' programme. The friend (hereafter referred to as John) was a senior sales consultant with an international information technology firm, as well as being a devoted husband and father of three school-aged children. The company was widely considered a market leader and, in his time at the company at least, had experienced consistently solid growth in both market share and overall profitability. However, like most companies operating in an increasingly globalized, cost-conscious marketplace, customer loyalty was harder to maintain and competition between companies was fierce. Sales had dropped markedly over the previous 12 to 18 months and everyone was under pressure to sell more, but of course to do this with increasingly tighter budgets. To make matters worse, a new manager had been appointed to lead the sales department and whilst being an outright genius when it came to winning new accounts, he was way out of his depth when it came to managing and leading people. Not only did he try to micro-manage seasoned sales staff, scrutinizing their every move, but he also introduced a series of performance incentives that effectively pitted colleague against colleague. John had approached his new manager on a number of occasions over these and other issues but, with their relationship rapidly deteriorating, he decided that the best course of action was to avoid the manager as much as possible. John spent considerably more time visiting clients and, in an effort to boost his flagging sales figures, was working in excess of 60 hours a week, trying to drum up new business whilst maintaining his existing client base.

John was not on his own in terms of his response to the situation and, being acutely aware of the declining morale within the department, the manager encouraged sales staff to take part in the company's new workplace health promotion programme. John knew little about why the programme had been introduced but, given the pressure he was under, was attracted to the menu of health checks that were on offer. He was particularly keen to take part in a one-on-one stress counselling session, if only as a temporary release from the constant grind of everyday work-life. However, John's enthusiasm for the programme quickly turned to frustration when confronted with the reality of what was actually involved.

John's responses to a 20-question stress test indicated that he was in the 'highly stressed' category. When asked what was contributing to the stress, John's quick but candid summary not only covered what was happening at work, but also included how the demands of work were impacting on his home-life, especially the quality of his relationships with his partner and children. It was at this point that John expected that the counsellor would show sympathy and compassion, perhaps acknowledge the difficulties he faced or even enquire about the strategies he was using to deal with the pressures. Instead, the counsellor seemed preoccupied with the time that had elapsed since their session began and quickly went into a pre-programmed, patronizing spiel about how John needed to relax more, perhaps go for a walk before or after work or join the local gym (and consume less coffee and alcohol!). The final insult came when the counsellor said that these steps could benefit everyone – himself, his family and the company – and that he was looking forward to seeing John in 6 months' time when they were scheduled to complete another round of health checks. If John could commit himself to a general strategy of 'working smarter, not harder', his results were sure to improve. John came out of the session feeling more disillusioned and frustrated, not so much with the counsellor, but more with the company. From his perspective, the firm had no intentions of looking at why employees might be feeling distressed and dissatisfied. The problem was clearly a matter for individual employees to deal with and workers simply had to find better ways of coping with the situation. To paraphrase from a song he had recently heard, John felt his head was being held under water and he was simply being told to breathe easy for a while.

This particular case raises a number of important questions that will be addressed in this chapter. First and foremost, what is workplace health promotion and what types of issues are tackled by WHP programmes? Work-based factors such as leadership styles, workloads, and decision-making-influence clearly had an impact on John's psychological well-being, but can these be classified as WHP-relevant issues? Or is WHP more about individual lifestyle choices (e.g., dietary intake, activity levels, or levels of alcohol consumption), which appeared to be the case in John's organization? A related question is: whose responsibility is it to protect and promote health at work and what roles should different stakeholders such as employers, employees, and specialist personnel (including occupational health psychologists) play in identifying and addressing the factors that contribute to health at work? The actions of John's organization suggest that health-related issues such as job stress are the responsibility of individual employees, but is this consistent with recognized guidelines on health promotion and WHP? Finally, how should WHP programmes be developed and what steps can organizations take to help ensure that the resulting initiatives actually promote employee health, rather than exacerbate stress, frustration, and resentment, which is what had occurred in John's case?

Although John's situation might seem an extreme example, this approach to promoting health at work appears to be closer to the norm rather than the exception. For instance, the active involvement and participation of all sections of the community (in this case the workplace community) has long been a stated principle of health promotion (WHO, 1986), yet a review of workplace health promotion programmes revealed that only 25% were implemented in response to employees' explicit needs and views and 14% included employees as partners in planning and implementing programmes (Harden, Peersman, Oliver, Mauthner, & Oakley, 1999). Similarly, international agreements on the promotion of health emphasize the importance of addressing the social, organizational, economic, and political conditions that shape health, rather than focusing exclusively on the symptoms of poor health (e.g., WHO, 1984, 1997). Yet organizations are much more likely to involve strategies directed at workers' lifestyle-related behaviours – such as those John took part in – and generally fail to consider the direct impact that working conditions have on employee well-being and/or their indirect influence on people's ability to adopt more stress-resistant behaviours (Caulfield, Chang, Dollard, & Elshaugh, 2004; Giga, Noblet, Faragher, & Cooper, 2003; LaMontagne, Louie, Keegel, Ostry, & Shaw, 2006; Murta, Sanderson, & Oldenburg, 2007).

In view of the large gap between WHP theory and practice, one of the key aims of this chapter is to provide students of occupational health psychology (OHP) a detailed, applied assessment of the relevant concepts, principles, and strategies. Ultimately, our hope is that OHP students can use this information to help bridge the divide between theory and practice and ensure that the way they approach WHP is consistent with the relevant guidelines, theories, and research findings.

## Defining Health and Health Promotion

*What do the terms 'health' and 'health promotion' refer to?*
*How does the definition of health influence health promotion practice?*
*What are the individual, social, economic, and political factors that impact on health?*

Any attempt to define workplace health promotion needs to begin with a clarification of the term 'health'. How health is defined will not only impact on the types of attributes that are targeted for protection and promotion, but will also influence the nature and scope of the factors that are thought to undermine or enhance people's health.

### Health

Early conceptualizations of health posited that 'health is the state of complete physical, mental and social well-being, not merely the absence of disease or infirmity' (WHO, 1946). Whilst this definition has been criticised for focusing on an idealised and largely unattainable set of end-points (Noack, 1987), it was one of the first officially recognized definitions to acknowledge that freedom from illness or disease is not the same as being healthy. People can be functioning in a biologically 'normal' way with no evident pathology, yet still lack the energy, drive, and all-round well-being to feel 'healthy'. The broader, more positive definition not only has significant implications for how health is measured and whether we monitor negative and/or positive outcomes, but also signals the need to move away from focusing solely on identifying and addressing the sources of ill-health. Consistent with the points that Bakker and Derks make in their chapter on positive occupational health psychology (Chapter 7), the emphasis on physical, mental, and social dimensions of well-being indicates that attempts to remove the causes of injury and disease will, at best, result in environments that cause no harm but will not necessarily lead to the development of conditions that promote positive health. Subsequent definitions of health have recognized that the dimensions of health should not be seen as an end point, but rather, have conceptualized health as a resource for undertaking everyday activities and for achieving a high quality of life. The view that health should be seen as a means to an end, rather than an end in itself, is captured in the following definition from the World Health Organization (WHO, 1984, p. 23):

> [Health is] the extent to which an individual or group is able, on the one hand, to realise aspirations and satisfy needs; and, on the other hand, to change or cope with the environment. Health is, therefore, seen as a resource for everyday life, not the object of living; it is a positive concept emphasizing social and personal resources, as well as physical capacities.

This definition has a number of important implications for the practice of health promotion. First, health is not just a unit of measurement that applies to individuals, but is also applicable to groups and, by extension, whole populations. Health promotion initiatives therefore need to be as concerned about group-based outcomes such as cohesiveness, harmony, and social inclusion/exclusion, not just individual-level outcomes (e.g., anxiety, optimism, and happiness). The second implication referred to in the above definition is that health outcomes represent resources that serve a very functional purpose. Forces that shape these resources (positively or negatively) ultimately impact on the individual's or group's ability to carry out everyday tasks and to fulfil important goals and aspirations. This resource-based perspective on health is emphasized in the Jakarta Declaration (WHO, 1997) which linked health to social and economic development and reinforced the need for governments, statutory authorities, private companies, and other relevant stakeholders to invest heavily in developing strategies that can protect and enhance health (Naidoo & Wills, 2000). The third point raised in the above definition is that the surrounding environment can impact on people's health and, in turn, that health is required to cope with or change environmental forces. Highlighting the dynamic interactions between people and their social, economic and physical environments suggests that any attempts to change people's health status need to take into account both environmental influences as well as personal and group-based capacities. Emphasizing personal attitudes and behaviours at the exclusion of environmental influences – which was the case for John – fails to recognize the dynamic, holistic nature of health.

The fourth and final implication stemming from the WHO (1984) definition involves the concept of control. By acknowledging that health is, in part, a reflection of people's ability to change their surrounding environments, this definition suggests that health promotion needs to assess the extent to which individuals and groups have decision-making control over the physical, social, and political environments in which they live and work. Feelings of powerlessness and helplessness should therefore be considered indicators of poor health along with more traditional measures such as high blood pressure or chronic anxiety. The emphasis on control in the WHO (1984) definition of health also suggests that health promotion should work with individuals and groups to enhance their span of control and increase their ability to influence the conditions and events that threaten or reinforce health resources. Notions of control and self-determination are in direct contrast to the medically-driven 'absence of disease' definition where health professionals are largely responsible for both the diagnosis and treatment of illness and people are expected to be passive recipients of these services.

## Health promotion

The contemporary view of health – with an emphasis on positive resources, dynamic interactions between people and their environments, and notions of control – is strongly reflected in the definitions of health promotion. The Ottawa Charter for Health Promotion provides one of the most commonly cited definitions of health promotion and has played a prominent role in the development of international guidelines on the practice of health promotion (Demmer, 1995; Nutbeam, 1998). According to this definition, health promotion refers to 'the process of enabling people to exert control over the determinants of health and thereby improve their health' (WHO, 1986, p. 1). This definition builds on and incorporates the core elements of health discussed in the previous section, in particular, the importance of identifying the underlying determinants of health and helping individuals and groups to gain control over these forces.

The term 'health determinants' refers to the range of personal, social, organizational, environmental, economic, and political factors that influence the health of individuals and groups. Dahlgren and Whitehead (2007) have diagrammatically grouped these determinants into a series of interrelated layers (see Figure 6.1), beginning with biological and hereditary factors (which determine an individual's predisposition to disease) and progressing out to individual lifestyle factors (e.g., dietary intake, activity levels, drug and alcohol misuse), social and community networks (e.g., health and welfare networks, support groups, community-based working parties), living and working conditions (e.g., housing, water and sanitation, education, and work environments) and general socio-economic, cultural, and environmental conditions (e.g., standards of living, labour market trends, levels of pollution, and natural resource depletion). Dahlgren and Whitehead also note that although individuals have some choice in the lifestyles they lead, the vast majority of the forces that shape well-being are outside the individual's direct span of control. This view is supported by research indicating that behavioural factors generally account for a small proportion of disease incidence, especially cardiovascular disease, as compared to society-level factors such as poverty, income distribution, access to material resources, decision-making influence, and civic participation (e.g., Feldman, Makuc, Kleinman, & Cornoni-Huntley, 1989; Marmot, Rose, Shipley, & Hamilton, 1978). Even lifestyle behaviours themselves are thought to be heavily influenced by socio-economic conditions with several studies indicating that negative environmental influences (such as hazardous or stressful working conditions) can either contribute directly to unhealthy behaviours or limit an individual's ability to make positive changes in health behaviours (e.g., Eakin, 1997; Green, 1988; Polanyi et al., 2000). The far-reaching effects of these environmental conditions are further reinforced by

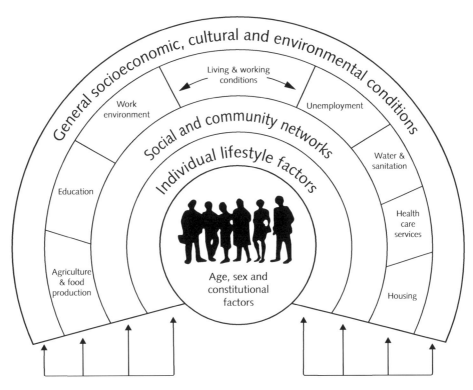

**Figure 6.1** Main health determinants (Dahlgren & Whitehead, 2007).

research indicating that lifestyle-oriented behaviour change strategies have had limited success in bringing about sustained behaviour change in community settings and have been least successful among blue-collar groups and other groups with low socio-economic status (e.g., Heaney & Goetzel, 1997; Rimer, Glanz, & Rasband, 2001).

The interplay between behavioural risk factors (such as smoking, sedentary behaviour) and negative living and working conditions (including poverty, lack of social support, and dangerous or stressful work environments) is illustrated in Labonte's (1992) 'socio-environmental approach to health' model (see Figure 6.2). This model suggests that attempts to prevent or reduce ill-health are likely to be unsuccessful if health promotion focuses exclusively on physiological or behavioural risk factors. Labonte's model also suggests that physiological and behavioural measures of ill-health – which are generally the focus of traditional, lifestyle-oriented health promotion programmes – are likely to be symptoms of underlying psychosocial risk factors and risk conditions. Therefore, by emphasizing individual lifestyles and diverting resources away from the underlying high risk conditions, programme planners may inadvertently harm health (Raphael, 2003).

The more holistic, socio-environmental view of health determinants is strongly represented in the strategy development guidelines included in the Ottawa Charter for Health Promotion. According to these guidelines, health promotion action

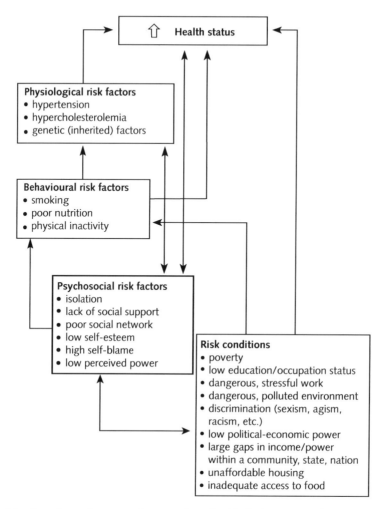

**Figure 6.2**   A socio-environmental approach to health (Labonte, 1992).

involves: (1) working with representatives from all sectors, not just the health sector, to ensure that policy-makers consider the health implications of their decisions (referred to as 'Building Healthy Public Policy'), (2) identifying the socio-environmental sources of poor health and using collaborative links with other sectors to create living and working conditions that are safe, stimulating, satisfying, and enjoyable ('Create Supportive Environments'), (3) empowering communities to identify and address health-related issues that are important to them ('Strengthening Community Action'), (4) providing or supporting personal and social development initiatives that enable people to exercise greater control over their health and their environments ('Develop Personal Skills'), and (5) encouraging the health sector to develop a much more preventative, proactive approach to addressing health issues and to move away from a largely reactive system that focuses almost exclusively on the provision of clinical and treatment services ('Reorient Health Services'). Collectively, the five action areas indicate that whilst physiological and behavioural risk factors are a key concern for health promotion (particularly through 'Developing Personal Skills'), the relevant strategies should complement (not replace) initiatives aimed at working with communities and other sectors to identify and address the underlying determinants of health.

## Summary

Contemporary health promotion practice is guided by a more holistic, positive concept of health that views individual and collective health as a means to achieving a high quality of life, not as an end in itself. Hence, promoting health is much more than identifying people at risk of developing chronic, lifestyle-related diseases and encouraging them to adopt healthier patterns of behaviour. Whilst disease prevention is still considered a key part of health promotion, the focus is now much more on identifying the individual, social, political, and economic factors that contribute to the health of individuals and groups. Furthermore, many of the issues that impact on health are not just beyond the control of individuals, they are also outside the influence of the health sector. Health promotion practitioners therefore need to work with relevant stakeholders (especially the individuals and communities most affected by the issue) to help build safer, fairer, and more satisfying environments in which to live, learn, and work.

## Promoting Health at Work: Individual and Settings-Based Approaches

*What are the key differences between the individual and the settings-based approaches to WHP?*
*What are the major criticisms directed at the individual, lifestyle-oriented approach and under what circumstances would it be appropriate to utilize the associated activities?*
*What factors are thought to contribute to the success of settings-based WHP initiatives?*

Many of the frameworks and guidelines for enhancing the health of individuals and communities emphasize the need to focus on working environments. The socio-environmental approach to health (Labonte, 1992) recognized that people's health status, as well as physiological and behavioural risk factors, are directly and indirectly influenced by work-related factors such as income inequities, low occupational status, dangerous or stressful working conditions, lack of social support, and low perceived power. Likewise, the Ottawa Charter for Health Promotion

(WHO, 1986) highlights the need to move away from focusing on disease prevention to addressing the settings in which people learn, work, play, and love. Given that most working adults spend anywhere between one and two-thirds of their waking hours at work, the sheer volume of time spent in this particular setting, coupled with the economic and social importance of employment in society, means that working environments are going to have a profound influence on people's physical, mental, and social well-being (Chu, Driscoll, & Dwyer, 1997; Gini, 2000; Noblet & Murphy, 1995).

Despite the pivotal role that workplaces play in shaping the health and quality of life experienced by employees, the practice of workplace health promotion has largely overlooked this role. As in the case study presented at the beginning of this chapter, WHP has tended to use the workplace as a convenient venue for reaching large numbers of working adults, identifying those who are at risk of experiencing lifestyle related diseases, and encouraging them to adopt healthier patterns of behaviour (LaMontagne, Keegel, & Vallance, 2007; Noblet, 2003; Shain & Kramer, 2004). Not only have these programmes operationalized health according to the narrow, 'absence of disease' definition, but they have also disregarded the health impact of the setting itself. In the following section we will examine the limitations of this lifestyle-focused approach and highlight some of the key criticisms that have been directed at the associated practices. We will then present a more comprehensive, settings-based approach to WHP that emphasizes the importance of identifying and addressing the full range of personal, social, organizational, and economic determinants of worker health. Traditional behaviour change programmes are still an important part of the settings-based approach to WHP and we will discuss the context in which these strategies are most appropriate.

## Individually-oriented WHP programmes

Individually-oriented WHP strategies are those that typically focus on the health-related knowledge, attitudes, and behaviours of employees and aim to provide them with information and guidance on how to lead healthier lives. These programmes became very popular in the 1970s and 1980s, particularly in the United States where many companies funded their employees' health insurance premiums and the private sector had a strong vested interest in reducing health care costs (Polanyi et al., 2000). The health costs borne by US companies increased by up to 20–30% per year during this period and by the mid-1990s health benefits represented 9% of corporate payrolls. Although company-sponsored health insurance was far less common in other industrialized countries, such as the UK, France, and Australia, escalating health care budgets world-wide gave governments a much greater incentive to consider ways of preventing ill-health (Harden et al., 1999; Noblet & Murphy, 1995). This was particularly true in the case of chronic diseases such as cardiovascular disease, adult onset diabetes, and some forms of cancer, where not only was the cost of treatment very high, but, being closely associated with behaviours such as cigarette smoking, sedentary activity, high fat diets and excessive stress, were considered to be largely preventable conditions.

The workplace was seen as a particularly important setting for undertaking disease prevention activities, not only because it gave public health authorities access to large numbers of working adults, but also because it enabled them to target those groups most vulnerable to lifestyle-related diseases – such as male, blue-collar workers – who were much less likely to visit their local general practitioner, community health service, or other formal health care agencies (Chu et al., 1997; LaMontagne, 2004; Linan et al., 2008). The workplace was also considered a particularly strategic setting for promoting healthier lifestyles as it provided the systems for communicating health-related messages in a cost-efficient manner (notice-boards, newsletters, company intranet) and as employees spent so much time at work, these messages had the potential to receive high levels of exposure (Harden et al., 1999). Finally, by drawing on the links between employee health and outcomes important to the organization (such as sickness-related absenteeism, productivity, reputation as an 'employer of choice'), there was some incentive for companies to support these initiatives, beyond mere altruism (O'Donnell, 2001).

The types of activities undertaken as part of worker-directed WHP programmes include:

- health screening programmes such as cholesterol tests, blood pressure checks, fitness appraisals, and other medically-oriented tests that are designed to detect the early signs of chronic, lifestyle-related disease;
- information and awareness raising activities (e.g., posters, brochures, memos) that are aimed at drawing attention to the consequences of harmful behaviours (such as smoking, alcohol and other drug misuse, and sedentary lifestyles) and encouraging people to adopt healthier ways of living;
- counselling and educational sessions that provide people with more specific guidance on how to reduce their risk of preventable disease (e.g., quit smoking counselling, healthy cooking seminars, coping-focused stress management classes);
- provision of facilities, services and/or incentives that support behaviour change and make 'healthier choices, easier choices' (e.g., more nutritious foods in the canteen, shower and changing facilities that encourage people to ride-to-work, allowing employees to undertake health checks during work time, and employer subsidized gym memberships) (O'Donnell, 2001; Polanyi et al., 2000).

A defining feature of the above activities is their emphasis on individual attributes, including physiological markers for lifestyle-related disease (e.g., high cholesterol levels) and the health-related knowledge, attitudes, and behaviours that may exacerbate the risk of disease (e.g., dietary intake). Characteristics of the workplace itself are generally not taken into account, except in cases where they may support 'healthy' behaviour change (e.g., shower facilities, time release to attend activities) (Golaszewski, Allen, & Edington, 2008). Another hallmark of many individually-oriented WHP initiatives is the way in which they are developed and the extent to which employees are involved in deciding which issues are addressed. As mentioned in the introduction to this chapter, available evidence indicates that many individually-oriented WHP initiatives are expert-driven with normative needs (i.e., based on scientifically derived knowledge) generally taking precedence over expressed needs (i.e., the views and wishes expressed by employees themselves) (Harden et al., 1999). Workers are also expected to be the recipients of the services and generally play a passive role in the initiation and delivery of the relevant activities.

Drawing on the definitions of health and health promotion discussed in the previous section, there are several areas where the individual approach departs from international guidelines, in particular, the Ottawa Charter for Health Promotion (WHO, 1986). According to the individualistic approach, health is equated with the absence of disease (rather than as a positive resource that includes physical, mental, and social dimensions) and the purpose of health promotion is to identify and address physiological and behavioural risk factors for disease (not to work with individuals and groups to take greater control over the full range of determinants). By focusing on individual attributes, this approach also assumes that health is largely within the control of individuals and that, by extension, workers are responsible for the level of well-being they experience. Furthermore, there is little community action, partnership building, or inter-sectoral collaboration as both the identification of needs and the development of strategies are driven by health professionals. In this context, health promotion is something that is done to people, not with them.

Not surprisingly, the individualistic approach to promoting health at work has received widespread criticism. These criticisms generally involve one or a combination of issues, namely: (1) the ethics of concentrating on individuals at the exclusion of underlying determinants, (2) the extent to which worker-directed activities meet international standards on occupational health and safety and health promotion, and (3) the effectiveness of worker-directed programmes, both in relation to achieving sustainable outcomes and programme reach. In terms of ethical concerns, several authors have been highly critical of the practice of focusing on individual employees whilst ignoring the influence of adverse working conditions (e.g., Corneil & Yassi, 1998; Daykin, 1998). In the case of job stress, for example, the European Agency for Safety and Health at Work (EU-OSHA, 2002) reports that individual symptoms of stress are often manifestations of organizational-level problems rather than personal coping deficiencies. Thus, by trying to teach employees to cope with stressful working conditions, proponents of this approach can be seen to be blaming the victim of poor communication channels, inadequate training, autocratic management styles, and other common sources of workplace stress. Occupational health and safety authorities and trade unions have also been very critical of these programmes, because of the victim-blaming mentality, and also because they may divert valuable resources away from what they consider to be the more serious and immediate work-based determinants of employee health (Blewett & Shaw, 1995; Ellis, 2001).

The second criticism often directed at the individual oriented approach is that strategies aimed at helping people adopt healthier lifestyles, without addressing the physical, social and organizational conditions that impact on worker health, contravene the occupational health and safety legislation that exists in many industrialized countries, including Australia, Canada, the European Union member states, Hong Kong, Malaysia, New Zealand, and the United States (Chu & Dwyer, 2002; Cousins et al., 2004). In the UK for example, employers must monitor both physical and psychosocial hazards and, as a result, a failure to address adverse working conditions, so far as is reasonably practical, is a breach of that legislation (Mackay, Cousins, Kelly, Lee, & McCaig, 2004). Overlooking the work-based sources of poor health is also a breach of internationally recognized health promotion and public health principles. The Ottawa Charter for Health Promotion (WHO, 1986) and the Luxembourg Declaration on Workplace Health Promotion in the European Union (ENWHP, 1997), for example, both emphasize the need to address the social, economic, and environmental determinants of health. Ignoring these principles is not considered unlawful; however, it does contravene internationally recognized guidelines on how WHP should be practised.

The final major criticism directed at the worker-oriented disease prevention strategies is that they often fail to achieve any significant health and/or productivity outcomes. Research examining the outcomes associated with employee-centred stress prevention strategies have found that, where benefits have been identified, such strategies tend to result in shorter-term psychological benefits that are not sustainable over a longer period and have little impact on organizational effectiveness (e.g., Pelletier et al., 1999; Whatmore, Cartwright, & Cooper, 1999). In terms of more general lifestyle-focused initiatives, such as smoking cessation programmes, healthy eating campaigns, and employer sponsored gym memberships, Allen (2001) reported that 80% of employees annually attempted lifestyle changes, but only 20% were successful. There are also concerns about the reach of these programmes and, in particular, their ability to attract people from high-risk groups. Participants in worker directed health promotion programmes are more likely to be younger, well-educated, female, non-smokers, and white-collar workers (LaMontagne, 2004; Thompson, Smith, & Bybee, 2005; Zavela, Davis, Cottrell, & Smith, 1988). Other research has found that whilst participation rates in worksite fitness centres were between 20% and 60%, those who led sedentary lifestyles, and had elevated blood pressure and/or heightened cholesterol levels were less likely to participate (Heaney, 1995). These results raise serious concerns regarding the ability of individualistic WHP programmes to reach the people most at risk of lifestyle-related illness. By helping the 'healthy get healthier', these programmes may be actually exacerbating health inequities, not reducing them.

## The comprehensive, settings-based approach to WHP

Whilst the individualistic approach to WHP uses the workplace as a venue for promoting healthier lifestyles, the aim of the settings-based approach is to create work settings that protect and promote health (Baric, 1993; Noblet & LaMontagne, 2006).

This latter approach not only takes into account characteristics of the job itself – the quantity and complexity of job demands, the level of decision-making control, the timeliness of feedback, guidance, and other forms of support – but also considers the context in which work takes place, including aspects of the physical (e.g., noise, unsafe equipment), social (e.g., quality of leader-member relationships, cultural norms), organizational (e.g., communication systems, training and development, promotional opportunities) and economic (i.e., salary levels, reward and recognition systems) environments. Characteristics of the individual – the knowledge, skills, experience, attitudes, and behaviours of employees – are also included in the settings approach as these can either contribute directly to health outcomes or interact with the physical, social and organizational factors to influence health. Importantly, these individual characteristics may include attributes that are specific to the job (e.g., technical competencies, knowledge of organizational systems), as well as attributes that relate more to people's lifestyles (e.g., dietary intake, alcohol consumption, general coping skills). The settings approach therefore supports the lifestyle-oriented WHP strategies; however, given the salience of job- and context-based forces (with which the employee is interacting on a daily basis), these lifestyle-directed strategies should complement (not replace) interventions addressing organizational characteristics.

Another important feature of the settings approach is the recognition given to external factors, including those relating to an individual's personal and family circumstances (e.g., parental responsibilities, financial commitments), as well as the broader socio-economic, cultural and political conditions (e.g., general economic conditions, national cultures, workplace legislation). These latter conditions impact on both individual and organizational characteristics and reinforce the more holistic, socio-environmental view of health referred to in the Ottawa Charter for Health Promotion (WHO, 1986). The range of individual, organizational, and extra-organizational factors included in the settings approach also reflects what Polanyi and colleagues (2000) refer to as the determinants of worker health (see Figure 6.3).

The determinants of worker health indicate that what happens outside the firm has a direct impact on internal policies, structures, and systems, and, in turn, what happens at a broad organization-wide level has a direct influence on the nature of the job and the more immediate psychosocial conditions in which the individual works. Whilst dimensions of the psychosocial environment ultimately influence worker health, the well-being of employees is also influenced by individual characteristics, in addition to non-work conditions and personal resources. Effectively, employee well-being (and the health of the organization overall) is influenced by a complex array of individual-, job-, organizational- and societal-level factors, and consistent with the socio-environmental view of health, the individual has limited control over these factors (Polanyi et al., 2000). A key implication of this limited control is that substantial, long-term health improvements cannot occur without the direct involvement and commitment of both employers and employees to addressing underlying determinants. Moreover, any attempts to promote health

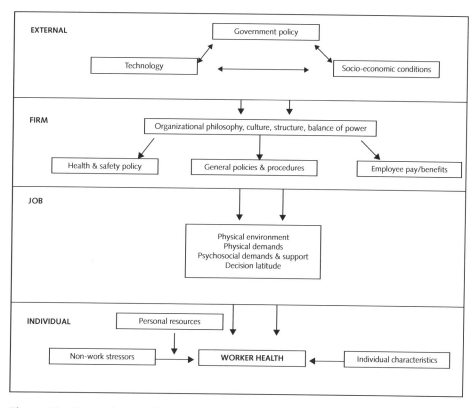

**Figure 6.3** Determinants of worker health (Polanyi et al., 2000).

need to be predicated on: (1) decision-makers having a sound understanding of the determinants that undermine and enhance health, (2) all organizational members being prepared to deal with the full range of health determinants, and (3) workers and management working together to identify, address and evaluate strategies to promote employee health.

The importance of joint employer-employee commitment to addressing the determinants of health is a guiding principle of contemporary WHP. The European Network for Workplace Health Promotion (ENWHP, 2004), for example, defines WHP as:

> the combined efforts of employers, employees and society to improve the health and well-being of people at work. This is achieved through a combination of: improving the work organization and the working environment; promoting the active partici-pation of employees in health activities, and; encouraging personal development.

Recognition of the broader determinants of health, and the need for dual work and worker-directed strategies are also evidenced in WHP strategy development frameworks. Noblet and Murphy's (1995) adaptation of the Ottawa Charter's five areas for health promotion action underlines the importance of creating working environments that are safer, fairer, and more satisfying while also equipping employees with the knowledge and skills for better managing increasingly more complex working and non-working lives. Inter-sectoral collaboration (i.e., management, human resources, occupational safety and health (OSH), finance, production) and workforce empowerment (through inclusive, participatory decision-making systems and processes) also represent important guiding principles for identifying and addressing the health-related needs of employees.

There is a growing body of evidence to suggest that initiatives aimed at addressing the broad range of determinants impacting on the health of employees, rather than focusing solely on health behaviours, can lead to more sustainable benefits for both employees and employers. Comprehensive stress prevention programmes, for example, which address both the organizational origins of stress at work as well as the symptoms of distress exhibited by individual employees, are much more likely to lead to favourable, long-term outcomes than programmes that focus solely on the individual (e.g., Kompier, Cooper, & Guerts, 2000; Michie & Williams, 2003). The inability of employee-centred programmes to achieve sustainable outcomes may be due, in part, to the return of favourably affected employees to unchanged (i.e., still stressful) work environments, resulting in the beneficial effects of the individual intervention being eroded (Nowack, 2000). When compared to traditional lifestyle education/counselling programmes, comprehensive WHP initiatives are also much more likely to capture the involvement of low-paid, blue-collar workers – a group that traditional lifestyle risk programmes had previously found difficult to reach – and to result in successful behaviour change (Sorensen et al., 2002). In addition, the benefits of comprehensive stress prevention programmes include outcomes that are relevant to the individual (e.g., enhanced psychological health, improved job satisfaction, reduction in ambulatory blood pressure) as well as the organization (e.g., reduced sickness absence, increased organizational commitment, improved job performance).

There are a number of factors that are thought to contribute to the success of the more comprehensive, settings-based initiatives. One common view is that a combined organizational and individual approach provides the opportunity to simultaneously prevent excessive stress and other indicators of poor health and, at the same time, help people better manage the effects of demanding and otherwise unhealthy working conditions. As acknowledged by Bond (2004, p. 147), comprehensive programmes provide a balance between organizational and individual-directed interventions which ensure that 'preventative benefits of the former can have a widespread impact across an organization, whilst the curative strengths of the latter can target those (fewer) people who have already succumbed to occupational ill-health'. Another key reason why multi-level strategies are thought to have more lasting effects is that they simultaneously target risk behaviours and risk conditions. High risk behaviours such as sedentary lifestyles and cigarette smoking are partly influenced by high risk conditions and, as indicated in Research Close-Up 6.1 on the Dutch Brabantia Project, attempts to address the risk behaviours are likely to lead to beneficial outcomes, if the risk conditions are also addressed (Maes, Verhoeven, Kittel, & Scholten, 1998). Finally, the processes used to develop comprehensive WHP initiatives can also help explain their success. Working with employees and using their insights and experiences to drive the needs assessment and strategy development process, for example, not only helps to provide a more accurate understanding of the key health determinants, but also enhances employees' commitment to whatever strategies are developed (Aust & Ducki, 2004; Kohler & Munz, 2006).

---

**RESEARCH CLOSE-UP      6.1   The Brabantia Project**

*Source:* LaMontagne, A. (2004). Integrating health promotion and health protection in the workplace. In R. Moodie & A. Hulme (Eds.), *Hands-On Health Promotion* (pp. 285–298). Melbourne: IP Communications.

The Dutch Brabantia Project illustrates the benefits of integrating individually-oriented health promotion with settings-based strategies targeting psycho-social work environments (Maes et al., 1998). This 3-year intervention in a Dutch manufacturing company included individual-level health education on a range of lifestyle and OSH topics, and a lunchtime physical activity programme. At the organizational and environmental levels, the intervention included supportive changes for individual-level lifestyle activities (e.g., creation of an on-site exercise facility) and work organization changes to reduce job stress (e.g., expansion of worker's decision authority over production processes). Evaluation showed that manufacturing employees had significantly greater changes in intervention compared to non-intervention control groups for cardiovascular health risks (decrease), psychological job demands (decrease), job control (increase), and ergonomic risks (decrease). In addition, these changes were paralleled by a significant drop in sickness absence in intervention (15.8% to 7.7%) versus control (14.3% to 9.5%) groups which, by the company's determination yielded a positive financial return on its investment in the project.

---

## Summary

The settings-based approach to WHP emphasizes the importance of creating working environments (physical, social, and organizational) that protect and promote the health of employees. Despite their limitations, individual lifestyle-oriented strategies are still considered worthwhile WHP strategies. However, worker-directed initiatives are much more likely to result in sustainable benefits when: (1) they are based on a detailed understanding of employees' needs, (2) all levels and sections of the organization are committed to addressing the determinants of health, and (3) they are couched within a comprehensive set of strategies that simultaneously address the organizational origins of health at work as well as the symptoms of poor health.

## Planning, Implementing and Evaluating Settings-based WHP Programmes

*What are the general steps that need to be considered when planning,
implementing and evaluating settings-based WHP programmes?
How can each of these steps – and the processes and methods
therein – strengthen or undermine programme effectiveness
(depending on if and how they're executed)?
What role/s can OHPs play in developing and evaluating WHP initiatives?*

Although WHP strategies that are based on employee involvement and empowerment are critical to the success of these programmes, there is a range of other process-oriented methods and techniques that can influence programme outcomes. In general, these methods indicate that the way in which WHP programmes are planned and developed can be just as 'health promoting' as the strategies that are designed to address particular health issues. In the following section we will describe the general steps for planning, implementing, and evaluating settings-based WHP programmes and highlight the processes that are particularly important in maximizing positive health outcomes.

As health professionals, organizations will often turn to OHPs (as well as other personnel with workplace health-related responsibilities) for guidance on how to address issues impacting on the well-being of employees. For example, a department manager may seek the advice of an OHP on how to deal with rising levels of sick-leave or declining levels of morale. Company executives may even expect OHPs to coordinate all organizational health initiatives and require them to lead the development of ongoing programmes. In either case, OHPs need to know not only what WHP is and how it can benefit employees, but also how to plan, implement and evaluate comprehensive, settings-based strategies.

The extent to which OHPs and other people involved in coordinating WHP programmes can understand and apply the various processes involved in planning, implementing, and evaluating WHP programmes will have a significant impact on the effectiveness of those programmes. As already indicated, programmes that overlook the needs and concerns of employees and exclude them from the decision-making process are unlikely to reach or engage large portions of the workforce (Aust & Ducki, 2004; Kohler & Munz, 2006). Likewise, a lack of support from managers and other senior personnel will have a dramatic effect on the resources allocated to the programme and, subsequently, will be pivotal in determining both the scope and quality of strategies developed (Nielsen, Fredslund, Christensen, & Albertsen, 2006). Overall, the programme planning and evaluation literature indicates that the strategies designed to protect and promote health are only as good as the processes used to plan and manage those initiatives and hence the people responsible for the initiatives need to have a sound working understanding of programme planning guidelines (Griffiths, 1999; Murta et al., 2007; Nielsen et al., 2006; Reynolds & Shapiro, 1991).

## Overview of planning framework

The programme planning framework presented in this section is based on that developed by Noblet and LaMontagne (2009). This framework consists of seven broad, interdependent steps: (1) gaining management support, (2) establishing a coordinating group (or identifying an existing group, if appropriate), (3) conducting a needs assessment and issue analyses, (4) identifying priority issues and setting intervention goals, (5) designing interventions and an action plan, (6) implementing interventions, and (7) evaluating implementation processes and intervention effectiveness. As illustrated in Figure 6.4, these seven steps are generally completed as part of an ongoing cycle, with each step informing and shaping the next. Once the programme is nearing the end of the first planning, implementation, and evaluation cycle, the information gained during the process and effectiveness evaluation is then directed back into the beginning of the next cycle and used to help plan subsequent interventions. The cycles are depicted as building on top of one another to illustrate the need for organizations to use the knowledge and skills learnt from previous interventions to inform the content of the proceeding cycle. Ultimately, the cyclical design aims to ensure that programme coordinators learn from past experiences and use a combination of prior learning and new knowledge to identify and address the changing needs of both employees and organizations.

*Gain management support*
The success of any WHP initiative will rest heavily on the extent to which all levels of the organization – senior executives, middle-management, supervisors, and employees – support the initiatives that have been established. Whilst an ongoing challenge for coordinators will be to develop, maintain, and expand this broad-based support, a key goal early in the programme lifecycle will be to gain the support of top-level management (Harden et al., 1999; Kohler & Munz, 2006; Kompier et al., 2000). At a pragmatic level, many of the tasks associated with identifying and addressing organizational health issues are resource intensive, time consuming, and potentially very disruptive. Coordinators will therefore need approval from key decision-makers to ensure they have the time, equipment, and

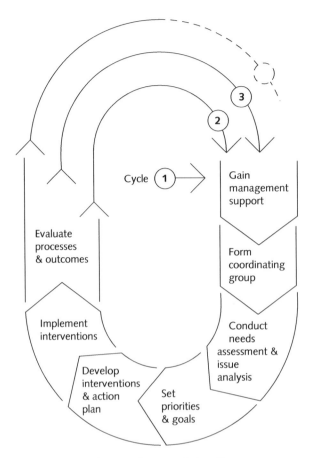

**Figure 6.4**   WHP programme planning framework (Noblet & LaMontagne, 2009).

other resources required to undertake the comprehensive programme development. At a more symbolic level, senior managers exert a strong influence on all
aspects of organizational functioning and gaining the support of top management
for WHP therefore sends out a message that management understands the
importance of employee health and is prepared to devote considerable time and
resources to identify and address priority health issues. Employees are unlikely to
become involved in, or support, organizational health-related initiatives if they feel
managers are only superficially interested in the programme and are not genuine in
their attempts to enhance employee health (Holt, Armenakis, Feild, & Harris,
2007). It is therefore critical that managers can see the benefits of undertaking
WHP interventions, appreciate the importance of designing programmes in a
comprehensive and systematic manner and are willing to invest considerable
time and resources to ensuring these initiatives are effective.

Gaining the understanding and support of high-level management is generally a
difficult task and, even in cases where managers have approached the coordinators
regarding organizational health concerns, they may not be aware of the complexity

of the issues involved or understand the time and resources required to tackle these issues effectively (Demmer, 1995; Health and Welfare Canada, 1991). An important step towards addressing this challenge is to increase management's awareness of the realities of what WHP strategies can and cannot achieve, acknowledge the typical steps that are taken when developing comprehensive programmes, and highlight the type of commitment that is required to achieve sustainable, long-term outcomes (Kohler & Munz, 2006). Providing managers with case studies that outline the benefits of organizational well-being programmes and the strategies to achieve these outcomes can help managers develop a practical understanding of what the programme could look like.

A major goal of the entire intervention development phase (Steps 1–5) is to gather the information required to generate widespread support among managerial personnel. Coordinators are therefore not expected to undertake an in-depth, data gathering exercise before seeking managerial support for the programme (Ganster & Murphy, 2000). Instead, they should aim to gather sufficient background information to demonstrate why employee health (or lack of it) is considered to be a key threat to organizational functioning and to highlight how effectively addressing this topic could result in substantial improvements for the organization.

### Establish (or identify) coordinating group

Once high-level support for the programme has been gained, the coordinators then need to assemble a group of people who, collectively, have the knowledge and the influence to undertake a detailed investigation into organizational health. Forming the coordinating group is an important way of building what Kotter (1995) refers to as a 'powerful guiding coalition'. The inability to create a sufficiently powerful guiding group is one of the key reasons why organizational development and change efforts fail (Jick, 2003; Kotter, 1995). So, while gaining the support of senior personnel is a critical step in the programme development process, it will be a largely wasted exercise if coordinators cannot then go on to capture the energy and enthusiasm of other relevant and influential members of the organization. Coordinators therefore need to approach the individuals and groups who are likely to have the most influence over health-related issues, including representatives from management, employees (e.g., union delegates), health and safety, and human resource management personnel. The determinants of organizational well-being often reside in work systems and processes (Noblet & LaMontagne, 2006; Noblet, Rodwell, & McWilliams, 2006) and, if the committee is going to design strategies that address these determinants, then it also needs to include representatives who have a strong systems-based understanding of the organization's operations, including line-supervisors, research and development experts, and quality control staff. 'Shop-floor' representation is another critical ingredient of the committee and coordinators need to ensure that all employees have the opportunity (through their representatives) to contribute to the planning and implementation of the programme (Kompier et al., 2000; Polanyi et al., 2000). Employees who are consulted and involved in planning and implementing a programme will be much more likely to be committed to the programme's aims (Arneson & Ekberg, 2005; O'Brien, 2002).

A relevant coordinating group may already exist in the organization – in the form of an occupational health and safety committee or a quality management body – in which case the coordinators should attempt to capitalize on existing mechanisms and seek their cooperation in addressing organizational well-being (Health and Welfare Canada, 1991). The advantages of using an existing committee include gaining relatively quick access to relevant and influential members of the organization, preventing the duplication of effort (which can easily occur when there is large functional overlap between groups), and utilizing the group's existing communication channels to quickly disseminate accurate information about the aims of the WHP initiatives. Finally, utilizing an existing committee helps to promote the view that strategies designed to protect and promote employee well-being should become a standard way of managing business, rather than add-on, discretionary functions that can be quickly eliminated when there is a change in key personnel or when there is a rationalization of resources (Health and Welfare Canada, 1991).

Utilizing an existing committee may not always be an effective developmental strategy, particularly when the committee has an overpowering reputation for achieving very little, lacks support from employees and other influential groups, and/or is poorly representative of the organization (Health and Welfare Canada, 1991). A key challenge for the coordinators is therefore to assess the capacity of existing coordinating groups to address organizational well-being and to consider the costs (in terms of time and energy) associated with trying to enhance this capacity. They should then estimate the relative value that can be gained by forming a new committee and, finally, make an informed judgment on which option is most appropriate.

### Conduct needs assessment and analyse health issues

Initiatives aimed at protecting and promoting employee health need to be based on a detailed understanding of the conditions and issues impacting on people's health, in particular, the number of people affected by the condition/issue, the severity of the effects and the range of factors that contribute to the issue (Goldenhar, LaMontagne, Katz, Heaney, & Landsbergis, 2001; Polanyi et al., 2000). Gathering data that can accurately identify the breadth and depth of the problem can help coordinators prioritize the problem areas (including high-risk groups and/or work conditions) and ensure that often scarce resources are channelled into those problems that are causing the most people the most concern (Demmer, 1995). Likewise, identifying contributory factors can help ensure coordinators are able to distinguish between symptoms and causes and can focus much of their energies on tackling the root source of the problem (Munz, Kohler, & Greenberg, 2001). Company-wide surveys, human resource records (rates of absenteeism, voluntary turnover figures, injury records), discussions with key stakeholders (line management, employees and their representatives, OSH staff, HR, etc.) can all be used to help identify, analyse, and prioritize health issues.

One of the most commonly identified problems associated with WHP programmes is that they are based on normative or expert-generated needs (e.g., lifestyle-related risk factors for chronic disease) and ignore the specific health concerns expressed by employees (e.g., Harden et al., 1999; LaMontagne, 2004; Noblet & LaMontagne, 2006; Shain & Kramer, 2004). An important challenge facing coordinators during this stage of the intervention development phase is therefore to identify the expressed needs of employees and, through issue analysis strategies, gain a detailed understanding of the range of individual and organizational factors that contribute to the problematic nature of these issues. The processes used to identify and analyse health needs can empower or disempower employees, depending on how they are designed, and another important task for coordinators is to develop needs assessment and issue analysis techniques that genuinely engage employees and convey the message that coordinators are working with them (not on them) (Nutbeam, 1998; Polanyi et al., 2000).

---

**RESEARCH CLOSE-UP     6.2   The Multi-Method Approach to Assessing Needs**

*Sources:* Doherty, L., & Manfredi, S. (2006). Action research to develop work-life balance in a UK university. *Women in Management Review, 21*(3), 241–259.

Kompier, M., Cooper, C., & Guerts, S. (2000). A multiple case study approach to work stress prevention in Europe. *European Journal of Work and Organizational Psychology, 9*(3), 371–400.

Studies involving organizational health issues generally support the use of multiple methods to identify and analyse people's needs. For example, a review of job stress prevention programmes implemented in eleven companies across Europe found that the participating organizations often used a combination of methods to effectively identify high risk groups and conditions. These methods ranged from 'first-line monitoring' (i.e., checklist and interventions) to questionnaires and the analysis of administrative data (e.g., sickness absence) (Kompier et al., 2000). Similarly, Doherty and Manfredi (2006) used organization-wide surveys and a series of focus group discussions to inform the development of work-life balance initiatives in a UK university. The survey helped to identify the extent to which staff felt that work-life issues were important to them, whilst the focus groups helped uncover the complex interplay of personal and organizational factors that contribute to the lack of work-life balance.

Another common fault of employee needs assessments is that they frequently focus on adverse or problematic working conditions. Indeed, the very title 'needs assessment' implies that coordinators should focus their attention on what is missing and/or in need of improvement. However, several WHP (Demmer, 1995) and organizational development models (French, Bell, & Zawacki, 2005) emphasize the importance of undertaking a broader 'situational analysis' that identifies both the strengths and weaknesses of working environments. Adopting this more balanced approach helps to keep the problematic issues in perspective and may prevent people from developing excessively negative or pessimistic mindsets. Identifying the positives can also help locate examples of where work units have developed more effective systems and structures, which may then be used to inform the development of interventions for other work units. Finally, an assessment of the organization's strengths encourages people to consider the full range of resources (i.e., knowledge, skills, processes, instruments, technologies) that are available in the organization. Internal resources are often overlooked or underestimated when developing strategies to address health-related concerns and a detailed situational analysis can help bring these resources to the fore and reduce the reliance on costly external services.

### Identify priorities and set goals

The identification and analysis of needs will generally result in a list of issues that could be addressed. However, the importance of these issues is likely to vary considerably, as is the feasibility of addressing them. As organizations are rarely in a position to address all issues simultaneously, the next key challenge confronting the coordinating committee will be to prioritize the issues identified in the needs assessment and pinpoint those that will receive more immediate attention.

The precise criteria for prioritizing issues are rarely considered in the WHP literature. Yet individual employees or groups may feel very strongly about when and how certain issues will be tackled, and equally, they may become very disillusioned and resentful if the coordination team is unable to present legitimate and transparent reasons why issues important to them were not addressed. Clearly, the organizing committee needs to develop a set of criteria that it will use to select issues and, given that the response to these judgments will heavily influence the acceptance of subsequent decisions, the committee should consult at all levels of the organization when developing these criteria. Some of the criteria that could be identified in this consultation process include: the severity of the health issue (in terms of its impact on people's well-being); the number of people affected by the issue; whether workplace laws (e.g., OSH and employee relations legislation) have prescribed tolerance limits; the level of understanding regarding how this issue should be addressed and the effectiveness of designated strategies; and the ability of the organization and its members to effectively address the issue given the constraints of time, resources and other contextual factors.

There is the natural tendency to prioritize highly problematic issues involving large numbers of people right at the beginning of the programme. However, in cases where a WHP programme is only just starting, the committee might be advised to tackle a small number of relatively straightforward issues first. Starting small gives the committee the opportunity to register some 'quick wins', to progressively build the partnerships and 'guiding coalitions' required to tackle the more complex issues, to give itself the time needed to develop a more detailed understanding of employees' needs and interests, and to use practical experience of what works to inform future intervention planning (Bowditch & Buono, 2005; Kotter, 1995).

Once the priority issues have been identified, the coordinating committee then needs to set intervention goals. These goals need to be informed by a detailed understanding of what is a realistic and achievable improvement and should be developed in conjunction with organizational members, their representatives, experts in the field, and the organizational health-related literature (especially previous intervention studies addressing this issue) (Shain & Kramer, 2004). The content of the goals themselves should express what individual or organizational changes the committee is aiming to achieve (e.g., a 12% increase in psychological well-being, or a 7% decrease in role ambiguity), who or what is the target of the initiatives and when the improvements are expected to be achieved (Naidoo & Wills, 2000). There will be some instances, such as when dealing with an emerging health issue and/or where there is little known about the effectiveness of possible interventions, where some or most of the aforementioned criteria cannot be incorporated into the goal. However, coordinating committees need to be accountable to the groups they represent. All stakeholders will want to know what the interventions are aimed at achieving, when the outcomes are expected to be achieved and whether the goals are realistic. Developing specific, measurable, and time-bound targets that articulate desired changes is an important way of communicating the aims of the programme and building both clarity and accountability into the interventions.

### Design interventions and action plan

Having established a clear set of well-informed and realistic goals, the coordinating committee now needs to develop the interventions that can achieve those goals. These interventions need to be based on the results of the needs assessment stage [Step 3] and should be directed at specific contributory factors identified in the process. Coordinators should also consult the relevant research and appropriate theoretical frameworks to identify the general strategies that could be used to address the contributory factors. The results of previous intervention research are particularly important in establishing a sound understanding of what has been found to be effective in addressing the issues identified. The people most affected by the health issues – employees themselves – are also likely to have a firm understanding of the extent to which different strategies can be effective (given the current organizational context) and they need to be heavily involved in developing the interventions (Kompier et al., 2000).

A problem frequently experienced by programme coordinators during this stage of intervention development is whether to adopt one size-fits-all 'pre-packaged' interventions or, along similar lines, allow outside consultants to assume sole responsibility for developing interventions (Ganster & Murphy, 2000; Kohler & Munz, 2006). The tendency to adopt generic interventions is not surprising, especially as few health-related intervention studies document the processes used to plan and implement these strategies (Goldenhar et al., 2001; Griffiths, 1999). However, the coordinators need to be aware that interventions are often very context dependent and they need to consult extensively with other members of the committee and the organization in general regarding their appropriateness (Hurrell & Murphy, 1996; Kompier et al., 2000). A strategy aimed at improving working conditions (e.g., a forward rotating shift schedule to replace a less healthy backward rotating schedule) may actually undermine employee well-being if it is imposed on employees in an authoritarian manner and without prior consultation and negotiation (Kompier et al., 2000).

---

### Box 6.1    Drawing on the Expertise of Outside Personnel

Organizational development (OD) consultants, independent occupational health practitioners, commercial WHP providers, and other organizational health experts can provide important guidance and advice at key stages of the programme (e.g., OD consultants can be very effective in facilitating the needs identification and issue analysis processes). However, a heavy reliance on external people or groups may result in the programme losing momentum or becoming inactive as soon as the outside people/groups cease their involvement. Coordinators need to recognize that capacity building is an important means for developing sustainable long-term WHP programmes and, if organizations are to develop the ability to identify and address their own problems, then organizational members need to take progressively greater ownership over the intervention development process. Outside consultants need to be chosen, therefore, not only on the basis of their technical capacities, but also on their willingness and ability to empower others.

---

Whilst the interventions outline the general strategies that will be adopted to achieve the programme goals (e.g., the introduction of self managed teams (SMTs) or the development of a new family-friendly rostering schedule), they do not specify the logistics of when and how these interventions will be undertaken, who will be responsible for overseeing their implementation, or the financial resources that have been allocated to support the intervention. An action plan provides this detail by documenting: (1) the particular methods that will be used to implement the interventions, (2) the timing of these methods, (3) the people responsible for introducing and monitoring the required tasks, and (4) the budget that has been set aside for each intervention (Burke, 2006; Health and Welfare Canada, 1991). The overall purpose of the action plan is to ensure that everyone has a clear and consistent understanding of exactly what the programme will look like in practice, when the associated methods/tasks will be undertaken, and by whom (Burke, 2006). As will be seen in the implementation stage, ambiguity and miscommunication regarding the specific methods used to undertake the interventions is likely to lead to interventions not being implemented as they were intended. Such an error can have costly implications for both the coordinators and the organization. In the extreme, the absence of a clear and detailed plan of action may lead to the organization withdrawing their support for the entire WHP programme.

*Implement strategies*

The many processes and methods described in the intervention development phase (Steps 1–5) have the dual purpose of (1) identifying where and how the health of employees can be improved, and (2) generating widespread support for and involvement in the designated interventions. However, as already noted, much of this momentum and support can be quickly lost if the interventions are poorly executed or haphazardly managed during the implementation phase.

There is ample evidence that weak, inconsistent, or non-existent implementation is a common problem across a range of organizational health domains, including OSH and WHP (Goldenhar & Schulte, 1994; Harden et al., 1999; Lipsey & Cordray, 2000; Nielsen et al., 2006; Saksvik, Nytro, Dahl-Jorgensen, & Mikkelsen, 2002). In the study by Saksvik and colleagues (2002), for example, process evaluation techniques were used to examine the implementation of job stress interventions across multiple organizations. The authors found that implementation methods that were supposed to be the same were, in fact, very different. In one particular instance, organizational interventions undertaken in two municipalities required that employees and their managers discuss problematic issues in the work environment together. These sessions were to be led by a neutral external facilitator; however, two of the five managers opted to run these sessions without the facilitator. This approach limited participants' ability to identify and discuss critical issues and had a major influence on the targets of the subsequent interventions.

The process evaluation research by Saksvik et al. (2002) and Nielsen et al. (2006) has identified a range of barriers to coordinators implementing strategies as they were intended, including: a lack of genuine enthusiasm for the interventions, particularly on the part of management; work demands that made it difficult for employees to take part in the activities; organizational change programmes including major restructuring and financial cutbacks that increased cynicism towards the project while adding to employees' workloads; traditional risk-aversive organizational cultures that undermined members' ability to learn from failure; a tendency to adopt the least difficult interventions (e.g., awareness raising) while ignoring those that are more resource intensive but can potentially have the greatest impact (e.g., stressor reduction strategies); unclear roles and responsibilities, and; and breakdowns in communication and cooperation.

There are numerous programme management strategies that can be employed to prevent these sorts of problems from occurring during the implementation phase or, if they do occur, to minimize their impact. These strategies include the following:

*Contingency planning.* Before the programme begins, coordinators need to identify where they might have difficulty either achieving the programme goals and/or implementing the action plan as intended (e.g., specific strategies fail to have the desired effect; turnover of key personnel, budget cutbacks). They then need to have a set of contingencies in place that can be quickly implemented if these problems occur.

*Process evaluation.* Checking mechanisms are required to ensure the interventions are being implemented in accordance with the action plan, that the various methods/tasks are completed to a high standard, that any barriers and obstacles to effective implementation are being identified and addressed, and that the interventions are generally being well received by the staff concerned (see following section for further details on process evaluation) (Goldenhar et al., 2001).

*Monitoring resources.* Coordinators need to carefully monitor resource use, particularly time and financial resources, at all stages of programme implementation (Burke, 2006; Demmer, 1995). Unexpected delays and costs are an inevitable part of any programme, however, if they are left unchecked or are not identified early enough, they could result in severe budget shortfalls and/or the implementation of poor quality initiatives.

*Internal communication.* Internal communication mechanisms (e.g., team meetings, feedback systems) should be established to ensure that there is a high level of coordination between initiatives, that the results of process evaluation are being shared among the coordinating group, and that team members remain clear about their respective roles in executing the action plan (Whitelaw, Martin, Kerr, & Wimbush, 2006).

*External communication.* The coordinating group also needs to communicate regularly with external stakeholders (e.g., managers, employees, HR personnel), particularly in regards to the progress being made (Demmer, 1995). External communication must be two-way and external individuals and groups should have ample opportunities for giving feedback and to contribute to the ongoing development of the programme. This two-way dialogue can help raise the profile of the programme, identify future opportunities and threats, reduce resistance to change, and maintain and/or increase support for the programme (Jick, 2003; Kotter, 1995).

*Identify changing needs.* Much of the long-term success of the WHP interventions will rest on the extent to which they meet employees' changing needs (Giga et al., 2003) and there should be sufficient flexibility built into the programme to accommodate these changes. The process evaluation strategies, as well as the internal and external communication systems, are important mechanisms for undertaking ongoing needs assessment.

*Evaluating the programme*

Programme evaluation is the systematic collection and analysis of information to allow informed decision-making about an approach, activity, or policy (Goldenhar & Schulte, 1994). In the WHP context, evaluation should provide the information required to assess the extent to which goals have been met, to determine whether the particular strategies were appropriate and efficient and to establish the reasons why or why not the strategies were successful. Ultimately, gathering this information is necessary to improve current and/or future strategies. Programme evaluation is often poorly undertaken in the organizational health arena (Goldenhar et al., 2001; Griffiths, 1999; Nutbeam, 1998) and, in an economic climate that places increasing emphasis on cost-effectiveness and evidence-based action, there is a clear need to improve the manner in which WHP initiatives are evaluated.

Evaluating WHP programmes can be challenging, both from a technical and a practical perspective, and coordinators should consult specialist evaluation and research methods publications when undertaking this task (including Taris et al.'s Chapter 10 in this textbook). Although providing in-depth guidance on programme evaluation is beyond the scope of this chapter, there are two critical issues that WHP programme coordinators need to take into account when planning to evaluate a comprehensive, settings-based WHP programme. These issues relate to the types of evaluation being undertaken and when the evaluation takes place.

In relation to evaluation types, there are three general forms of evaluation that collectively assess the effects associated with specific strategies and the processes used to plan and implement the strategies themselves. Much of the intervention research involving strategies designed to protect and promote health has tended to focus on the short- and long-term effects of specific strategies (Griffiths, 1999; Murta et al., 2007; Nielsen et al., 2006; Reynolds & Shapiro, 1991). These forms of evaluation are referred to as impact and outcome evaluation, respectively, and capture immediate to short-term changes in attitudes, behaviours, practices, conditions, and policies (i.e., impact evaluation) as well as changes that are sustained over a longer time period (i.e., outcome evaluation). As already highlighted, the processes used to develop and manage workplace health interventions play a major role in the success of specific strategies, and in the absence of sound process evaluation, intervention-based studies that focus solely on effects/outcomes fail to adequately consider the role that contextual factors (e.g., management support, programme reach, competing projects) played in contributing to those outcomes (Griffiths, 1999; Murta et al., 2007; Nielsen et al., 2006; Reynolds & Shapiro, 1991). Understanding why certain initiatives experienced more, or less, success is central to the ongoing cycle of learning and renewal underpinning the planning framework (see Figure 6.1) and, hence, coordinators are urged to integrate extensive process evaluation into their programmes.

A key implication of the need to assess planning and implementation processes, in addition to the impact and outcome of WHP strategies, is that evaluation should take place at all stages of the programme cycle, not just towards the end or immediately after the implementation phase (which is what is implied with evaluation being the final step in the programme planning cycle). With this in mind, programme coordinators need to plan and develop their evaluation methods well before the programme implementation phase begins. In terms of impact and outcome evaluations, they should assess the extent to which programme goals were achieved. Thus the type of data collected, as well as the specific data collection methods, should be developed at the same time as the programme goals are being established. This approach not only helps to ensure coordinators collect data that is specific to their particular goals but also forces coordinators to assess whether they have the capacity to collect the necessary data in the first place. Process evaluation is more of an ongoing task and, while coordinators have a limit to the amount of data they can gather and review, attempts should be made to assess the methods and techniques involved in all stages of the programme life-cycle (even evaluation methods themselves).

Although the seven steps are presented in a neat linear sequence, with one step informing the next, the reality of planning and evaluating interventions is generally more chaotic than this framework suggests. Coordinators often need to 'back-track' (e.g., when the processes used to design interventions [Step 5] uncover concerns or ideas that weren't properly investigated in the needs assessment step [Step 3]), or leap ahead (e.g., when issue analysis techniques [Step 3] reveal relatively simple, straight forward solutions [Step 5] that can be implemented [Step 6] without the development of a detailed action plan), and/or to undertake several steps simultaneously (e.g., using the results of the process evaluation [Step 7] undertaken during the implementation stage [Step 6] to demonstrate strong interest in the intervention and, in turn, to encourage key employees to join the coordinating committee and ensure it has broad representation [Step 2]). It is also important to emphasize that interventions are developed and implemented in complex social and organizational settings and that any events in the surrounding environment (e.g., changing strategic priorities, new operational procedures, budget cuts) can trigger changes in the way the intervention is developed or the content of the intervention itself. This does not suggest that attempting to under-take rational, organized planning is a futile exercise, but rather that coordinators need to be flexible in their approach. Moreover, the planning and evaluation framework should be regarded more as a check-list of systematic activities and tasks that need to be considered when developing, implementing and assessing WHP programmes.

## Summary

The overall aims of the seven steps outlined in the programme planning framework are to identify and analyse the health needs of employees (including both positive and negative influences on health), to develop interventions that address those needs (using a combination of prior research, expert opinion and workers' own insights) and then to evaluate the effectiveness of the interventions (including the processes used to plan and implement the interventions). The results of the evaluations are then fed back into the cycle and are used to help improve current and/or future interventions. The involvement and support of key groups (particularly managers and employees) is crucial to the ongoing success of the interventions and a further aim of the seven steps is therefore to generate broad-based support for the WHP initiatives and ensure they have the resources (people, time, finances) in place to sustain appropriate initiatives well into the future. While the various stages in the planning framework are presented in a sequential manner, programme coordinators need to be flexible in their approach in order to effectively accommodate the unpredictable and idiosyncratic nature of organizational life.

## SUMMARY AND CONCLUSIONS

The following is a summary of the major points covered in this chapter:

- There is a large gap between WHP theory and practice and OHPs can play a key role in bridging this divide.
- Contemporary views of WHP are based on internationally recognised definitions of 'health' and 'health promotion' and practitioners need to be familiar with these definitions in order to appreciate what WHP is aiming to achieve and how.
- Health is conceptualized as a resource for everyday life, not the object of living; it is a positive concept emphasizing social and personal resources, as well as physical capacities.
- Health is shaped by a broad range of individual, social, economic and political factors and, as many of these factors are outside the control of individuals, a key goal of health promotion is to identify the underlying determinants of health and help individuals and groups to gain control over these forces.
- The individually-oriented approach to WHP focuses heavily on the 'absence of disease' definition of health and tends to use the workplace as a convenient venue for identifying those who are at risk of experiencing lifestyle-related diseases and encouraging them to adopt healthier patterns of behaviour.
- Several criticisms have been directed at the individual approach, namely the tendency to concentrate on individual behaviours at the exclusion of underlying determinants, failing to meet international standards on occupational health and safety and health promotion, and not delivering sustainable outcomes (both in terms of programme reach and effectiveness).
- The settings-based approach to WHP emphasizes the importance of creating working environments (physical, social and organizational) that

protect and promote the health of employees. Worker-directed strategies still have a role to play in these programmes, however, only when they complement (not replace) strategies aimed at building safer, fairer and more satisfying workplaces.

- The way in which WHP programmes are planned and developed can be just as 'health promoting' as the strategies that are designed to address particular health issues, hence, practitioners need to be familiar with the wide range of processes and methods that can be employed when planning, implementing, and evaluating WHP programmes.

- The programme planning framework discussed in this chapter includes seven broad, interdependent steps: (1) gaining management support; (2) establishing a coordinating group (or identifying an existing group, if appropriate); (3) conducting a needs assessment and issue analyses; (4) identifying priority issues and setting intervention goals; (5) designing interventions and an action plan; (6) implementing interventions; and (7) evaluating implementation processes and intervention effectiveness.

There is a clear need for WHP practice to move from the individually-oriented approach of 'doing health promotion in the work setting' to the more comprehensive, settings-based model that aims to create working environments that protect and promote health. Given the importance of work and workplaces in people's lives, many would argue that substantial improvements in the health of individual employees, their families and whole communities would not be possible without this shift being made. Occupational health psychologists have the potential to make many valuable contributions to the development of this more contemporary approach, both in terms of promoting greater awareness of the settings-based model and in actively working with managers, employees, and their representatives to develop comprehensive WHP initiatives. However, as has been indicated in the latter half of this chapter, planning and implementing WHP programmes that respond to the needs of employees and employers is a complex task that requires sustained, coordinated efforts from a range of workplace personnel. OHPs and other workplace health professionals therefore need to work closely with managers, employees, and their representatives to ensure that health-related issues are identified and addressed in a systematic manner and that, ultimately, these strategies enhance the health both of organizations and their members.

## Suggestions for Further Reading

ENWHP (2004). *Making the case for workplace health promotion: Analysis of the effects of WHP.* Belgium: European Network for Workplace Health Promotion (ENWHP). Presents lines of argument and case studies that can be used to promote the benefits of WHP.

LaMontagne, A. (2004). Integrating health promotion and health protection in the work-place. In R. Moodie & A. Hulme (Eds.), *Hands-on health promotion* (pp. 285–298). Melbourne: IP Communications. Provides a detailed description of how individually-oriented behaviour change programmes can be integrated with more traditional workplace health and safety strategies.

Noblet, A., & LaMontagne, A. D. (2006). The role of workplace health promotion in addressing job stress. *Health Promotion International, 21*(4), 346–353. Highlights the role that settings-based approach can play in preventing and/or reducing occupational stress.

Saksvik, P., Nytro, K., Dahl-Jorgensen, C., & Mikkelsen, A. (2002). A process evaluation of individual and organizational occupational stress and health interventions. *Work & Stress, 16*(1), 37–57. An example of a growing number of studies that assess the processes used to plan and implement job stress interventions.

## References

Allen, J. (2001). Building supportive cultural environments. In M. O'Donnell (Ed.), *Health promotion in the workplace* (3rd ed.). Albany, NY: Delmar Thomson Learning.

Arneson, H., & Ekberg, K. (2005). Evaluation of empowerment processes in a workplace health promotion intervention based on learning in Sweden. *Health Promotion International, 20*(4), 351–359.

Aust, B., & Ducki, A. (2004). Comprehensive health promotion interventions at the workplace: Experiences with health circles in Germany. *Journal of Occupational Health Psychology, 9*(3), 258–270.

Baric, L. (1993). The settings approach: Implications for policy and strategy. *The Journal of the Institute of Health Education, 31*(1), 17–24.

Blewett, V., & Shaw, A. (1995). Health promotion, handle with care: Issues for health promotion in the workplace. *Journal of Occupational Health and Safety, Australia and New Zealand, 11*, 461–465.

Bond, F. (2004). Getting the balance right: The need for a comprehensive approach to occupational health. *Work and Stress, 18*(2), 146–148.

Bowditch, J., & Buono, A. (2005). *Organization development and change* (6th ed.). Hoboken, NJ: John Wiley & Sons.

Burke, R. (2006). *Project management: Planning and control techniques* (5th ed.). Burke Publishing (internet publisher).

Caulfield, N., Chang, D., Dollard, M., & Elshaugh, C. (2004). A review of occupational stress interventions in Australia. *International Journal of Stress Management, 11*(2), 149–166.

Chu, C., Driscoll, T., & Dwyer, S. (1997). The health-promoting workplace: An integrative perspective. *Australian and New Zealand Journal of Public Health, 21*(4), 377–385.

Chu, C., & Dwyer, S. (2002). Employer role in integrative workplace health management: A new model in progress. *Disease Management & Health Outcomes, 10*(3), 175–186.

Corneil, D., & Yassi, A. (1998). Ethics in health protection and health promotion. In J. Stellman (Ed.), *Encyclopaedia of Occupational Health and Safety* (Vol. 1, pp. 19.18–19.22). Geneva: International Labour Office.

Cousins, R., Mackay, C., Clarke, S., Kelly, C., Kelly, P., & McCaig, R. (2004). 'Management Standards' and work-related stress in the UK: Practical development. *Work & Stress, 18*(2), 113–136.

Dahlgren, G., & Whitehead, M. (2007). *Policies and strategies to promote social equity in health: Background document to WHO – Strategy paper for Europe.* Stockholm: Institute for Future Studies.

Daykin, N. (1998). Workplace health promotion: Benefit or burden to low-paid workers. *Critical Public Health, 8*(2), 153–166.

Demmer, H. (1995). *Worksite Health Promotion: How to go about it.* Copenhagen: World Health Organization (Europe).

Doherty, L., & Manfredi, S. (2006). Action research to develop work-life balance in a UK university. *Women in Management Review, 21*(3), 241–259.

Eakin, J. M. (1997). Work-related determinants of health behavior. In D. Gochman (Ed.), *Handbook of health behavior research I: Personal and social determinants* (pp. 337–357). New York: Plenum Press.

Ellis, N. (2001). *Work and health: Management in Australia and New Zealand.* South Melbourne: Oxford University Press.

ENWHP (1997). *Luxembourg Declaration on Workplace Health Promotion (Updated in June 2005).* Luxembourg: European Network for Workplace Health Promotion.

ENWHP (2004). *Making the case for workplace health promotion: Analysis of the effects of WHP.* Belgium: European Network for Workplace Health Promotion (ENWHP).

EU-OSHA (2002). *How to Tackle Psychosocial Issues and Reduce Work-Related Stress.* Luxembourg: European Agency for Safety and Health at Work (EU-OSHA).

Feldman, J., Makuc, D., Kleinman, J., & Cornoni-Huntley, J. (1989). National trends in educational differentials in mortality. *American Journal of Epidemiology, 129*, 919–933.

French, W., Bell, C., & Zawacki, R. (2005). *Organization development and transformation: Managing effective change* (6th ed.). New York: McGraw-Hill Irwin.

Ganster, D., & Murphy, L. (2000). Workplace interventions to prevent stress-related illness: Lessons from research and practice. In C. Cooper & E. Locke (Eds.), *Industrial and organizational psychology* (pp. 34–51). Oxford: Blackwell Publishers.

Giga, S., Noblet, A., Faragher, B., & Cooper, C. (2003). Organisational stress management interventions: A review of UK-based research. *The Australian Psychologist, 38*(2), 158–164.

Gini, A. (2000). *My job my self: Work and the creation of the modern individual.* New York: Routledge.

Golaszewski, T., Allen, J., & Edington, D. M. A. (2008). Working together to create supportive environments in worksite health promotion. *American Journal of Health Promotion, 22*(4), 1–10.

Goldenhar, L., LaMontagne, A., Katz, T., Heaney, C., & Landsbergis, P. (2001). The intervention research process in occupational health and safety: An overview from the National Occupational Research Agenda Intervention Effectiveness Research Team. *Journal of Occupational and Environmental Medicine, 43*(7), 616–622.

Goldenhar, L., & Schulte, P. (1994). Intervention research in occupational health and safety. *Journal of Occupational Medicine, 36*(7), 10–22.

Green, K. (1988). Issues of control and responsibility in worker's 'health'. *Health Education Quarterly, 15*, 473–486.

Griffiths, A. (1999). Organizational interventions: Facing the limits of the Natural Science Paradigm. *Scandinavian Journal of Work, Environment and Health, 25*(6), 589–596.

Harden, A., Peersman, G., Oliver, S., Mauthner, M., & Oakley, A. (1999). A systematic review of the effectiveness of health promotion interventions in the workplace. *Occupational Medicine, 49*(8), 540–548.

Health and Welfare Canada (1991). *Corporate health model: A guide to developing and implementing the workplace health system in medium and large businesses.* Ottawa: Health and Welfare Canada.

Heaney, C. (1995). Are employees who are at risk for cardiovascular disease joining worksite fitness centres? *Journal of Occupational and Environmental Medicine, 37,* 718–724.

Heaney, C., & Goetzel, R. (1997). A review of health-related outcomes of multi-component worksite health promotion programs. *American Journal of Health Promotion, 11,* 290–308.

Holt, D., Armenakis, A., Feild, H., & Harris, S. (2007). Readiness for organizational change. *The Journal of Applied Behavioral Science, 43*(2), 232–255.

Hurrell, J., & Murphy, L. (1996). Occupational stress intervention. *American Journal of Industrial Medicine, 29,* 338–341.

Jick, T. (2003). Implementing change. In T. Dick & M. Peiperl (Eds.), *Managing change: Cases and concepts* (pp. 174–219). New York: McGraw-Hill.

Kohler, J., & Munz, D. (2006). Combining individual and organizational stress interventions: An organizational development approach. *Consulting Psychology Journal: Practice and Research, 58*(1), 1–12.

Kompier, M., Cooper, C., & Guerts, S. (2000). A multiple case study approach to work stress prevention in Europe. *European Journal of Work and Organizational Psychology, 9*(3), 371–400.

Kotter, J. (1995). Leading change: Why transformation efforts fail. *Harvard Business Review, March–April,* 59–67.

Labonte, R. (1992). Heart health inequalities in Canada: Modules, theory and planning. *Health Promotion International, 7*(2), 119–128.

LaMontagne, A. (2004). Integrating health promotion and health protection in the workplace. In R. Moodie & A. Hulme (Eds.), *Hands-on health promotion* (pp. 285–298). Melbourne: IP Communications.

LaMontagne, A. D., Keegel, T., & Vallance, D. A. (2007). Protecting and promoting mental health in the workplace: Developing a systems approach to job stress. *Health Promotion Journal of Australia, 18*(3), 221–228.

LaMontagne, A., Louie, A., Keegel, T., Ostry, A., & Shaw, A. (2006). *Workplace stress in Victoria: Developing a systems approach.* Melbourne: Victorian Health Promotion Foundation.

Linan, L., Bowling, M., Childress, J., Lindsay, G., Blakey, C., Pronk, S., et al. (2008). Results of the 2004 National Worksite Health Promotion Survey. *American Journal of Public Health, 98*(8), 1503–1509.

Lipsey, M., & Cordray, D. (2000). Evaluation methods for social intervention. *Annual Review of Psychology, 51,* 345–375.

Mackay, C., Cousins, R., Kelly, P., Lee, S., & McCaig, R. (2004). 'Management standards' and work-related stress in the UK: Policy background and science. *Work & Stress, 18* (2), 91–112.

Maes, S., Verhoeven, C., Kittel, F., & Scholten, H. (1998). Effects of a Dutch wellness program: The Brabantia Project. *American Journal of Public Health, 88,* 1037–1041.

Marmot, M., Rose, G., Shipley, M., & Hamilton, P. (1978). Employment grade and coronary heart disease in British civil servants. *Journal of Epidemiology and Community Health, 32,* 244–249.

Michie, S., & Williams, S. (2003). Reducing work related psychological ill health and sickness absence: A systematic literature review. *Occupational and Environmental Medicine, 60*(1), 3–9.

Munz, D., Kohler, J., & Greenberg, C. (2001). Effectiveness of a comprehensive worksite stress management program: Combining organizational and individual interventions. *International Journal of Stress Management, 8*(1), 49–62.

Murta, S., Sanderson, K., & Oldenburg, B. (2007). Process evaluation in occupational stress management programs. *American Journal of Health Promotion, 21*(4), 248–254.

Naidoo, J., & Wills, J. (2000). *Health promotion: Foundations for practice* (2nd ed.). London: Bailliere Tindall.

Nielsen, K., Fredslund, H., Christensen, K., & Albertsen, K. (2006). Success or failure? Interpreting and understanding the impact of interventions in four similar worksites. *Work & Stress, 20*(3), 272–287.

Noack, H. (Ed.) (1987). *Concepts of health and health promotion.* Copenhagen: World Health Organization.

Noblet, A. (2003). Building health promoting work settings: Identifying the relationship between work characteristics and occupational stress in Australia. *Health Promotion International, 18*(4), 351–359.

Noblet, A., & LaMontagne, A. (2009). The challenges of developing, implementing, and evaluating interventions. In S. Cartwright & C. Cooper (Eds.), *The Oxford handbook of organizational well-being.* Oxford: Oxford University Press.

Noblet, A., & LaMontagne, A. D. (2006). The role of workplace health promotion in addressing job stress. *Health Promotion International, 21*(4), 346–353.

Noblet, A., & Murphy, C. (1995). Adapting the Ottawa Charter for health promotion to the workplace setting. *Health Promotion Journal of Australia, 5*(3), 18–22.

Noblet, A., Rodwell, J., & McWilliams, J. (2006). Organisational change in the public sector: Augmenting the demand control model to predict employee outcomes under new public management. *Work & Stress, 20*(4), 335–352.

Nowack, K. (2000). Screening and management of the workplace for CVD risk: Individual stress management – effective or not. *State of the Art Reviews: Occupational Medicine, 15*(1), 231–233.

Nutbeam, D. (1998). Evaluating health promotion: Progress, problems and solutions. *Health Promotion International, 13,* 27–43.

O'Brien, G. (2002). Participation as the key to successful change – a public sector case study. *Leadership and Organization Development Journal, 23*(8), 442–455.

O'Donnell, M. (Ed.). (2001). *Health promotion in the workplace.* Albany, NY: Delmar Thomson Learning.

Pelletier, K., Rodenburg, A., Vinther, A., Chikamoto, Y., King, A., & Farquhar, J. (1999). Managing job strain: A randomized, controlled trial of an intervention conducted by mail and telephone. *Journal of Occupational and Environmental Medicine, 41*(4), 216–223.

Polanyi, M. F. D., Frank, J. W., Shannon, H. S., Sullivan, T. J., Lavis, J. N., Bertera, R. L., et al. (2000). Promoting the determinants of good health in the workplace. In B. Poland, L. W. Green & I. Rootman (Eds.), *Settings for health promotion: Linking theory and practice* (pp. 138–174). Thousand Oaks, CA: Sage Publications.

Raphael, D. (2003). Barriers to addressing the societal determinants of health: public health units and poverty in Ontario, Canada. *Health Promotion International, 18*(4), 397–405.

Reynolds, S., & Shapiro, D. (1991). Stress reduction in transition: Conceptual problems in the design, implementation and evaluation of worksite stress management interventions. *Human Relations, 44,* 717–733.

Rimer, B., Glanz, K., & Rasband, G. (2001). Searching for evidence about health education and health behavior interventions. *Health Education and Behavior, 28*, 231–248.

Saksvik, P., Nytro, K., Dahl-Jorgensen, C., & Mikkelsen, A. (2002). A process evaluation of individual and organizational occupational stress and health interventions. *Work & Stress, 16*(1), 37–57.

Shain, M., & Kramer, D. M. (2004). Health promotion in the workplace: Framing the concept; reviewing the evidence. *Occup Environ Med, 61*(7), 643–648.

Sorensen, G., Stoddard, A., LaMontagne, A., Hunt, M., Emmons, K., Youngstrom, R., et al. (2002). A comprehensive worksite cancer prevention intervention: Behavior change results from a randomised controlled trial in manufacturing worksites. *Cancer Causes and Control, 13*, 493–502.

Thompson, S., Smith, B., & Bybee, R. (2005). Factors influencing participation in worksite wellness programs among minority and underserved populations. *Family & Community Health, 28*(3), 267–273.

Whatmore, L., Cartwright, S., & Cooper, C. (1999). United Kingdom: Evaluation of a stress management programme in the public sector. In M. Kompier & C. Cooper (Eds.), *Preventing stress, improving productivity: European case studies in the workplace.* London: Routledge.

Whitelaw, S., Martin, C., Kerr, A., & Wimbush, E. (2006). An evaluation of the Health Promoting Health Service Framework: The implementation of a settings based approach within the NHS in Scotland. *Health Promotion International, 21*(2), 136–144.

WHO (1946). *World Health Organization Constitution.* Geneva: World Health Organization.

WHO (1984). *Report of the Working Group on Concepts and Principles of Health Promotion.* Copenhagen: World Health Organization (WHO).

WHO (1986). *Ottawa Charter for Health Promotion. Charter for action presented at the first international conference on health promotion.* Ottawa, Canada: World Health Organization (WHO).

WHO (1997). *The Jakarta Declaration on Health Promotion into the 21st Century.* Geneva: World Health Organization (WHO).

Zavela, K., Davis, L., Cottrell, R., & Smith, W. (1988). Do only the healthy intend to participate in worksite health promotion? *Health Education Quarterly, 15*, 259–267.

# 7

# Positive Occupational Health Psychology

## Arnold B. Bakker and Daantje Derks

### CHAPTER OUTLINE

This chapter introduces positive occupational health psychology (POHP). We discuss the negativity bias, and consider why a focus on positive job characteristics, well-being, and positive behaviours is important. After introducing the emerging concept of work engagement, we describe research findings on several POHP-topics, including the design of jobs to do good, job crafting, and positive spillover from work to home. Additionally, we review the first positive interventions in occupational health psychology.

## Introduction

Imagine you are working as a waiter in a restaurant. Today at work you have served many customers who complained about their dish. This is absolutely not your day, and the bad thing about it is that you have had such days regularly during the past few months. Complaining customers mean more (and more difficult) work and less time to talk to your colleagues. You start to wonder whether you should continue with this job, given that work has become rather stressful.

In Chapter 3, Mike O'Driscoll and Paula Brough discussed the wealth of occupational health psychology research that has examined the associations between work organization and health. It is notable that most research has focused on risk factors in the workplace such as high job demands and resulting stress-related diseases (for example, burnout and cardiovascular diseases). In Chapter 4, Raymond Randall and Karina Nielsen similarly observed that the vast majority of intervention research and practice concerns the detection and amelioration of occupational health problems rather than the measurement and reinforcement of positive aspects of work. In this chapter we respond to this situation by advocating an integrated approach which balances attention between positive and negative aspects of work and well-being. Specifically, this chapter is devoted to *positive occupational health psychology* (POHP) and the presentation of insights into optimal functioning at work. If occupational health psychology (OHP) researchers and practitioners wish to improve working conditions, it is not enough to help those who experience stress. The majority of 'normal' employees also need examples and advice to reach a richer and more fulfilling existence (see Seligman & Csikszentmihalyi, 2000). Thus, to return to our restaurant example, waiters may learn to be optimistic through training, and become self-efficacious through the use of positive emotions in customer interactions.

The chapter consists of three parts. In the first part, we discuss the negativity bias in psychology, and the emerging positive psychology approach. We describe why a focus on positive job characteristics, well-being, and positive behaviours is important. In the second part, we give examples of positive occupational health phenomena and research, including work engagement, job resources, psychological capital, positive job design, job crafting, and positive spillover. In the third part, we review positive interventions in occupational health psychology.

## From Negative to Positive
. . . . . . . . . . . . . . . . . . . . . . . . . . . . . . . . . . . . . . . . . . . . . . . . . . . . . . . . . .

*Why is there a negativity bias in psychology?*
*What is Positive Psychology?*
*Why is Positive Occupational Health Psychology important?*

### Negativity bias in psychology

For centuries, the focus in the field of psychology has been on negative aspects in human beings and society at large (Seligman, 2002). Whereas clinical psychologists spent most of their time on the study, diagnosis, and treatment of pathologies, social psychologists focused on illusions, biases, and errors of the human being. In a similar vein, evolutionary psychologists emphasized the selfishness in our battle to survive, and some cultural psychologists have been creative in interpreting helping behaviour as a selfish act    arguing that true altruism does not exist.

In general, people (with or without a background in psychology) are inclined to look at the dark side of life. Moreover, phenomena that are positive at first glance can quite easily be interpreted as negative. For example, when a neighbour offers to help rebuild our house, we may be suspicious and look for hidden motives. We simply seem poor at accepting and appreciating help from others without wondering why they are offering help and what they want from us in return.

It is evident that organizational life has been influenced by this negativity bias as well. Human resource departments and occupational health services try to 'help' sick employees to return quickly to work in order to reduce absence costs; they offer training programmes to fix individual shortcomings. Moreover, if employees lack certain competencies, it may often seem easier to replace them than to invest in tailor-made training programmes. Competent managers who are able to provide constructive and positive feedback are scarce. People often just forget to say positive things or take them for granted. It seems difficult to compliment employees for good work or progression. Being critical is sometimes confused with being negative and discouraging.

However, in the competitive battle between organizations, employee contribution becomes a critical business issue, because in trying to produce more output with less employee input, companies have no choice but to try to engage not only the body but the mind and soul of every employee. Obviously, this goal is not achieved with the prevailing four Ds approach (damage, disease, disorder, and dysfunction) that focuses on preventing poor performance, low motivation, unwell-being, ill-health, and disengagement (Bakker & Schaufeli, 2008). Additionally, employees' expectations of their job have changed as well. The best employers are no longer those that promise lifetime employment and a good retirement fund, but rather those that provide their employees with opportunities, resources, and flexibility for sustainable growth (Luthans, Youssef, & Avolio, 2007).

## Origin of the negative

What is the origin of the negativity bias? Why are positive emotions neglected relative to negative emotions? First, and perhaps most important, there are evolutionary reasons. The evolutionary value of negative emotions is clear and well known. But until recently it was not clear how positive emotions fit in. Negative emotions lead to immediate action: anger creates the urge to attack, and fear the urge to escape. These urges indicate physiological readiness of the body that enables the individual to act immediately. Negative emotions have adaptive value in that they narrow our thought-action repertoire to those that best promoted our ancestor's survival in life-threatening situations (Fredrickson, 2003). In other words, these repertoires are 'programmed' in our brain to recurrent problems that our ancestors faced. This all occurs automatically and unconsciously.

Second, it is important to note that there are more negative emotions than positive emotions. Consider, for example, the six cross-culturally identified facial expressions resembling basic emotions (Ekman, 1973; Ekman, Friesen, & Ellsworth, 1982). These 'Big 6' are: anger, disgust, fear, joy, sadness, and surprise. The balance between good and bad is on the negative side. Also, the names and words people use to describe negative emotions exceed the ones for positive emotions. This indicates that negative emotions are more salient in society than positive ones. It should of course be noted that negative emotions signal potentially severe problems for individuals and society. These problems may range from depression, violence, eating disorders, and phobias, to stress-related physical disorders (Fredrickson, 2004). In contrast, positive emotions do not so easily generate societal problems, and the positive problems that do exist (e.g., excessive mania) have lower priority in the research field.

The context of positive emotions is generally speaking not a life-threatening one. The facial expressions and urges to act are not that specific or obviously relevant to survival. The question that remained unanswered for a long time is: if positive emotions do not directly contribute to the survival of our ancestors, why do they exist at all? Barbara Fredrickson is a pioneer in the field of positive psychology who has outlined the value of positive emotions using her *broaden-and-build theory* (Fredrickson, 2001). She argues that positive emotions solve problems concerning personal growth and development. The broaden-and-build theory states that positive emotions broaden an individual's momentary mindset, and by doing so help to bring about enduring personal resources (Fredrickson, 2003). It is important to note that personal resources acquired during this process are enduring and long lasting. Through experiencing positive emotions like joy, gratitude, and hope, people become more resilient, creative, knowledgeable, socially integrated, healthy individuals (Fredrickson, 2001). One step ahead is the *undoing hypothesis* which states that positive emotions are not only capable of helping people deal with negative emotions and reducing the resonance of a particular unpleasant event by placing it in a broader context, but also may 'correct' or 'undo' the after effects of negative emotions. See Research Close-Up 7.1 for a detailed description of the experimental research Barbara Fredrickson conducted on this topic.

---

**RESEARCH CLOSE-UP        7.1        An Experimental Test of the Undoing Hypothesis**

*Source:* Fredrickson, B. L., Mancuso, R. A., Branigan, C., & Tugade, M. M. (2000). The undoing effect of positive emotions. *Motivation and Emotion, 24,* 237–258.

### Introduction

Fredrickson (1998) argued in her broaden-and-build theory that positive emotions may promote survival in the long run by building resources that can be drawn on when coping with inevitable threats in the future. Whereas negative emotions narrow thought-action repertoires, positive emotions do the opposite. They broaden thought-action repertoires leading to a wider range of thoughts and actions than is typical (e.g., play, explore). The *undoing hypothesis* (Fredrickson & Levenson, 1998) states that positive

Research Close-Up 7.1 *(Cont'd)*

emotions may undo or correct the after effects of negative emotions. In other words, positive emotions can promote cardiovascular recovery and down-regulate lingering negative emotions and the psychological and physiological preparation for specific action that they generate (Fredrickson, Mancuso, Branigan, & Tugade, 2000). The researchers set up an experiment to test whether positive emotions can speed recovery from the cardiovascular reactivity that remains after experiencing a negative emotion.

## Method

*Participants*

The sample included 95 university students (50% women) recruited for a study on emotions. 71 were European American and 24 were African American.

*Design and procedure*

Participants were given 60 seconds to prepare a 3-minute speech on 'why you are a good friend'. They were also told that there was a 50% chance that 'the computer' would select them as the lucky one to deliver their speech. If so, a 3-minute timer would appear on the video monitor, cueing them to look straight into the camera and begin their speech, speaking loud and clear. The taped speeches would later be shown to and evaluated by students in another study. If 'by chance' they were not selected, a video clip would start on the monitor. Here the manipulation started. Two film clips elicited two distinct positive emotions. 'Waves' showed ocean waves breaking on the beach, which elicited contentment. 'Puppy' showed a small dog playing with a flower, which elicited amusement. 'Cry' showed a young boy crying over the death of his father, triggering sadness. Finally, 'Sticks' showed an abstract dynamic display of coloured sticks, which elicited virtually no emotion (control condition). The film was followed by a blank screen for 3 minutes. The participants were videotaped during the entire experiment and their bodily reactions were monitored using physiological sensors. The duration of cardiovascular reactivity was measured as the time elapsed (in seconds) from the start of the film clip until the cardiovascular arousal on each measure returned to the defined baseline for that participant.

## Results

As predicted, both positive emotion groups exhibited faster recovery than the sadness group and the neutral group. The difference between contentment and amusement was not significant.

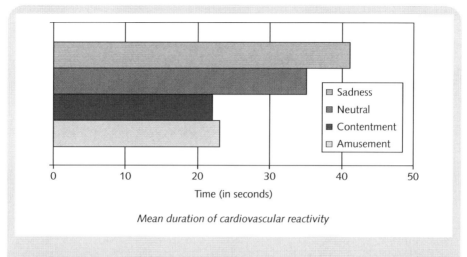

Time (in seconds)

*Mean duration of cardiovascular reactivity*

## Discussion

These findings support the undoing hypothesis for two distinct types of positive emotions: a low activation pleasant state of contentment and a higher activation pleasant state of amusement. These positive emotions – although distinct in their phenomenology and activation level – share the ability to regulate lingering negative emotional arousal that can be health damaging.

## Positive psychology

Positive psychology emerged in the late 1990s with a renewed emphasis on what is right with people in contrast to the preoccupation psychology has had over the years with what is wrong with people (Seligman & Csikszentmihalyi, 2000; Snyder & Lopez, 2002). This approach rehabilitated the focus on positivity and people's strengths and virtues (Peterson & Seligman, 2004), and was specifically initiated by Martin Seligman's presidential address at the American Psychological Association in 1998 (Seligman, 1998a).

Positive psychology is an attempt to adopt a more open and appreciative per-spective regarding human potentials, motives, and capacities (Sheldon & King, 2001). Positive psychology and organizational theory merge in the new approach of positive organizational behaviour (POB) defined as 'the study and application of positively oriented human resource strengths and psychological capacities that can be measured, developed, and effectively managed for performance improvement in today's workplace' (Luthans, 2002, p. 59; see also Bakker & Schaufeli, 2008; Cooper & Nelson, 2006; Wright, 2003). For psychological capacities and strengths to be included in this concept they have to meet certain criteria. Specifically, they must be positive and relatively unique to the field of organizational behaviour, they must be theory- and research-based, measurable, state-like or developmental, and related to work performance outcomes (Luthans, Youssef, & Avolio, 2007).

Typically, POB involves the study of individual positive psychological conditions and human resource strengths that are – in one way or another – related to employee well-being or performance improvement. Research may focus, for example, on the cognitive capacities of creativity and wisdom, and the affective capacities of work engagement and humor in the workplace. POB studies also examine the role of states like self-efficacy, optimism, hope, resilience, and other personal resources utilized in coping with organizational demands or in fostering performance. Further, POB researchers are interested in peak performance in organizations (like work-related flow), and examine the conditions under which employees thrive.

Researchers who simultaneously started the *Positive Organizational Scholarship* (POS) movement have provided a conceptual framework for organizing and integrating their research on positive organizations (Cameron, Dutton & Quinn, 2003). POS is defined as:

> the study of that which is positive, flourishing, and life-giving in organizations. Positive refers to the elevating processes and outcomes in organizations. Organizational refers to the interpersonal and structural dynamics activated in and through organizations, specifically taking into account the context in which positive phenomena occur. Scholarship refers to the scientific, theoretically derived, and rigorous investigation of that which is positive in organizational settings. (Cameron & Caza, 2004, p. 731)

Similar to POB, but different from positive psychology, the primary emphasis of POS is on the workplace and on the accomplishment of work-related outcomes. Although partly overlapping, POB is primarily concerned with individual psychological states and human strengths that influence employee performance (Luthans, 2002), whereas POS is primarily concerned with the positive aspects of the organizational context that influence employees' ability to thrive (Cameron, 2005).

Positive Occupational Health Psychology (POHP) includes both approaches – POB and POS – and has its own specific emphasis. Occupational health and well-being are central to the POHP approach, but of course, researchers and organizations are simultaneously interested in causes of occupational health (e.g., job design) and possible consequences (e.g., performance). Important is that the focus is – again – on the positive side of work life, and not limited to the negative side (e.g., risk factors, job demands, burnout). The original definition of OHP proposed by the US National Institute of Occupational Safety and Health (NIOSH) captures the field rather well; accordingly, OHP concerns 'the application of psychology to improving the quality of work life, and to protecting and promoting the safety, health, and well-being of workers' (Schaufeli, 2004, p. 503). Although this definition focuses on the positive side of OHP by mentioning quality of work life, and the promotion of safety, health and well-being, research has typically followed the four Ds approach instead. This approach examines

damage, disease, disorder, and dysfunction and focuses on preventing poor performance, low motivation, impaired well-being, ill-health, and disengagement.
According to Bakker and Schaufeli (2008), OHP needs a radical shift away from
the four Ds. A focus on POHP illuminates how work contexts (such as jobs, units,
work groups, professions, and organizations) affect, and are affected by positive
relationships, positive emotions, and positive meanings (see Fredrickson & Dutton,
2008). In sum, POHP is the study and application of optimal functioning in the
workplace. It promotes occupational health and flourishing, and examines how
positive phenomena (contexts, personal resources) can be used to protect against
occupational risks.

## Usefulness of the positive

Failing to recognize the positive aspects of work is neglectful, and as Turner,
Barling, and Zachartos (2002, p. 715) have argued 'it is time to extend our
research focus and explore more fully the positive sides, so as to gain full
understanding of the meaning and effects of working.' However, in order to
make a substantive contribution to organizational science, POHP will need to
show the added value of the positive over and above the negative. Moreover, we
agree with Tetrick (2002), who convincingly argued that it is very unlikely that
the same mechanisms that underlie employee ill-health and malfunctioning
constitute employee health and optimal functioning. Hence, POHP may contribute by supplementing the traditional negative model with a distinct wellness
model that focuses on the positive. By not exclusively focusing on the positive
side but by taking a more comprehensive perspective that includes positive *as
well as* negative aspects, criticisms of positive psychology's one-sided positivity
bias and its separating positive from negative experiences and emotions are
counteracted (Fineman, 2006).

A ground-breaking study making this point in an organizational setting is
Fredrickson and Losada's (2005) study among business teams. They empirically
demonstrated that positive communication and expressions of support among
team members distinguished flourishing teams over languishing teams. Specifically,
in their observational research with sixty management teams, the authors identified fifteen teams that clearly produced better results (as indicated by profitability;
customer satisfaction; and 360-degree evaluations by superiors, peers, and subordinates) based upon their speech acts. Positive speech was coded for encouragement, support, and appreciation, while negative speech was coded for disapproval,
cynicism, and sarcasm. Sixteen teams with mixed verbal interactions had average
performance, while nineteen teams with negative verbal interactions showed
inferior performance. Moreover, results showed that the successful teams exhibited
verbalization of more positive affect and a wider range of ideas and initiatives,
while teams with average or no success were more constrained in range of affect
and ideas. The poorest performing teams where tightly bounded, uncreative and
generally negative in outlook. In conclusion, this study illustrates how positive

organizational behaviour can outweigh negative behaviour. Such a theoretical approach clearly adds to our overall knowledge regarding organizational behaviour and its outcomes.

Meanwhile, recent studies in the organizational and occupational (health) psychology domain have convincingly shown that positive organizational phenomena can make a unique contribution to explaining organizational outcomes over and above negative ones. In the second part of this chapter, we will discuss several of these POHP studies.

## Summary

The focus of psychology has long been on the negative aspects of life. Broaden-and-build theory posits that positive emotions play a central role in people's lives because such emotions contribute to personal growth and development. Positive Occupational Health Psychology is the study and application of optimal functioning in the workplace. It promotes occupational health and flourishing, and examines how positive phenomena (contexts, personal resources) can be used to protect against occupational risks.

## Examples of Positive Occupational Health Psychology

*What is work engagement?*
*What roles do job resources have?*
*Which components of psychological capital can be distinguished?*
*What is job crafting, and why is it important?*

### From burnout to engagement

Ironically, it is research on burnout that stimulated most contemporary research on work engagement. In contrast to those who suffer from burnout, engaged employees have a sense of energetic and effective connection with their work, and instead of stressful and demanding they look upon their work as challenging. Two different but related schools of thought exist that consider work engagement as a positive, work-related state of well-being or fulfilment. According to Maslach and Leiter (1997), engagement is characterized by energy, involvement, and efficacy – the direct opposite of the three burnout dimensions. They argue that in the case of burnout energy turns into exhaustion, involvement into cynicism, and efficacy into ineffectiveness. By implication, engagement is assessed by the opposite pattern of scores on the three dimensions of the Maslach Burnout Inventory (MBI; Maslach, Jackson, & Leiter, 1996): low scores on exhaustion and cynicism, and high scores on professional efficacy.

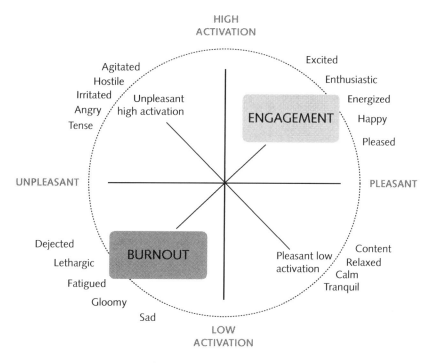

**Figure 7.1** Burnout versus work engagement (adapted from Russell & Carroll, 1999).

The alternative view considers work engagement as an independent, distinct concept that is negatively related to burnout. Consequently, work engagement is defined and operationalized in its own right as 'a positive, fulfilling, work-related state of mind that is characterized by vigour, dedication, and absorption' (Schaufeli, Salanova, González-Romá, & Bakker, 2002, p. 74; see also Schaufeli & Bakker, 2010). That is, in engagement, fulfilment exists in contrast to the voids of life that leave people feeling empty as in burnout. Vigour is characterized by high levels of energy and mental resilience while working, the willingness to invest effort in one's work, and persistence even in the face of difficulties. Dedication refers to being strongly involved in one's work, and experiencing a sense of significance, enthusiasm, inspiration, pride, and challenge. Absorption is characterized by being fully concentrated and happily engrossed in one's work, whereby time passes quickly and one has difficulties with detaching oneself from work. See Figure 7.1 for a graphical display of the conceptualization of burnout and work engagement in a circumplex of emotions (Russell & Carroll, 1999).

Accordingly, vigour and dedication are considered direct opposites of exhaustion and cynicism, respectively, the two core symptoms of burnout. The continuum that is spanned by exhaustion and vigour has been labelled 'energy', whereas the continuum that is spanned by cynicism and dedication has been labelled 'identification' (González-Romá, Schaufeli, Bakker, & Lloret, 2006). Hence, work engagement is characterized by a high level of energy and strong identification with one's work, whereas burnout is characterized by the opposite: a low level of energy and poor identification with one's work (see also Demerouti & Bakker, 2008). In addition, based on in-depth interviews (Schaufeli et al., 2001), absorption was identified and included as the third constituting aspect of work engagement.

Various studies have demonstrated associations of employee engagement with meaningful organizational outcomes such as in- and extra-role behaviour (Halbesleben & Wheeler, 2008), intention to leave and organizational commitment (Schaufeli & Bakker, 2004), financial turnover at the end of the work shift (Xanthopoulou, Bakker, Demerouti, & Schaufeli, 2009b), reduced sickness absenteeism (Schaufeli, Bakker, & Van Rhenen, 2009), and service quality as rated by customers (Salanova, Agut, & Pieró, 2005). In conclusion, studies on employee engagement add to our understanding of positive organizational processes – also vis-à-vis negative processes – and show the relevance of the concept for organizational outcomes. As such, employee engagement is a promising new avenue for future POHP research (see also, Bakker & Demerouti, 2008; Bakker, Schaufeli, Leiter, & Taris, 2008).

### Pioneer    Wilmar B. Schaufeli

Wilmar B. Schaufeli (1953–), a pioneer in burnout and engagement research, received his Bachelor and Master degrees in Clinical Psychology at the University of Groningen, The Netherlands. In 1988 he received his PhD on the psychological consequences of unemployment, *cum laude* from that same university. From 1989 to 1994 he worked as assistant and associate professor at Radboud University Nijmegen and was then appointed full-professor of Clinical and Organizational Psychology at Utrecht University. Schaufeli is visiting professor at Jaume I University in Castellón de la Plana, Spain (since 2002), and at Loughborough University Business School (since 2004). He received the Work Wellness Award from North West University, South Africa. His extensive research on burnout formed the basis for research on work engagement. Schaufeli has published more than 300 journal articles and book chapters. Together with Arnold Bakker, he defined work engagement as a positive, fulfilling, affective-motivational state of work-related well-being that is the opposite of job burnout. Based on this conceptualization, the Utrecht Work Engagement Scale (UWES) was developed that includes three interrelated dimensions: vigour, dedication, and absorption. The UWES is used worldwide and has stimulated engagement research in over 30 countries.

## Job demands and resources

Recent POHP-studies have started to investigate how the *combination* of stressful and motivating job characteristics influences negative and positive aspects of well-being. According to the Job Demands–Resources (JDR) model (Bakker & Demerouti, 2007) working conditions can be classified in two general categories (i.e., job demands and job resources) that are applicable to virtually all occupations. Job demands require effort and are therefore associated with physiological and psychological costs, such as fatigue, whereas job resources foster personal growth, learning, development, and have motivational qualities. Bakker, Demerouti, and Euwema (2005), in their study among about 1,000 Dutch college teachers, found that job resources buffered the impact of job demands on burnout (exhaustion and cynicism). Specifically, they found that job demands such as work overload, emotional demands, and physical demands did *not* result in high levels of burnout if employees experienced job resources, such as autonomy, performance feedback, social support, or coaching from their supervisor.

Xanthopoulou et al. (2007) reported similar findings in a study among employees from two homecare organizations. The findings revealed, for example, that patient harassment interacted with autonomy and support (both job resources) in predicting exhaustion; and with autonomy, support, and professional development in predicting cynicism. Autonomy proved to be the most important buffer of job demands for both burnout dimensions, followed by support and opportunities for professional development. Conditions where job demands were high and job resources were low resulted in the highest levels of burnout (exhaustion and cynicism). Put differently, in cases where the levels of job resources were high, the effect of job demands on the core dimensions of burnout was significantly reduced. To illustrate, Figure 7.2 displays the interaction between job demands and job resources and well-being.

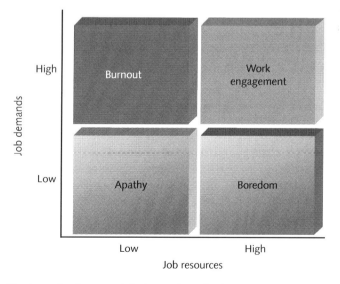

**Figure 7.2** The interplay between job demands and job resources.

What is the role of job resources in this burnout process? Job resources are assumed to play either an intrinsic motivational role because they foster employees' growth, learning, and development, or an extrinsic motivational role because they are instrumental in achieving work goals. In the former case, job resources fulfil basic human needs, such as the needs for autonomy, relatedness, and competence (Deci & Ryan, 1985). For instance, proper feedback fosters learning, thereby increasing job competence, whereas decision latitude and social support satisfy the need for autonomy and the need to belong, respectively.

Job resources may also play an *extrinsic* motivational role, because resourceful work environments foster the willingness to dedicate one's efforts and abilities to the work task (Meijman & Mulder, 1998). In such environments it is likely that the task will be completed successfully and that the work goal will be attained. For instance, supportive colleagues and performance feedback increase the likelihood of being successful in achieving one's work goals. In either case, be it through the satisfaction of basic needs or through the achievement of work goals, the outcome is positive and engagement is likely to occur (Schaufeli & Bakker, 2004).

### Salience of job resources

According to conservation of resources (COR) theory (Hobfoll, 2001), people seek to obtain, retain, and protect things they value, including, for instance, material, social, personal, or energetic resources. The theory proposes that stress experienced by individuals can be understood in relation to potential or actual loss of resources. More specifically, Hobfoll and Shirom (2000) have argued that: (1) individuals must bring in resources in order to prevent the loss of resources, (2) individuals with a greater pool of resources are less susceptible to resource loss, (3) those individuals who do not have access to strong resource pools are more likely to experience increased loss ('loss spiral'), and (4) strong resource pools lead to a greater likelihood that individuals will seek opportunities to risk resources for increased resource gains ('gain spiral'). Additionally, Hobfoll (2002) argues that resource gain acquires its saliency in the context of resource loss. This suggests that job resources become more salient and gain their motivational potential when employees are confronted with high job demands (e.g., workload, emotional demands, and mental demands) because they can help goal accomplishment.

Hakanen, Bakker, and Demerouti (2005) tested this interaction hypothesis in a sample of Finnish dentists employed in the public sector. It was hypothesized that job resources (e.g., variability in required professional skills, peer contacts) are most beneficial in maintaining work engagement under conditions of high job demands (e.g., workload, unfavourable physical environment). The dentists were split in two random groups in order to cross-validate the findings. A set of hierarchical regression analyses resulted in seventeen out of forty significant inter-actions (40%), showing, for example, that variability in professional skills boosted work engagement when qualitative workload was high, and mitigated the negative effect of qualitative workload on work engagement.

Conceptually similar findings have been reported by Bakker, Hakanen, Demerouti, and Xanthopoulou (2007). In their study among Finnish teachers working in elementary, secondary, and vocational schools, they found that job resources act as buffers and diminish the negative relationship between pupil misbehaviour, representing a demanding aspect of work and work engagement. In addition, they found that job resources particularly influenced work engagement when teachers were confronted with high levels of pupil misconduct. A series of moderated structural equation modeling analyses resulted in fourteen out of eighteen possible two-way interaction effects (78%). In particular, supervisor support, innovativeness, appreciation, and organizational climate were important job resources for teachers that helped them cope with demanding interactions with students. Again, these studies shed light on the fascinating interplay between positive and negative characteristics of the work environment (see Figure 7.2).

## Designing jobs to do good

Yet another interesting example of POHP is recent work on how organizations can design jobs that allow employees to make positive contributions to the lives of others, and also to connect with those who benefit from their work. Grant (2007, 2008) argued that in addition to individual differences (e.g., agreeableness, empathy, interpersonal concern, and altruistic personality), contextual forces and situational cues could have a powerful influence on the motivation to do good. An understanding of how work contexts can fulfil and strengthen the motivation to do good is important since the research evidence shows that the motivation to do good can promote behaviours that benefit other people and the organization at large, such as task commitment, effort, persistence, and helping behaviour (Grant, 2007). Additionally, the motivation to do good can benefit the self by promoting increased satisfaction (Lyubomirsky, Sheldon, & Schkade, 2005) and improved health and longevity (Brown, Nesse, Vinokur, & Smith, 2003).

Grant (2008) conducted three studies. In Study 1, he developed a self-report survey that assessed six dimensions of prosocial job characteristics, suitable either for reporting on beneficiaries in general or the specific beneficiaries of a given occupation (e.g., 'guests' for lifeguards, 'citizens' for police officers). The results of confirmatory factor analyses showed that the prosocial job characteristics scale has good psychometric properties. The findings show that it is possible to distinguish job opportunities for impact on beneficiaries (magnitude, frequency, and scope), and job opportunities for contact with beneficiaries (frequency, breadth, and depth). In Study 2, Grant used structural modeling to test the hypothesis that prosocial job characteristics predict a variety of other-focused psychological states, including employees' perceived impact on beneficiaries, their affective commitment to beneficiaries, as well as their prosocial motivation. Finally, in Study 3, he used a multitrait-multimethod approach with job incumbents and observers as sources of information to provide more rigorous evidence for the validity of this new conceptualization of job design. In developing and validating this new

### Pioneer    Deo J. W. Strümpfer

Deo J. W. Strümpfer (1928–), a pioneer in positive occupational health psychology, is Professor Extraordinary of Psychology, University of Pretoria and Professor Emeritus of Industrial and Organizational Psychology, University of Cape Town, South Africa. He received his Masters degree in Psychology at the University of Potchefstroom, South Africa, and received his PhD in 1959 from Purdue University, West Lafayette, Indiana, USA. He taught at the universities of Potchefstroom (11 years), Port Elizabeth (12 years), Witwatersrand (5 years), and Cape Town (11 years). Strümpfer had visiting posts at the universities of Regina (Canada), Ben Gurion (Israel), and Western Cape. He is one of the scholars who examined the origins of health in the workplace, by following the perspectives of *fortigenesis* and *salutogenesis*. These perspectives focus on factors that support human health and well-being rather than on factors that cause disease (pathogenesis). The terms salutogenesis and fortigenesis come from the Latin *salus* = health and *fortis* = strength, and the Greek *genesis* = origin. Strümpfer's research has focused on flourishing and the role of resilience in coping with organizational stressors.

measure, Grant paved the way for future investigators to discover how organizations might better design jobs to unleash or create employees' motivations to do good, which can both energize the process of work and contribute to individual and group flourishing (Fredrickson & Dutton, 2008).

### Psychological capital

Work and how it is carried out in organizations is fundamentally about relationships between the organization and the customer, but also about relationships between organizations and employees (Larson & Luthans, 2006). People make the difference, and therefore it is important to focus on people's self-beliefs. Luthans and colleagues define *psychological capital* (PsyCap) as 'an individual's positive psychological state of development that is characterized by: (1) having confidence (self-efficacy) to take on and put in the necessary effort to succeed at challenging tasks; (2) making a positive attribution (optimism) about succeeding now and in the future; (3) persevering toward goals and, when necessary, redirecting paths to goals (hope) in order to succeed; and (4) when beset by problems and adversity, sustaining and bouncing back and even beyond (resiliency) to attain success' (Luthans, Youssef, & Avolio, 2007, p. 3). They believe that these four core constructs are keys to higher performance. Table 7.1 presents a definition of the four PsyCap components.

One of the inclusion criteria of positive psychological constructs, including Psychological Capital, is that it can be effectively managed for performance

**Table 7.1** The four components of PsyCap

| PsyCap variables | Definition | Development |
| --- | --- | --- |
| Self-efficacy | Individuals' confidence about their abilities to mobilize the motivation, cognitive resources, and courses of action needed to successfully execute a specific task within a given context (Stajkovic & Luthans, 1998) | E.g., Enactive mastery, vicarious learning, verbal persuasion |
| Hope | A cognitive set that is based on a reciprocally derived sense of successful agency and pathways (Snyder et al., 1991) | E.g., Setting personally valuable, realistic goals, defining sub-goals, creating multiple ways to achieve goals and to work around obstacles |
| Optimism | An attributional style that explains positive events as personal, permanent, and pervasive and negative events as external, temporary, and situation-specific (Seligman, 1998b) | E.g., ABCDE approach. Identify Adversity, recognize self-defeating Beliefs, realize the Consequences of these beliefs, Dispute counter-productive beliefs, and Experience the Energy |
| Resilience | One's ability, when faced with adversity, to rebound or 'bounce back' from a setback or failure (Block & Kremen, 1996) | E.g., Provide support to recover from adversity, thrive when faced with positive change |

improvement. However, the scope of studies measuring the impact of PsyCap on job performance is still very small. Luthans, Avolio, Avey, and Norman (2007) conducted a study to test the hypothesis that an employees' level of PsyCap is positively related to their performance and job satisfaction. The sample consisted of employees of both service and technology manufacturing companies. To measure performance they used actual performance evaluations based on objective data and managerial ratings. Results showed that PsyCap had a positive relationship with both performance and job satisfaction. Furthermore, overall PsyCap showed stronger results for both satisfaction and performance than each of the four individual components, providing evidence for PsyCap as a higher-order construct (Luthans et al., 2007).

Luthans, Norman, Avolio and Avey (2008) examined whether PsyCap can mediate the relationship between supportive organizational climate and performance. They defined supportive organizational climate as 'the overall amount of perceived support employees receive from their immediate peers, other departments and their supervisor that they view as helping them to successfully perform their work' (Luthans et al., 2008, p. 225). This can, in the light of the Job Demands-Resources model (Bakker & Demerouti, 2007), also be interpreted as providing extra job resources in the capacity of social support. Luthans and colleagues hypothesized a positive relationship between PsyCap and performance.

Additionally, they expected that PsyCap would fully mediate the relationship between supportive organizational climate and performance. They used two separate samples to test these hypotheses: one student sample with self-reports of performance and an employee sample with objective measures of performance based on figures and managerial ratings. The results showed a positive relationship between PsyCap and performance in both samples. Additionally, Luthans et al. found initial evidence for a full mediation of PsyCap in the supportive organizational climate and employee performance relationship.

Xanthopoulou and her colleagues examined *daily* PsyCap. In their diary study among flight attendants, Xanthopoulou, Bakker, Heuven, Demerouti, and Schaufeli (2008) examined whether daily fluctuations in colleague support predicted day-levels of job performance through self-efficacy (one PsyCap component) and work engagement. Forty-four flight attendants filled in a questionnaire and a diary booklet before and after consecutive flights to three intercontinental destinations. Results of multi-level analyses revealed that both colleague support and self-efficacy had an indirect effect on in-role performance through work engagement.

In a similar vein, Xanthopoulou, Bakker, Demerouti, and Schaufeli (2009b) investigated how daily fluctuations in job resources (i.e., autonomy, coaching, and team climate) were related to daily changes in employee's self-efficacy, self-esteem, and optimism (i.e., daily PsyCap; they call this personal resources), work engagement, and company financial returns. Forty-two employees working in three branches of a fast food company completed a questionnaire and a diary booklet over five consecutive workdays. Consistent with hypotheses, multi-level analyses revealed that day-level job resources had an effect on work engagement through day-level PsyCap, after controlling for general levels of personal resources and engagement (Figure 7.3). Day-level work engagement, in turn, had a positive relationship with daily financial returns. Additionally, previous days' coaching had a positive, lagged effect on following days' work engagement (through following days' optimism), and on following days' financial returns. Thus, when supervisors communicated to their subordinates how well they performed on their assigned tasks, and suggested better ways for doing so, employees' optimism was boosted, and consequently they were likely to become more engaged and productive.

Taken together, these studies show that psychological capital is positively related to performance. People make the difference, particularly when they are self-efficacious, optimistic, hopeful, and resilient.

## Job crafting

Many studies in the field of OHP assume that working conditions can have a major impact on employees. However, employees are not necessarily passive recipients but may influence their own work environment. Employees may actively change the design of their jobs by choosing tasks, negotiating different job content, and assigning meaning to their tasks or jobs (Parker & Ohly, 2008). This process of employees shaping their jobs has been referred to as job crafting (Wrzesniewski &

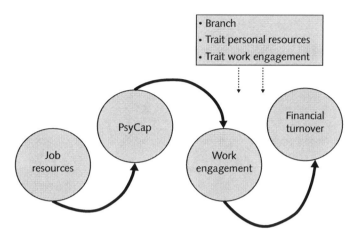

**Figure 7.3**   Psychological Capital (PsyCap) at work (see Xanthopoulou et al., 2009b).

Dutton, 2001). It is defined as the physical and cognitive changes individuals make in the task or relational boundaries. Physical changes refer to changes in the form, scope or number of job tasks, whereas cognitive changes refer to changing how one sees the job. Changing relational boundaries means that individuals have discretion over whom they interact with while doing the job. As a consequence of job crafting people may be able to increase their person-job fit.

Wrzesniewski, McCauley, Rozin, and Schwartz (1997) suggest that employees who view their work as a calling are more likely to engage in job crafting because work is more central in their lives. There is indeed some research showing that engaged employees are the most active job crafters. For example, Hakanen, Perhoniemi, and Toppinen-Tanner (2008) conducted a two-wave 3-year panel study among 2,555 Finnish dentists to examine the effect of work engagement on personal initiative and job resources. Among other things, their results showed that work engagement had a positive impact on personal initiative and job resources. Thus, engaged workers are more inclined to tailor their jobs in line with their needs than non-engaged workers.

Xanthopoulou, Bakker, Demerouti, and Schaufeli (2009a) carried out a two-wave longitudinal study among 163 employees with a 2-year time interval. It was hypothesized that job and personal resources, and work engagement, are reciprocal over time. Indeed, results showed that resources and work engagement are mutually related. Thus, personal resources (i.e., self-efficacy, self-esteem, and optimism) and job resources (i.e., job autonomy, supervisory coaching, performance feedback, and opportunities for professional development) had a positive influence on work engagement. Work engagement, in turn, had a positive impact on personal and job resources. All effects (causal and reversed-causal) were equally strong. These findings support the notion that engaged employees' successfully adapt their work environment.

As a final example, Bakker and Bal (in press) tested a model of *weekly* work engagement. Teachers were asked to fill in a weekly questionnaire every Friday during five consecutive weeks. Results largely confirmed the hypotheses, by showing that week-levels of autonomy, exchange with the supervisor, and opportunities for development (but not social support) were positively related to weekly engagement, which, in turn, was positively related to weekly job performance. Moreover, momentary work engagement was positively related to job resources in the subsequent week. These findings show how intra-individual variability in employees' engagement can predict weekly changes in job characteristics.

---

### RESEARCH CLOSE-UP 7.2 A Diary Study on Recovery, Work Engagement, and Proactive Behaviour

*Source:* Sonnentag, S. (2003). Recovery, work engagement, and proactive behaviour: A new look at the interface between nonwork and work. *Journal of Applied Psychology, 88*, 518–528.

#### Introduction

How one feels and behaves at work is affected by life outside work. Research has shown that periods of rest from work are important for maintaining well-being at work, decreased work stress, and burnout (e.g., Eden, 2001; Westman & Etzion; 2001). Sonnentag (2003) argues that because the effects of vacations fade quickly, people may need additional opportunities for recovery in the evening after a normal working day. Recovery attained during leisure time in the evening has an effect on how individuals experience the subsequent workday, and is crucial for work engagement. Work engagement is highly relevant for employee well-being and affects work behaviour in a positive way (e.g., Demerouti, Bakker, de Jonge, Janssen, & Schaufeli, 2001). Work engagement can fluctuate on a daily level (Kahn, 1990) and is expected to affect proactive behaviour at work.

#### Method

*Participants*
147 employees of six public service organizations returned questionnaires and daily surveys. Sixty-five per cent of the respondents were men, 35% were women. Average age was 39 years.

*Design and procedure*
The study was based on a within-subjects design and examined whether recovery during leisure time on a specific day had an impact on work engagement and proactive behaviour on the subsequent workday. The daily survey measured day-level recovery, work engagement, and proactive behaviour (pursuit of learning and personal initiative). Participants responded to the daily survey on five subsequent workdays. Each day started with a section to be filled out in the morning, at the beginning of the workday, and a section at the end of the workday.

## Results

The effects of recovery on work engagement and proactive behaviour were analysed with multi-level models. Results showed that day-level recovery contributed significantly to the prediction of day-level work engagement, independent of the level of general ('trait') work engagement. Sonnentag also found evidence for day-level work engagement as a mediator in the relationship between day-level recovery and day-level proactive behaviour (both personal initiative and pursuit learning).

## Discussion

This study shows that recovery has a positive effect on work engagement and proactive behaviour, with work engagement serving the role of mediator in this relationship. Employees who have recovered sufficiently during evening hours after work experience more work engagement on the next workday. This increase in work engagement, in turn, helps them in taking initiative and pursuing learning goals. These findings illustrate that people benefit from short rest periods that occur in the evening after work. In conclusion, it seems that daily recovery from work-related stress is helpful to supplement the effect of vacations.

## Positive spillover

Research in the work-family interface domain has focused almost exclusively on the negative impact of work on the home situation. However, several scholars have argued that workers may also benefit from combining 'work' and 'family' and that these benefits may outweigh the costs (e.g., Hochschild, 1997; Kirchmeyer, 1993). Positive spillover refers to a process whereby experience or participation in one role increases quality or performance in the other role. Work-family enrichment occurs when involvement in work provides benefits such as skill growth, which has a positive effect on the family. Family-work enrichment occurs when involvement within the family results in the creation of a positive mood, feeling of support, or feeling of success, which can help that individual to function more efficiently and confidently at work.

There is, indeed, ample empirical evidence for this positive spillover process. For example, Crosby (1982) found that married employed women with children were more satisfied with their jobs than single employed women or married employed women without children. In addition, Barnett's (1998) review shows that full-time workers experience better health than their reduced-hours counterparts. In a classic longitudinal study, Moen, Dempster-McClain, and Williams (1992) showed that occupying multiple roles in 1956, participating in volunteer work on an intermittent basis, and belonging to a club or organization were positively related to various measures of health in 1986. In addition, a longitudinal study in the United States showed that white married women who decreased their labor force participation from full-time to low part-time or homemaker reported a significant increase in distress symptoms over a 3-year period (Wethington & Kessler, 1989). Conversely, those women who increased their labor force participation from homemaker or part-time worker to full-time worker reported a significant decrease in emotional distress (see also Barnett & Gareis, 2000; Herold & Waldron, 1985; Verbrugge, 1989).

## Summary

Several examples of POHP have been demonstrated in recent studies. The research evidence shows that it makes sense to focus on work engagement, and to supplement the focus on job demands, with a focus on job resources. Additionally, recent POHP studies have focused on positive job design, psychological capital, job crafting, and positive spillover from work to the home domain.

## Positive Interventions

*What is a micro intervention?*
*What is a macro intervention?*
*What are the benefits of positive interventions?*

By 'positive interventions' we mean interventions that meet the criteria of positive organizational behaviour (Luthans, 2002). Interventions are positive if they are open to development and change (i.e., state-like as opposed to fixed and trait-like), measurable, and if there is a strong link with performance improvement. It is useful to make a distinction between different levels of impact of an intervention. Micro interventions are usually interventions on the individual level that have relatively little impact on daily organizational life: a short training session, for example. However, this does not automatically imply that they cannot have long lasting, positive consequences. Interventions on the macro level can involve a whole organization or employment sector.

Leiter and Maslach (2010) argue that there are clear benefits to be yielded by the use of a positive framework. One is motivational, in that people are often more enthusiastic about working to make things better, rather than having to deal with unpleasant problems. Further, they argue that an organization that is focused on engaging its employees, and becoming a workplace of choice, may have a more positive image than one that is grappling with burnout. Indeed, many organizations have found that a focus on burnout poses a liability for them, and so they have avoided acknowledging that there may be problems or that they are undertaking any efforts to deal with it. The opportunity to address these issues by focusing on the positive goal of work engagement provides organizations with a less risky, and potentially more successful, process of change (Leiter & Maslach, 2010).

## Micro interventions

Luthans and his colleagues developed a micro-intervention to develop psychological capital (Luthans, Avey, Avolio, Norman, & Combs, 2006). Each PsyCap construct received its own unique approach. For 'hope' development they used a three-folded strategy embedded in a goal-oriented framework. This included goal setting, generating multiple pathways, and managing obstacles. A facilitator explained that an ideal goal entails a concrete end point to measure success, an active framework, and sub-goals to celebrate small wins as well as large ones. The sub-goaling strategy is based on the stepping concept in Snyder's hope training (Snyder, 2000). The authors argued that the development of optimism is fostered within self-efficacy training and the hope programme can also have a positive impact on optimism (Luthans et al., 2006). Bandura (1997) emphasized the importance of goal orientation and framing in building efficacy. Therefore, they integrated the goal exercise for building hope with the sources that are important in building efficacy. In building resilience, participants identified recent personal setbacks within their work domain. They were instructed to write down their spontaneous reactions to the identified setbacks. The facilitator helped in mentally framing the setback in an ideal way and elaborated on examples of a staunch view of reality. This gave the participants more insight into the realistic impact of their setbacks and helped them to see the bigger picture. In comparison with a control group, the experimental group accomplished a significant rise in their psychological capital level. Longitudinal data are still not available which means that at this moment the performance effects cannot be determined (Luthans et al., 2006).

Luthans, Avey, and Patera (2008) questioned whether Psychological Capital could be developed with a short-term, highly focused, *online* intervention. They tested their online intervention with a pre-test, post-test control group experimental design. The intervention consisted of two online sessions which started after the participants logged in to a website developed for this purpose. The first session consisted of an introductory presentation of the positive capacities of resilience and efficacy and how each capacity is applicable in the workplace in general and their job in particular. Additionally, participants could watch short video fragments displaying examples of resilience and efficacy in dramatized settings. The last phase of the first session entailed a consideration of personal work-related situations in their own organizations (Luthans et al., 2008). In the second session, the focus was on the development of hope and optimism. The participants started by considering personal goals. After that, they watched a presentation by the facilitator on the importance of personal values and the realistic challenge of achieving goals and accomplishing tasks. Then, participants had to write down several tasks that are realistically challenging, applicable to their work situation, and personally valuable. The next task consisted of breaking the main goals into smaller, easier achievable, sub-goals. The pathway component of hope was covered by the identification and generation of multiple ways to accomplish the same goal. The control group received an alternate decision-making exercise. Psychological capital was measured both in advance of the intervention and afterwards using the 24-item PsyCap Questionnaire (Luthans, Avolio, Avey, & Norman, 2007). Results showed that the 'treatment' group experienced a significant increase in their PsyCap, whereas the control group did not. This indicates that it is possible to build PsyCap through a short web-based training intervention (Luthans et al., 2008).

As a final example of a micro intervention, Fredrickson, Cohn, Coffey, Pek, and Finkel (2008) developed an intervention to test the build hypothesis of broaden-and-build theory (Fredrickson, 2001). The build hypothesis states that positive emotions set people on trajectories of growth that, over time, build consequential personal resources. Fredrickson and her colleagues set up a field experiment with random allocation to the treatment condition or waitlist control condition. The aim of the study was to test whether positive emotions, induced through loving-kindness meditation (LKM), could build consequential personal resources. The researchers also wanted to examine whether these resources hold positive consequences for the person's mental health and overall life satisfaction. In total, 139 information technology professionals filled out an initial survey that assessed their life satisfaction, depressive symptoms, and personal resources. Additionally, both groups completed daily surveys of their emotional experiences and meditation practice for nine weeks (including one week before and one week after the workshops). At the end of the period they filled out a final questionnaire that assessed the same variables as the initial one. The meditation training involved six 60-minute group sessions and was led by a stress management specialist. Participants were instructed to practice LKM at least five days a week at home, using guided recordings. The results confirmed the build hypothesis: increases in positive emotions were associated with higher levels of personal resources; personal resources, in turn, significantly increased life satisfaction and decreased the level of depressive symptoms (Fredrickson et al., 2008). This experiment is the first, to our knowledge, to empirically prove that experiencing positive emotions can have enduring effects, build resources, and make a true difference in people's lives.

## Macro interventions

An example of a macro level intervention can be found in a study on the effects of a healthy work organization intervention (DeJoy, Wilson, Vandenberg, McGrath-Higgins, & Griffin-Blake, 2009). The intervention was designed to build capacity for employee participation and problem solving and to create a healthier work organization. In each intervention store an employee problem-solving team, the ACTion team, was organized. These teams developed action plans using a five stage problem-solving process. In the familiarization stage the roles and responsibilities of the team members were explained and discussed. In the skill-building phase the ground rules for the team were set and the roles determined. The team set a weekly meeting to discuss progress. In the prioritization phase a facilitator helped the team to identify and prioritize problems and issues. A detailed action plan to address the identified priorities and to meet the team goals was developed during the action phase. Finally, in the reaction phase the team members reviewed the action plan, monitored progress, and communicated with each other and the rest of the employees about the steps being taken to refine and adjust the overall plan. Overall, the worksites that received the intervention fared better than the control worksites. Job satisfaction and organizational commitment declined at the same pace in both groups. However, stress levels increased significantly in control companies and stayed relatively stable in the intervention companies. The results showed that employees in the experimental condition considered themselves healthier and safer at work than those in the control condition. Overall, the findings of this study suggest that participatory, capacity building interventions hold promise for improving work organizations.

Schaufeli and Salanova (2008) argue that work engagement in employees can be encouraged through effective human resource management. They describe three HR strategies with a different focus that may enhance work engagement. Note that they have not empirically tested these strategies yet. The first strategy is called *employee development agreement,* the main goal of which is to optimize the fit between the employee and the organization. Schaufeli and Salanova argue that this can be achieved by following three steps: (1) assessing values, preferences, and goals (both professional and personal); (2) subsequently, negotiating a written contract (the agreement) that acknowledges these goals and necessary resources provided by the organization to accomplish them; and (3) monitoring this agreement system-atically on goal achievement and discussing re-goaling strategies, if necessary. This strategy might be successful because it focuses both on personal goals and the necessary resources to accomplish these goals (Schaufeli & Salanova, 2008). The second strategy contains a wellness audit. This implies that employer and employee evaluate together the level of wellness experienced by the employee. With this information a decision is facilitated about what improvement measures should be taken. The third strategy involves the organization of workshops to promote work engagement by augmenting personal resources. The focus of the workshops should be towards optimizing the quality of work and the level of employee functioning (Schaufeli & Salanova, 2008). The common ground that these strategies share is that they all focus on the motivational potential of job resources.

## Summary

Positive interventions are state-like, measurable, and developmental. Additionally, there should be a strong link with performance. The benefit of a positive framework is that people are more motivated to make things better instead of fixing things that have gone wrong. Micro interventions focus on the development of psychological capital, whereas macro interventions focus on structural changes in the work environment (e.g., an increase in job resources).

## SUMMARY AND CONCLUSIONS

Let us go back to the example at the start of this chapter. We asked you to imagine that you were working as a waiter in a restaurant, and that you were often confronted with complaining customers. You started to wonder whether you should continue with this job, since work had become rather stressful. Although a focus on the reduction or prevention of stressors continues to be of high importance, we argued that occupational health psychologists should also focus on positive aspects of working life. From a Positive Occupational Health Psychology (POHP) perspective, employees may use optimism and humor to deal with complaining customers. Additionally, organizations can design resourceful workplaces and foster employee engagement. Such positive qualities contribute to employee health, well-being, and job performance. In sum:

- Negative emotions have adaptive value in that they narrow our thought-action repertoires to those that best promoted our ancestor's survival in life-threatening situations.
- Broaden-and-build theory states that positive emotions broaden an individual's mindset and by doing so help to develop enduring personal resources.
- Positive psychology rehabilitated the focus on people's strengths and virtues.
- POHP is the study and application of optimal functioning in the workplace. It promotes occupational health and flourishing, and examines how positive phenomena (contexts, personal resources) can be used to protect against occupational risks.

- POHP is a complementary perspective that takes both positive and negative aspects in consideration.
- Engaged workers are characterized by high levels of energy (vigour), high involvement in their job (dedication), and by being fully concentrated and happily engrossed in their work (absorption).
- Work engagement is associated with numerous positive outcomes; e.g., reduced sickness absenteeism, improved service quality, organizational commitment, and financial turnover.
- Job resources are motivating and can buffer the negative effects of high job demands. Such resources become particularly salient in the context of high job demands.
- Psychological capital (PsyCap) is characterized by self-efficacy, optimism, hope, and resiliency. One of the key inclusion criteria is that it can be effectively managed for performance improvement.
- Organizations may build work engagement by offering job resources. However, employees can also mobilize their own resources and have an impact on their work environment. This is called job crafting.
- Positive spillover refers to a process whereby experience or participation in the work (family) role increases the quality or performance in the family (work) role.
- Positive interventions are state-like, measurable, developmental, and there is a strong link with performance.
- An example of a positive intervention is an online micro intervention to develop overall PsyCap in employees.

## Suggestions for Further Reading

Aspinwall, L. G., & Staudinger, U. M. (Eds.) (2002). *A psychology of human strengths: Fundamental questions and future directions for a positive psychology.* Washington D.C.: American Psychological Association.

Bakker, A. B., & Leiter, M. P. (Eds.) (2010). *Work engagement: A handbook of essential theory and research.* New York: Psychology Press.

Macik-Frey, M., Quick, J. C., & Nelson, D. L. (2007). Advances in occupational health: From a stressful beginning to a positive future. *Journal of Management, 33,* 809–840.

Snyder, C. R., & Lopez, S. (Eds.). (2002). *Handbook of positive psychology.* New York: Oxford University Press.

## References

Bakker, A. B., & Bal, P. M. (in press). Weekly work engagement and performance: A study among starting teachers. *Journal of Occupational and Organizational Psychology.*

Bakker, A. B., & Demerouti, E. (2007). The Job Demands-Resources model: State of the art. *Journal of Managerial Psychology, 22,* 309–328.

Bakker, A. B., & Demerouti, E. (2008). Towards a model of work engagement. *Career Development International, 13*, 209–223.

Bakker, A. B., Demerouti, E., & Euwema, M. C. (2005). Job resources buffer the impact of job demands on burnout. *Journal of Occupational Health Psychology, 10*, 170–180.

Bakker, A. B., Hakanen, J. J., Demerouti, E., & Xanthopoulou, D. (2007). Job resources boost work engagement, particularly when job demands are high. *Journal of Educational Psychology, 99*, 274–284.

Bakker, A. B., & Schaufeli, W. B. (2008). Positive organizational behavior: Engaged employees in flourishing organizations. *Journal of Organizational Behavior, 29*, 147–154.

Bakker, A. B., Schaufeli, W. B., Leiter, M. P., & Taris, T. W. (2008). Work engagement: An emerging concept in occupational health psychology. *Work & Stress, 22*, 187–200.

Bandura, A. (1997). *Self-efficacy: The exercise of control.* New York: Freeman.

Barnett, R. C. (1998). Toward a review and reconceptualization of the work/family literature. *Genetic, Social and General Psychology Monographs, 124*, 125–182.

Barnett, R. C., & Gareis, K. C. (2000). Reduced-hours employment: The relationship between difficulty of trade-offs and quality of life. *Work and Occupations, 27*, 168–187.

Block, J., & Kremen, A. M. (1996). IQ and ego-resiliency: Conceptual and empirical connections and separateness. *Journal of Personality and Social Psychology, 70*, 349–361.

Brown, S. L., Nesse, R. M., Vinokur, A. D., & Smith, D. M. (2003). Providing social support maybe more beneficial than receiving it: Results from a prospective study of mortality. *Psychological Science, 14*, 320–327.

Cameron, K. S. (2005). Organizational effectiveness: Its demise and re-emergence through positive organisational scholarship. In K.G. Smith & M.A. Hitt (Eds.), *Great minds in management: The process of theory development.* New York: Oxford University Press.

Cameron, K. S., & Caza, A. (2004). Contributions to the discipline of positive organizational scholarship. *American Behavioral Scientist, 47*, 731–739.

Cameron, K. S., Dutton, J., & Quinn, R. (Eds.) (2003). *Positive organizational scholarship.* San Francisco: Berrett-Koehler.

Cooper, C. L., & Nelson, D. L. (Eds.) (2006). *Positive Organizational Behavior: Accentuating the positive at work.* Thousand Oaks, CA: Sage.

Crosby, F. (1982). *Relative deprivation and working women.* NewYork: Oxford University Press.

Deci, W. L., & Ryan, R. M. (1985). *Intrinsic motivation and self-determination in human behavior.* New York: Plenum.

DeJoy, D. M., Wilson, M. G., Vandenberg, R. J., McGrath-Higgins, A. L., & Griffin-Blake, C. S. (2009). *Journal of Occupational and Organizational Psychology.*

Demerouti, E., & Bakker, A. B. (2008). The Oldenburg Burnout Inventory: A good alternative to measure burnout and engagement. In J. Halbesleben (Ed.), *Handbook of stress and burnout in health care* (pp. 65–78). Hauppauge, NY: Nova Science Publishers.

Demerouti, E., Bakker, A. B., de Jonge, J., Janssen, P. P. M., & Schaufeli, W. B. (2001). Burnout and engagement at work as function of demands and control. *Scandinavian Journal of Work Environment and Health, 27*, 279–286.

Eden, D. (2001). Vacations and other respites: Studying stress on and off the job. In C. L. Cooper & I. T. Robertson (Eds.), *International review of industrial and organizational psychology.* (pp. 121–146). Chichester, UK: Wiley.

Ekman, P. (1973). Cross-cultural studies of facial expressions. In P. Ekman (Ed.). *Darwin and facial expression* (pp. 169–222). New York: Academic Press.

Ekman, P., Friesen, W. V., & Ellsworth, P. (1982). What emotion categories or dimensions can observers judge from facial behavior? In P. Ekman (Ed.), *Emotion in the human face* (pp. 39–55). New York: Cambridge University Press.

Fineman, S. (2006). On being positive: Concerns and counterpoints. *Academy of Management Review, 31*, 270–291.

Fredrickson, B. L. (1998). What good are positive emotions? *Review of General Psychology, 2*, 300–319.

Fredrickson, B. (2001). The role of positive emotions in positive psychology: The broaden-and-build theory of positive emotions. *American Psychologist, 56*, 218–226.

Fredrickson, B. (2003). The value of positive emotions. *American Scientist, 91*, 330–335.

Fredrickson, B. (2004). The broaden-and-build theory of positive emotions. *Philosophical transactions of the Royal Society of Biological Sciences, 359*, 1367–1377.

Fredrickson, B. L., Cohn, M. A., Coffey, K., Pek, J., & Finkel, S. M. (2008). Open hearts build lives: Positive emotions, induced through meditation, build consequential personal resources. *Journal of Personality and Social Psychology, 95*, 1045–1062.

Fredrickson B., & Dutton, J. (2008). Unpacking positive organizing: Organizations as sites of individual and group flourishing. *Journal of Positive Psychology, 3*, 1–3.

Fredrickson, B. L., & Levenson, R. W. (1998). Positive emotions speed recovery from the cardiovascular sequalae of negative emotions. *Cognition and Emotion, 12*, 191–220.

Fredrickson, B. L., & Losada, M. F. (2005). Positive affect and the complex dynamics of human flourishing. *American Psychologist, 60*, 678–686.

Fredrickson, B. L., Mancuso, R. A., Branigan, C., & Tugade, M. M. (2000). The undoing effect of positive emotions. *Motivation and Emotion, 24*, 237–258.

González-Romá, V., Schaufeli, W. B., Bakker, A. B., & Lloret, S. (2006). Burnout and work engagement: Independent factors or opposite poles? *Journal of Vocational Behavior, 62*, 165–174.

Grant, A. M. (2008). Designing jobs to do good: Dimensions and psychological consequences of prosocial job characteristics. *Journal of Positive Psychology, 3*, 19–39.

Grant, A. M. (2007). Relational job design and the motivation to make a prosocial difference. *Academy of Management Review, 32*, 393–417.

Hakanen, J. J., Bakker, A. B., & Demerouti, E. (2005). How dentists cope with their job demands and stay engaged: The moderating role of job resources. *European Journal of Oral Sciences, 113*, 479–487.

Hakanen, J. J., Perhoniemi, R., & Toppinen-Tanner, S. (2008). Positive gain spirals at work: From job resources to work engagement, personal initiative and work-unit innovativeness. *Journal of Vocational Behavior, 73*, 78–91.

Halbesleben, J. R. B., & Wheeler, A. R. (2008). The relative roles of engagement and embeddedness in predicting job performance and intention to leave. *Work & Stress, 22*, 242–256.

Herold, J., & Waldron, I. (1985). Part time employment and women's health. *Journal of Occupational Medicine, 27*, 405–412.

Hobfoll, S. E. (2001). The influence of culture, community, and the nested-self in the stress process: Advancing conservation of resources theory. *Applied Psychology: An International Review, 50*, 337–370.

Hobfoll, S. E. (2002). Social and psychological resources and adaptation. *Review of General Psychology, 6,* 307–324.

Hobfoll, S. E., & Shirom, A. (2000). Conservation of resources theory: Applications to stress and management in the workplace. In R. T. Golembiewski (Ed.), *Handbook of organization behavior* (2nd ed., pp. 57–81). New York: Dekker.

Hochschild, A. (1997). *The time bind.* New York: Metropolitan.

Kahn, W. A. (1990). Psychological conditions of personal engagement and disengagement at work. *Academy of Management Journal, 33,* 692–724.

Kirchmeyer, C. (1993). Nonwork-to-work spillover: A more balanced view of the experiences and coping of professional women and men. *Sex Roles, 28,* 531–552.

Larson, M., & Luthans, F. (2006). Potential added value of psychological capital in predicting work attitudes. *Journal of Leadership and Organizational Studies, 13,* 45–62.

Leiter, M. P., & Maslach, C. (2010). Building engagement: The design and evaluation of interventions. In A. B. Bakker & M. P. Leiter (Eds.), *Work engagement: A handbook of essential theory and research.* New York: Psychology Press.

Luthans, F. (2002). Positive organizational behaviour: Developing and managing psychological strengths. *Academy of Management Executive, 16,* 57–72.

Luthans, F., Avey, J. B., Avolio, B. J., Norman, S. M., & Combs, G. M. (2006). Psychological capital development: toward a micro-intervention. *Journal of Organizational Behaviour, 27,* 387–393.

Luthans, F., Avey, J. B., & Patera, J. L. (2008). Experimental analysis of a web-based training intervention to develop positive psychological capital. *Academy of Management Learning & Education, 7,* 209–221.

Luthans, F., Avolio, B. J., Avey, J. B., & Norman, S. M. (2007). Psychological capital: Measurement and relationship with performance and satisfaction. *Personnel Psychology, 60,* 541–572.

Luthans, F., Norman, S. M., Avolio, B. J., & Avey, J. B. (2008). The mediating role of psychological capital in the supportive organizational climate—employee performance relationship. *Journal of Organizational Behavior, 29,* 219–238.

Luthans, F., Youssef, C. M., & Avolio, B. J. (2007). *Psychological capital: Developing the human competitive edge.* Oxford, UK: Oxford University Press.

Lyubomirsky, S., Sheldon, K. M., & Schkade, D. (2005). Pursuing happiness: The architecture of sustainable change. *Review of General Psychology, 9,* 111–131.

Maslach, C., Jackson, S. E., & Leiter, M. (1996). *Maslach Burnout Inventory. Manual* (3rd ed.). Palo Alto, CA: Consulting Psychologists Press.

Maslach, C., & Leiter, M. P. (1997). *The truth about burnout: How organizations cause personal stress and what to do about it.* San Francisco, CA: Jossey-Bass.

Meijman, T. F., & Mulder, G. (1998). Psychological aspects of workload. In P. J. D. Drenth & H. Thierry (Eds.), *Handbook of work and organizational psychology, Vol. 2: Work psychology* (pp. 5–33). Hove: Psychology Press.

Moen, P., Dempster-McClain, D., & Williams, R. M. (1992). Successful aging: A life-course perspective on women's multiple roles and health. *American Journal of Sociology, 97,* 1612–1638.

Parker, S. K., & Ohly, S. (2008). Designing motivating jobs. In R. Kanfer, G. Chen, & R. Pritchard (Eds.), *Work motivation: Past, present, and future.* SIOP Organizational Frontiers Series.

Peterson, C., & Seligman, M. E. P. (2004). *Character strengths and virtues.* Oxford, UK: Oxford University Press.

Russell, J. A., & Carroll, J. M. (1999). On the bipolarity of positive and negative affect. *Psychological Bulletin, 125, 1,* 3–30.

Salanova, M., Agut, S. & Peiró, J. M. (2005). Linking organizational resources and work engagement to employee performance and customer loyalty: The mediation of service climate. *Journal of Applied Psychology, 90,* 1217–1227.

Schaufeli, W. B. (2004). The future of occupational health psychology. *Applied psychology: An International Review, 53,* 502–517.

Schaufeli, W. B., & Bakker, A. B. (2004). Job demands, job resources and their relationship with burnout and engagement: A multi-sample study. *Journal of Organizational Behavior, 25,* 293–315.

Schaufeli, W. B., & Bakker, A. B. (2010). The conceptualization and measurement of work engagement: A review. In A.B. Bakker & M.P. Leiter (Eds.), *Work engagement: A handbook of essential theory and research.* New York: Psychology Press.

Schaufeli, W. B., Bakker, A. B., & Van Rhenen, W. (2009). How changes in job demands and resources predict burnout, work engagement, and sickness absenteeism. *Journal of Organizational Behavior, 30,* 893–917.

Schaufeli, W. B. & Salanova, M. (2008). Enhancing work engagement through the management of human resources. In K. Näswall, M. Sverke & J. Hellgren (Eds.), *The individual in the changing working life* (pp. 380–404). Cambridge: Cambrigde University Press.

Schaufeli, W. B., Salanova, M., Gonzáles-Romá, V., & Bakker, A. B. (2002). The measurement of engagement and burnout: A two sample confirmatory factor analytic approach. *Journal of Happiness Studies, 3,* 71–92.

Schaufeli, W. B., Taris, T. W., Le Blanc, P., Peeters, M., Bakker, A. B., & De Jonge, J. (2001). Maakt arbeid gezond? Op zoek naar de bevlogen werknemer [Does work make happy? In search of the engaged worker]. *De Psycholoog, 36,* 422–428.

Seligman, M. E. P. (1998a). Positive social science. *APA Monitor, 29,* 5.

Seligman, M. E. P. (1998b). *Learned optimism.* New York: Pocket Books.

Seligman, M. E. P. (2002). *Authentic Happiness.* New York: Free Press.

Seligman, M., & Csikszentmihalyi, M. (2000). Positive Psychology: An introduction. *American Psychologist, 55,* 5–14.

Sheldon, K. M., & King, L. (2001). Why positive psychology is necessary. *American Psychologist, 56,* 216–217.

Snyder, C. R. (2000). *Handbook of hope.* San Diego: Academic Press.

Snyder, C. R., Harris, C., Anderson, J. R., Holleran, S. A., Irving, L. M. Sigmon, S. T., Yoshinobu, L., Gibb, J., Langelle, C., & Harney, P. (1991). The will and the ways: Development and validation of an individual-differences measure of hope. *Journal of Personality and Social Psychology, 60,* 570–585.

Snyder, C. R., & Lopez, S. (Eds.). (2002). *Handbook of positive psychology.* New York: Oxford University Press.

Sonnentag, S. (2003). Recovery, work engagement, and proactive behavior: A new look at the interface between nonwork and work. *Journal of Applied Psychology, 88,* 518–528.

Stajkovic, A. D., & Luthans, F. (1998). Social cognitive theory and self-efficacy: Going beyond traditional motivational and behavioral approaches. *Organizational Dynamics, 26,* 62–74.

Tetrick, L. E. (2002). Individual and organizational health. In D. Ganster & P. L. Perrewe (Eds.), *Research in organizational stress and well-being* (Vol. 3, pp. 107–141). Greenwich, CN: JAI Press.

Turner, N., Barling, J., & Zacharatos, A. (2002). Positive psychology at work. In C.R Snyder & S. Lopez. (Eds.), *The handbook of positive psychology* (pp. 715–730). Oxford: Oxford University Press.

Verbrugge, L. M. (1989). The twain meet: Empirical explanations of sex differences in health and mortality. *Journal of Health and Social Behavior, 30,* 282–304.

Westman, M., & Etzion, D. (2001). The impact of vacation and job stress on burnout and absenteeism. *Psychology and Health, 16,* 595–606.

Wethington, E., & Kessler, R. C. (1989). Employment, parental responsibility, and psychological distress. *Journal of Family Issues, 10,* 527–546.

Wrzesniewski, A., McCauley, C., Rozin, P., & Schwartz, B. (1997). Jobs, careers, and callings: People's reactions to their work. *Journal of Research in Personality, 31,* 21–33.

Wrzesniewski, A., & Dutton, J. E. (2001). Crafting a job: Revisioning employees as active crafters of their work. *Academy of Management Review, 26,* 179–201.

Wright, T. A. (2003). Positive organizational behavior: An idea whose time has truly come. *Journal of Organizational Behavior, 24,* 62–65.

Xanthopoulou, D., Bakker, A. B., Demerouti, E., Schaufeli, W. B. (2009a). Reciprocal relationships between job resources, personal resources, and work engagement. *Journal of Vocational Behavior, 74,* 235–244.

Xanthopoulou, D., Bakker, A. B., Demerouti, E., & Schaufeli, W. B. (2009b). Work engagement and financial returns: A diary study on the role of job and personal resources. *Journal of Occupational and Organizational Psychology, 82,* 183–200.

Xanthopoulou, D., Bakker, A. B., Dollard, M. F., Demerouti, E., Schaufeli, W. B., Taris, T. W., & Schreurs, P. J. G. (2007). When do job demands particularly predict burnout? The moderating role of job resources. *Journal of Managerial Psychology, 22,* 766–786.

Xanthopoulou, D., Bakker, A. B., Heuven, E., Demerouti, E., & Schaufeli, W. B. (2008). Working in the sky: A diary study on work engagement among flight attendants. *Journal of Occupational Health Psychology, 13,* 345–356.

# 8

# The Physical Workspace
## An OHP Perspective

Phil Leather, Tony Zarola,
and Angeli Santos

### CHAPTER OUTLINE

Occupational health psychology (OHP) has at its core a concern with the role and interplay of psychological, social, and organizational aspects of work in impacting upon both individual and organizational health. As Cox, Baldursson, and Rial González (2000) point out, this focus brings together a number of areas of applied psychology including health psychology, work and organizational psychology, social psychology, and environmental psychology. In this chapter, we focus especially on the contribution of environmental psychology to issues of occupational health and well-being.

## Introduction

Although research in this area is growing, the 'environmental psychology of the workplace' remains a relatively underdeveloped aspect of occupational health psychology (OHP). Our goal in writing this chapter is therefore both to summarize the current state of knowledge in the area and to set out an explanatory framework which might profitably advance OHP research and interest in it. This framework builds upon the work of Leather and colleagues at the Institute of Work, Health and Organisations, University of Nottingham (see, for example, Leather, Pyrgas, Beale, & Lawrence, 1998; Leather, Beale, & Sullivan, 2003; Leather, Beale, Santos, Watts, & Lee, 2003), as well as leading 'environmental' researchers elsewhere (see, for example, Evans & Johnson, 2000; Evans & McCoy, 1998; McCoy, 2002; McCoy & Evans, 2005; Ulrich, 1991; Vischer, 2007). Once established, we use this framework to explore and illustrate the impact of the physical work environment upon occupational health by reference to three specific topic areas: open-plan office designs, windows in the workplace, and noise.

To facilitate what will possibly be the reader's first encounter with the environmental psychology of the workplace, the answers to five key questions constitute the underpinning structure to this chapter:

1. What is environmental psychology?
2. What concepts and theories does environmental psychology use to help explain the impact of the physical environment upon employee – and organizational – health and well-being?
3. What framework, if any, can serve to integrate and inform the contribution of environmental psychology to OHP?
4. What evidence is there to support the claim that the physical work environment plays an important role in influencing employee health and well-being and to what extent does this evidence support the use of any unifying framework?
5. What conclusions can be drawn about the impact of the physical work environment upon well-being and behaviour and what are some of the possible avenues and directions for further scientific research and inquiry into the environmental psychology of the workplace?

The research and other literature presented here is necessarily selective and illustrative rather than exhaustive. Our purpose is not to try and capture all that is known about the impact of physical workspace upon individual or organizational health but rather to make the case that the physical environment in which work is carried out constitutes both an important influence upon employee health and a necessary focus for OHP.

We concentrate in this chapter primarily – although not exclusively – upon office work. If for no other reason, this focus is warranted by the fact that the majority of workers in many more economically developed countries now work in offices. McCoy (2002), for example, comments that over 50 per cent of US workers are now engaged in office work. Despite our emphasis upon office work, we will draw attention to other workplaces – and indeed other physical settings – wherever possible. The lessons that can be learned from looking at one setting, or place, are often easily and equally transferable to another.

## What is Environmental Psychology?

*How can environmental psychology be defined?*
*Why is the transaction between a person and their physical environment important?*

Heimstra & McFarling (1978) define environmental psychology as the study of the *interrelationship* between behaviour and the physical environment. Their use of the term 'interrelationship' emphasizes the fact that the relationship between the physical environment and behaviour is dynamic and reciprocal, i.e., while behaviour is influenced by the physical environment, it is also human behaviour which helps to create and shape that environment.

Imagine, for example, that you are sitting on the train trying to read a detailed scientific paper, e.g., one that contains a plethora of multivariate statistics. You are hoping for a relative amount of peace and quiet to help you maintain your focus and concentration upon the paper. A person sitting near you then proceeds to play music via a personal stereo. Although the actual sound level that is audible to you is not great, the muted sound of the music being played soon 'gets on your nerves', becomes increasingly distracting, and prevents you from taking in what you are reading. This simple scenario illustrates neatly the dynamic and reciprocal nature of person-environment relationships. On the one hand, your ability to satisfactorily accomplish your reading task is directly impacted upon by the level of sound in the carriage environment and yet it is the goal-directed behaviour of someone else (i.e., to listen to their music) that in part creates the salient physical environment for you.

Canter and Craik (1981) further advance our understanding of what is involved in the relationship between person and environment. In their view, environmental psychology analyses the transactions and interrelationships of human experiences and actions with pertinent aspects of the socio-physical surroundings. Their use of the term *transactions* again signifies a two-way relationship between the physical environment and aspects of human behaviour. More importantly, their additional emphasis upon *experiences* and *actions* points to both the goal-directed nature of people's behaviour in different physical environments and the importance of the perceived environment as the basis upon which the quality or appropriateness of any environment is to be judged. Put simply, it is not so much the objective characteristics of the physical environment *per se* that influence behaviour, but our perception of those characteristics and the extent to which we appraise them as being congruent or incongruent with our current needs and goals.

To take a simple example, consider the issue of social density, i.e., the ratio of people to available space. The perception of what constitutes a suitable or appropriate level of social density will differ markedly, not only from one social situation to another, e.g., from a pop concert to a lecture, but even within the same social situation as our needs and goals change, e.g., when we are being criticized rather than praised at work, or when we need a time for quiet concentration at work as opposed to a time to interact and work collaboratively with others.

Another important point about Canter and Craik's (1981) definition is that it draws attention to the need for environments to be fit for their social purpose as judged by those who carry out the necessary tasks and activities to be pursued there. The critical assessment of whether a workplace is fit for purpose is therefore not that made by an architect or designer but that made by those who work there. Put simply, users' appraisals of physical settings – e.g., workplaces, libraries, and hospitals – are at the very centre of the relationship or transaction between people and the physical environment. It is for this very reason that post-occupancy evaluation, i.e., the systematic assessment of buildings and other settings as they are actually used (Zimring, 2002), is fundamental to much environmental psychology investigation.

Importantly, environmental appraisal is influenced by both individual differences and socio-cultural factors. Furnham (1997), for example, speculates on how office workers' job satisfaction and performance are likely to be influenced by the degree of fit or match between their personality and the environmental attributes they are presented with in open and closed-office plan arrangements (see Chapter 2 for a discussion on Person-Environment Fit theory). Given their desire for arousal and stimulation, extroverts, he suggests, are likely see the noise, movement, and variety of an open-plan office arrangement as more suited to their needs. The introvert, on the other hand, is likely to prefer closed office environments with limited external stimulation. Where the extravert might be expected to work best – and report higher job satisfaction – in an open office, the introvert will work best – and be most satisfied – in a closed office.

The appraisal of any physical setting is as much a product of socio-cultural factors as it is of either individual differences or indeed technical specifications alone. Design specifications are fundamentally social judgments. Think for a few moments about prison design. What social values might underpin the possible design for a prison? Sommer (1976) notes that one of two competing goals typically underpins prison design: incapacitation and retribution versus reform and rehabilitation. These competing philosophies advance different design specifications for the buildings, amenities, facilities, and physical character required in a prison, e.g., austere prison cells in the former and classroom settings in the latter. Historically, the incapacitation philosophy dominates, such that prison design often takes on the character of fortress-like buildings that symbolize penitence and spawn impersonality (Veitch & Arkkelin, 1995).

The assessment and evaluation of any workplace or other behaviour setting is therefore the product of an amalgam of individual, social, and cultural influences all of which combine and interact such that the appraisal of the physical environment cannot be dissociated from its psychological, social, and cultural context. As Levy-Leboyer (1982) puts it, 'the physical environment simultaneously symbolizes, makes concrete, and conditions the social environment'.

What does all this mean for an environmental psychology of the workplace? First, from an OHP perspective, it means that any environmental psychology of the workplace is fundamentally about identifying those physical qualities of the workplace which influence employee well-being and behaviour. Second, it means that whatever physical qualities or design elements might be 'under the microscope', e.g., sound and noise, spatial layout, windows, views, colour, or architectonic details, they cannot be considered in isolation from their full social and organizational context. Workplaces are designed with a specific social purpose in mind, i.e., the efficient accomplishment of designated tasks in a manner conducive to employee health, safety, well-being, and productivity. The impact of physical design elements cannot therefore be reliably and validly assessed without due consideration being given to the simultaneous impact of such things as individual differences, the demographic characteristics of the workforce, the nature of the tasks to be accomplished, and the organizational structures and processes that the physical workplace is designed to support (McCoy, 2002).

Third, since the ultimate arbiter and judge of the quality of any given work environment is not those who designed it but those who use it, so concepts such as worker comfort and their satisfaction with the physical work environment become critical concerns. It is the appraised environment which is critical rather than the objective environment (Hedge, 1982) although there are likely to be identifiable relationships between the two. Again, however, any assessment of the appraised workplace environment must give due attention to the individual and social factors which are known to influence appraisal processes, e.g., aspects of personality and other individual differences; the needs, goals, and motives of those involved; the characteristics of the task at hand; and the broader social values that help to shape our views and images of workplaces.

We turn now to a brief overview of some of the early models, theories, and concepts that environmental psychologists have used to try and explain the impact of the physical environment upon human behaviour both in the workplace and elsewhere.

## Early Explanations of Environment–Behaviour Relationships in Environmental Psychology

*What early theories were used to understand the person-physical environment transaction?*
*What are the implications of these theories for the nature of the transaction?*
*What are the limitations of these early theoretical perspectives?*

### Arousal level

One of the longest standing explanations of how the physical environment impacts upon behaviour is through its impact upon levels of arousal. Arousal can be characterized as lying on a continuum from sleep to heightened wakeful activity (Berlyne, 1960) and comprises physiological, behavioural, and psychological aspects, e.g., heart rate, motor activity, and emotional response respectively. Environmental conditions can bring about changes in arousal level as, for example, when we experience discomfort and agitation on an overcrowded bus or train. Conversely, we might experience a significant reduction in arousal when having the opportunity to take a pleasant stroll. Arousal is, in essence, an intervening variable between environmental stimuli and behaviour.

Importantly, the arousal model makes discrete predictions about the effects of arousal upon task performance. Specifically, the Yerkes-Dodson Law (1908) posits

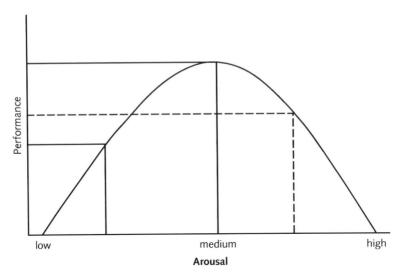

**Figure 8.1** Yerkes-Dodson model of the relationship between arousal and performance.

an 'inverted U' relationship between arousal and performance (see Figure 8.1) such that performance is maximal at intermediate levels of arousal and gets progressively worse as arousal moves below or above this optimum point.

The optimum level of arousal for maximal performance is, of course, dependent in part upon the nature of the task. It is easier, for example, to transcribe or copy notes while exposed to other people's conversation than it is to undertake mathematical calculations. For complex tasks, therefore, optimum performance occurs at lower levels of arousal, as shown in Figure 8.2.

There is a ready application of this arousal approach to the workplace. Open-office designs, for example, might lead to elevated arousal levels through the increased social and aural stimulation that often go with them (Maher & von Hipple, 2005; Oldham, 1988). An open-plan office arrangement necessarily places employees in close proximity, often with unregulated interpersonal access to each other. In addition to this increased social stimulation, each worker is necessarily exposed to the many sources of sound that can emanate in an open-office, e.g., from telephones, others' conversations, and the plethora of office equipment. The impact of any elevated arousal level resulting from these open-office conditions will ultimately depend upon the nature of the task that is being undertaken, as well as the employees' experience and competence in the task and their ability to screen out or inhibit distractions (Maher & von Hipple, 2005).

### Environmental load

The basic idea here (Cohen, 1978) is that human beings have limited information processing capacity, i.e., they are limited in the extent to which they can process multiple and competing incoming stimuli. When faced with multiple inputs that

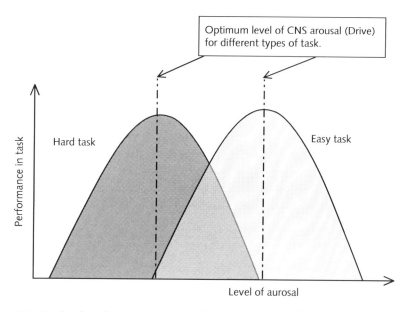

**Figure 8.2** Optimal performance points within the Yerkes-Dodson law.

exceed our processing capacity, each requiring an adaptive response, a monitoring process within our cognitive system attempts to decide what coping strategy to employ. The 'normal' human strategy in this situation is to (1) ignore those inputs that are deemed to be less relevant to the task at hand, and (2) devote more attention to those inputs that are seen as relevant. The final point to note is that the amount of attentional capacity available is not constant, but fluctuates depending upon what we are doing. It might, for example, become depleted after a period of prolonged demands, such as writing a complex scientific report, whereupon it becomes difficult to do anything further that requires much attention.

Milgram (1970) used the environmental load model to explain the deterioration of social life in large urban areas. He suggests that the 'unfriendliness' many believe to be true of city dwellers is in fact the product of their being overwhelmed by the amount of social stimulation present there. Hence, such phenomena as bystanders ignoring others in distress are, he concludes, due in part to an environmental overload in which the hustle and bustle of city life requires so much attention that there is little remaining for peripheral social concerns which are, by and large, simply ignored. A similar reasoning might be used to explain the behaviour of those who work in an open-plan office and simply choose to 'keep themselves to themselves' rather than engage in trivial conversation with their colleagues.

While environments may be socially very stimulating they can also provide an understimulating physical environment. In the workplace, for example, the playing of music by textile (garment) machinists might be seen as a means of increasing the environmental stimulation to help them cope with an otherwise rather monotonous work experience. Of course the arousal model could also be invoked here, i.e., playing background music supplements the low level of arousal derived from monotonous work and so elevates arousal closer to the level required for maximal performance.

## Adaptation level theory

Both the arousal and environmental load approaches assume that too much or too little environmental stimulation has undesirable effects on behaviour and emotions. Explicitly or implicitly, both approaches contend that an intermediate level of stimulation is ideal. This is the basic tenet in Wohlwill's (1974) adaptation level theory of environmental stimulation which holds that human beings prefer an optimal level of any form of environmental stimulation, e.g., noise, temperature, social density, or scenery. As an illustration, most people would agree that a cramped and overcrowded office makes for a very unpleasant work experience and yet neither do we seek social isolation.

Wohlwill (1974) suggests that at least three categories of environment-behaviour relationships conform to this optimal level hypothesis – sensory stimulation, social stimulation, and movement – with too much or too little of each being undesirable. Each of these three categories is held to vary along three key dimensions: intensity (amount), diversity (variety), and pattern (degree of order and structure). Based upon past experience, each person is believed to have their own optimal level of stimulation, whether sensory, social, or movement. Importantly, this optimal level of stimulation can and does change, e.g., how many people who move from a quiet location to live close to a major highway at first complain about the noise but sooner or later seem to get used to it and indeed filter it out?

It is the ability for optimal stimulation level to shift as a function of continued exposure to a stimulus that is termed 'adaptation'. Adaptation is where we adjust our response to environmental stimuli, as opposed to adjustment (Sonnenfeld, 1966), where we change the stimulus itself, e.g., when we control office temperature by altering a thermostat or opening or closing a window. Adaptation levels change both between and within individuals.

The increasing relocation of office work from closed to open-plan arrangements makes for an interesting case study regarding the application of adaptation level theory to the workplace. In particular, if adaptation level theory is correct, then any initial dissatisfaction to such relocation should dissipate over time as people adapt to their new arrangements. Conversely, if workers do not adapt to open-plan working arrangements then any negative impact should remain constant, if not increase, over time. We will touch on some research evidence that has a bearing on this topic later in this chapter.

## Behaviour-constraint approach

There are three basic elements in the behaviour-constraint approach: perceived loss of control, reactance, and learned helplessness. The starting point in this approach is the idea that something about the environment limits or interferes with our ability to do the things we wish to do, e.g., we cannot accomplish a given work task because we are constantly being interrupted by telephone calls or unwanted distraction from the noise around us. This constraint can be both an actual impairment, e.g., the rush hour congestion that brings the traffic to a standstill, or a belief that the environment is placing a constraint upon us, e.g., when those in privately rented homes believe the building of an eco-town nearby will have a disastrous impact upon their standard and quality of life. What is important is our interpretation of the situation as being one in which we are losing – or have lost – control.

The effects of a perceived loss of control are, first, the experience of discomfort and negative affect, then second, some attempt at reasserting control over the situation. This is known as psychological reactance (Brehm, 1966; Brehm & Brehm, 1981). Note, for example, the common practice on busy trains of passengers deliberately leaving a coat or case on the seat beside them, as if to prevent others having close proximity to them. Similarly, the adornment of the office with personal items and memorabilia might be seen as a means of reasserting our own sense of identity and control within the workplace.

Where repeated efforts to reassert control result in failure, we start to believe that our actions have no effect on the situation and so stop trying to regain control even when actual control might have been restored. This is what Seligman (1975) termed 'learned helplessness', i.e., we learn, or more correctly learn to believe, that we are helpless. An easy environmental illustration of this phenomenon is the problem of the elderly giving up the fight against the cold in the winter months.

### The role of cognitive mediation in models of environment–behaviour relationships

Cognitive mediation plays an important role in the arousal, environmental load, adaptation level, and behaviour-constraint approaches. When aroused, for example, we seek information about our internal state. We try to interpret the nature of the arousal and reasons for it. Is it, for example, due to the people around us, to some perceived threat in the environment, or to some physical aspect of the environment? In short, how we interpret matters is critical. Similarly, monitoring, evaluation, and decision-making processes are central within the environmental load approach. As adaptation level theory has it, optimal levels of stimulation change as we change our interpretation and appraisal of current conditions. In the behaviour-constraint approach it is the perception of a loss of control that triggers attempts to regain it.

As we noted in our discussion of the nature and definition of environmental psychology, it is the appraised environment rather than the objective environment that matters. This emphasis on appraisal can be seen to figure prominently in the majority of models and approaches used to explain environment–behaviour relationships. Arguably the cornerstone of these appraisal processes is a judgment of whether the environment fits with and supports our current needs and concerns. When environmental conditions do fit current needs and purposes then the accomplishment of goals is made easier; when they don't fit then the achievement of goals becomes more difficult. Put another way, a poorly fitting work environment adds to the demands of the task while a supportive work environment helps in coping with these demands. This is the language of stress, the integrating concept to which we now turn.

## Stress: A Framework for the Contribution of Environmental Psychology to OHP

*How can the concept of stress help us to understand the person – physical environment transaction?*
*How can a stress perspective inform the design of the physical work environment?*

A concern with the environment is at the heart of stress theory. Specifically, all biological systems, including of course human beings, must self-regulate in the context of changing environmental conditions (Evans & Cohen, 1987). Stress emanates from particular appraisals of and reactions to those conditions, i.e., where environmental conditions are seen as threatening the well-being, integrity, or existence of the organism (Evans, 1982). Environmental conditions have a negative impact upon well-being when (1) they are appraised as being harmful in some way and (2) coping resources are seen as being limited, deficient, or unavailable.

Stress can be thought of as an imbalance between the perceived demands of any situation on the one hand and our perceived ability to meet or cope with those demands on the other (Cox, 1998). Stress results either when perceived demands exceed perceived coping ability (overload) or when our perceived abilities are grossly underutilized in what we have to do (underload). Stress is therefore a process and relationship rather than an entity. Anything which impacts upon this balance between perceived demands and perceived ability to cope becomes a part of what we might conveniently term the overall stress equation. Within models of work-related stress, the availability of social support and the existence of constraining organizational policies and personal expectations are seen as especially important in influencing the perceived balance between demands and the ability to cope with them (Cox, 1998).

Vischer (2007) notes that studies of workplace stress tend to focus on psychosocial influences in the work environment to the relative exclusion of the physical environment. She notes, however, that if stress derives from some degree of person–environment 'misfit' then the physical resources of the workspace are potentially important contributors to this, e.g., through poorly designed office furniture and equipment, lack of space, the noise generated by distraction, and so on. McCoy & Evans (2005) similarly characterize as stressful those situations where elements of the physical environment interfere with the task performance and the attainment of work objectives.

Evans (2001) points to three potential roles of the physical environment in the aetiology of stress:

1. where aspects of the physical environment (e.g., noise, distraction and a lack of space) load or pressure the system as when crowding creates excessive stimulation;
2. where aspects of the physical environment damage or ameliorate coping resources, e.g., where chronic noise exposure leads to learned helplessness;
3. where aspects of the physical environment serve to elicit unhealthy coping strategies, e.g., where noisy work conditions result in increased substance abuse.

Indeed, Lazarus & Folkman (1984) drew attention to two broad classes of coping resources: properties of the person and properties of the environment. Where occupational stress research usually construes the latter as the social environment, as in the availability social support, it is our contention that the design and affordance of the physical workplace must be taken equally into account.

From a stress perspective then, aspects of the physical environment could have both a direct and indirect effect upon health and well-being, i.e., they might in themselves generate stress, or they might combine and interact with psychosocial elements (e.g., the content and context of work) in the derivation of their impact (Griffiths, 1998). Prolonged exposure to workplace noise would be a simple example of a direct effect, while having an accessible space for quiet and distraction-free work when needed would be an example of an indirect effect, i.e., the importance of a particular design specification (peace and quiet) depends upon the nature of the task to be accomplished. In short, the physical workspace should support the job to be done, albeit form the user's perspective.

Ulrich (1991) and Evans and McCoy (1998) have both pointed out that the design of many buildings, including the workplace, emphasizes functional effectiveness and typically works against user well-being since it is unsuited to the psychological needs of users. An alternative design goal, they argue, is one that promotes wellness through physical surroundings which are 'psychologically supportive' to the needs, goals, and motives of the user. Stress plays a key explanatory role in this idea of a 'supportive' physical environment. In particular, to promote wellness, workspace design should foster better coping with task demands and thereby less likelihood of stress. Workspace design can fulfil this supportive role, they variously suggest, through assisting in coping with the task at hand; by not raising obstacles to coping with the task at hand; by not creating added stress in themselves; and by utilizing known stress reducing elements, e.g., facilitating access to social support, positive distractions, and giving people a sense of control over their physical-social surroundings (Evans & McCoy, 1998; Ulrich, 1991).

What evidence is there, then, that the physical environment might lead to negative well-being and behavioural outcomes when it is 'unsupportive' and improved well-being and behavioural outcomes when it is 'supportive'? This is the question to which we now turn.

## The Physical Work Environment, Well-Being, and Behaviour

*What is the evidence for there being associations between the physical work environment and well-being?*
*How does stress theory help us to understand these associations?*

For too long, the design of the workplace was often taken by researchers and practitioners alike as a given, i.e., as something that we simply accepted and 'got on with'. Ornstein (1990) succinctly and cleverly captured this unsatisfactory state of affairs when she wrote that 'there is a general tendency among psychologists and managers to ignore the physical setting (much like the proverbial fish that does not notice the surrounding water)'. That the physical design of the workplace could have important consequences for human health and behaviour was frequently unseen, despite a growing body of evidence that the physical environment in which work is completed – often referred to as the physical workspace or the physical work environment – has a marked and measurable impact upon both employee well-being and other work outcomes (Vischer, 2007).

In this section we review some of the evidence in support of this claim that the physical work environment plays an important role in influencing employee health, well-being, and behaviour. In doing so we use stress as an explanatory heuristic to help guide our exploration. In line with the framework outlined above we therefore look for:

- evidence of the importance of the appraised environment;
- evidence that design elements in the workplace might act as either stressors or coping resources;
- evidence of interactions between physical and psychosocial factors;
- evidence that the physical environment can have both direct and indirect effects;
- evidence that coping with unsatisfactory workspaces is detrimental to well-being.

We focus in this review upon three specific design aspects of the workplace: open-plan office designs, windows in the workplace, and noise.

### Open-plan office

As more and more organizations relocate their office staff into large open-plan offices, questions are increasingly being asked about both the quality of working life that is experienced in such workplaces and their appropriateness as a basis for effective work performance. Fully open-plan office designs are shared workplaces with modular furniture and no barriers between workstations. Semi-open or cubed office designs utilize moveable partitions that partially screen office occupants from each other. By contrast, the traditional or closed office has floor to ceiling walls and a door thereby providing a separate and fully private workspace for the office occupant.

The espoused benefits of the open-plan office derive from engineering and economic considerations (Yildirim, Akalin-Baskaya, & Celebi, 2007). In simple terms, open-plan arrangements enable the accommodation of a greater number of employees in a smaller amount of space, thereby saving on building, maintenance, and running costs. In addition, they create flexible space in that floor layout can be easily reconfigured in response to changing working arrangements. Set-up and renovation times are therefore reduced.

In addition to these economic benefits, some commentators have suggested that the absence of internal barriers between workers is conducive to improved employee interaction, communication, and sociability (Allen & Gersberger, 1973; Brooks & Kaplan, 1972; Zahn, 1991) with a consequent possibility of improved satisfaction, morale and productivity (Maher & von Hippel, 2005; Yildirim, et al., 2007). On the other hand, open-plan office designs have also been associated with a range of negative impacts, especially increased workplace noise; increased disturbance, distraction, and interruption; loss of privacy and an increase in perceived crowding which, in turn, are believed to result in reduced functional efficiency, decreased performance, diminished satisfaction, and an increase in physiological and psychological stress (Evans & Johnson, 2000; Lee & Brand, 2005; Vischer, 2007; Yildirim, et al., 2007).

Carlopio & Gardner (1992) make the important point that the impact of any objective characteristics of the physical work environment upon such outcomes as satisfaction and performance will depend upon a number of intermediary variables, especially an individual's perception (appraisal) of them and the nature of the task at hand. Perception and appraisal are examples of mediator variables (Baron & Kenny, 1986) in that they explain how the environment impacts upon well-being, i.e. through the meaning and interpretation we ascribe and attribute to it. Task demands, on the other hand, are an example of a moderator variable (Baron & Kenny, 1986) in that they help explain when the environment has its impact, i.e., when certain task conditions are also present.

In line with a moderation model, Carlopio & Gardner (1992) hypothesize that the negative impact of the open-plan office upon satisfaction will be greatest for those undertaking complex jobs since these are more sensitive to disruption and distraction. They compared 228 managerial, professional, and clerical employees working in open, cubed, or traditional offices in a large bank. Confirming their hypothesis, their results showed that managers were most satisfied with the work site in traditional offices than in cubed or open offices. Clerks, on the other hand, were most satisfied in open offices and cubes, while professionals appeared equally satisfied in traditional or cube environments and less satisfied in open settings. Similarly, supervisors' satisfaction with the work site increased progressively from open to cube to traditional office environments, while non-supervisors were more satisfied in cube than open environments, but least satisfied in traditional offices.

The implication of Carlopio & Gardner's (1992) results is that the office environment needs to 'fit' the tasks to be undertaken there. The type of arrangement most appropriate for one set of tasks, e.g., clerical, might be very different to that best suited to a different set of tasks, e.g., managerial. Of key concern here is the balance or imbalance between the degree of privacy, quiet, and distraction-free seclusion needed for satisfactory task accomplishment and the degree of privacy, quiet, and distraction-free seclusion afforded by particular office arrangements. Indeed, Brill et al. (2001) report that the ability to do distraction-free solo work is amongst those environmental qualities having the greatest impact upon work performance and job satisfaction. Maher & von Hippel (2005) argue that it is precisely the inherent loss of space and inevitable increase in contact with co-workers that drives the negative attitudinal and behavioural responses of employees to the open-plan office. By design open-plan arrangements bring people into close proximity with each other thereby making it difficult to avoid inter-personal contact and maintain privacy.

Privacy can be defined as the ability to control incoming stimulation and interpersonal contact and to limit outgoing information (Sundstrom et al., 1982). As such, privacy is closely associated with any physical features which allow voluntary isolation form visual and auditory commerce with others, e.g., walls, screens and partitions, doors, and the physical distance between colleagues. Importantly, privacy is a psychological phenomenon that is closely related to the degree of enclosure afforded by any workspace design but not entirely dependent upon it. Sundstrom et al. (1982), for example, found that while closed offices were not surprisingly rated as more private than open offices, perceptions of privacy were also associated with job rank, i.e., managers rated a closed office as more private than secretaries. With higher organizational rank comes greater control over social contact. A manager can enter a secretary's office more readily than a secretary can enter a manager's office. Privacy is, in effect, the product of an appraisal process which takes a number of simultaneous factors into account.

From a stress perspective a lack of workplace privacy should have a cumulative negative impact over time, i.e., the damage done to well-being should increase as coping resources become increasingly taxed from exposure to a chronic stressor. This is in contrast to the prediction that might be made on the basis of adaptation level theory, according to which we might expect any negative impact to lessen as people get used to any particular set of environmental conditions. Using a sample of 130 secretaries and administrative assistants, Duvall-Early and Benedict (1992) found that the relationship between privacy and both (1) general satisfaction and (2) many components of job satisfaction, e.g., reward, advancement opportunities, supervision, and the like, *strengthened* over time. In other words, those without adequate perceived privacy reported increasingly diminishing levels of satisfaction over time.

Not only do these results favour the stress perspective over a model of adaptation, but they beg the question as to why the perception of the physical workplace might be linked to satisfaction with as such diverse work aspects as social status, company policies, authority, and independence? One possible reason why the physical workplace is so important is that it is appraised by staff as symbolizing the status and importance placed in them by the organization. In essence, the quality and maintenance of the physical work environment is seen as a message that management sends to staff about how they are valued by the organization (McCoy, 2002). A better quality physical workplace therefore implies a more highly valued and respected workforce. The significance of the physical work environment is therefore closely tied to the importance of management behaviour, i.e., the provision of a decent and well maintained physical work environment is itself seen as a statement of a supportive management.

Interestingly, Duvall-Early and Benedict (1992) also report that perceived privacy and actual enclosure – assessed in terms of the presence or absence of walls, partitions, doors, and the proximity or visibility of co-workers and supervisors – correlated at $r = 0.71$, $p<0.001$. Squaring a correlation coefficient gives us the coefficient of determination, i.e., the percentage of variance in one variable that can be accounted for the variance in another. Hence, only 50 per cent of the variance in perceived privacy was accounted for by enclosure, pointing again to the fact that the appraisal of the physical environment takes into account factors over and above purely physical elements.

In line with stress theory, one such additional factor likely to influence the appraisal of the open-plan office is individual differences. We have already noted Furnham's (1997) speculation concerning the possible contribution of extroversion and introversion in influencing workers' adaptation to open-plan office designs. Maher and von Hippel (2005) note that some people are better able than others to cope with excessive stimulation, hence another important individual difference likely to influence employees' reactions to the open-plan office is the ability to inhibit distraction. The ability to block unwanted stimuli and concentrate on the work task at hand is, they argue, fundamental to selective attention which presupposes two complementary processes, i.e., attention and inhibition.

This idea builds upon the work of Mehrabian (1977) who distinguished between screeners and non-screeners. Screeners are those who can effectively employ prioritisation to reduce overstimulation, whereas non-screeners cannot do this and so become over-aroused. Those who are effective at screening incoming information, prioritizing inputs and inhibiting distraction are therefore hypothesized to have less negative reactions to the auditory and social stimulation inherent in the open-plan office, particularly when engaged in complex tasks which require a high level of attention and concentration.

In partial support of this hypothesis and based upon a sample of 109 participants from two open-plan offices – one a Municipal Council and the other an architecture and design firm – Maher & von Hippel (2005) found that: (1) employees with better inhibitory ability perceived the open-plan office as more private; (2) stimulus screening ability (measured using Mehrabian's (1977) Stimulus Screening Scale) correlated with both manager-rated performance and job satisfaction; and (3) inhibitory ability (measured using The Stroop Test) impacted on job satisfaction, but not performance, when perceived privacy was low and job complexity high. Curiously, scores on the Stimulus Screening Scale and scores on The Stroop Test did not correlate, suggesting either that stimulus screening and inhibitory ability are distinct and independent processes or that the Strrop Test is a poor means of operationalizing inhibitory ability. Interesting also was the somewhat counter-intuitive finding in Maher and von Hippel's (2005) study that poor stimulus screening only had a negative impact on job satisfaction when privacy was *high* and complexity high (rather than when privacy was low and complexity high). In explaining this rather odd result, Maher and von Hippel point to the fact that the partitions in use at the research sites provided visual privacy but failed to block noise. Noise, they add, might be deemed to be more intrusive when there are no visual cues to determine its source. Open-plan office partitions might therefore create problems as well as solve them!

Perceived control plays a vital role in the aetiology of environmental stress. Evans et al. (1994), for example, note that control can moderate the relationship between environmental conditions and employee reactions, while Lee & Brand (2005) point to the positive association between high work control and job satisfaction, work performance, and psychological well-being. Reactions to open-plan working arrangements should therefore be more positive when employees have greater environmental control. Lee and Brand (2005) investigated this hypothesis on a sample of 228 participants working predominantly in a variety of open-office arrangements in five different organizations covering motor vehicle supply, general services administration, manufacturing, telecommunications, and marketing.

Their results showed that perceived control – assessed by items such as 'I can determine the organization/appearance of my work area' and 'The variety of work environments needed for my job is available to me' – did indeed have a significant and positive influence on both job satisfaction and group cohesiveness. From their results, it appears that perceived control is a matter of having some means of adjusting, altering, or modifying environmental conditions either through what one is able to do in or to one's own workspace (e.g., personalize or (re)arrange it) or through having access to a sufficient pool of different types of workspaces to call upon as necessary.

## Windows in the workplace

There is a widespread desire for windows in the workplace, with better comfort ratings being given by building occupants with greater access to windows (Vischer, 1996). Windowless or underground workplaces, on the other hand, attract a number of negative reactions including diminished satisfaction and increased health complaints (Butler & Biner, 1989; Hollon et al., 1980; Wotten et al., 1982; Wyon, 1981; Wyon & Nilsson, 1980). Employee surveys point to a number of reasons underpinning the desire for windows, including weather information, illumination, sunlight, better mood effects, aesthetics and appearance, ventilation, temperature control, and information about the outside world (Butler & Biner, 1989; Sundstrom, 1986; Wyon & Nilsson, 1980).

That there is more to window access than simple preference is evidenced by the fact that views of natural elements have consistently been found to be advantageous to health across a range of settings including hospitals (Ulrich, 1984), and prisons (Moore, 1982; West, 1986) as well as workplaces (Finnegan & Solomon, 1981; Leather et al., 1998; Ruys, 1970; Yildrim, Akalin-Baskaya, & Celebi, 2007).

Heerwagen & Orians (1986) suggested that the desire for windows was so great that workers in windowless offices would attempt to compensate for their absence by adorning the office walls, dividing partitions etc with 'nature themes' (e.g., pictures of landscapes and the like). Their own findings corroborated this view, i.e., they found more visual materials in windowless offices compared to offices with windows. Biner, Butler, Lovegrove, and Burns (1993), however, failed to confirm this so called 'compensation hypothesis', finding no difference in nature theme adornments between windowed and windowless offices. Rather, their data suggested that people adorn their workspaces with such things as pictures of people, nature, and plants for three principal reasons: personal aesthetics, personal remembrances, and to personalize the workspace.

Boubekri, Hulliv, and Boyer (1991) argue that the value of windows in the workplace derives directly from the sunlit area they give rise to, i.e., the issue is one of the quality of illumination – natural versus artificial light – rather than its intensity. Their results showed that sunlight penetration was indeed related to relaxation but only when participants were sitting sideways to window. They also reported an inverted U shaped relationship between sunlight penetration and relaxation, i.e., too little or too much sunlight are equally problematic.

Leather et al. (1998) note that windows in the workplace give rise to three potential influencing mechanisms on well-being and behaviour: general level of illumination, illumination quality (sunlight penetration), and view (the percentage or rural elements in accessible view). They incorporated measures of each in a single study. In order to investigate the possibility that windows might have both direct and indirect effects upon well-being and behaviour, job strain was also measured (Karasek, 1979). A series of correlation and hierarchical multiple linear regression analyses were then conducted to try to establish (1) the impact of each potential influencing mechanism and (2) whether its impact was direct (i.e., independent of level of job strain) or indirect (i.e., resulted from its interaction with levels of job strain). Three outcome measures were used in their study – job satisfaction, intention to quit the organization, and self-reported general well-being – while gender, adaptation and job status were all controlled for in their statistical analyses.

Level of illumination – measured objectively using a light meter – was not found to correlate with any of the outcome measures. Sunlight penetration was found to have a direct effect upon job satisfaction, intention to quit, and self-reported well-being but no indirect effects. View, on the other hand, had no direct effects but interacted with job strain to influence both intention to quit and aspects of self-reported well-being. Having a view of rural elements, they found, helped to suppress the negative impact of job strain upon both intention to quit and well-being. In line with the idea that elements of the physical environment might contribute to coping resources, it seems that a view of nature can help in coping with job strain. The direct effect of sunlight, they suggest, is possibly a matter of melatonin secretion and circadian rhythms.

In somewhat similar vein, Yildrim, Akalin-Baskaya, and Celebi (2007) explored the possibility that access to a window might help workers cope with the overstimulation and lack of privacy inherent in the open-plan office. Their results showed that those employees whose workspace was nearer to a window had a more positive perception of the worksite than those whose workspace was further away. Those who were further from a window also complained more of being disturbed by their colleagues; while those with ready access to a window – and whose workspace had the benefit of high partitions providing a reasonable level of privacy – reported higher satisfaction with the worksite. Having access to a window, it seems, helps to compensate for the negative effects of the open-plan office.

## Workplace noise

Whereas sound is an objective fact, noise, typically defined as unwanted sound, is a psychological phenomenon. Noise, in other words, is sound that is appraised as unwanted, unpleasant, or in some other way distracting. Noise is not dependent upon the intensity or sound level of the noise but its meaning given our current goals and circumstances. Frequently, noise is seen as an environmental stressor (Evans & Johnson, 2000), exposure to which is associated with a range of negative outcomes including impaired physical health (e.g., hearing damage, elevated neuro-endocrine and cardio-vascular responses, hypertension, and ischaemic heart disease); poorer psychological health (e.g., mental instability, depression, and overall nervousness, anger, and aggression); impaired quality of life (e.g., disturbed daily activities and sleep disruption); and impaired language development, cognition, and learning in children (Bronzaft, 2002; Evans & Lepore, 1993; Hiramatsu, 1999; Hiramatsu, Yamamoto, Taira, Ito, & Nakasone, 1997; Passchier-Vermeer & Passchier, 2000).

Research on the non-auditory effects of noise, i.e., its impact upon motivation and performance, physiological change, annoyance, and so on, shows that cardio-vascular responses to noise habituate unless the individual is noise sensitive and/or is engaged in highly demanding tasks. Exposure to uncontrollable noise has also been shown to lead to a post stressor effect (deficit) in subsequent task performance, an effect believed to result from learned helplessness. This interpretation is supported by research showing that manipulations of perceived control over the noise largely ameliorate any negative motivational or performance after-effects (Evans & Johnson, 2000).

The majority of research on the non-auditory effects of noise has tended to focus upon the impact of loud noise either in the laboratory or where people live or study close to such high intensity sources as major airports. Only recently have published studies emerged on the consequences of exposure to low-intensity noise such as that characteristic of the modern office. This, despite the fact that exposure to noise is reported to be one of the most commonly reported stressors in the office environment (Sundstrom, Town, Rice, Osborn, & Brill, 1994).

Evans & Johnson (2000) report a significant increase in epinephrine at the end of a three hour experimental task in 'noisy' (55dB) versus 'quiet' (40dB) experimental conditions. This 'noisy' condition was also associated with a statistically significant decrease in attempts at solving unsolvable puzzles and with a significant decrease in postural adjustment during the task. They conclude that the after-effects of diminished motivation found in exposure to loud noise are also to be found in exposure to low intensity noise. They note also, however, that the impact of noise exposure on outcomes or dependent measures is not always consistent, e.g., in their study no significant changes in self-reported stress, cortisol, or norepinephrine were found despite the significant differences in epinephrine, motivation and postural adjustment. Their overall conclusion is that it is not sound intensity that matters but the controllability of the noise.

Leather, Beale, and Sullivan (2003) investigated the impact of low intensity noise on 128 UK local government clerical workers in two matched city centre offices. Objective and questionnaire data were collected relating to three predictor variables: objective noise level, subjective rating of noise, and job strain. Three outcome or dependent measures were assessed: job satisfaction, organizational commitment, and self-reported health and well-being. The objectively assessed sound levels in the two offices ranged from 45 to 63dB with a median of 55dB.

A median split was used to divide participants into 'low' and 'high' noise levels (below and above the median respectively). A similar procedure was used to divide participants into 'low' and 'high' job strain categories. The resulting $2 \times 2$ matrix was analysed using a two-way between subjects analysis of variance to explore the direct and indirect effect of noise on job satisfaction, organizational commitment, and self-reported health and well-being respectively. The results showed that noise had no main effect on any of these three outcomes but did interact with job strain to produce a statistically significant interaction on each. Job strain also had a significant direct effect on all three outcomes. On the basis of their results, Leather, Beale, and Sullivan (2003) conclude that while low levels of noise might not be stressful in themselves, they can make a contribution to the overall stress equation. In effect, even a low level of background noise can make it more difficult to cope with an otherwise stressful job or set of work tasks.

## SUMMARY AND CONCLUSIONS

In writing this chapter we set ourselves the goals of outlining the part played by the design of the physical environment in respect of OHP's focus upon the interplay of psychological, social, and organizational aspects of work in impacting upon individual and organizational health. In doing so, we sought both to review some of the evidence that the design of the physical workspace has a discernible effect on employee well-being and behaviour and to provide a general explanation, or framework, to guide interpretation of an environmental psychology of the workplace.

What is hopefully clear from the evidence reviewed in respect of the open-plan office, windows in the workplace, and the negative impact of even relatively low intensity noise is that the physical environment of the workplace does indeed have a marked and measurable impact upon worker well-being and behaviour. Research exploring other aspects of the physical environment, e.g., indoor air quality (Milton, Glencross, & Walters, 2000) and lighting (Veitch & Newsham, 2000), demonstrates a similar impact of the physical environment upon employee health and behaviour.

What has hopefully also been made apparent is the need, in researching the impact of the physical workspace, to consider and examine the possibility that the physical environment has both direct and indirect effects upon employee well-being and behaviour. In short, the physical workspace might impact upon behaviour both independently of psychosocial aspects of work and in combination with them. The direct effect of sunlight yet indirect effect of view reported by Leather et al. (1998) is a case in point, as is the need to take task characteristics and individual differences into account in determining the non-auditory impact of noise, as opposed to its direct impact upon hearing loss. The full impact of the physical environment of the workplace can only be known when both direct and indirect effects are accounted for (Evans, Johansson, & Carrere, 1994).

While an increasing amount of evidence points to the demonstrated impact of the physical workspace upon well-being and behaviour there is still much to be known. One area of possible future inquiry is to fully unpack the meaning, mechanisms, and significance of control over the physical workspace. While some form of mastery or functional control over environmental conditions is one obvious mechanism of control, so too are the ability to personalize the workspace (e.g., adorn or decorate it to one's own taste and inclination) (Wells, 2000) and employee involvement in the design process itself (e.g., participatory ergonomics) (McCoy, 2002).

The issue of office personalisation brings to the fore the possibility that the physical workspace has both functional and symbolic influence. In his famous dictum, Kurt Lewin argued that behaviour is a function of person by environment (Fiske, 2004). While, to date, much of the emphasis in work psychology has been to construe the environment in social terms, the argument here is not only that we should give due account to the physical environment but that the physical and social environments are inextricably intertwined (Bonnes & Secchiaroli, 1995). Thus a supportive physical environment (Evans & McCoy, 1998; Ulrich, 1991) might be construed as part and parcel of a supportive social and organizational environment. In essence, the quality and character of the physical environment at work is read as a message or communication of the value, status, and worth ascribed to those who work there (McCoy, 2002). The investigation of symbolic workspace is a further likely area of fruitful research endeavour.

Since teamwork is becoming ever more important in the modern workplace (Mumford, Iddekinge, Morgeson, & Campion, 2008) the manner in which physical workspace can support team identity, development, cohesion, and performance is another critical area of future inquiry (McCoy, 2002). How, for example, can the spatial organization of the workplace, the physical resources available to employees and the use of colour, signs, and other architectonic details be used to support such outcomes as team communication and collaboration, knowledge sharing, collective personalization, team-based creative expression, and collaborative performance?

The concept of stress, we believe, provides a useful heuristic for exploring the impact of the physical environment of the workplace, not least because it holds appraisal processes at its core, accommodates and integrates physical and psychosocial elements within a single explanatory framework, and gives due weight to individual differences and other moderating factors. Just as importantly, the concept of stress provides a simple means of making sense of what the physical workspace should and should not do to support individual and organizational health and effectiveness. As McCoy (2002, p. 457) puts it:

> The physical environment of work should not exacerbate ... problems. Indeed, it should provide methods of coping with and managing this stress. The physical workplace ... can support the people who work there by acknowledging psychological and physiological needs specific to the individual, their tasks, and the social and cultural context of their work.

Such concerns are at the very heart of OHP.

## Suggestions for Further Reading

Evans, G. W., Johansson, G., & Carrere, S. (1994). Psychological factors and the physical environment: Inter-relations in the workplace. In C. N. Cooper, & I. T. Robertson (Eds.), *International review of industrial and organizational psychology* (Vol. 9, pp. 1–29). Chichester, UK: Wiley.

Halpern, D. (1995). *Mental health and the built environment: More than bricks and mortar?* London: Taylor & Francis.

McCoy, J. M. (2002). Work Environments. In R. B. Bechtel, & A. Churchman (Eds.). *Handbook of environmental psychology.* New York: Wiley.

Ornstein, S. (1990). Linking environmental and industrial/organizational psychology. *Organizational Psychology, Vol. 5* (pp. 1995–2228). Chichester: Wiley.

Vischer, J. (2007). The effects of the physical environment on job performance: towards a theoretical model of workspace stress. *Stress and Health, 23,* 175–184.

# References

Allen, T. J., & Gerstberger, P. G. (1973). A field experiment to improve communications in a product engineering department: The nonterritorial office. *Human Factors, 15,* 488–498.

Baron, R. M., & Kenny, D. (1986). The moderator-mediator variable distinction in some social psychological research: Conceptual, strategic, and statistical considerations. *Journal of Personal and Social Psychology, 51,* 1173–1182.

Berlyne, D. E. (1960). *Conflict, arousal and curiosity.* New York: McGraw Hill.

Biner, P. M., Butler, D. L., Lovegrove, T. E., & Burns, R. L. (1993). Windowlessness in the workplace: A re-examination of the compensation hypothesis. *Environment and Behavior,* 25(2), 205–227.

Bonnes, M. & Secchiaroli, G. (1995). *Environmental psychology: A psycho-social introduction.* London: Sage.

Boubekri, M., Hull, R. B., & Boyer, L. L. (1991). Impact of window size and sunlight penetration on office workers' mood and satisfaction: A novel way of assessing sunlight. *Environment and Behavior, 23,* 474–493.

Brehm, J. W. (1966). *A theory of psychological reactance.* New York: Academic Press.

Brehm, S. S., & Brehm, J. W. (1981). *Psychological reactance: A theory of freedom and control.* New York: Academic Press.

Brill, M., Weidemann, S., Alard, L., Olson, J., & Keable, E. (2001). *Disproving widespread myths about workplace design.* Jasper, IN: Kimball International.

Brooks, M. J., & Kaplan, A. (1972). The office environment: Space planning and affective behaviour. *Human Factors, 14,* 373–391.

Bronzaft, A. L. (2002). Noise Pollution: A Hazard to Physical and Mental Well-Being. In R. B. Bechtel, & A. Churchman (Eds). *Handbook of environmental psychology.* New York: Wiley.

Butler, D. L., & Biner, P. M. (1989). Effects of setting on window preferences and factors associated with those preferences. *Environment and Behavior, 21,* 17–32.

Canter, D. V., & Craik, K. H. (1981). Environmental psychology. *Journal of Environmental Psychology, 1,* 1–11.

Carlopio, J. R., & Gardner, D. (1992). Direct and interactive effects of the physical work environment on attitudes. *Environment and Behavior, 24,* 579–601.

Cohen, S. (1978). Environmental load and the allocation of attention. In A. Baum, J. E. Singer, & S. Valins (Eds.), *Advances in environmental psychology* (Vol. 1, pp. 1–29). Hillsdale, NJ: Erlbaum.

Cox, T. (1998). Work-related stress: from environmental exposure to ill health. In R. McGaig, & M. Harrington (Eds.), *The changing nature of occupational health.* Norwich: HSE Books.

Cox, T., Baldursson, E., & Rial González, E. (2000). Occupational health psychology. *Work & Stress, 14,* 101–104.

Duvall-Early, K., & Benedict, J. O. (1992). The relationship between privacy and different components of job satisfaction. *Environment and Behavior, 24,* 670–679.

Evans, G. W. (2001). Environmental stress and health. In, A. Baum, T. Revenson, & J. E. Singer (Eds.). *Handbook of health psychology.* Hillsdale, NJ: Erlbaum.

Evans, G. W., & Cohen, S. (1987). Environmental stress. In D. Stokols, & I. Altman (Eds.), *Handbook of environmental psychology* (Vol. 1, pp. 571–610). New York: Wiley-Interscience.

Evans, G. W., & Johnson, D. (2000). Stress and open-office noise. *Journal of Applied Psychology, 85 (5),* 779–783.

Evans, G. W., & Lepore, S. J. (1993). Nonauditory effects of noise on children: A critical review. *Children's Environments, 10,* 31–51.

Evans, G. W., & McCoy, J. M. (1998). When buildings don't work: The role of architecture in human health. *Journal of Environmental Psychology, 18,* 85–94.

Evans, G. W., Johansson, G., & Carrere, S. (1994). Psychological factors and the physical environment: Inter-relations in the workplace. In C. N. Cooper, & I. T. Robertson (Eds.), *International review of industrial and organizational psychology* (Vol. 9, pp. 1–29). Chichester: Wiley.

Finnegan, M. C. & Solomon, L. Z. (1981). Work attitudes in windowed vs. windowless environments. *Journal of Social Psychology, 115,* 291–292.

Fiske, S. T. (2004). *Social beings: Core motives in social psychology.* NJ: Wiley.

Furnham, A. (1997). *The psychology of behaviour at work: The individual in the organization.* Hove: Taylor-Francis.

Griffiths, A. (1998). The psychosocial work environment. In R. McGaig, & M. Harrington (Eds.), *The changing nature of occupational health.* Norwich: HSE Books.

Hedge, A. (1982). The open plan office: A systematic investigation of employee reactions to their work environment. *Environment and Behavior, 14*(5), 519–542.

Heerwagen, J. H., & Orias, G. H. (1986). Adaptions to windowlessness: A study of the use of visual décor in windowed and windowless offices. *Environment and Behavior, 18,* 623–639.

Heimstra, N. W., & McFarling, L. H. (1978). *Environmental psychology.* CA: Brooks/Cole.

Hiramatsu, K. (1999). *A report on the aircraft noise as a public health problem in Okinawa.* Okinawa, Japan: Okinawa Prefectural Government, Department of Culture and Environmental Affairs.

Hiramatsu, K., Yamamoto, T., Taira, K., Ito, A., & Nakasone, T. (1997). A survey of health effects due to aircraft noise on residents living around Kadena air base in the Ryukyus. *Journal of Sound and Vibration, 205,* 451–460.

Hollon, S. D., Kendall, P. C., Norsted, S., & Watson, D., 1980. Psychological responses to earth sheltered multilevel and above ground structures with and without windows. *Underground Space, 5,* 171–178.

Karasek, R. A. (1979). Job demands, job decision latitude, and mental strain: Implications for design. *Administrative Science Quarterly, 24,* 285–306.

Lazarus, R. S., & Folkman, S. (1984). *Stress, appraisal, and coping.* New York: Springer.

Leather, P., Beale, D., & Sullivan, L. (2003). Noise, psychological stress and their interaction in the workplace. *Journal of Environmental Psychology, 23,* 213–222.

Leather, P., Beale, D., Santos, A., Watts, J., & Lee, L. (2003). Outcomes of environmental appraisal of different hospital waiting areas. *Environment and Behavior, 35*(6), 842–869.

Leather, P, Pygras, M., Beale, D., & Lawrence, C. (1988). Windows in the workplace: Sunlight, view and occupational stress. *Environment and Behavior, 30,* 739–762.

Lee, Y., & Brand, J. L. (2005). Effects of control over office workspace on perceptions of the work environment and work outcomes. *Journal of Environmental Psychology, 25,* 323–333.

Levy-Leboyer, C. (1982). *Psychology and environment.* London: Sage.

Maher, A., & von Hippel, C. (2005). Individual differences in employee reactions to open-plan offices. *Journal of Environmental Psychology, 25,* 219–229.

McCoy, J. M. (2002). Work Environments. In R. B. Bechtel, & A. Churchman (Eds.), *Handbook of environmental psychology.* New York: Wiley.

McCoy, J. M., & Evans, G. W. (2005), Physical work environment, in J. Barling, K. Kelloway, & M. Frone (Eds.), *Handbook of work stress,* Thousand Oaks, CA: Sage.

Mehrabian, A. (1977). A questionnaire measure of individual differences in stimulus screening and associated differences in arousability. *Environmental Psychology and Nonverbal Behavior, 1,* 89–103.

Milgram, S. (1970). The experience of living in cities. *Science, 167,* 1461–1468.

Milton, D. K., Glencross, P. M., & Walters, M. D. (2000). Risk of sick leave associated with outdoor air supply rate, humidification and occupation complaints. *Indoor Air, 10(4),* 212–221.

Moore, E. O. (1982). A prison environment's effects on health care service demands. *Journal of Environmental Systems, 11,* 17–34.

Mumford, T. V., Van Iddekinge, C. H., Morgeson, F. P., & Campion, M. A. (2008). The team role test: Development and validation of a team role knowledge situational judgment test. *Journal of Applied Psychology, 93 (2),* 250–267.

Oldham, G. (1988). Effects of changes in workspace partitions and spatial density on employee reactions: A quasi-experiment. *Journal of Applied Psychology, 73,* 253–258.

Ornstein, S. (1990). Linking environmental and industrial/organizational psychology. In C. L. Cooper, & I. T. Robertson (Eds.), *International Review of Industrial and Organizational Psychology* (Vol. 5, pp. 195–228). Chichester: John Wiley & Sons.

Passchier-Vermeer, W., & Passchier, W. F. (2000). Noise exposure and public health. *Environmental Health Perspectives, 108,* 123–131.

Seligman, M. E. P. (1975). *Helplessness.* San Francisco: Freeman.

Sonnenfeld, J. (1966). Variable values in space and landscape: An inquiry into the nature of environmental necessity. *Journal of Social Issues, 22,* 71–82.

Sundstrom, E. (1986). *Work places: The psychology of the physical environment in offices and factories.* New York: Cambridge University Press.

Sundstrom, E., Herbert, R. K., & Brown, D. W. (1982). Privacy and communication in an open-plan office. *Environment and Behavior, 14,* 543–559.

Sundstrom, E., Town, J. P., Rice, R. W. Osborn, D. P., & Brill, M. (1994). Office noise, satisfaction and performance. *Environment and Behavior, 26,* 195–222.

Ulrich, R. S. (1984). View through a window may influence recovery from surgery. *Science, 224,* 420–421.

Ulrich, R. S. (1991) Effects of interior design on wellness: Theory and recent scientific research. *Journal of Health Care Interior Design, 3,* 97–10.

Veitch, R., & Arkkelin, D. (1995). *Environmental psychology: An interdisciplinary perspective.* Englewood Cliffs, NJ: Prentice-Hall.

Veitch, R., & Newsham, G. R. (2000). Exercised control, lighting choices, and energy use: An office simulation experiment. *Journal of Environmental Psychology, 20(3),* 219–237.

Vischer, J. (1996). *Workspace strategies: Environment as a tool for work.* New York: Chapman & Hall.

Vischer, J. (2007). The effects of the physical environment on job performance: Towards a theoretical model of workspace stress. *Stress and Health, 23,* 175–184.

Wells, M. (2000). Office clutter or meaningful personal displays: The role of office personalisation in employee and organisational well-being. *Journal of Environmental Psychology, 20,* 239–255.

West, M. J. (1986). Landscape views and stress responses in the prison environment. Unpublished Master's thesis, University of Washington, Seattle.

Wohlwill, J. F. (1974). Human response levels to environmental stimulation. *Human Ecology, 2,* 127–147.

Wyon, D. (1981). Upplevelse av vistelse i fönsterlösa lokaler. In M. Küller (Ed.), *Icke Visuella Effekter av Optisk Strålning. Symposium i Lund 6 maj, 1981Lund, Miljöpsykologiska Monografier,* Nr. 2, pp. 17–21.

Wyon, D., & Nilsson, I. (1980). Human experience of windowless environments in factories, offices, shops and colleges in Sweden. In J. Krochmann (Ed.), *Proceedings of the Symposium on Daylight: Physical, psychological and architectural aspects,* pp. 216–225.

Yerkes, R. M., & Dodson, J. D. (1908). The relation of strength of stimulus to rapidity of habit-formation. *Journal of Comparative Neurology and Psychology, 18,* 459–482.

Yildirim, K., Akalin-Baskaya, A., & Celebi, M. (2007). The effects of window proximity, partition height, and gender on perceptions of open-plan offices. *Journal of Environmental Psychology, 27,* 154–165.

Zahn, L. G. (1991). Face to face communication in an office setting: The effects of position, proximity and exposure. *Communication Research, 18,* 737–754.

Zimring, C. (2002). Postoccupancy Evaluation: Issues and Implementation. In R. B. Bechtel, & A. Churchman (Eds.), *Handbook of environmental psychology.* New York: Wiley.

**9**

# Corporate Culture, Health, and Well-Being

## Gerard Zwetsloot and Stavroula Leka

### CHAPTER OUTLINE

In preceding chapters, the changing world of work and the challenges and opportunities that this presents to occupational health were discussed at length. This chapter focuses on an often-overlooked element of organizational life – corporate culture – as a determinant of health and well-being, and as a variable to be manipulated for the promotion of occupational health. The culture of organizations has a significant – but often unnoticed – influence on the decisions and behaviour of individuals and the organization as a whole. Shared values are a main element of corporate culture, and are important for the identity and cohesion of organizations; they are linked with business ethics and are important for corporate social responsibility (CSR).

## Introduction

*What is the importance of organizational culture
in relation to employee well-being?*

While managers usually do their best to design and run companies in a rational and planned way, the reality is often different: personal convictions, habits, emotions, conflicts, values, and mental models all play a role in decision-making and the actual behaviour of people and organizations. Also, occupational health and well-being, as well as the motivation, productivity, and creativity of people at work, are greatly influenced by organizational values and organizational culture.

Everybody knows that people have to breathe all the time and will die very soon after breathing stops. However, it is naive to assume that breathing is 'the meaning of life'. There are obviously more important values in human life. Similarly, companies need to make money. If they stop making money, they will die (or be taken over). Increasingly, managers have become aware that there is more to organizational life than the imperative to make money. By defining and pursuing corporate values, and contributing to social and/or ecological sustainability, companies give meaning to their existence, thereby improving their status in society (and often their profit margin). Occupational health is an important social issue and a responsibility of every organization. In this chapter we will therefore explore the links between corporate culture, occupational health, and well-being.

## Key Issues and Definitions in Corporate Culture and Corporate Health

*What is corporate culture?*
*How is corporate culture defined?*

The culture of an organization comprises the (often tacit) values, norms, opinions, attitudes, taboos, and visions of reality that have an important influence on the decision and behaviour of organizations. Increasingly, explicit core values of organizations are recognized as main determinants of the organization's identity, and guide corporate strategies. The organization is then regarded as a social community that shares some values etc. (e.g., McKinsey's 7-S model: see Figure 9.1).

McKinsey's 7-S model illustrates the idea that shared values are underlying company strategy, structure, and systems (the hard side of business) but also the company skills, staff, and style (the soft side of business).

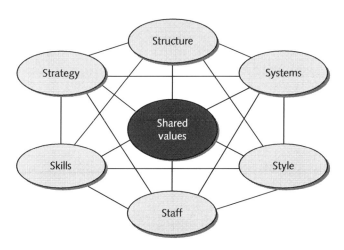

**Figure 9.1**   McKinsey's 7-S model.

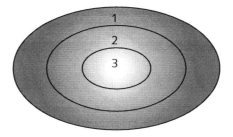

1  Artefacts

2  Espoused core values

3  Basic assumptions

**Figure 9.2**  The three levels of organizational culture (Schein, 2002).

The culture of an organization determines 'how we do things around here'. Often the knowledge of the culture remains partly unconscious or subconscious. The culture is usually transferred to new members of the group or organization by means of implicit socialization processes.

Schein (2002) clarified that there are always different layers in a culture (see Figure 9.2). He distinguishes three levels that are closely related: basic assumptions, espoused core values and artefacts (including aspects of behaviour).

*Basic assumptions* cannot be directly observed or perceived, but they are the core aspects of an organization's culture. *Espoused core values* are the core values that the organization and its top management proclaim to be important. Finally, *artefacts* are phenomena co-determined by corporate culture; they can easily be observed or measured, but it is not so easy to clarify the link with the two underlying layers of culture. Culture is not a static item that can easily be measured, but rather a set of patterns that can be identified and understood. Ethnographic methods (e.g., discourse analysis) and observational methods are often more effective in this respect than surveys (surveys are not very useful to get insight into unconscious or subconscious factors).

As human values are important determinants of corporate culture, there is a direct link with business ethics and with corporate social responsibility. Business ethics is defined in Wikipedia as a form of applied ethics that examines ethical principles and moral or ethical problems that arise in a business environment. It applies to all aspects of business conduct and is relevant to the conduct of individuals and business organizations as a whole. The European Commission defined corporate social responsibility as the incorporation of social and environmental concerns into business operations and into their interactions with stakeholders (EC, 2001).

Through human values, the rational aspects of health management can be complemented with value-based approaches (Zwetsloot, 2003). Company strategies become broader than the traditional focus on financial goals only, as social, ecological, and ethical concerns are becoming increasingly important. Organizational culture is greatly influenced by leadership style. An example is the concept of servant leadership, developed by Greenleaf (2002), whereby managers are aware that work and business are not an aim in themselves, but rather means to realize something meaningful. Human and social values are seen as an integral part of business. The world and people should be respected and well treated. Managers have the opportunity to help their employees to further develop themselves, for the benefit of people, business, and society at large.

Let us first consider some definitions. As discussed in Chapter 6, *Health* has been defined by the World Health Organization as a complete state of physical, mental and social well-being, not merely the absence of disease or infirmity (WHO, 1948). The WHO definition of health clearly expresses that health and well-being are interdependent and closely related. However, the concept health is usually often associated with the medical profession, focusing on cure and prevention of diseases, and paying attention to groups at risk for such diseases, often with an emphasis on physical health. The concept of well-being is mostly associated with mental and social aspects of health, and with human resource management.

The concept health is also used to refer to the 'health' of organizations: *organizational health*. However, there are several definitions in this respect. A definition of a healthy organization derived from an individual health perspective is given by the Enterprise for Health network as one whose culture, management, working climate, and other business practices create an environment that promotes the health, effectiveness, and performance of its employees. From a business perspective, De Geus (1997) introduced the concept of 'the living company' and researched the mortality and life expectancy of firms. In this way, De Geus identified four basic characteristics of healthy companies: they are sensitive to their environment (and are always learning to adapt); they are cohesive with a strong sense of identity; they are tolerant to activities in the margin and to decentralized initiatives and experiments; and they are conservative in financing.

Obviously the above are relevant to the *values* of the organization: core beliefs that guide and motivate attitudes and actions. Before we continue with the meaning of corporate culture for health and well-being, we first consider changes in policies and practices in the promotion of health and well-being at work.

## The Promotion of Occupational Health and Well-Being: From Policy to Practice

*What changes have taken place in recent times in regard to organizational perspectives on workplace health promotion?*

Traditionally, the focus of occupational health was on risk reduction and control. This view regarded ill-health as problematic for the individual and costly for the organization. As a result, the reduction of ill-health and return-to-work following illness are the traditional goals of occupational health policies. However, increasingly, it is recognized that health and well-being should (also) be regarded as a resource, as an important aspect of the organization's human and social capital. The policies and practices of organizations are therefore changing, and increasingly companies pursue a double goal: promoting health and well-being of the individual employees, while strengthening organizational health. This development from a traditional health management perspective towards an integrated health management approach is presented in Box 9.1.

---

**Box 9.1 The shift from traditional health management towards the integrated management of health and well-being**

*Source:* adapted from Frick & Zwetsloot, (2007). From safety management to corporate citizenship – an overview of approaches to health management. In U. Johansson, G. Ahonen, & R. Roslander (Eds.), *Work, health and management control* (pp. 99–134). Stockholm: Thomson Fakta.

| Traditional health management | Integrated health management |
|---|---|
| *From reactive problem-solving* | *to proactive solutions and positive challenges* |
| Focus on risk-reduction and on solving problems. | Focus also on the positive value for business and proactive action to improve health. |
| Mainly, reactions to costs, other problems, and legislative requirements. | Mainly, recognition of health as a business resource. |
| *From a mainly medical, regulatory* Health issues are seen as individual and operational problems, despite a mandatory duty for a preventive management. | *to a business perspective* Health is a company asset that needs to be part of the business strategy. |
| Health is associated with problems that managers often are, but do not feel, responsible for. | Health is associated with company benefits and productivity that are the core responsibility of managers. |
| Medicalization of people's ill health. | De-medicalization with emphasis on subjective and positive health. |
| Only comprising activities that are explicitly meant to influence health. | Comprising activities that have an implicit or explicit impact on health. |
| Little impact on company image, except as specific scandals and negative labour relations. | Positive impact on the image of the company and its brands. |
| *From fragmented activities* Focusing on specific issues for specific target groups and addressing specific operational risks. | *to an integrated approach* Integrated approach, with a focus on the strategic business importance for management to control health. |
| Management sees illness, complaints, and absenteeism as closely related and ignores, | Health is recognized as a continuum, where there is no one-to-one |

for example, presenteeism and non-absence-related injuries.

relationship between illness/symptoms and absenteeism. The focus is on capabilities and work ability instead of disabilities and absenteeism.

*From attention to people with health problems*
Focus only on employees who have risky jobs, suffer from working disabilities, or frequent or long-term illness.

*to caring for all personnel as well*
Focus also on all employees and their personal development (related to HRM).

*From cost*
Measures for reduction of sickness absence and control of risks are seen only as costs.

*to a sound investment*
Measures for reduction of sickness absence, including providing some costly measures as CSR, are seen as investments in healthy people and a healthy company as a business resource.

Costs are incurred for corrective action, cure, and post care despite the duty to prevent risks at the source.

Costs for proactive and preventive health activities are regarded as a sound investment (and prevention is also much cheaper than corrections).

*From seeing health as a private issue*

Managers see it as the responsibility of the individual worker to protect himself or herself against health risks, despite their legal duty to prevent all work-related risks.

*to seeing it as an organizational issue*
Promoting and protecting employee health is a business issue, involving both managing risk prevention and helping employees to take care of their health.

Box 9.1 illustrates that the way health and well-being and their management are perceived and managed are rapidly developing. As a result, many different perceptions of health and health management play a role in company practices. Nowadays, the scope of health management is broader than avoiding occupational health risks at work. The distinction between occupational and public health issues is blurring, as many health problems have both work-related and other causes. Besides preventing risks at work, workplace health promotion has become important, and health management aims also to keep people at work (maintain work ability and develop employability), and enhance their productivity. Work is thereby no longer seen as mainly a threat to health, but increasingly as a condition that is favourable to health (Black, 2008).

The resource perspective on health emphasizes that health is closely related to the functioning of people and that healthy people are thus a human and business resource. From this perspective, health promotion is understood as a means to increase the human and social capital of the organization. This links the management of health and well-being to human resources management and productivity management. The societal meaning of health links it to corporate social responsibility.

## Corporate Social Responsibility and the Promotion of Health and Well-Being
......................................................................

*What is CSR?*
*What is the policy imperative for CSR?*

Corporate social responsibility (CSR) has many definitions but, in essence, it is based on the integration of economic, social, ethical and environmental concerns in business operations. A major social concern is for the welfare of key stakeholders in the business, especially employees (HSE, 2005). One important distinction between different types of CSR policies and activities is whether they are 'internal' in that they are targeted at management and employees of the firm itself, or 'external' in that they are targeted at outside groups such as suppliers, the society, or the environment (Bondy et al., 2004).

The internal dimension of CSR policies covers socially responsible practices concerning employees, relating to their safety and health, investing in human capital, managing change, and financial control. Recent occupational safety and health (OSH) promotion strategies by the European Commission (EC) and the European Agency for Safety and Health at Work (EU-OSHA) have attempted to link OSH with CSR, establishing a business case of strategic importance for organisations (EC, 2001, 2002; Zwetsloot & Starren, 2004). Health and safety at work is seen as an essential component of CSR and companies are increasingly recognizing that they cannot be good externally, while having poor social performance internally (ibid.). CSR is also identified as a critical component for engaging small and medium-sized enterprises (SMEs) to move the area of OSH forward (HSE, 2005).

Recent international and national CSR initiatives are complemented by innovative safety and health initiatives that go beyond traditional OSH issues and have either an implicit or explicit relationship with CSR. They change the context of safety and health at work at company level. Zwetsloot and Starren (2004), in a report for EU-OSHA, categorized these initiatives as:

- raising awareness, awards and ethical initiatives;
- exchange of knowledge: best practice, networks, pilot projects, and guidelines;
- standardization and certification;
- reporting (external) and communication;
- innovative partnerships, NGOs, public and private;
- ethical trade initiatives ('fair trade');
- financial sector involvement/financial incentives.

The nature of the relationship between CSR and OSH varies widely among the initiatives. Some refer explicitly to OSH items while others focus only on new social issues that have no tradition in companies, or on totally voluntary aspects (such as use of unfair labour practices by suppliers in developing countries or new European Union (EU) member states). Initiatives for promoting CSR are predominantly private and voluntary, while OSH initiatives are often dominated by legal regulation and governmental action. Relevant external stakeholders from a health and well-being perspective are, for example, family members, consumers, neighbours, or potential employees of the company, etc. In CSR, as in the promotion of health and well-being, there is a tendency to start with problem solving and risk management. Increasingly this focus is followed up by attention towards the creation of added-value (preferably for the company, its people, its stakeholders, and society at large).

## Corporate Culture and Health Management

*What issues need to be considered in the implementation of health management initiatives?*
*What is the CSR business case?*

Increasingly, CSR is becoming a *strategic* platform for health and safety management in enterprises. Companies that are perceived to be frontrunners in supporting human, social, and mental resources are often viewed as 'employers of choice'. A lot of organizations address such issues not purely as an obligation in law, but through a framework of common (business) sense and social responsibility. In doing so, many of these companies go beyond their legal obligations in relation to health management and view the promotion of well-being as part of their usual business practices.

### Health management and the importance of implementation of processes

The management of health and well-being requires systematically planned activities (like the ones for psychosocial risk management described in Chapter 5). This can and should be integrated in the management systems the company may have to manage general risks, e.g., via integrating it in OSH management systems, or in the planning and control cycle, or other existing procedures. For their realization, the plans and measures have to be *implemented*. Implementation processes are therefore an interesting area of research.

### The importance of internalization of values and responsible behaviour

However, the management of health is also about ethics and values, about doing the right things (as complementary to doing things right – see Zwetsloot, 2003), i.e., it is about awareness, responsible behaviour, and walking the talk. Plans and technical or organizational measures are usually not very helpful in bringing about such behavioural change. Behaviour is usually greatly influenced (positively or negatively) by social interactions (including leadership) and the organizational culture. In fact these factors greatly influence behaviour in an informal but often surprisingly effective way, i.e., 'how things are done around here'. While the keyword for systems and plans is implementation, for values and for ethical and behavioural aspects it is *internalization*. As part of CSR policy many companies provide training to their employees about corporate values and how to deal with ethical dilemmas. Values and ethical dilemmas related to health and well-being can easily be integrated into such CSR approaches.

Several health theories or models emphasize the importance of social cultural environmental factors in determining health and well-being, as well as associated behaviours. Examples are social ecological models (Stokhols et al., 1996), social learning theories (Bandura, 1986) and cognitive behavioural models like the theory of planned behaviour (Fishbein & Ajzen, 1975). In other literatures, the social environment is acknowledged as a co-determining factor for psychosocial health, e.g., in the job strain-stress model (Karasek & Theorell, 1990), job demands-job resources model (Demerouti et al., 2001). Social factors generally acknowledged as important for psychosocial health include social support (Thoits, 1995) and rewards (Siegrist, 1998). Peterson and Wilson (2002) presented a culture-work-health model to clarify that both individual and organizational health are greatly influenced by the organization's culture.

There is also a literature clarifying that organizational culture is an important determinant of workplace health (social-ecological theories for workplace health promotion, and health management approaches (Goetzel et al., 2007; Golaszevski et al., 2008); see also Chapter 6 on workplace health promotion; according to the latter, a new generation of health management systems is needed, that help to create a social context wherein health and the work environment are interacting mutually positively).

A related issue is organizational social capital (Hasle et al., 2007; Kouvonen et al., 2006; Kristensen et al., 2007; Oksanen et al., 2008). Hasle (2007) operationalized organizational social capital as trust, justice, and cooperation, and demonstrated a direct positive impact on psychosocial health.

With respect to occupational *safety* there is already a tradition, both in research and practice, to pay attention to, and try to influence, the organizational culture (Hale & Hovden, 1998). Thereby there is a lot of attention on the way safety is embedded in organizational practices, and how it is influenced by the leadership of (higher-level) managers (Parker et al., 2006). Many high reliability organizations nowadays strive explicitly for a 'safety culture', e.g., via the 'hearts and minds' programme developed for Shell (Hudson, 2001). There are several definitions of a safety culture. They focus, to varying degrees, on the way people think and behave in relation to safety (e.g., Cooper, 2000; Hale, 2000). Most definitions tend to reflect the view that safety culture is something an organisation 'is' rather than something it 'has' (Choudry, 2007).

The International Labour Organization (ILO) has a vision on decent work and a global preventative health and safety culture. According to the ILO, work is central to people's well-being. In addition to providing income, work can pave the way for broader social and economic advancement, strengthening individuals, their families, and communities. Such progress, however, hinges on work that is decent. Decent work sums up the aspirations of people in their working lives. The promotion of a preventative health and safety culture is key in this respect (ILO, 2009).

### Promoting responsible and healthy work practices

At a stakeholders' meeting on Integrated Health Management in the Netherlands in November 2005, some front-runner companies discussed their ambitions, motives, and goals with regard to health and health activities (Zwetsloot & Van Scheppingen, 2007). One of the main conclusions was that health for these companies is seen as a strategic asset, the motor of development and innovation. For these companies, the reason to invest in health is that they assume that health is a resource to achieve their business targets. These companies point out that they need (physically and mentally) healthy and vital people. Healthy people who work in safe, healthy, and stimulating conditions for these companies are the main prerequisites for productivity, flexibility, continuity, and innovation – the key to surviving as a company. From a business perspective, health for these companies is experienced as an asset that creates added value in terms of innovation and development, besides reducing various costs (e.g., sickness absence costs and medical costs). The following section focuses on one key CSR business network in Europe and discusses some of its activities in relation to health and well-being.

## A Business Network for CSR: CSR Europe

CSR Europe is the leading European business network for corporate social responsibility with around 75 multinational corporations and 25 national partner organizations as members. Its mission is to support member companies in integrating CSR into the way they do business, every day. CSR Europe sees the issue of health and well-being in the workplace as core to CSR objectives. It asserts that the business case ought to be soundly made, at moral, financial and other levels, but that this still needs to be communicated more efficiently in the language of business. One of the network's activities is the CSR Laboratory on Well-being in the Workplace. It aims to identify the key areas related to well-being issues in the workplace as well as mainstreaming and coordinating policy initiatives through discussions of best practices and development of associated tools. The Laboratory brought companies together, in 2007 and 2008, to understand, share and identify best practices, to facilitate an understanding of managerial performance, as well as highlight supporting tools and techniques. They developed a guide to capture the necessity of well-being strategies in the workplace, showcase best practices from participating companies, discuss reintegration theories and initiatives, and provide a comprehensive list of resources on various aspects of well-being theory, implementation and EU or national policies. Box 9.2 presents some key tips the Laboratory developed for implementing a successful well-being strategy.

## Box 9.2   CSR Europe's Tips for Implementing a Successful Well-Being Strategy

*Source:* CSR Europe (2008). *Wellbeing in the workplace: A guide with best practices and tips for implementing a successful wellbeing strategy at work.* Available at: www.csreurope.org/data/files/toolbox/wellbeing_guide.pdf.

Ensure top-level management understanding, endorsement and engagement in the establishment of a global well-being strategy.

Fully inform and involve employee representative bodies/trade unions as partners in the development and actions of the well-being policy.

Implement the global well-being policy locally by addressing the needs of the employees and respecting the country culture and legislation.

Mainstream well-being in daily business operations by making it cross-departmental and operational (e.g., move beyond HR/Health & Safety and incorporate within site objectives and business plan).

Identify and assess the root causes of poor well-being and promote and support best practices of good well-being.

Train managers and employees on risk factors (e.g., work organization, management style, the external environment in which the business operates, and individual resilience) appropriate for the organization, in order to facilitate prevention, early detection and awareness-raising at all levels. Manage with the applicable organizational processes and tools.

Provide independent and confidential communication channels through which employees can report on well-being issues.

Be aware of culturally appropriate terminology and adjust communication accordingly (e.g., well-being versus mental health).

Include questions about well-being in company surveys and provide employees with feedback on aggregate findings and proposed measures for improvement.

Ensure at all times confidentiality of individual employee data.

Ensure full organizational engagement of outsourced occupational health and well-being services (where applicable) in alignment with the service level agreement and business needs.

Recognize that employee responsibility and involvement forms a key element of a successful well-being programme.

The tips for implementing a successful well-being strategy are applicable for all organizations. However, the approach might need to be adjusted depending on the organization's size, resource availability, and allocation.

# The Business Case for Well-Being at Work

*What are the arguments in favour of promoting well-being at work?*

Absenteeism, staff turnover, productivity and staff satisfaction are well-being-related concerns that most businesses today struggle to overcome – and the costs of not doing so are surprisingly high. Health and well-being are central to the lives of individuals. Both are related themes that touch on all aspects of life, including the workplace.

Addressing well-being and the management of chronic illnesses has traditionally fallen upon national governments, and to a lesser extent, non-governmental organizations. While governments and non-governmental organizations aim to raise the general understanding on the importance of well-being at work, until now there has been relatively little awareness among employees and employers. Fortunately, well-being issues at work are gaining importance and greater attention on the business agenda.

Various reports highlight the importance of well-being strategies in the workplace. The Fourth European Survey on Working Conditions, published in February 2007 (EuroFound, 2007), reports that 62 per cent of European employees work to tight deadlines, while 60 per cent work at high speeds, compared to 19 per cent of those surveyed in 1990. Additionally, 28 per cent of the European workforce admits to suffering from health problems not related to occupational accident, and 35 per cent, on average, feel that their job puts their health at risk. A draft Consensus Paper on Mental Health at Work by the European Commission estimates that employment costs related to mental health disorders in 2004 were approximately 132 billion EUR. Such statistics demonstrate that poor health can reduce employee productivity and business profitability. It also highlights that positive employee well-being can significantly improve the internal welfare of an organization. Poor employee health can translate into increased absenteeism and reduced levels of productivity. Moreover, employees experiencing stress, chronic disease, or other productivity-decreasing factors cannot operate as efficiently, resulting in reduced motivation, engagement and health. Therefore, defining a strategy that addresses well-being issues within the workplace is in the best interest of businesses.

CSR Europe's Laboratory project resulted also in a booklet with chapters on (1) the business case for health and well-being at the workplace; (2) best practices for (a) prevention, (b) identification and support, (c) integration; and (3) well-being resources. In each concrete example they firstly define the business issue/problem, followed by the benefits for the company, and the benefits for the employee.

An important tip is to ensure that the policies and tools are properly deployed at all levels of the organization. It is a multi-disciplinary process (involving specialists and managers). Creating a network of 'ambassadors' among health safety and environment, human resources, and business representatives to implement corporate guidelines and foster local approaches on sites, with regular appraisal of results as part of a long-term strategy is also important.

## Case Study 9.1: The European Enterprise for Health Network

*Sources:* EfH (2008). *Enterprise for Health Network: Achieving Business Excellence – Health Wellbeing and Performance.* Bertelsmann Stiftung and BKK.

EfH (2009). *Information on the Enterprise for Health network.* Available at: www.enterprise-for-health.org/index.php?id=126.

European Enterprise for Health (EfH) is a network of around twenty European enterprises from different branches of industry in eleven countries. The network and its members are committed to the development of a corporate culture based on partnership and a modern company health policy. The companies participating in the EfH network share an important basic conviction: 'Activities of a corporate culture based on partnership and a company health policy are investments in the future of an enterprise. They ensure competitiveness in the long term by building-up and maintaining innovative human wealth.'

The EfH members share their experience on structuring and implementing corporate culture based on partnership and a company health policy amongst one another and in this way improve their own efforts. At the same time, EfH advocates its basic conviction to outsiders. Many companies have to reorganize and streamline their workflows in the wake of tougher international competition. Against this backdrop, the Network members perceive the further development of a corporate culture based on partnership and a company health policy as part of their social responsibility.

### Corporate culture based on partnership

A corporate culture based on partnership is characterized by openness, mutual respect, and trust in working life. One essential element of a corporate culture based on partnership is health and person-promoting work design. A corporate culture based on partnership is, at the same time, a basic condition for an exemplary company health policy. A corporate health policy comprises all activities to maintain and improve health at the workplace. Health is understood here as a management task and not as a limited responsibility of individuals. Health at the workplace can only arise if all company players combine forces and interact. They work closely together with those responsible in the fields of occupational safety and health and environmental protection, workplace health promotion, and quality management.

The company health policy creates the basic conditions for healthy working conditions and health-promoting behaviour of the employees by means of healthy work design, employee participation, and trend-setting concepts for staff development. These include the following topics which the members of the EfH network have set themselves as key activities:

- development of a corporate culture based on partnership;
- health and personality-promoting design of work and its environment;
- working time organization and new organizational forms of work;
- knowledge management – future strategy of how the company deals with knowledge and information;
- development of individual health competence of the employees; healthy work design for older employees;
- work-life balance/transitions within working life and transitions into and out of working life;
- social responsibility of companies in the neighbourhood and society;
- integration of all the aspects mentioned into management systems and HR management.

## What role does health play at the workplace?

Healthy working conditions derived from a corporate culture based on partnership not only make a crucial contribution to the health of the employees but they also govern the economic success of a company. For it is only with a highly motivated and healthy workforce that companies can survive against competition in the long term: the employees are the key potential for the development of innovative products and services and play a decisive role in customer satisfaction.

> The discussion on corporate culture also has an ethical dimension, which is characterized by two poles. At the one end of the spectrum there is the paradigm of the personal responsibility of every individual for his living conditions and thus also for his health. At the other end is the paradigm of solidarity emphasizing the responsibility of the community. (Prof. Dr. Jean-François Caillard, Scientific Advisor of the EfH Network)

Today, there is a consensus in the EfH Group which justifies investments in a corporate culture based on partnership and a company health policy. The member companies make these investments because:

- they share and support the values of a health-related corporate culture based on partnership;
- the effects of the social and demographic development call for a corporate culture oriented towards participation and health – especially with a view to the effects on the labor markets;
- they can improve productivity and growth as a result and develop sustainable customer relations.

EfH companies are convinced that there is a strong need for a new direction in the development of business strategy which can be best described by the notion of a *healthy organization:* an organization whose culture, management, working climate, and other business practices create an environment that promotes the health, effectiveness, and performance of its employees. Healthy organizations are financially successful and have healthy workforces. Healthy organizations are able to balance economic performance goals with employee health and wellness goals and can adapt the balance within the context of a continuously changing economic and social environment.

This conviction is driven by commonly shared values and both practical and scientific evidence. This central value is expressed by EfH's commonly shared belief that the quality in work including the human capital is *the* decisive factor for the economic and social success of our companies and society at large. Practical experience and research evidence clearly show that employee health, economic growth, and productivity can be improved by tackling the critical factors, which means making changes to job design, production systems, organizational systems, human resource management practice, and the overall corporate culture.

## Values which matter: Driving socially responsible leadership

Successful leadership today needs a clear value base which provides direction and offers a sense of coherence to all stakeholders. The key value is centred in the belief that social cohesion and successful economic performance need each other. This includes all levels of action: enterprises, local communities, countries, and supra-national regions such as the European Union. Views on the role of human resources, management practices, and corporate culture become critical fields for investment which help ensure the necessary flexibility and capabilities to manage change and continuously adapt to new environments.

High performance workplaces ensure that people are enabled to get involved in continuous learning. Work intensification – and its impact on the level of stress and health – is known to be the most important barrier to implementing a learning culture in many businesses. In particular, highly educated professionals, technical workers, managers, and other knowledge workers, who are regarded as the most strategic contributors to innovation and productivity improvements yet who are simultaneously affected by high levels of job stress and work intensification, require a high level of work quality, which in turn includes a healthy work environment.

Several challenges have been identified by the EfH network: the challenges of an ageing workforce, work-life balance, technological change, diversity, flexible work, knowledge management, lifelong learning, and the promotion of a healthy lifestyle. By tackling each of these challenges, the goal is to improve:

- the employees' work motivation;
- their deployment flexibility;

- their identification with the company;
- their general willingness to perform;
- their own initiative to improve workflows and environmental conditions;
- creativity with respect to product and service improvements.

With these effects on the workers, their contribution can be increased especially in the critical value-added processes through improved planning capability of the processes as a result of lower sickness rates and reduced staff turnover, shorter development times for products and services, reduced likelihood of faults or errors. As a result, supporting individual resources and the healthy design of the working environment are becoming a task for management. If supervisors above all have a crucial influence on their employees' perception of stress, then they assume a key position in this connection and they are called upon to act as honourable examples.

The exchange of experience between the members of the EfH network led to the conclusion that a greater focus is needed for the following topics:

- the intensification of work;
- mental health (the Achilles' heel of a knowledge-based economy);
- a value-oriented management and leadership;
- a step towards a healthy company.

In the past, the promotion of health and well-being at the workplace often concentrated on the individual behaviour of employees. Healthy companies are now going one step further: they are also looking after the ability of each individual not only to be and remain prepared for change in times of upheaval but also to be able to actively support such change. This approach combines work organization, work design, supportive leadership, learning, innovation, and health.

## SUMMARY AND CONCLUSIONS

In this chapter we have shown that organizations and business networks are increasingly acknowledging the relevance of corporate culture and corporate social responsibility for the functioning of organizations, and for promoting (or managing) health and well-being. Key to the development of organizational culture is the development of shared values, thereby integrating them into the 'basic assumptions' of the organization. While there is already a tradition of fostering 'safety cultures' in organizations, the attention on the impact of culture on health and well-being is relatively new.

The resource perspective on health and well-being is also rather new, and is clearly different from the medical profession's focus on ill-health and return to work. The latter focus is usually limited to the 5 per cent of the employees that are 'at risk'. From a resource perspective it is more important to focus on the health and well-being of 100 per cent of the employees, as this will improve their mental and social functioning and thereby their productivity and creativity. The examples from the networks of CSR Europe and Enterprise for Health show that it is important for companies to learn from each other in this new challenge. In this way, companies pursue a double dividend from their investments in policies and practices for health and well-being, to the benefit of individual employees, the organization, and – often implicitly – for society at large.

## Suggestions for Further Reading

CSR Europe (2008). Wellbeing in the workplace: A guide with best practices and tips for implementing a successful wellbeing strategy at work. Available at: www.csreurope.org/data/files/toolbox/wellbeing_guide.pdf.

Enterprise for Health Network (2008). Achieving business excellence – Health wellbeing and performance. Bertelsmann Stiftung and BKK.

Schein, E. (2002). A conceptual model for managed culture change. In E. Schein (Ed.), *Organizational culture and leadership* (3rd ed.). Chichester: Jossey-Bass.

Zwetsloot, G. I. J. M., Leka, S., & Jain, A. (2009). Corporate social responsibility and psychosocial risk management. In S. Leka, & T. Cox (Eds.), *The European Framework for Psychosocial Risk Management*: PRIMA-EF (pp. 96–114), Nottingham, UK: I-WHO Publications.

Zwetsloot, G. I. J. M., & Starren, A. (2004). *Corporate social responsibility and safety and health at work*. Research report from the European Agency for Safety and Health at Work, Issue 210, Bilbao.

## References

Bandura, A. (1986). *Social foundations of thought and action: A social cognitive theory.* Englewood Cliffs, NJ: Prentice Hall.

Black, C. (2008). *Working for a healthier tomorrow: A review of Britain's working age population.* Norwich: The Stationery Office.

Choudry, R. M., Fang, D., & Mohamed, S. (2007). The nature of safety culture: A survey of the state of the art. *Safety Science, 45,* 997 1012.

Cooper, M. D. (2000). Towards a model of safety culture. *Safety Science, 36,* 111–136.

De Geus A. (1997). *The living company – Habits for survival in a turbulent business environment.* Boston: Harvard Business School Press.

Demerouti, E., Bakker, A.B., Nachreiner, F., & Schaufeli, W.B. (2001). The job demands resources model of burnout. *Journal of Applied Psychology, 86,* 499–512.

European Commission (EC) (2001). *Promoting a European Framework for CSR – Green Paper.* Commission of the European Communities, COM (2001) 366 final, Brussels.

European Commission (EC) (2002). *Communication from the Commission concerning CSR: A business contribution to sustainable development.* European Commission, COM (2002) 347 final, Brussels.

European Foundation for the Improvement of Living and Working Conditions (Euro-Found) (2007). *Fourth European Working Conditions Survey.* Luxembourg: Office for Official Publications of the European Communities.

Fishbein, M., & Ajzen, I. (1975). *Belief, attitude, intention, and behavior: An Introduction to theory and research.* Reading, MA: Addison-Wesley.

Frick, K., & Zwetsloot, G. I. J. M. (2007). From safety management to corporate citizenship – an overview of approaches to health management. In U. Johansson, G. Ahonen, & R. Roslander (Eds.), *Work, health and management control* (pp. 99–134). Stockholm: Thomson Fakta.

Goetzel, R. Z., Shechter, D., Ozminkowski, R. J., Marmet, P. F., Tabrizi, M. J., & Roemer, E. C. (2007). Promising practices in employer health and productivity management efforts: findings from a benchmarking study. *Occupational & Environmental Medicine, 49(5)*, 583.

Golaszeweski, T., Allen, J., & Edington, D.W. (2008). The art of health promotion. *The American Journal of Health Promotion, 22*(4), 1–10.

Greenleaf, R. (2002). *Servant leadership: A journey into the nature of legitimate power and Greatness.* Nahwah, NJ: Pauliss Press.

Hale, A. R. (2000). Editorial: Culture's confusions. *Safety Science, 34*, 1–14.

Hale, A., & Hovden, J. (1998). Management and culture: the third age of safety. A review of approaches to organizational aspects of safety, health and environment. In: A. M. Feyer, & A.Williamson (Eds.). *Occupational injury: Risk, prevention and intervention.* London: Taylor & Francis.

Hasle, P., Kristensen, T. S., Møller, N., & Olesen, K.G. (2007). Organisational social capital and the relations with quality of work and health – a new issue for research. International Congress on Social Capital and Networks of Trust, 18–20 October 2007, Jyväskylä, Finland.

HSE (2005). *Promoting health and safety as a key goal of the Corporate Social Responsibility agenda.* Health and Safety Executive. Research Report 339.

Hudson, P. (2007). Implementing a safety culture in a major multi-national. *Safety Science, 45*(6), 697–772.

ILO (2009). Information on decent work and a health and safety culture. Available at: www.ilocarib.org.tt/portal/index.php?option=com_content&task=view&id=1138&Itemid-=1141.

Karasek, R., & Theorell, T. (1990). *Healthy work: Stress, productivity and the reconstruction of working life.* New York: Basic Books.

Kouvonen, A., Kivimaki, M., Vahtera, J., Oksanen, T., Elovainio, M., Cox, T., Virtanen, M., Pentti, J.,Cox, S. J., & Wilkinson R. G. (2006). Psychometric evaluation of a short measure of social capital at work. *BMC Public Health, 6*, 251.

Kristensen, T.S., Hasle, P., Pejtersen, J. H., & Olesen, K. G. (2007). Organisational social capital and the health and quality of work of the employees: two empirical studies from Denmark. International Congress on Social Capital and Networks of Trust, 18–20. October 2007, Jyväskylä, Finland.

Oksanen, T., Kouvonen, A., Kivimäki, M., Pentti, J., Virtanen, M., Linna, A., & Vahtera, J. (2008). Social capital at work as a predictor of employee health: Multiple evidence from work units in Finland. *Social Science & Medicine, 66*, 637–649.

Parker, D., Lawrie, M., & Hudson, P. (2006). A framework for understanding the development of organisational safety culture. *Safety Science, 44,* 551–562.

Peterson, M., & Wilson, J.F. (2002). The culture-work-health model and work stress. *American Journal of Health Behavior, 26,* 16–24.

Schein, E. (2002). A conceptual model for managed culture change. In E. Schein (Ed.), *Organisational Culture and Leadership* (3rd ed.), Jossey-Bass.

Siegrist, J. (1998). Adverse effects of effort-reward imbalance at work. In C. Cooper (Ed.), *Theories of organisational stress.* Oxford: Oxford University Press.

Stokhols, D., Pelletier, K. R., & Fielding, J. E. (1996). The ecology of work and health: Research and policy directions for the promotion of employee health. *Health Education Quarterly, 23*(2), 137–158.

Thoits, P.A. (1995). Stress, coping and social support processes: Where are we, what next? *Journal of Health & Social Behavior,* 53–79.

WHO (1948). World Health Organization Constitution, Geneva: WHO.

Zwetsloot, G. I. J. M. (2003). From management systems to corporate social responsibility. *Journal of Business Ethics, 44,* 201–207.

Zwetsloot, G. I. J. M., & van Scheppingen, A. (2007). Towards a strategic business case for health management. In U. Johansson, G. Ahonen, & R. Roslander (Eds.), *Work, health and management control* (pp. 183–213). Stockholm: Thomson Fakta.

Zwetsloot, G. I. J. M., & Starren, A. (2004). *Corporate social responsibility and safety and health at work.* European Agency for Safety and Health at Work. Luxembourg: Office for Official Publications of the European Communites.

# 10

# Research Methods in Occupational Health Psychology

Toon W. Taris, Annet H. de Lange,
and Michiel A. J. Kompier

### CHAPTER OUTLINE

Occupational health psychologists must possess a working knowledge of the most important research methods used in their field. This chapter addresses the basics of the scientific method: that is, what separates scientific from common-sense approaches. We distinguish between qualitative and quantitative methods and discuss when these are best suited for one's goals. We provide typical research designs and address a number of pitfalls that may apply. Finally, we deal with the issues of the reliability and validity of the measures that are used in occupational health psychology.

## Introduction

Suppose that the management of a large information technology company asks you to conduct a study on the health and well-being of their 10,000 employees. These workers hold different jobs, work at various locations, and differ in their background characteristics (age, family status and gender). Where would you start? You might enter the coffee room and chat with several employees over their lunch boxes, but you could also conduct interviews with a specific set of workers (e.g., union members or department leaders), send out questionnaires to all employees (e.g., using a web-based questionnaire), or, alternatively, confine yourself to examining absence figures across various groups of employees. Many such choices have to be made before you can report to the top management on their personnel's well-being, and the quality of these decisions determines the degree to which the interventions that may be conducted on the basis of your research will improve the quality of the employees' work lives.

Clearly this is not an easy task, and students in occupational health psychology (OHP) should be prepared to deal with complex decisions on how to go about things. This implies that they should possess a working knowledge of the basics of scientific research, that is, the systematic, replicable, and valid methods used to expand the knowledge of the phenomena relevant to those working in OHP. Scientific research starts with a *research question* that defines the purpose of the study. Based on this question, the researcher's knowledge and skills and all sorts of practical constraints (e.g., the budget available for the study and the degree to which the organization is willing to cooperate with the researcher), a *research design* is chosen (that is, the approach to collecting the data that will be used to address the research question). Finally, after the data have been collected and analysed, conclusions would be drawn on the phenomenon of interest, leading to interventions to ameliorate possible problems.

In this chapter we address the important steps you must take in designing and conducting research in OHP. As research in this area is usually (albeit not exclusively) conducted within organizations, in this chapter we mainly focus on research that is conducted in organizational contexts. However, many of the issues discussed here can readily be generalized towards other situations. Below we first discuss the nature of the research process, followed by a discussion of several qualitative and quantitative research designs. Finally, we address the measurement of concepts in OHP.

## Research and the Research Process

*What is science?*
*What are the goals of science?*
*What is a research question, and why is it important?*
*What is a scientific theory?*

### The scientific method

The scientific approach refers to the process or method that is used to generate a body of knowledge concerning a phenomenon of interest. In contributing to this knowledge, researchers test hypothetical propositions about the presumed relations among natural phenomena in a systematic, controlled, empirical, and critical way (Kerlinger & Lee, 2000). This approach could lead to the achievement of various goals (Christensen, 1994). First, researchers may want to provide an accurate *description* of the phenomenon of interest. For example, one could examine levels of burnout (a state of excessive work-related fatigue, cynicism towards work, and a lack of work-related efficacy) across different departments of an organization. However, it would be interesting to relate differences in levels of burnout to other phenomena as well, such as differences in work load, personality, or factors such as age and gender. In that case a second goal emerges, namely *explanation*: e.g., does having a high work load contribute to the occurrence of burnout? And are particular persons (e.g., those with high scores on neuroticism) more prone to experiencing high levels of burnout than others? If so, we may be able to anticipate which workers may come to experience burnout; *prediction* is the third goal of science. Without the ability to predict, OHP professionals have little to offer to the organizations asking for their advice. Finally, the fourth goal of science is to *obtain control* of the phenomenon of interest. That is, ideally we are able to manipulate the causes of the occurrence of this phenomenon. For example, in the case of burnout we may want to know how we can prevent burnout from occurring, e.g., by designing jobs in such a way that work stress is minimized or by developing selection methods that optimize the fit between the job and the worker hired to do the job.

Summarizing, we have attained some degree of scientific understanding only if we are able to describe, explain, predict, and control a particular phenomenon reasonably well. One way of summarizing the four goals of science is to say that we aim to develop a *theory* for the phenomenon of interest. Kerlinger and Lee (2000) defined a theory as a set of interrelated constructs (concepts), definitions, and propositions that presents a systematic view of phenomena by specifying relations among variables, with the purpose of explaining, predicting, and controlling the phenomena. Indeed, Kerlinger and Lee feel that the four goals of science discussed above are actually subsumed under a single major objective of science, namely theory development. Without an emphasis on theory development, science would be nothing more than a search for answers, lacking any framework or carefully controlled process. It is theory that allows us to explain, interpret and control the world around us, and it is as important to fundamental as to applied researchers in OHP.

Note that this does not necessarily mean that science must always start from theory. The deductive approach (in which researchers begin their studies with deriving a set of theory-based expectations or hypotheses regarding the phenomenon of interest before they collect their data) is not better or 'more scientific' than the inductive approach (where hypotheses can be construed as generalizations that are based on individual instances and observations). Indeed, the inductive approach has a long history in science. For example, the seventeenth-century philosopher Sir Francis Bacon argued that science should start with empirical observation and induction by enumeration (the generalizing from instances of phenomena to experimentally testable laws). The inductive approach is still popular today, and can fruitfully be integrated with a deductive approach: based on casual observation, researchers may develop a set of ideas (induction) that may subsequently be tried and tested (deduction) using data collected to test and refine these ideas.

## Questions and hypotheses

Every study begins with a research question. The basic aim of such a question is to guide the study: what is the phenomenon that interests us, and what do we want to do with it – describe it, explain it, predict it or gain control over it? For example, a descriptive research question might ask 'how many people in this organization suffer

**Pioneer**     Frederick N. Kerlinger (1910–1991)

Frederick N. Kerlinger was born in New York City. After graduating in 1942 from New York University (majors in education and philosophy), he joined the army to become second lieutenant (1946). He returned to the United States in 1950, where Kerlinger earned degrees in educational psychology from the University of Michigan. In 1955 he was offered the chair of the doctoral programme in research and measurement of New York, where he stayed until his retirement in 1974. Subsequently he moved to the Netherlands where he chaired the Methods Department of the University of Amsterdam. After returning to the United States in 1981 he joined the School of Education at the University of Oregon. Kerlinger is best known for his textbook on *Foundations of behavioral research* (1964), in which he provided an extremely influential account of how science 'works' in the behavioural sciences.

from high levels of burnout, as compared to the level of burnout in the general population?' An explanatory research question could be 'does work load affect levels of burnout?' The latter question specifies a particular influence on burnout, suggesting that work load may well be a causal agent that leads to burnout. In order to obtain an answer to this question, researchers should collect data on at least employees' levels of burnout and work load. It is preferable to translate a research question into a *hypothesis* on the outcomes of a study; hypotheses can either be confirmed or be rejected, meaning that it is possible to test one's theory much more precisely than would be possible on the basis of a research question. It also means that researchers are forced to think about the phenomenon they are examining: what, exactly, do they expect to occur? And which mechanisms may account for these outcomes? Thus, drawing on existing theory and research, researchers will articulate their best guess concerning the study's outcome, for example, 'high work load will lead to elevated levels of burnout'. In practice most applied work takes such a deductive, hypothesis-testing approach. As Spector (2008) argues, the research question and the corresponding hypotheses form the basis of many studies in OHP: without a specific and well-formulated question it is difficult to design a study that will provide an adequate answer to it. Conversely, when the research question clearly states the study goal and the phenomenon of interest, it is relatively straightforward to choose an appropriate design for the study addressing it.

## Summary

The scientific approach refers to the process or method that is used to generate a body of knowledge concerning the phenomenon we want to study. It has various goals, including the description, explanation, prediction and control of the phenomenon, and these four goals may be construed as contributing to one overarching goal, namely theory development. This does not mean that science must always start from theory (deduction); indeed, often observation forms the starting point for a scientific study (induction). Every study begins with a research question that aims to guide the study. When this question clearly states the study goal and the phenomenon of interest, it is relatively straightforward to specify study hypotheses, and to choose an appropriate design for the study that will test these.

# Designing a Study

*What is a research design?*
*What decisions are involved in choosing a research design?*
*What is the difference between experimental and non-experimental designs?*
*How can alternative explanations for a particular finding be ruled out?*

A number of decisions must be made before we can actually conduct a study. Basically, these decisions refer to:

- the *setting* in which the study will be conducted: is it a laboratory or a field study?
- the type of participants that will be in the study;
- the constructs of interest: how can we operationalize constructs like burnout or job satisfaction into measurable variables?
- if there are different conditions in the study (e.g., a condition in which the participants are 'manipulated' in some way, versus a control condition in which nothing special happens), the assignment of participants to these conditions; and
- the data collection mode, that is, the way in which information on the variables of interest will be collected.

In conjunction, the answers to these issues determine the *research design*, that is, the basic plan for the study to be conducted.

## Setting and participants

A study can be conducted in the laboratory or the field. In a *field setting* the phenomena of interest are not manipulated by the researcher. For example, organizations are field settings in which employee behaviour can be studied 'as it occurs', without any intervention from the researcher. Conversely, the *laboratory* is an artificial setting in which the phenomena that interest us do not normally occur; these have to be created by the researcher. This distinction does not entirely coincide with that between *experimental* and *non-experimental* research. In experimental research the participants are assigned to one of at least two conditions.

In the experimental (or treatment) condition some aspect of the situation is manipulated by the researcher, whereas in the control condition nothing is changed. The two groups are then compared on the concepts that interest us: if the groups did not differ before the treatment but do thereafter *and* if other explanations for such a difference can be ruled out, the treatment has been shown to causally affect the study variables. This is a common way of conducting research in a laboratory setting, in which other factors that may affect the participants' responses can be controlled. However, experimental designs also occur in OHP. For instance, the effectiveness of intervention programmes is best studied using a *quasi-experimental* design. For example, an organization may institute a new health promotion programme at one plant location but not at another, taking measures of employee health and well-being before and after the institution of the programme at both locations. Superficially this looks like an experiment that is conducted in a field setting, the crucial difference being that participants are not randomly assigned to the experimental (new health programme) and control (business as usual) conditions. This means that it is harder to exclude alternative explanations for differences in the study outcomes between the two groups, as it is quite possible that the experimental and control group differ in more respects than only the health promotion programme they are subjected to.

Pure laboratory studies are rare in OHP, presumably because the work setting is not easily transferred to the laboratory, random assignment of participants to conditions is difficult (see Kompier & Kristensen, 2001), and because the participants in such studies are unlikely to be workers – but it is not impossible. For example, Deelstra and her colleagues (2003) examined the effects of providing instrumental social support on health experimentally in a simulated office environment (i.e., a laboratory that was equipped like any normal office, with computers, telephones, desks, chairs, and so on), among 48 temporary office workers, finding that unwanted social support may have negative effects on worker well-being. Conversely, non-experimental and quasi-experimental designs are very common in OHP. For example, many studies that examine the effectiveness of work stress prevention programmes employ a quasi-experimental design, in that groups of workers participating in the prevention programme are contrasted with other workers who do not. Common non-experimental designs in OHP include observational designs (in which the researcher observes the participants' behaviour and takes notes of what is observed: e.g., how often the participant takes a rest break or communicates with their co-workers) and survey designs (studies in which the participants complete questionnaires). These and other research designs are discussed in more detail below.

## Design: Concepts and variables

A *concept* is a property of people or things that can vary across the people or things that interest us. For instance, size or weight are properties of people. In OHP we are usually interested in concepts such as physical complaints, absence days, or work load. These concepts must be operationalized, that is, the researcher should decide upon how these concepts are measured. After the concepts have been operationalized they are referred to as *variables*.

When examining questions like: 'What is the influence of social support in the development of burnout', we can distinguish between the *independent* variable social support (i.e., the presumed cause) from the *dependent* variable burnout (the effect). Independent variables are the concepts that are either varied by the researcher (in quasi- and experimental designs) or measured (in non-experimental research) as an antecedent to other variables. The dependent variable is the variable of interest, that is, what we design our study to assess. Thus, we are usually interested in the effect of the independent variable on the dependent variable.

Note that the distinction between dependent and independent variables is a conceptual one. Although we are usually interested in drawing causal inferences (the independent variable is assumed to influence the dependent variable causally), the strength of our research design determines the degree to which such inferences are warranted. For example, the assumed dependent and independent variables are often measured at the same point in time. This implies that the temporal order of these concepts cannot be established, meaning that a positive association between work load and burnout can be interpreted theoretically in terms of 'having a high work load leads causally to high levels of burnout', but also as 'workers suffering from burnout tend to experience their work load as heavier'. Whether we can distinguish between these two accounts depends on the strength of our design, i.e., whether alternative explanations for a particular association between a pair of variables can be ruled out.

## Control

It occurs only rarely that a particular result obtained in a study can be explained in just a single way: usually several explanations for this result can be thought of. *Control* refers to the set of procedures that allow researchers to rule out alternative explanations for their findings, other than the hypotheses they intend to test. To ensure that we can draw a causal inference about the effect of our independent variable on the dependent variable in our study, we need to be able to exercise control over the study. For instance, we may want to know whether experiencing high levels of work stress increases the likelihood that workers will be absent from their jobs. We might conduct a survey in which we ask employees (1) whether they experience work stress, and (2) how many days they were absent from their job in the preceding year. We might find that the higher the work stress, the greater the number of days they were absent. However, with this sort of design there may be many uncontrolled variables that could be the real cause of absence. For instance, it would seem possible that the employees with higher absence rates are in different types of jobs than those with lower absence rates. If the high-absence workers are all in high-risk jobs and the low-absence workers are all in white collar jobs, it is difficult to conclude that work stress is the prime cause of absence – rather, it is possible that the high levels of absence in the high-risk group are due to a higher chance of experiencing accidents at work. Thus, type of job is an alternative explanation for the association between work stress and absence rates, meaning that job type should in some way be controlled for in order to rule out the possibility that job level and not job stress is the prime antecedent of absence.

There are several procedures that can be used to control for the effects of variables that do not interest us. For the most part these procedures involve either holding constant or systematically varying the levels of one or more variables. For example, in the stress-absence example above, we might hold type of job constant by collecting data for just a single occupation. Thus, all participants would have the same job, meaning that all participants have the same risk of experiencing accidents. Alternatively, we may include job type as an additional independent variable in our study design. In that way we could examine whether job stress contributed to sickness absence, net of the effects of job type.

In experimental studies, a standard way to control for factors other than the variables of interest is to assign the participants in a non-systematic way ('at random') to the experimental and control conditions. Although all participants will have their own idiosyncrasies and differ from each other in many respects, on average the participants in both groups will be more or less equivalent in their characteristics: if the samples used are large enough, the two groups should be approximately the same in terms of ability, age, gender, motivation, and so forth. Unfortunately, random assignment of participants is impossible in field studies (as here the researcher does not manipulate the independent variable, there are no experimental or control groups) and difficult in quasi-experiments. For example, although we can implement a health promotion programme in one plant location (the experimental group) but not in another (the control group), it is possible that workers of these plants differ in other respects than the location of their work as well, including the products manufactured (which could lead to differences in required skill level, pay and expected continuity of labour), quality of the management, and the neighbourhood in which the plants' workers live. In such cases it is important to consider which additional variables could affect the study's findings, and these should preferably be included in the study design in order to control for their effects. In this vein, the *internal validity* of the study (i.e., the degree to which we can draw causal inferences about our variables) can be increased.

## Summary

In order to conduct a study, a number of decisions must be made that refer to the research design, that is the setting (laboratory or the field), type of participants, variables to be assessed or varied, assignment of participants to the study conditions (i.e., random or non-random) and data collection mode (to be discussed below) that will be used. Basically, a good research design allows researchers to rule out alternative explanations for their findings, other than the hypotheses they intend to test. To ensure that causal inferences about the effect of our independent variable on the dependent variable in a study are warranted, one must be able to control for the effects of variables that may otherwise affect the study outcomes. For the most part, these procedures involve either holding constant or systematically varying the levels of one or more independent variables.

## Data Collection in Occupational Health Psychology

*What are qualitative and quantitative designs?*
*When should we prefer a qualitative design to a quantitative design,*
*and vice versa?*
*What are typical qualitative and quantitative designs?*

After the research question and study hypotheses have been established and the focal variables have been chosen, it is time to focus on the mode of data collection. This section focuses on the most common methods of data collection in OHP. Some considerations relevant to the choice of data collection have already been mentioned in passing, but below we provide a more systematic overview of various modes of data collection.

Organizational phenomena may be studied using a wide variety of designs. It is common to juxtapose qualitative against quantitative designs. Basically, the difference between these two approaches is that quantitative approaches to examining issues in OHP emphasize its quantifiable nature and are concerned with prediction (e.g., of absence figures, levels of burnout, and so forth), classification of workers in high versus low-risk groups, or otherwise measuring distinct elements or dimensions of health and its antecedents in as objective a way as possible. Quantitative approaches tend to emphasize the testing of theory-driven hypotheses, measurement using standardized instruments, and data analysis using advanced statistical techniques. Conversely, qualitative approaches seek to characterize its rich, emergent, constructed and multi-dimensional nature using ethnographic approaches, often requiring 'psychological immersion' in an organization (such as observation of workers and in-depth interviewing) or employing a case-study approach (see Brewerton & Millward, 2001). Qualitative approaches are often used in a hypothesis-generating fashion, emphasising data exploration and the context-boundness of the phenomenon of interest, and results are often reported in narrative form.

These two classes of approaches differ in a number of respects, including philosophical orientation, question development, involvement of the researcher, tools, flexibility, and contextual influences (Bachiochi & Weiner, 2002). Clearly, it is beyond the scope of this chapter to provide an exhaustive discussion of the differences between these two. Indeed, rather than discuss these differences in detail, it is perhaps more useful to indicate when qualitative designs should be preferred to quantitative designs. According to Bachiochi and Weiner, four questions can help researchers decide whether a quantitative or a qualitative approach is best suited for their needs:

- *Is the context central to the research question?* If the specific context of the study is a key driver in the research process and/or in the interpretation of the findings, then a qualitative approach may be appropriate. For instance, we may be interested in examining the antecedents of sickness absence among certified nurses. This may require an in-depth examination of their work situation, hopefully yielding insight into the factors that could lead to elevated levels of absence. Although the findings of such a study may not be generalizable to other professions, it can provide useful information on how to reduce absence rates among nurses.
- *Is the participant's interpretation central to the research question?* Closed-ended questions, e.g., Likert-type statements that require participants to indicate how much they agree or disagree with these, may not provide the participants with sufficient opportunity to express fully why they feel the way they do. Thus, researchers may allow participants to provide answers and interpretations that were initially not anticipated. For instance, participants in a focus group may indicate that the main reasons for a high absence rate are not the high work load, the lack of opportunity for skill use or having to deal with aggressive clients, but rather lack of flexibility in their working times. This factor may not have been expected by the researcher or identified in previous quantitative research where these causes of absence were not included in the set of questions asked.
- *Is depth or richness of the data essential?* The answer to this question may seem obvious ('yes, of course rich data are essential'), but in practice it may be difficult to achieve the desired level of detail. Fortunately, many hypotheses may be tested using relatively restricted data sets. For example, in order to obtain a working understanding of the health risks in the work situation of office technology users, a relatively simple questionnaire tapping standard psychological stressors (such as work load, social support, and job autonomy) and measures of well-being may already provide a good understanding of these associations. Conversely, for research questions requiring greater depth, case studies, interviews or other qualitative approaches may provide the opportunity to collect the necessary detailed information. For example, whereas it is well-known that supervisor support is an important determinant of subordinate burnout, we may be interested in mapping the precise behaviors that contribute to the occurrence of burnout among subordinates. A combination of approaches (e.g., a qualitative pilot study combined with a quantitative survey) may provide the depth needed while still offering the sample size needed for drawing broader conclusions.
- *Is the research exploratory?* The nature of the research question may not readily lend itself to clear operational definitions, especially when a new area of research is explored. In such cases it is often better to start off with a qualitative approach, charting the domain and determining the relevant dimensions of the phenomenon of interest.

Based on such findings a quantitative follow-up may be conducted. Further, the topic may cause some degree of discomfort among the participants (such as bullying or sexual harassment at work). In such cases, a qualitative approach may lead to findings that may otherwise be missed: e.g., in survey research participants may well skip uncomfortable questions or provide a socially desirable answer to these.

## Qualitative approaches

### Observational methods

An obvious way to collect data is to observe employees in their organizational setting. Observation may occur both in laboratory and field settings when we are interested in some behaviour that can be observed, counted or measured. Observations can be either with (*obtrusive* observation) or without (*unobtrusive* observation) the employees' knowledge. In the first case researchers may observe employees doing their jobs for a particular period of time, with the employees being aware of the fact that the researcher was collecting data on some aspect of their functioning on the job. With unobtrusive methods, the workers under study may be aware that the researcher is present, but they would not know that they were being studied. For example, a consultant may attend a meeting to observe the leadership style of the CEO and his or her interaction with the subordinates, which could be the basis of a measure of the quality of the interaction with the supervisor (a possible determinant of job stress).

One important drawback of the obtrusive observational design is that researchers may affect the phenomenon being studied: the mere fact that employees know that the researcher is monitoring their performance may be sufficient to increase or decrease their motivation to work hard. This is one reason why unobtrusive designs are to be preferred to obtrusive designs, although it should be noted that unobtrusive designs may be problematic because of ethical and legal requirements to respect people's privacy. A further problem with these designs is that they are usually time-consuming, both in terms of collecting and coding the data. Thus, this design is especially useful if data are collected on relatively small samples, examining issues that cannot be addressed using a more efficient design.

### Interviews and focus groups

Focus groups are a method for qualitative data collection in which pre-selected groups of people (such as employees, clients, managers) have a facilitated discussion with the purpose of answering specific research questions. Interviews are typically conducted for the same purpose, but involve one-on-one sessions between an interviewer and the interviewee (Bachiochi & Weiner, 2002). Focus groups and interviews are often used prior to a quantitative study to identify the topics that should be included in this research. They are generally not used to provide representative data for a large population (quantitative approaches are often much better suited for that purpose). This also means that the conclusions of this type of research cannot be generalized too broadly; the findings are based on a limited and not necessarily representative group of participants.

Researchers intending to conduct an interview or focus group study must deal with a number of issues. First, it is important that *key groups* to be included in the study are selected, and one should decide which and how many members of these groups will be contacted for participation. The number of sessions (or interviews) to be held is determined by the point at which *theoretical saturation* is achieved, that is, when new sessions (interviews) do not lead to new information. Furthermore, it is important that a *script* is available, i.e., a structured guide or protocol that describes the course of the session and that may contain the introductory statements to be used (e.g., the goal of the session, how results will be used, and instructions for participants), the questions to be asked (usually in an open-ended format), and closing information. Of course, there are also practical issues to consider, for instance, how long will the sessions take, and will sessions be recorded or will notes be taken. Finally, researchers should consider the way the data will be analysed. As the data collected using focus groups and interviews will usually be of a textual nature (e.g., transcripts, notes, etc.), this will involve some sort of *content analysis*. Basically, the aim of content analysis is to give insight in the type of answers given by the participants, as well as the frequency of these answers. For example, in a focus group study on the sources of high job stress among firefighters, researchers might hope to obtain an idea of the type of events that elicit high levels of stress in that profession (type of stressors), as well as whether these events affect all participants equally strongly (frequency of mentioning these stressors).

*Case studies*

A case study can be defined as an examination of a single individual, group, company or society (Babbie, 1998). Researchers who develop case studies do not necessarily favour one data collection method over another. For example, data can be collected via observation, structured or semi-structured interviews, or archival research. Typically, the data set comprises a mix of verbal and numeric information, possibly including quantitative approaches (such as a personnel survey) as well. For example, Liu, Spector, and Shi (2008) combined qualitative information (stressful incidents) and quantitative information (an employee survey) in their study of gender differences in experienced job stress among university employees.

As case studies are defined in terms of the object to be studied (that is, the specific group under investigation), the issue of sampling is a central concern in the research design. Case study researchers usually follow a purposeful sampling strategy, in that objects are chosen specifically for the potential they offer for understanding the issue being researched. For example, researchers may not strive towards obtaining a random sample of all employees of a particular organization, but may contact specific employees instead. For instance, in a case study on sexual harassment in an organization, researchers may interview several current and former female workers or the organization (have they had experiences with harassment? how do they experience the organization's policy regarding incidents of harassment?), as well as the head of the HR department (what is the organization's policy in this respect? have any complaints been filed over the past couple of years?). Keyton et al. (2006) examined how Mitsubishi dealt with the claims of sexual harassment made by female employees, examining both the company and union responses to these, finding that organizations that presumptively support values such as honesty, fairness, and respect react and renegotiate these values when organizational incidents reveal value lapses.

Case studies are not typically used to test hypotheses, but they can be useful for description, for generating hypotheses, as well as for illustrating and understanding specific processes and associations (see Yin, 1994). For example, Israel and her colleagues presented four case studies to illustrate their model of occupational stress, safety and health, and discuss the implications of this model for the development of prevention interventions (Israel, Baker, Goldenhar, & Heaney, 1996).

*Action research*

Action research may be considered as a special instance of the case study design. Basically, the idea in this approach is that knowledge creation (by conducting research within a particular organization) is combined with intervention. According to Lewin (1951), the best way to understand a social system is to first introduce change into it and then observe its effects (Locke & Golden-Biddle, 2003). Action researchers thus distinguish themselves from other researchers by their dual purposes of advancing knowledge on the one hand and providing practical advice on

## Box 10.1   Action Research

An interesting combination of quasi-experimental and action research was described by Le Blanc, Hox, Schaufeli, Taris, and Peeters (2007). The aim of their study was to evaluate the impact of a team-based burnout intervention programme, which was conducted among the staff of 29 oncology wards. Before the programme started, immediately after it was completed and 6 months later quantitative surveys were conducted, in which information was collected on the participants' work situation and well-being. Nine wards were assigned to the experimental (intervention) group; the other wards served as controls.

The intervention programme for the experimental wards was designed and implemented using action-theoretical principles. As a first step, at each ward interviews with the key stakeholders (head nurses, physicians, coordinators, and team leaders) were conducted, during which the programme was clarified and information about key characteristics of the context in which the ward operated was collected. A kick-off meeting for the staff of each of the experimental wards served the same purpose. In this way the local context in which the interventions would be conducted could be taken into account. The training programme itself consisted of 6 monthly sessions of 3 hours

## Box 10.1   (*Cont.*)

each. In the first session the findings of the first questionnaire on the participants' work situation was fed back to the participants. The remaining sessions all consisted of an educational and an action part. During the educational part, general issues relating to work stress were discussed, and during the action part, participants formed problem-solving teams that collectively designed, implemented, evaluated and reformulated action plans to cope with the most important stressors in their work situation. In this way each experimental ward created its own unique intervention. Comparison of the post-intervention scores to the pre-intervention scores revealed that levels of burnout had decreased significantly for the experimental wards, whereas such was not the case for the control wards. Thus, it was concluded that the intervention program had been effective in increasing worker well-being.

the other. As a research process, action research is often conceived as an interactive and multi-phased process. The process starts with problem diagnosis and data gathering, after which an intervention is planned and implemented. This is followed by an evaluation of the effects of the intervention (leading to knowledge creation), which may lead to another cycle of intervention, and so forth. In comparison to other modes of research, the roles of the researcher and the participants are quite different in action research. Participants are considered as active shapers of their environment, not just passive recipients of environmental influences; researchers are change agents that participate in the change process as well as creators of knowledge about the change process. Box 10.1 presents an example of a diary study.

## Summary

Many phenomena in OHP may be studied using a variety of designs. A main distinction is that between quantitative versus qualitative approaches. Quantitative approaches tend to emphasize the testing of theory-driven hypotheses, measurement using standardized instruments, and data analysis using advanced statistical techniques. Conversely, qualitative approaches are often used in a hypothesis-generating mode, seeking to characterize the rich, emergent, constructed and multidimensional nature of the phenomenon of interest using an observational or case-study approach. A qualitative approach becomes more appropriate when the context or participant's interpretations are central to the research question, when answering this question requires very detailed data, or when the research has an exploratory, hypothesis-generating focus.

# Quantitative approaches

........................................................................

*What is the difference between quasi- and true experiments?*
*What competing explanations can be controlled by using a pre-test-post-test*
*control group design?*
*What is the difference between cross-sectional and longitudinal designs?*
*Why is it important to have a high response rate?*

Although qualitative approaches may well be useful in OHP, it cannot be denied that most published research in this area has a strong quantitative focus. Below several designs are discussed, including experimental and quasi-experimental designs, and cross-sectional and longitudinal survey studies.

*Quasi- and true experiments*

In a *true experiment* there are two or more independent variables and one or more dependent variables, as well as random assignment of the participants (Stone-Romero, 2002). Typically, at least one of the independent variables is manipulated by the researcher, i.e., this variable has at least two levels (the experimental and the control level or condition). Due to the practical difficulty of assigning participants randomly to conditions, such true designs are relatively rare in OHP. However, *quasi-experimental designs* are much more common. In such designs one or more of the features of a true experiment have been compromised; most often the requirement of random assignment to the conditions has been dropped.

For example, Bond, Flaxman, and Bunce (2008) examined the effects of a control-enhancing intervention programme on mental health and absence rates. Participants were employees of two customer service centres of a large financial services organization. The programme was implemented in one of these centres, and before and after implementation health and absence measures were taken from both, showing that the intervention programme was effective. This type of design is commonly known as a quasi-experimental (or non-equivalent) pre-test-post-test control group design. It is quasi-experimental as participants were not randomly assigned to the conditions, and the groups may not be equivalent in terms of the properties of the members of these groups: as the levels of the main independent variable (i.e., receipt of the intervention programme) are manipulated across conditions, there is an experimental (intervention) versus a control (no intervention) group; as measures were taken before and after the intervention, this is a pre-post-test design.

In spite of the absence of random allocation of participants, the non-equivalent pre-test-post-test control group design is a strong design, in that it allows researchers to rule out a number of important competing explanations for the study findings (see Shadish, Cook, & Campbell, 2002). The most important of these are listed below:

- *History.* It is possible that events or developments, other than the researcher's intervention programme, are responsible for an improvement of health and well-being of the employees of the two customer service centres of Bond et al. (2008); for example, the introduction of new technology may affect participants' working conditions. Insofar as such events apply equally strongly to both centres, their effects will not bias the effects of the intervention. However, if the poor-performing director of the centre where the intervention programme was implemented was replaced during the programme, this would be a plausible rival hypothesis for the idea that the intervention programme led to an improvement on the outcome variables.

- *Maturation.* A change in the outcome variables may be due to development of the participants, and not the treatment: participants may become older and wiser, more experienced, and so forth. In the Bond et al. case, such processes would apply equally well to the participants in both the control and the intervention group, meaning that this alternative explanation of the findings can be ruled out.

- *Testing.* In principle, being subjected to a test (e.g., completing a questionnaire) may affect participants' answers to subsequent measurements. For example, participants may 'learn' from taking a test (e.g., they may become more familiar with the type of problems posed in intelligence tests), or being asked about their absence rates may lead participants to realize that they have been absent excessively often during the preceding year, and that they should attempt to adopt a more healthy way of living (by exercising more often, quit smoking, or get more sleep). Although such a change in lifestyle could result from completing a questionnaire at the pre-test, this would apply equally strongly to both the experimental and the control group, meaning that this rival explanation would not account for the effect of the intervention.

- *Instrumentation.* Comparison of pre-test with post-test scores implies that the measurement instruments are identical, otherwise across-time changes may be due to a change in the instruments that have been used. For example, if at the pre-test measures were taken using paper-and-pencil questionnaires and at the post-test using an internet-based questionnaire, differences between the pre and post-test could result from the difference in the measurement devices used. However, even if different types of measures were used at the pre and the post-test, this would probably affect the intervention and the control group equally strongly, again meaning that the effect of the intervention programme will not be biased.

- *Selection and regression to the mean.* Finally, the treatment difference could be due to a pre-existing difference on some other variable. It is conceivable that the intervention group was selected on the basis of a high need for the intervention (e.g., the participants in this group reported high levels of stress and health complaints). It is likely that these excessively high scores are at least partly due to random influences and unreliability of the measures. It is possible that these factors will diminish or disappear after some time, meaning that the intervention group will more or less automatically report lower levels of stress and health complaints on the post-test measure (a phenomenon known as regression to the mean: extreme scores tend to become more normal across time, see

Campbell & Kenny, 2003). However, due to the presence of a pre-test and a control group it is possible to examine the credibility of this explanation: if at baseline the control and intervention groups obtained equal scores on the pre-test, it is unlikely that selection and regression to the mean account for the effects of Bond et al.'s intervention programme.

---

**Pioneer    Donald T. Campbell (1916–1996)**

Donald T. Campbell was born in Grass Lake, Michigan, the son of a farmer. After high school Campbell worked on a turkey farm before completing his undergraduate education at Berkeley, graduating first in the class of 1939. He served in the Naval Reserve in World War II, after which he returned to Berkeley to receive his doctorate in social psychology in 1947. Campbell did his main research at Northwestern University in Evanston, Illinois. His long-lasting interest was the study of knowledge: how it is acquired, recognized, evaluated, refined and passed on. His paper with Donald Fiske entitled 'Convergent and discriminant validation by the multitrait-multimethod matrix' is the most widely cited paper in the *Psychological Bulletin* in the past 50 years, whereas his volume with Thomas D. Cook on quasi-experimentation has become the research bible in intervention research. When he took up his last academic post in 1982 at Lehigh University, he was designated 'university professor' with faculty listings in the departments of psychology, education, sociology and anthropology.

---

*Non-experimental designs*

If you want to know how people feel about something, the first thing that comes to mind is to ask them. This is the basis of one of the simplest research designs, namely the survey design. This design involves the selection of a sample of participants (such as the employees of a particular organization), who are then asked to complete a questionnaire consisting of a series of questions that are designed to tap the variables of interest. Surveys are very often used in OHP, for various reasons. First, if researchers are interested in how workers perceive their work situation or how they feel about their health (i.e., subjective perceptions of matters), there is no better source of information about these issues than the workers themselves. Second, surveys are usually easy to administer, e.g., by handing out paper-and-pencil questionnaires, or through the intra- or internet. Third, they can be administered to large groups of people at the same time. Finally, they can provide respondents with a feeling of anonymity. This could lead to more honest answers and a higher response rate, especially when the questionnaire addresses sensitive issues.

On the negative side, surveys are not well-suited for all concepts that could interest an OHP researcher. For example, whereas it is possible to ask people about the frequency and duration of their spells of sickness absence in the previous year, the answers to such questions tend to be unreliable (e.g., Van der Vaart & Glasner, 2007). Similarly, reports on their own functioning tend to be biased: for instance, Taris (2006) found that worker's self-reported performance (as measured in terms of a global evaluation of one's own functioning at work) was not significantly correlated with objective performance measures (e.g., evaluations of peers, customers, and supervisors). Thus, for some concepts other modes of data collection may be preferable; e.g., information about sickness absence may be obtained from company files.

### Cross-sectional and longitudinal designs

Most survey studies are cross-sectional, meaning that all data are collected at (and for) a single point in time. The major drawback of such a design is that the temporal order among the variables is not known, meaning that we cannot unambiguously establish whether – say – high work load leads causally to high levels of exhaustion, or that high levels of exhaustion bring about a change in the perception of one's work load. Therefore, cross-sectional designs are of limited use in furthering the goals that are of most interest to OHP researchers, i.e., explaining, predicting and controlling the phenomena of interest. In these respects, *longitudinal designs* are often much more useful. In such designs data are collected for the same set of participants for (but not necessarily at) two or more occasions, allowing for the examination of intra-individual change across time. For example, using a longitudinal design, researchers could relate turnover (i.e., a change of employer during the observed time interval) to specific circumstances at work at the first study wave. In this way one could see whether being bullied at work predicts turnover. Similarly, a high work load at the first study wave could be related to health at a later point in time, controlling for health status at the first wave of the study.

Clearly, longitudinal designs are extremely useful in examining the temporal relationships among variables. However, in order to be able to realize this potential even longitudinal designs must meet a number of requirements. Based on common insights from general and longitudinal research methodology (e.g., Menard, 2008; Taris, 2000), De Lange, Taris, Kompier, Houtman, and Bongers (2003) formulated various design criteria to evaluate the quality of longitudinal research, including the basic design of the study (e.g., the number of measures of the study variables and the length of the interval between the study waves) and the non-response analysis.

*Study design.* Figure 10.1 presents a complete panel design for two variables X and Y. Using this design it is possible to examine the lagged effects of these two variables on each other, distinguishing between the temporal effects of variable X on Y ($X_1 \rightarrow Y_2$), and vice versa ($Y_1 \rightarrow X_2$). The advantage of this design as compared to a cross-sectional design is that they allow for a fuller understanding of

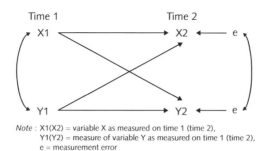

Note : X1(X2) = variable X as measured on time 1 (time 2),
       Y1(Y2) = measure of variable Y as measured on time 1 (time 2),
       e = measurement error

**Figure 10.1**   The complete panel design.

the relationships between variable X and Y. For example, it is often assumed that high job demands lead causally to high levels of fatigue, and this reasoning could be tested by relating fatigue (measured at T2) to Time 1 job demands, controlling for Time 1 fatigue (this is referred to as an *incomplete* panel design, as only fatigue has been measured twice). In this way it is possible to see whether Time 1 job demands predict part of the variance of Time 2 fatigue, partialling out the Time 1-Time 2 stability of fatigue. However, whereas it is likely that demands affect fatigue across time, it is also possible that fatigue leads causally to higher job demands. For example, fatigued workers may possess less energy than non-fatigued workers, and this could lead them to evaluate their work load as heavier. Thus, in order to gain a sound understanding of the possibly reciprocal relationships between pairs of variables, a longitudinal design – preferably a complete panel design – is indispensable.

Unfortunately, even a complete panel design may be unable to demonstrate causal effects of variables over time if the interval between the study waves does not correspond with the 'true' causal lag between the variables, that is, the period that it takes for the causal variable to take effect on the outcome variable. If the interval between the study waves is too small, effects will not be significant because the causal process has not yet had enough time to unfold itself. A too-large interval will lead to bias as well, for example, because changes are often repeatable: participants may change their attitudes several times during a particular interval, or changes may only be temporary. Hence, it is imperative that the time lag between the study waves closely approximates the real causal lag. However, as the length of this lag is usually unknown, it may be difficult to satisfy this assumption (Taris, 2000).

*Diary studies.* One special instance of a longitudinal design is the so-called diary study. This design is especially suitable when one wants to learn about the fine-grained temporal relations between the variables of interest. The label 'diary' may be somewhat misleading. Ordinary diaries (the type written by Anne Frank, Samuel Pepys, and Bridget Jones) usually present a somewhat ad-hoc, impressionistic and unstructured record of what happened during the day. However, the aim of a diary *study* is the standardized and structured collection of activities and psychological reactions on a day-to-day basis and at particular well-defined times (Bolger, Davis & Rafaeli, 2003; Semmer, Grebner, & Elfering, 2004; Sonnentag, 2001). The term 'diary' thus implies a day-to-day perspective. Through this method, it is possible to assess mood states and activities of participants shortly after they actually conducted their (work) activities. This minimizes the need for retrospection and therefore the effects of recall bias (Bolger et al., 2003). Diary data may be collected by means of daily surveys, but it is also possible to employ modern means of communication. For example, many current diary studies use palmtop computers or PDAs (Personal Digital Assistants) to collect the data. The participants are expected to carry these with them, completing short diaries at frequent intervals during the day. Box 10.2 presents an example of a diary study.

## Box 10.2   A Diary Study

A recent example of a diary study is a study into daily overtime work by Beckers et al. (2008). Beckers and her co-workers collected data among 120 Dutch faculty members in a nine-day diary study: they collected precise data on the participants' daily (24 hours) overtime, work and non-work activities and work and non-work experiences. The study aim was to find out *when* faculty workers work overtime, *what activities* (e.g., research, teaching, other) were undertaken during overtime, and *how overtime was experienced* (e.g., pleasurable or stressful). Analysis of variance was used to analyse the data. The study's findings showed that overtime was very prevalent among faculty members but unevenly distributed over the week. Working overtime was common on Sunday and Monday and uncommon on Friday and Saturday. The type of overtime activities during the weekend differed from those during the workweek. Specifically, during weekend-overtime work, relatively much time was spent on research as compared to teaching-related activities. Further, overtime activities were experienced differently than activities during regular work hours: overtime work was experienced as less effortful and stressful than regular work hours, and weekend-overtime as less pleasurable than regular hours and evening-overtime.

This detailed day-to-day mapping and evaluation of overtime work thus contributed to a better understanding of overtime work by demonstrating meaningful patterns of overtime over the (work)week, and meaningful associations between overtime activities and time-contingent experiences.

*Response rates.* According to Spector (2008), perhaps the biggest problem in conducting a survey is assuring that a sufficiently high response rate is obtained.

Basically, the issue is how many of those who were intended to be part of the sample (the study population) do actually contribute data to the study (Taris, Scheurs, & Sepmeijer, 2004, for a discussion). It is important that this response rate (which is usually expressed as a percentage) is as high as possible, for a variety of reasons. For example, a high response rate means that many people are represented in the findings. This increases the credibility of the conclusions and recommendations of the study: CEOs cannot easily discard a study's findings if 90 per cent of the workers in a company indicate that they suffer from burnout, something that would be easy were a study to be based on 5 per cent of the workers. There are also more mundane reasons for striving towards a high response rate. For example, statistical tests are *more powerful* if they are applied on a large data set: obviously, in a given organization a high response rate will lead to a larger data set than a low response rate, thus increasing the usefulness of the data collected. *Outliers* (that is, participants with extreme values on the study variables) will have stronger effects on the study findings in small samples than in large samples. Finally, it is possible that those who do not respond to an invitation to participate in a survey differ systematically from those who do, that is, *non-response* may be *selective*. This may well lead to findings that do not generalize beyond the sample. Previous research revealed that survey non-response is associated with a wide array of factors, including high levels of depression, low education, and low decision latitude, low organizational commitment and job satisfaction, low organizational support, and personality variables such as low conscientiousness (Taris & Schreurs, 2007). Thus, non-response might be a problem in many organizational surveys, leading to restriction-of-range effects (that is, selective study attrition increases the homogeneity of the sample, making it more difficult to detect associations between variables) and biased descriptive statistics (non-respondents differ systematically from respondents).

The best solution to minimize the severe consequences of possible selectivity is to maximize response rates. Obviously, if there is no non-response, there will be no selective non-response either. Unfortunately, 100% response rates are extremely difficult to achieve. What, then, is an adequate response rate? Unfortunately, it is difficult to say when a particular response rate is acceptable. The main issue is the degree to which the sample is representative for the study population, and without information on the population it is difficult to say whether the sample is representative or not. Of course, one may compare figures on the composition of the population to that of the sample (e.g., percentage females, distribution of participants across age groups, jobs and departments), but such an approach does not directly focus on the study variables, meaning that bias may be present, even if the sample and study population resemble each other strongly in terms of such background variables. However, researchers have proposed some guidelines as to what response rates are acceptable. For example, based on an analysis of 490 survey studies that were published in 2000 and 2005 in seventeen refereed academic journals, Baruch and Holtom (2008) found that the average response rate for studies that utilized data collected from individuals was 52.7%

with a standard deviation of 20.4. They argued that studies with a response rate that is more than one standard deviation below the mean response rate (i.e., 32.4%) should be critically judged. These figures apply to cross-sectional research: no corresponding research has been conducted for longitudinal research, but it may be expected that the average response rates in such studies will be lower than in cross-sectional studies (Taris, 2000). Clearly, it makes sense to invest quite some effort into optimizing response rates, e.g., by keeping questionnaires as short as possible, or by rewarding participants in some way for their cooperation.

## Summary

Quantitative research designs may be true or quasi-experimental studies or field studies. Participants in true experiments are randomly assigned to the conditions of interest, but this is not always possible in OHP. In quasi-experiments (such as many intervention studies) there are at least two different conditions, but participants are not usually randomly assigned to these. Field studies can be classified as cross-sectional (single-shot) and longitudinal approaches (where measures are taken for at least two occasions). A major issue in field studies is assuring that a sufficiently high response rate is obtained: this will prevent problems with the statistical power of tests (i.e., their ability to detect effects) as well as with the degree to which sample-based findings can be generalized to the population of interest.

## Measurement and Psychometrics

*What is meant by the reliability of a variable?*
*What is meant by the validity of a variable, and how can it be assessed?*

Basically, measurement is the process of assigning numbers to characteristics of people, events or things, using rules in such a way as to represent specified attributes of these people, events or things (Stevens, 1968). For OHP, this often means that we are quantifying individuals along some attribute. An attribute is a dimension along which individuals can be measured and along which they vary, for example, number of health complaints, work load, or number of absence days. In order to do so we need an instrument to measure the location of individuals on this dimension, i.e., we must assign numbers to individuals that indicate how much or how little of an attribute they possess (Levy, 2003). One of the critical steps in planning a study is deciding how the study variables will be measured: ultimately, the quality of our measures will determine how strong our conclusions can be. Two aspects of our measures are of central importance: their reliability and their validity.

## Reliability

The reliability of a measure is the consistency or stability of a measure across repeated observations of a characteristic on the same subject, assuming that the underlying or 'true' score of this subject on this characteristic is stable across time. In order to be reliable, a measure should show little variation from observed score to observed score; if observations differ each time the subject is assessed, the measure is said to be unreliable. Reliability is an important issue, as we cannot adequately describe, explain, predict, or control attitudes, behaviour, performance or health with a variable that is not measured very well. This implies that the reliability of our variables provides an upper bound on the accuracy of our conclusions: our findings cannot be accurate or useful if our variables have been measured badly.

What makes our measures reliable or unreliable? According to *classical measurement theory,* scores on a variable consist of two components: true score and error. The true score represents the characteristic that interests us, the error component is just that – error, comprising random influences on the observed score. Normally an individual's score on a measure will not perfectly represent their true score on the characteristic of interest. For example, people may misunderstand a question or the answering categories provided for a question or assign a different meaning to these: how often should one experience a particular health complaint (say, heart palpitations) in order to check the 'sometimes' alternative for an item tapping that complaint? Note that such misunderstandings could arise even if researchers were to provide objective frequencies as answering categories for such a question, as people would have to recall the average frequency with which they experienced such complaints. Thus, there will virtually always be some potential for errors to occur.

However, as these errors are assumed to be independent of the true score, they are as likely to increase as to decrease the observed scores on our variables. This implies that if multiple observations of a variable are taken, the errors of these will cancel each other out: after averaging these observations, the errors will disappear and the resulting mean will approximate the true score. This reasoning suggests a simple way to increase the reliability of our measures, that is, to take multiple measures of the concepts of interest: when the number of items in a test increases, the reliability of that test will increase correspondingly. This is one of the reasons why the instruments used in OHP often consist of multiple items.

The reliability of a measure can be expressed in various ways. One common way to assess reliability, Cronbach's alpha, is a measure of the *internal consistency* of a measure. This refers to the interrelatedness of the test items. As these items are assumed to tap the same thing, they should be highly related: items that do not correlate highly with the other items of a test may be measuring a different thing and are usually omitted. As a rule of thumb, alpha should be at least .60 when measuring concepts at the group level; many researchers prefer a reliability of

.70 (Nunnally & Bernstein, 1994: note that for individual diagnosis alpha should be much higher, preferably 0.90 or better). Another often-used reliability index is the *test-retest reliability*, referring to the stability of test scores across time, assuming that the underlying true scores did not change. For instance, we may administer a test tapping work load to the members of an organization and then administer the same test to the same group four weeks later. Assuming that the work load did not change across that time interval, the scores of the participants should be about the same at both occasions (as expressed in a high correlation coefficient).

---

### Pioneer    Jum C. Nunnally, Jr. (1924–1982)

Jum C. Nunnally, Jr. was born in Binghamton, Alabama. He graduated from high school in 1942 after which he flew transport aircraft in World War II. After the war he returned to Binghamton, where he graduated in 1949 from the local college. Successively he obtained a PhD in Psychology from the University of Chicago (1952), graduating on an analysis of the therapy-induced changes in the factor structure of a client's self-description. His career then took him to the University of Illinois (1954) and finally to Vanderbilt University, where he accepted a full professorship in 1960. Nunnally is best known for his influential textbook entitled *Psychometric theory*, in which he discussed important issues in measurement avoiding unnecessarily complex mathematics.

---

### Validity

It is one thing for a measure to be reliable, but that does not imply that the scores on this variable represent a valid indication of a person's standing on the dimension of interest. The validity of a test is most appropriately considered in terms of its *construct validity*, that is, the degree to which a test measures the construct it was intended to measure. A construct is an abstract quality, meaning that it cannot directly be observed (unlike concepts such as level of education and gender), and that is difficult to measure. Construct validity may be demonstrated by several types of evidence (see Table 10.1). The *face validity* of a measure is high if it appears to assess what it was designed to measure. E.g., job-related fatigue may be tapped with items such as 'I feel exhausted at the end of the work day'. One problem with this type of validity is that it depends on the perspective of the person judging it: whereas I may feel that my measures have high face validity (or else I would be using different measures), others could well disagree. Therefore, this type of evidence is insufficient to demonstrate the validity of our measures.

**Table 10.1**  Types of validity

| Type | | | Key question |
|---|---|---|---|
| | • Face validity | | Does the measure look like what it should assess? |
| | • Content validity | | Does the measure cover the entire underlying concept, as it is theoretically defined? |
| Construct validity | | Predictive validity<br>• convergent<br>• divergent | Does the measure predict the future criterion that it should predict (convergent validity) and not the future criterion it should not predict (divergent validity)? |
| | • Criterion validity | Concurrent validity<br>• divergent<br>• convergent | Does the measure predict the current criterion that it should predict (convergent validity) and not the current criterion it should not predict (divergent validity)? |

*Content validity* refers to the degree to which a test covers a representative sample of the characteristic being assessed. For instance, burnout is theoretically defined as a syndrome of high levels of job-related exhaustion, high levels of cynicism towards one's job and low levels of job-related self-efficacy (Maslach & Jackson, 1981). Thus, a valid measure of burnout should cover these three domains, and a measure that only covers one of these dimensions does a poor job of adequately covering the entire concept. Like face validity, content validity is often assessed by asking experts (such as fellow occupational health psychologists) to evaluate a measure.

The *criterion-related validity* of a measure refers to the degree to which this measure relates to other concepts that are theoretically assumed to be associated with this measure. One type of criterion-related validity is *predictive validity,* referring to the extent to which test scores obtained at one point in time predict criteria observed in the future. For example, theoretically it may be assumed that a measure of burnout predicts future sickness absence and turnover. Another type of criterion-related validity is the *concurrent validity,* referring to how well a test predicts a criterion that is measured at the same time as the test is conducted. For instance, a measure of burnout should correlate highly with work load and stress. Further, *convergent validity* can be demonstrated by showing that one measure of a particular concept correlates highly with other measures of the same concept. For example, a new measure of burnout has high convergent validity if it is strongly associated with existing measures of burnout. In contrast, its associations with theoretically dissimilar measures such as gender or pay level should be low (*divergent validity*).

## Summary

To be useful, the measures used in OHP research should be both reliable and valid. The reliability of a measure refers to the degree that this measure is stable across repeated observations of a characteristic on the same participant, assuming that the true score of this participant on this characteristic does not change. The validity of a measure can be established by demonstrating its face, content and criterion validity. In conjunction these three forms of validity provide evidence for the fourth and most important criterion, namely the construct validity of the measure. To the criteria of reliability and validity we might add a third, namely the *utility* of a measure. This refers to the practical applicability and the balance between the costs and benefits of a measure. Some ways of measuring stress may be reliable and valid, but – in the context of a particular study – quite impractical or overly expensive. For example, measuring cortisol levels may be a good way to obtain an objective impression of worker stress, but workers may be unwilling to participate in such a study whereas the organization they work for may be unwilling to pay for the extra costs. Thus, in practice one must frequently compromise between the validity and reliability of a measure on the one hand, and its utility on the other.

## SUMMARY AND CONCLUSIONS

Let us now return to the example we began with, that is, the occupational health psychologist who was asked by the management of a large IT firm to conduct a study on the health and well-being of their employees. Which issues should be considered before this study could actually be conducted?

- The scientific approach refers to the process or method that is used to generate a body of knowledge concerning a phenomenon deemed to be of interest. In generating (or contributing to) this body of knowledge researchers rely on formal, systematic observation to help them find answers to the questions that interest them.
- Before starting a study, it is vitally important to decide upon the goal of and basic research question for the study: will the study have a hypothesis-testing or exploratory goal? And does the researcher intend to describe, explain, predict or control the phenomenon of interest? In an applied context, it is vitally important that the study goal and research questions match with the interests of the organization, imposing practical constraints on the study's aims.

- Based on the goals and research question(s), researchers should decide upon the research design for the study: its setting (laboratory or the field), the type of participants involved, the variables to be assessed or varied, the way of assigning participants to the study conditions (i.e., random or non-random) and the data collection mode (e.g., a qualitative or a quantitative approach) that will be used.
- A good research design allows researchers to rule out alternative explanations for their findings, other than the hypotheses they intend to test. This means that researchers must be able to control for the effects of variables that are of little substantive interest.
- A main distinction can be made between quantitative versus qualitative approaches. Quantitative approaches emphasize the testing of theory-driven hypotheses and data analysis using advanced statistical techniques. Qualitative approaches are often used in an hypothesis-generating mode. Such an approach becomes more appropriate when the context or participant's interpretations are central to the research question, when answering this question requires very detailed data, or when the research has an exploratory, hypothesis-generating focus.
- Quantitative research designs may be true or quasi-experimental studies or field studies. Participants in true experiments are randomly assigned to the conditions of interest. In quasi-experiments participants are not usually randomly assigned to these. Field studies can be either cross-sectional (data are collected for one occasion) or longitudinal (measures are taken for at least two occasions).
- A major issue in field studies is assuring that a sufficiently high response rate is obtained: this will prevent problems with the statistical power of tests (i.e., their ability to detect effects) as well as with the degree to which sample-based findings can be generalized to the population of interest.
- The measures used should be reliable (stable across repeated observations of an unchanging characteristic on the same subject), valid (measure what it intends to measure), and useful in the context under study.
- The validity of a measure can be established by demonstrating its face, content and criterion validity. In conjunction these three forms of validity provide evidence for the fourth and most important criterion, namely the construct validity of the measure.

## Suggestions for Further Reading

Menard, S. (2008). *Handbook of longitudinal research: Design, measurement, and analysis.* London: Academic Press.

Nesselroade, J. R., & Baltes, P. B. (Eds.) (1979). *Longitudinal research in the study of behavior and development.* New York: Academic Press.

Robson, C. (2002). *Real world research: a resource for social scientists and practitioner-researchers* (2nd ed.). Malden, MA: Blackwell.

Rogelberg, S. G. (Ed.) (2002). *Handbook of research methods in industrial and organizational psychology.* Malden, MA: Blackwell.

Shadish, W. R., Cook, T. D., & Campbell, D. T. (2002). *Experimental and quasi-experimental designs for generalized causal inference.* Boston: Houghton-Mifflin.

Stevens, J. (1996). *Applied multivariate statistics for the social sciences.* Mahwah, NJ: Lawrence Erlbaum Associates.

Taris, T. W. (2000). *A primer in longitudinal data analysis.* London: Sage.

# References

Babbie, E. (1998). *The practice of social research.* Belmont (CA): Wadsworth.

Bachiochi, P. D., & Weiner, S. P. (2002). Qualitative data collection and analysis. In S. G. Rogelberg (Ed.), *Handbook of organizational research methods* (pp. 161–183). Malden, MA: Blackwell.

Baruch, Y., & Holtom, B. C. (2008). Survey response rate levels and trends in organizational research. *Human Relations, 61,* 1139–1160.

Beckers, D. G. J., Van Hooff, H. L. M., Van der Linden, D., Kompier, M. A. J., Taris, T. W., & Geurts, S. A. E. (2008). A diary study to open up the black box of overtime work among university faculty members. *Scandinavian Journal of Work, Environment and Health, 34,* 213–223.

Bolger, N., Davis, A., & Rafaeli, E. (2003). Diary methods: Capturing life as it is lived. *Annual Review of Psychology, 54,* 579–616.

Bond, F. W., Flaxman, P. E., & Bunce, D. (2008). The influence of psychological flexibility on work redesign: Mediated moderation of a work reorganization intervention. *Journal of Applied Psychology, 93,* 645–654.

Brewerton, P., & Millward, L. (2001). *Organizational research methods.* London: Sage.

Campbell, D. T., & Kenny, D. A. (2003). *A primer on regression artifacts.* New York: The Guilford Press.

Christensen, L. B. (1994). *Experimental methodology.* Boston: Allyn & Bacon.

De Lange, A. H., Taris, T. W., Kompier, M. A. J., Houtman, I. L. D., & Bongers, P. M. (2003). The *very* best of the millennium: Longitudinal research on the Job demands-Control model. *Journal of Occupational Health Psychology, 8,* 282–305.

Deelstra, J. T., Peeters, M. C. W., Schaufeli, W. B., Stroebe, W., Zijlstra, F. R. H., & Van Doornen, L. P. (2003). Receiving instrumental support at work: when help is not welcome. *Journal of Applied Psychology, 88,* 324–331.

Israel, B. A., Baker, E. A., Goldenhar, L. M., & Heaney, C. A. (1996). Occupational stress, safety, and health: Conceptual framework and principles for effective prevention interventions. *Journal of Occupational Health Psychology, 1,* 261–286.

Kerlinger, F. N., & Lee, H. B. (2000). *Foundations of behavioral research* (4th ed.). Orlando: Harcourt College Publishers.

Keyton, J., Cano, P., Clounch, T. L., Fischer, C. E., Howard, C., et al. (2006). Ethical storm or model workplace? In S. May (Ed.), *Case studies in organizational communication: Ethical perspectives and practices* (pp. 153–168). Thousand Oaks: Sage Publications.

Kompier, M. A. J., & Kristensen, T. S. (2001). Organizational work stress interventions in a theoretical, methodological and practical context. In J. Dunham (Ed.), *Stress in the workplace: Past, present and future* (pp. 164–190). London: Whurr Publishers.

Le Blanc, P. M., Hox, J. J., Schaufeli, W. B., Taris, T. W., & Peeters, M. C. W. (2007). Take care! Evaluation of a team-based burnout intervention program for oncology care providers. *Journal of Applied Psychology, 92*, 213–227.

Lewin, K. (1951). *Field theory in social science.* New York: Harper & Row.

Liu, C., Spector, P. E., & Lin, S. (2008). Use of both qualitative and quantitative approaches to study job stress in different gender and occupational groups. *Journal of Occupational Health Psychology, 13*, 357–370.

Locke, K., & Golden-Biddle, K. (2002). An introduction to qualitative research: Its potential for industrial and organizational psychology. In S. G. Rogelberg (Ed.), *Handbook of research methods in industrial and organizational psychology* (pp. 99–118). Malden, MA: Blackwell.

Maslach, C., & Jackson, S. (1982). *The Maslach Burnout Inventory.* Palo Alto: Consulting Psychologists Press.

Nunnally, J. C., & Bernstein, I. H. (1994). *Psychometric theory* (3rd ed.). New York: McGraw-Hill.

Semmer, N. K., Grebner, S. & Elfering, A. (2004). Beyond self-report: using observational, physiological, and situation-based measures in research on occupational stress. In P. L. Perrewé and D. C. Ganster (Eds.), *Research in occupational stress and well-being: Emotional and physiological processes and positive intervention* strategies (pp. 205–263). Amsterdam: Elsevier.

Shadish, W. R., Cook, T. D., & Campbell, D. T. (2002). *Experimental and quasi-experimental designs for generalized causal inference.* Boston: Houghton-Mifflin.

Sonnentag, S. (2001). Work, recovery activities, and individual well-being: A diary study. *Journal of Occupational Health Psychology, 6*, 196–210.

Spector, P. E. (2008). *Industrial and organizational behaviour* (5th ed.). Malden, MA: Wiley.

Stevens, S. (1968). Measurement, statistics, and the schemapiric view. *Science, 161*, 849–856.

Stone-Romero, E. F. (2002). The relative validity and usefulness of various empirical research designs. In S.G. Rogelberg (Ed.), *Handbook of research methods in industrial and organizational psychology* (pp. 77–98). Malden, MA: Blackwell.

Taris, T. W. (2000). *A primer in longitudinal data analysis.* London: Sage.

Taris, T. W. (2006). Is there a relationship between burnout and objective performance? A critical review of 16 studies. *Work & Stress, 20*, 316–334.

Taris, T. W., & Schreurs, P. J. G. (2007). How may nonresponse affect findings in organizational studies? The tendency-to-the-positive effect. *International Journal of Stress Management, 14*, 249–259.

Taris, T. W., Schreurs, P. J. G., & Sepmeijer, K. J. (2004). Web-based data collection in occupational health psychology. In J. Houdmont and S. McIntyre (Eds.), *Occupational health psychology: Key papers of the European Academy of Occupational Health Psychology* (pp. 398–406). Maia (POR): ISMAI.

Van der Vaart, W., & Glasner, T. (2007). Applying a timeline as a recall aid in a telephone study: A record check study. *Applied Cognitive Psychology, 21*, 227–238.

Yin, R. K. (1994). *Case study research: Design and methods* (2nd ed.). Thousand Oaks: Sage.

# 11

# Future Directions in Occupational Health Psychology

## Jonathan Houdmont and Stavroula Leka

### CHAPTER OUTLINE

This chapter examines the direction that activity in occupational health psychology might take as the discipline matures into its third decade. It begins by considering what has been achieved in the discipline's early years before discussing important areas for development across the interdependent domains of research, education, and professional practice.

## Introction

The chapters of this book have illustrated various facets of contemporary theory, evidence, and professional practice in occupational health psychology (OHP). Collectively, they paint a picture of a thriving discipline characterized by a vision to protect and promote worker health; one that is replete with theoretically and empirically grounded processes and procedures by which that vision might be realized. The quantity and quality of OHP activity that has emerged in the 20 years since Raymond, Wood, and Patrick (1990) coined the term 'occupational health psychology' is testament to the efforts of a dedicated international cohort of individuals and institutions. Impressive progress has been made across the research, education, and professional practice domains. The ever-growing body of scientific OHP research finds support from numerous funding bodies that place value on studies which seek to apply psychological principles and practices towards facilitating our understanding and ability to effectively manage the dynamic relationship between work and health. This research finds its voice in the pages of two respected journals that are explicitly dedicated to the discipline (*Journal of*

*Occupational Health Psychology* and *Work & Stress*) alongside a host of supplementary publication outlets. Graduate education and training in OHP has been offered since the mid 1990s, and students continue to navigate towards the numerous programmes in ever increasing numbers. Finally, it is possible to identify a growing constituency of OHP graduates that is offering its services to organizations and, in doing so, establishing the foundations of an OHP career pathway and professional network.

Yet despite these successes, activity across the three domains remains unequal, and each has not always informed and influenced the others as could and should be the case. While research output has developed at a rapid rate, educational opportunities have expanded only gradually despite student demand. The slow rate at which universities have introduced OHP programmes has no doubt also contributed to the paucity of efforts to establish professional career pathways and governance structures for practitioners which, in turn, has limited opportunities for OHP graduates to develop a practice-oriented career. Given the inconsistent rate of progress on research, education, and practice in this young specialty it is worthwhile considering what needs to be done in respect of each to maximize OHP's contribution to meeting contemporary occupational health challenges. Thus, the following sections consider possible future directions in these interdependent areas of activity.

## Where Next for Research?

*What factors will influence the future direction of OHP research?*
*Which issues should OHP researchers address?*
*What barriers to publication do OHP researchers encounter?*

### The future direction of OHP research

Cooper and Dewe (2004) have suggested that 'the history of stress is also a history of occupational health psychology' (p. 107). However, as the chapters of this book have shown, OHP research has moved beyond its traditional focus on stress to address a broad range of psychosocial issues at work using a plethora of theoretical perspectives and research methodologies. To ensure the cohesive and integrated maturation of the field it is important that we ask ourselves what issues, perspectives, and methodologies ought OHP research navigate towards in the future. Like the teenager considering the abundance of choices and opportunities that attend imminent adulthood, OHP has come of age and such questions become inevitable. Perhaps surprisingly, these are questions that, with a limited number of exceptions (e.g., Macik-Frey, Quick, & Nelson, 2007; Schaufeli, 2004; Taris, 2006), few have considered. It would appear that researchers have rarely had the opportunity (or, possibly, the inclination) to raise their head above the parapet to scan the horizon for what it holds, not only for their topic of study, but for the discipline as a whole.

Wilmar Schaufeli of Utrecht University (The Netherlands) is one of the few to have attempted a rigorous examination of future topics that OHP researchers might address. In his 2004 paper on 'The future of occupational health psychology' (available at www.schaufeli.com), he suggests that future research trends are likely to be shaped by *external factors* that have a bearing on the organization of work, and *internal factors* associated with developments in the nature of scientific inquiry. In relation to the former, Schaufeli points to a model of the organization of work delineated by the US National Institute for Occupational Safety and Health (NIOSH) (Sauter et al., 2002) (available at www.cdc.gov/niosh) that identifies three contexts which have a bearing on worker health and safety. The evolving character of these contexts suggests a three-pronged research agenda concerned with surveillance of the changing organization of work, the effects of these changes, and interventions for the promotion of safety and health (Figure 11.1). The NIOSH research agenda has gained widespread respect and influence, derived in large part from its grounding in a large-scale consultation that captured the opinions of some 500 individuals and organizations including employers, employees, safety and health professionals, public agencies, and industry and labour organizations.

In tandem with external factors, Schaufeli suggests that internal factors associated with developments in the nature of scientific inquiry within the discipline are likely to play a role in directing the attention of researchers towards five broad types of research. These include: (1) fundamental explanatory research that seeks to improve our understanding of psychological processes and mechanisms, (2) descriptive research that presents facts (such as work-related illness prevalence rates), (3) the development of tools for organizational application, (4) intervention research that evaluates both outcomes and processes, and (5) organizational change research. Among these research categories, it is important to note in particular the need for further intervention research. Intervention studies are essential to the development of our ability to design work that is health-promoting. However, few intervention studies have been published and many of those that have reached the pages of a journal have demonstrated disappointing results (Macik-Frey et al., 2007). Figure 11.2 illustrates the paucity of intervention studies in OHP research. Analysis of the 631 papers published in the *Journal of Occupational Health Psychology* and *Work & Stress* between 1996 and 2006 revealed that only 7.2% and 6.4% respectively involved a longitudinal design (Kang, Staniford, Dollard, & Kompier, 2008). Kang and colleagues suggest that the paucity of longitudinal study designs in OHP research may reflect the limited translation of research to practice, a limited evaluation of it, or a lack of research that reaches journal publication standards.

Macik-Frey et al. (2007) similarly scanned the horizon for topic areas that hold promise for the future of OHP and, consistent with Schaufeli (2004), concluded that the changing character of work organization is likely to determine future research foci. Four areas were identified for particular attention: technology advances, virtual work, globalization, and the ageing workforce.

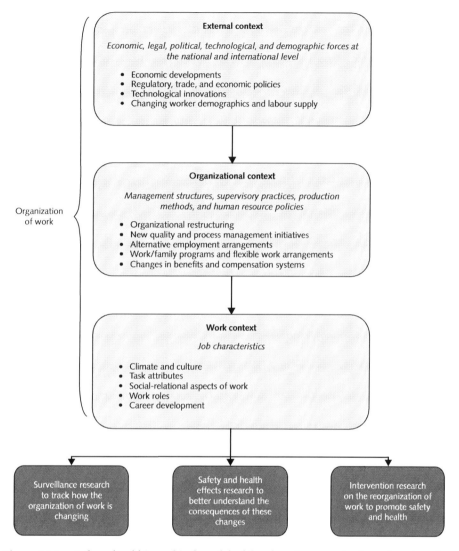

**Figure 11.1** A three-level hierarchical model of the changing organization of work and an attendant scientific agenda (Sauter et al., 2002).

Given the rapid nature of change in the content and context of work, analysis of these topic areas, and others, is likely to require researchers to revisit, and where necessary revise, theoretical models that have been heavily relied upon thus far in OHP research. For example, some have claimed that the theoretical perspectives which have dominated the study of work-related stress – Karasek's (1979) Demand–Control model and Siegrist's (1996) Effort–Reward Imbalance model – 'are still relevant but they certainly need to be refined, supplemented and interpreted in the new working life context' (Theorell, 2006, p. 113). Theorell and others have pointed to the need for augmentations of existing theoretical models of

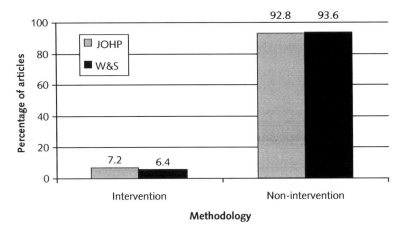

**Figure 11.2** Frequency of intervention vs. non-intervention designs in OHP research published in between 1996 and 2006 in the *Journal of Occupational Health Psychology* and *Work & Stress* (Kang, Staniford, Dollard, & Kompier, 2008).

the work-related stress construct that enhance the consideration of the psychosocial work environment by taking into account forces external to the organization, such as globalization, new cognitive demands, and modern information and communication technologies. This is an argument developed by Wallis and Dollard (2008) who similarly noted the need for models to account for external factors such as free market forces, technological, and environmental demands that may impact upon worker well-being.

### Positive occupational health psychology

If 100 OHP researchers were asked to scan the horizon to identify a single topic worthy of future research attention it is likely that an equal number of topics would be identified. Such is the nature of research that addresses health as it relates to the rapidly changing world of work. However, there appears to be growing consensus among researchers on one particular point: that as the discipline matures the research emphasis must shift from a focus on negative concepts to the positive.

There is no denying that much OHP research has focused on what is wrong with work, the so-called four Ds approach centred on damage, disease, disorder, and dysfunction. The degree to which research has concentrated on illness as opposed to wellness was illustrated in a review of topics addressed in studies that appeared in the *Journal of Occupational Health Psychology* (Macik-Frey et al., 2007). Among the articles published between 1996 and 2006, only two dealt with positive health or positive psychology as it relates to workers' health and well-being. Schaufeli (2004), among others, has argued that having focused for too long on ill-health and negative constructs such as burnout, workplace violence, and substance abuse, it is time to turn our attentions to positive concepts including job satisfaction, intrinsic motivation, and work-related self-esteem. It is argued that in doing so the discipline will reorient its focus from fixing what is wrong about work to developing that which is good.

The trend towards positive OHP research is strong, relentless, and encouraged by journal editors (e.g., Barling, 2005; Tetrick, 2006). Indeed, such is the enthusiasm for positive OHP that the absence of a chapter dedicated to the topic within the initial outline for this textbook sent many of the reviewers into a spin! There can be little doubt that the influence of positive OHP will spread in years to come; rightly, perhaps, given that it is embedded in Raymond, Wood, and Patrick's (1990) original vision for OHP as a specialty that:

> beyond the basics of assuring that adequate mechanisms exist to deal with the negative consequences of work stress ... has a responsibility to take on a more proactive role in advocating and developing healthful environments and policies that will enhance the positive aspects of work. (p. 1159)

Moreover, the positive OHP perspective accords with Münsterberg's (1913) assertion that what would become known as OHP 'offers no more inspiring idea than this adjustment of work and psyche by which mental dissatisfaction in the work, mental depression and discouragement, may be replaced ... by overflowing joy and perfect inner harmony' ('The future development of economic psychology' section, para. 5).

## Publication challenges

An often-overlooked factor that has an influence on researchers' decision-making in respect of the identification of suitable topics for investigation is that of journal publication policies. As mentioned previously, OHP is serviced by two dedicated journals. Each receives many more submissions than can be published. Fortunately, numerous other scientific journals welcome OHP research, though not all recognize the OHP specialty in explicit terms. Scientific journals do a great service towards the dissemination of OHP research. This has become truer than ever following the incorporation of personal subscriptions to the two dedicated OHP journals within the membership packages of the European Academy of Occupational Health Psychology (EAOHP) and the Society for Occupational Health Psychology (SOHP); an innovation that has valuably enhanced the ability of practitioners to access research that has historically been available only to those with right of entry to university libraries.

The publication policies of established journals are often embedded in traditional notions of what makes good science. Though journal editorial boards might reasonably be expected to uphold scientific standards, stringent acceptance criteria can inadvertently conspire against the publication of research produced by students and practitioners that may involve forms of research design and statistical analysis that are fit for purpose while being less sophisticated than those typically employed by professional academics. There is growing evidence to suggest that less-than-optimal research designs can nevertheless reveal unique insights (Nielsen, Randall, & Christensen, 2010). Traditional publication criteria may also discourage policy research and scientific inquiry concerning OHP education and training. Furthermore, complex scientific language and statistical analysis, often stipulated as a requirement within journal publication policies, can render OHP research the exclusive preserve of a highly trained and experienced academic constituency.

The paucity of publication outlets for research written for and by practitioners is an issue worthy of further consideration. It has been estimated that between 1 and 3 per cent of journal articles in fields related to OHP are written by practitioners (Anderson, Herriot, & Hodgkinson, 2001). This is a matter for concern given that professional practice can thrive only when supported by publications that help practitioners to keep abreast of scientific developments that have a bearing on their work with organizations. Restrictive journal submission criteria can preclude practice-oriented submissions, rendering traditional journals inappropriate for the publication of such research. Fortunately, in recent times the challenge in publishing practitioner-oriented research has been acknowledged by publishers. This has resulted in the establishment of various publications that serve the practitioner community alongside the academic. Examples include the *European Journal of Work and Organizational Psychology* (Psychology Press) that seeks to publish articles 'that are relevant to the real-world situations faced by professionals' (González-Romá, 2009, p. 5) and requires authors to dedicate a portion of each paper's discussion section to the study's practical implications; the *International Journal of Workplace Health Management* (Emerald) launched in 2008; and *Contemporary occupational health psychology: Global perspectives on research and practice* (Wiley-Blackwell), a biennial book series launched in 2010 and produced collaboratively by the EAOHP and SOHP. These publications, and others, have an important role in ensuring that OHP research remains pragmatic rather than pedantic; in other words, practical in orientation while upholding sound scientific research principles.

The embedding of journal publication policies within a traditional scientific paradigm may conspire not only against the publication of practitioner-oriented works but also those produced by experienced professional researchers. Töres Theorell, EAOHP fellow and influential figure within the OHP community, has written candidly about the challenge in conducting research that has real-world application and that upholds the standards of scientific rigor required for publication in the leading journals. In his words, 'journals may become so preoccupied with technical properties of assessments that they lose perspective on what may actually be important' (2006, p. 114). Theorell cites the example of a study he co-authored that examined how conflicts were solved in a large multinational company. The manuscript was rejected by a journal on the grounds that (1) the issue of how conflicts were solved had been addressed through one question only, and (2) due to the cross-sectional, questionnaire-based nature of the study, both explanatory (independent) variables and outcome (dependent) variables had been measured using the same instrument, raising the possibility of an overestimation of associations between variables: the so called common method variance problem. Theorell and colleagues accepted the possibility of common method variance in their study but noted that the new and previously unexplored nature of the research question suggested that value could be found in the study as an exploratory first step in a new avenue of scientific enquiry. On the journal editor's criticism of the use of a single-item measure of approaches to conflict resolution, the authors expressed concern at the preference evident in the selection policy of some journals for evidence of complex psychometrically tested measures. While in some contexts the use of sophisticated measurement instruments that hold demonstrated psychometric reliability and validity will be appropriate, in other cases, such as the study described here in which the organizational context constituted the core of the independent variable, their use may be less relevant. This is an issue of relevance to other topic areas. For example, in the study of work-related stress there is growing evidence to suggest that single-item measures involving a question along the lines of 'on a scale of one to five, how stressful do you find your job' may hold predictive power of equivalence to more complex measurement approaches (Smith, 2001; Smith, Johal, Wadsworth, Davey Smith, & Peters, 2000). At present, the use of the single-item approach to the measurement of work-related stress is limited to a handful of studies (e.g., Smith, Wadsworth, Moss, & Simpson, 2004; Wadsworth, Dhillon, Shaw, Bhui, Stansfeld, & Smith, 2007). However, should evidence continue to emerge to attest to the validity and reliability of the approach, journal editors may be forced to reconsider their policies.

Ultimately, it is incumbent upon the international community of occupational health psychologists to encourage one another in their research endeavours, to welcome research on a vast array of topics and conducted in a range of contexts, and to find value in a host of research methodologies, both traditional and non traditional. If we fail on this score we risk forcing a narrowing of approach that will result in a bland research landscape. We need to avoid inflexibility in our understanding of what constitutes good science, constantly remind ourselves that OHP is an applied discipline, and ensure that research does not become detached from organizational practice. If we fail to privilege the intimate research–practice linkage we risk creating research that is 'so rigorous that we lose sight of what is important' (Theorell, 2006, p. 115).

## Summary

Future research trends in OHP are likely to be determined by external forces related to developments in work organization and forces internal to the discipline associated with the evolution of science. A number of outlets exist for the publication of OHP research. Some of these may favour studies based on a traditional scientific research paradigm and, in consequence, generate barriers to the publication of research produced for and by practitioners. OHP is an applied branch of science; the international community needs to ensure that appropriate publication opportunities exist for the dissemination of practice-oriented research.

# Where Next for Education?

*Can an educational OHP curriculum be discerned?*
*How might OHP programmes be accredited?*
*What ought to be the role of the discipline's representative*
*bodies in the regulation of education?*

Education and training are central to the sustainable development of any discipline; a consistent flow of graduates from university programmes ensures the continuation and evolution of research and professional practice. Without education and training that prepares graduates with knowledge and understanding of theory, evidence, and research design and evaluation, the quality and quantity of OHP activities would inevitable suffer and, in all likelihood, eventually cease.

In recognition of the crucial importance of education and training to the future of OHP as a scientific and applied field, in 2002 the EAOHP published a strategy document on *The Promotion of Education in Occupational Health Psychology in Europe.* Published following a 12-month consultation process that sought to establish and integrate the views of members, the document set out to provide a foundation and structure to guide educational developments. To this end, it presented six objectives as important for the sustained expansion and promotion of OHP education and training. These concerned the development of (1) a core educational syllabus, (2) a mechanism for identifying, recognizing and listing undergraduate and graduate OHP courses and programmes, (3) structures to support the extension of current provision, (4) ways of enhancing convergence in current provision, (5) ways of encouraging regional cooperation between education providers across the regions of Europe, and (6) ways of ensuring consistency with North American developments in education and promoting worldwide cooperation in education. Progress across the six objectives has been variable (Houdmont, Leka, & Cox, 2007). The analysis that follows facilitates a consideration of what remains to be done.

## A core curriculum for education in occupational health psychology

As has been noted, OHP cannot be sustained on the strength of research activity alone; opportunities are required for individuals to carve careers centred on the application of psychological principles and practices in the organizational context. As such, an imperative can be identified for the development of professional training pathways that have at their root an educational curriculum on which there is agreement surrounding key topic areas. Owing to the youthfulness of the discipline and the paucity of guidance on curriculum matters provided by its representative bodies, there exists a lack of consistency across OHP curricula in terms of the topics that are addressed. Such variability makes it difficult to discern the key characteristics of a curriculum.

Although the need to identify key topic areas that might be included in an OHP curriculum was recognized early by the EAOHP, limited progress has been made towards that end. Pragmatic and conceptual explanations for the lack of progress can be identified. The fact that individuals who commit themselves to working on behalf of representative bodies usually do so on a voluntary basis while juggling the demands of a career in OHP often means that developments fail to materialize with desired expediency. Lack of progress might also be attributed to challenges associated with three complex questions identified as being of central importance to the definition of an OHP curriculum (Sinclair, 2006). These concern: (1) on what knowledge, skills, and abilities should OHP education focus; (2) how might OHP programmes address the needs and concerns of multiple stakeholder groups including employers, trade unions, practitioners, and academics; and (3) how might and to what extent should OHP integrate knowledge from other disciplines? Irrespective of the nature of the challenges, it is incumbent upon the representative bodies to grasp the thorny issues of curriculum development and programme accreditation if they are to fulfil their *raison d'être*.

Stimulated by the EAOHP strategy document and a call from NIOSH for:

> Steps . . . to be taken within the academic community and professional organizations to nurture and formalise the subject of organization of work and health as a distinct multidisciplinary field of study, and to provide the multidisciplinary training to ensure that students are prepared for research on organization of work and health (NIOSH, 2002, p. 25)

several researchers have sought to define OHP topic areas within educational curricula. One approach to examination has involved analysis of existing curricula. Scrutiny of topics addressed in twelve US doctoral OHP training programmes revealed one topic taught across programmes: introduction to the discipline of OHP; work-related stress was the second most prevalent topic area, taught at seven institutions (Fullagar & Hatfield, 2005). A similar analysis of the content of eleven US doctoral curricula identified six topic areas that appeared consistently: (1) survey (overview) of occupational safety and health, (2) job stress theory, (3) organizational risk factors for occupational stress, injury, and illness, (4) physical and psychological health implications of stressful work, (5) organizational interventions for the reduction of work-related stress, and (6) research methods and practices in public/occupational health and epidemiology (Barnes-Farrell, 2006). These topic areas are consistent with the seven broad areas identified by Macik-Frey et al. (2007) as representing the major research themes addressed in papers published in the *Journal of Occupational Health Psychology*. It might be reasonable to assume that consistency between OHP curricula and published research themes has arisen owing to programme designers having relied on the latter to inform the former.

Themes in the published research certainly provide an indication of important topics that ought to perhaps be included in educational curricula. However, given that many factors drive research foci beyond the intrinsic interest or importance of a topic, themes in the research literature cannot provide guidance on the topics that are fundamental to the discipline; nor can they offer a comprehensive account of OHP topics. Thus, a curriculum that reflects the key themes in published OHP research may be inadequate.

Moreover, the applied nature of OHP renders it important that curricula do not merely reflect the topics that academics study but encompass the issues of interest and concern to practitioners. To that end, programme designers in the US and Europe have sought to identify key topic areas from the practitioner perspective. This line of research was initiated in the US with a survey of 1,100 human resource managers, public health professionals, and experts in disciplines allied to OHP (Schneider, Camara, Tetrick, & Sternberg, 1999). Though it revealed a need for OHP education and training, the survey stopped short of delineating a curriculum. Schneider and colleagues' study laid the groundwork for the development of OHP curricula in the US in the late 1990s, including the doctoral programme at the University of Houston. Keen to ensure that the Houston curriculum met the needs of local employers, 141 human resource managers and 27 trade union representatives were surveyed on their organization's concern about various OHP-related topics (Tetrick & Ellis, 2002). Respondents were required to indicate the degree of organizational concern associated with 31 OHP-related topics derived from the authors' knowledge of the OHP literature and human resource practices in the US. Results showed that the top ten concerns of human resource managers included accidents, attendance, changing technology, education and training, employee commitment, physical well-being, psychological well-being, safety, teamwork, and workplace injuries. Within the list of concerns generated by trade union representatives, priority was given to issues of immediate and direct relevance to employees such as job security, work-related stress, retirement, and workload. This line of research was further developed in the US through a survey of 67 safety and health practitioners and nine OHP academics/researchers in a study that sought to assess both the types of organizations that OHP practitioners work within and the nature of health and safety issues they are charged with addressing (Sinclair, Hammer, Oeldorf Hirsch, & Brubaker, 2006). Survey responses revealed the ten most important OHP-related issues included accidents, safety climate, personal protective equipment, compliance with US Occupational Safety and Health Administration regulations, fire safety, repetitive strain injuries, ergonomics, traumatic injuries, workers' compensation, and noise/hearing protection. Owing to the nature of the sample the results were biased towards the perceptions of practitioners, many of whom worked in safety-related occupations. Thus, the study offered a tentative indication of the topics that might be considered important to an OHP curriculum from the viewpoint of a particular constituency.

Only one European study can be identified that has elicited the views of practitioners on these questions. Leka, Khan, and Griffiths (2008) conducted a two-wave project that involved a Delphi study with 30 national-level occupational safety and health experts in Britain, and a questionnaire that was administered to 1,679 occupational safety and health practitioners. The study sought to identify emerging and future occupational health priorities, and occupational health (and safety) practitioner training needs in the British context. Results from the Delphi study showed that subject matter experts' top five emerging and future workplace health priorities included common mental health problems (anxiety, depression, and stress), sickness absence (monitoring, management, return to work, rehabilitation, and presenteeism), musculoskeletal disorders, engaging and advising small and medium sized enterprises, and the evaluation of workplace health interventions. Survey results revealed that practitioners identified eight priority areas in terms of emerging and future workplace health issues: common mental health problems, the use of government guidance on the management of work-related stress, the identification of emerging risks, planning for major events (e.g., pandemics), work-related driving, work-life balance, immigrant and migrant workers, and non-standard workplaces (e.g., flexiwork, telework). Together, these studies provide useful guidance on topics that might be addressed within a curriculum that seeks to prepare graduates for professional practice.

The studies described above share the intention of canvassing stakeholder opinion on topic areas that might be considered important to an OHP curriculum. In light of this aim, it is perhaps surprising that only one study can be identified (Sinclair et al., 2006) that has attempted to elicit views from within the academic community. This is an important constituency whose views bring considerable weight to bear in the design and implementation of university curricula. Sinclair and colleagues' study provided a useful preliminary indication of the views of the academic OHP community; however, care must be taken in generalizing results drawn from a restricted sample of nine academics all of whom worked in the US higher education system. In recognition of the imperative for the development of consensus on the definition of curriculum areas in OHP, and the paucity of research that has sought to elicit the views of OHP academics in this regard, the EAOHP and the SOHP together designed and administered a study that aimed to identify the topic areas perceived by OHP academics to be: (1) 'important', and (2) 'core' to an educational curriculum in the discipline (Houdmont, Leka, & Bulger, 2010). Forty-nine OHP academics from seventeen countries completed a questionnaire that required respondents to indicate the importance of 68 topics to an OHP curriculum on a 5-point scale that ranged from [1] 'not important' to [5] 'extremely important'. A cut-off of 3.5 was applied for the identification of topics that might be considered essential, or 'core', to a curriculum. Seven topic areas met this criterion: combating psychosocial risk, interventions to promote health, organizational research methods, psychosocial work environment, stress theory, stress interventions, and work design and health. Interestingly, North American and European differences in the definition of OHP (see Chapter 1)

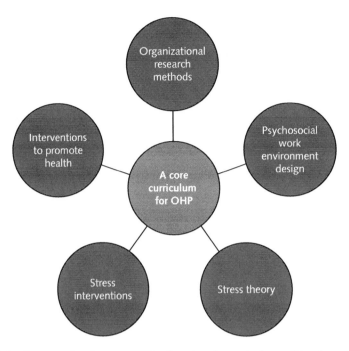

**Figure 11.3** Core topics in an OHP educational curriculum (Houdmont, Leka, & Bulger, 2010).

presented no barrier to consensus: eleven topics were identified by both groups as 'important' and a further five as 'core'. The core topics are illustrated in Figure 11.3. The observant reader will note that a chapter in this textbook is dedicated to each of these five core areas.

## Mechanisms for the accreditation of occupational health psychology programmes

OHP's representative bodies do not, at present, operate mechanisms for the accreditation of OHP educational programmes. This may be attributable to a perceived lack of consensus among OHP academics on key topic areas. However, results from Houdmont et al.'s (2010) study, described above, provide a basis upon which the development of programme accreditation criteria might be initiated. Accreditation would, in all likelihood, be welcomed by many academics and institutions; it would constitute an important step forward in the standardization of OHP educational provision (while allowing for flexibility that recognizes variance in institutional research expertise and the needs of employers across regions), send a positive message about a programme's quality to prospective students and employers, and facilitate the professionalization of practice-oriented careers in OHP. Given recent advances in the definition of topic areas within OHP curricula, the time might be right for the EAOHP and SOHP to embark upon the development of accreditation criteria.

## Structures to support the promotion
## of current OHP educational provision

It is unreasonable to expect programme providers to accept sole responsibility for the promotion of OHP education. The discipline's representative bodies must have a role in supporting the promotion of current provision. This might be achieved in a number of ways, four of which were advocated by the EAOHP (2002) in its strategy document. Namely, (1) the provision of information on programme content on the representative bodies' websites, (2) programme listings on the representative bodies' websites, (3) reference to programmes and provider information within educational networks, and (4) assistance in the marketing of new programmes through the websites of the representative bodies and the International Coordinating Group for Occupational Health Psychology (ICG-OHP). All four proposals have been implemented to varying degrees. It is important that these initiatives continue. In the US, the SOHP's Education and Training Committee has been particularly active in its attempt to establish and maintain a comprehensive and up-to-date list of OHP programmes available across the globe. In addition, the Committee has conducted research to investigate the training needs of OHP graduates with a view towards the results being used to inform future education provision. Though funds are restricted, EAOHP and SOHP could also usefully collaborate to promote OHP education at the international conferences of disciplines allied to OHP, and international graduate study fairs.

## Convergence of provision

In addition to facilitating the development of standardized training pathways, convergence in the structure and broad content of OHP provision across national boundaries might support the smooth exchange of students and staff between institutions and ensure the portability and recognition of qualifications across borders. Though desirable, convergence is not easily achieved given regional and national differences in funding systems, the structure of the academic year, and the operation of accreditation and licensing structures.

Nevertheless, current European developments concerning the harmonisation of psychological education and training could have an important bearing on the shape, structure, and content of education and training in OHP. These developments centre on the European Certificate in Psychology (EuroPsy): a qualification for psychologists working in Europe that is designed to be of equivalence to doctoral-level training. In essence, EuroPsy is intended to provide:

> a standard of academic education and professional training which informs clients, employers and colleagues that a psychologist can be considered to have gained the necessary competencies for the provision of psychological services. EuroPsy aims to set a common standard of competence in all the countries where it is issued. It promotes the free movement of psychologists across the countries of the European Union. (European Federation of Psychologists' Associations, 2006, p. 9)

EuroPsy is awarded upon completion of a 3+2+1 professional training model that comprises a first degree in psychology, a 2-year full-time Master's degree in a psychological specialty, and a minimum of 1 year of full-time supervised practice as a psychologist-practitioner in training. At the time of writing EuroPsy is yet to be rolled out across Europe and its potential impact on OHP provision can only be speculated upon. Nevertheless, its introduction will, in all likelihood, support the convergence of provision for the good of the discipline.

Promise for the future convergence of education might also be found in the notion of a professional doctorate in occupational health psychology (DOHPsy). A research degree with substantial taught and organizational-placement components, the DOHPsy is equivalent in status and challenge to a traditional PhD, and confers the title 'Dr' on the successful candidate, while being more appropriate for those following a professional rather than academic career path. So called PsyD programmes in professional psychology have been popular in a limited number of psychological specialties for some time. The clinical psychology professional doctorate is particularly well established; US data for 2003–4 revealed that clinical PsyD students represented approximately 25% of all new doctoral students in psychology (Norcross, Kohout, & Wicherski, 2005). In recent times the PsyD model has gained popularity in other areas of psychology, and its eventual infiltration of graduate education and training in OHP would appear inevitable. Innovation of this type is to be warmly welcomed if it serves to empower graduates with the confidence and competence required to operate as highly effective OHP practitioners in a diverse range of employing-organizations.

### Regional cooperation between educational providers

Cooperation and collaboration between psychologists has featured in the successful development of psychological science since Geneva played host to the first International Congress of Applied Psychology in 1920. Today, these same features characterize the very best in OHP research and education. Numerous inter-university arrangements exist to support the exchange of OHP students and staff. In Europe, many of these operate with the support of the European Commission.

Despite there being widespread evidence of cooperation between institutions in respect of OHP education, much of this activity is restricted to regional pockets. In Europe, for example, OHP educational provision mirrors the traditional clustering of OHP research activity in the north-western corner of the map. Similarly, on the American continent, the majority of OHP research emanates from North America. The distribution of OHP research was systematically analysed by Kang et al. (2008) who found that 462 of the 631 papers published in the Journal of Occupational Health Psychology and Work & Stress between 1996 and 2006 emanated from North America and Western Europe (Figure 11.4). The under-representation of central and southern European countries in OHP research and education is acute.

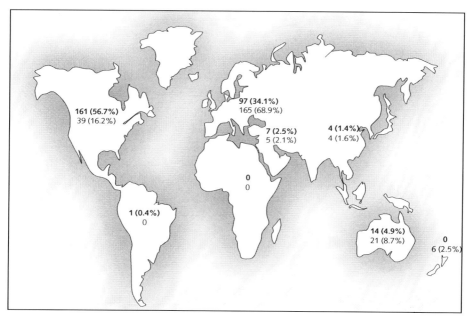

**Figure 11.4**  Global distribution of OHP research: 1996–2006. Figures in bold represent the *Journal of Occupational Health Psychology*; figures not in bold represent *Work & Stress* (Kang, Staniford, Dollard, & Kompier, 2008).

Furthermore, in those countries where OHP is reasonably well developed, activity has tended to cluster around a small number of institutions. This clustering of activity is detrimental to the global development of OHP education, research, and professional practice. It could be argued that as a result of the clustering of activity, those regions where OHP might have the greatest untapped potential, such as in developing economies, are failing to benefit from the discipline. Indeed, it is a matter for regret that Kang and colleagues' study revealed that over an 11-year period not a single study in the two leading OHP journals was located in an African nation.

It is therefore important that efforts are made to address the uneven clustering of OHP activity with a view towards maximizing its organizational impact. Educational provision offers an obvious starting point. Although a growing number of programmes exist, barriers to the implementation of new provision remain. Not least among such barriers may be uncertainty on the part of faculty members of the potential market for OHP programmes and challenges associated with programme implementation. These issues point towards the need for collaboration and cooperation between existing and new educational providers that is focused on the sharing of best-practice and establishment of integrated programmes, all the while supported by the discipline's representative bodies.

## Ensuring consistency with North American developments and promoting international cooperation

OHP educational initiatives in North America and Europe have traditionally evolved independently of one another. This independence does not reflect a rejection of the other's approach; rather, it represents the disparity between educational systems and the level at which programmes have been targeted. Nevertheless, since the early days of OHP, the discipline's European and North American protagonists have sought to innovate collaboratively. In respect of education this was recognized in 2002 in the EAOHP's strategy document which observed that 'While a degree of friendly rivalry may spur action and innovation, it is important that the European Academy works with APA and NIOSH and other relevant bodies as they emerge . . . to guarantee the promotion of the discipline through education' (p. 11). That approach, characterized by friendly and constructive cooperation, continues to be the modus operandi of interactions between OHP's European and North American representative bodies. This has resulted in a number of joint EAOHP-SOHP initiatives that have included research on the definition of OHP curriculum areas (Houdmont, Leka, & Bulger, 2008) and the establishment of a biennial book series *Contemporary occupational health psychology: Global perspectives on research and practice* (Houdmont & Leka, 2010). In recent times, cross-continental collaboration has received an additional boost following the revival in 2006 of the International Coordinating Group for Occupational Health Psychology (ICG-OHP) which exists to encourage collaboration between current and emerging representative groups in shaping the future of OHP. As interest in the establishment of new OHP programmes grows, the role of the ICG-OHP is likely to develop.

## Summary

Education and training is recognized by the discipline's representative bodies as key to the long-term sustainability of research and professional practice. Stimulated in part by influential reports from the EAOHP and NIOSH, researchers have begun to investigate the possible constitution of a core educational curriculum. Activities such as this will take on increasing importance in the next decade as steps are taken to standardize educational provision with a view towards facilitating the development of recognized professional training pathways for aspiring occupational health psychologists.

## Where Next for Professional Practice?

*Why has OHP professional practice lagged behind research and education?*
*How might professional practice be further developed?*

Schaufeli (2004) noted that 'OHP is both a scientific discipline and an applied field. That is, OHP tries to understand the underlying psychological processes, and seeks to improve occupational health, safety, and well-being' (pp. 503–504). Despite the uncontested position that OHP research is meaningless if not put into practice in the organizational context, developments in the support and formalization of professional practice have lagged behind those in research and, to a lesser extent, education. Indeed, there is by no means consensus on the question of whether there should be such a thing as a practitioner occupational health psychologist, a point illustrated in a series of interviews conducted with five leading figures from the North American OHP community (Sinclair, 2009). Responses to the question of whether there might ever be occupations with the OHP job title revealed mixed opinion. Lois Tetrick, editor of the *Journal of Occupational Health Psychology*, offered an answer that summed up the contrasting perspectives:

> Is there a need for jobs with the title of Occupational Health Psychologist? I guess I distinguish between the body of knowledge and an occupation. Is it necessary for a person who studies English to have a job that is titled 'English-or'? This doesn't exactly translate, but I think it demonstrates my point. On the other hand, if there were a demand in industry/government for Occupational Health Psychologists – who actually were OHPs and with duties that reflect OHP, not just a subset such as one might find among the related disciplines – then I do believe that OHP will be making a difference in reaching its goal of a safe and healthy work environment for workers. (p. 15)

There may be a number of reasons for the lack of progress made on the formalization of professional practice. Traditionally, most OHP practice has been conducted by academics on a consultancy basis as a supplement to, or as part of, their university work. Such individuals may have little incentive to establish formal regulatory structures given that they are generally not reliant on consultancy work as a primary income source, and, perhaps more importantly, in the eyes of organizations, their authority and credentials arise as a by-product of academic qualifications, position, reputation, and societal status, rather than membership of professional bodies or licensed status.

Nevertheless, as discussed in Chapter 1, in recent times professional practice in OHP has begun to flourish as individuals (often graduates of OHP programmes) have established themselves in business as a practising occupational health psychologist, or secured employment within an organization's occupational health or human resource division. The initiative of a small band of individuals has had a snowball effect; in some regions employment vacancy advertisements that make explicit reference to the services of an occupational health psychologist are no longer uncommon.

The growth in employment opportunities for OHP practitioners has been facilitated by a number of contemporary developments. Among these can be identified the establishment of OHP job descriptions that reflect common OHP research themes, topics taught within OHP curricula, and typical occupational health challenges, particularly those of a psychosocial nature. The OHP job description advanced by Fullagar and Hatfield (2005) (see Chapter 1) was, so far as the authors are aware, the first of its kind. Not only did it reflect the topics covered in North American OHP curricula in addition to the knowledge, skills, and abilities required by various OHP-related positions to which OHP practitioners might apply, it maintained consistency with Adkins' (1999) list of core competencies for OHP practice. These include the assertion that practice should be: (1) grounded in theory, (2) informed by a business plan capable of predicting financial and psychological benefits, (3) focused at the organizational 'systems' level that recognizes the dynamic and complex transaction between people and their environment rather than focusing at the individual level of analysis, and (4) open to transcending traditional boundaries and using knowledge and skills derived from a variety of domains. Fullagar and Hatfield's job description offers a valuable touchstone for future activities centred on the development of OHP practice.

The development of professional practice in OHP is to be welcomed given the applied nature of the questions addressed by the science. Indeed, it is somewhat surprising that unlike other related professions little has been done to establish a standardized training pathway, CPD provision, and governance structures for OHP practice. An opportunity exists for the discipline's representative groups to develop these elements, and others associated with the support of professional practice, in collaboration with national, regional, and international regulatory bodies. Failure to do so might lead to undirected growth in OHP professional practice that is fragmented, ungoverned, unsustainable, and ultimately damaging to the reputation of OHP. The possible future role of the representative bodies in the facilitation of professional practice is discussed below using three exemplars: professional training pathways, continuing professional development, and the regulation of professional practice.

## Professional training pathways

Many country-specific psychological regulatory bodies offer a pathway for the education and training of practitioners in disciplines allied to OHP. Few, if any, recognize OHP as a discrete specialty that warrants its own pathway and professional status. This situation results in prospective practitioners facing a requirement to train and qualify in a discipline related to but separate from OHP. In the UK context, for example, many prospective OHP practitioners report having felt compelled to pursue training in occupational psychology rather than OHP because the well-established occupational psychology training pathway leads to recognized professional status (Chartership) under the regulation of the British Psychology Society. No comparable system is offered in respect of OHP.

For OHP professional practice to establish itself as a career of choice for applied psychologists it is imperative that the discipline's representative bodies seek to actively engage with national, regional, and international regulatory bodies with a view towards the establishment of recognized training pathways. As previously discussed, the emergence of the professional doctorate may hold promise in this respect. However, prior to the initiation of discussions, the representative bodies would be well advised to ensure that consensus can be identified among the OHP community on the important features of OHP as a discipline. The absence of consensus would serve to weaken OHP's position at the negotiating table. Should formal regulation prove difficult to achieve in the existing climate, the EAOHP and SOHP might do well to consider the introduction of programme accreditation mechanisms independent of the involvement of regulatory bodies as a short–medium term solution.

## Continuing professional development

Taris (2006) noted that within OHP 'the degree to which a particular notion is cherished is not necessarily equalled by the degree to which it is supported empirically' (p. 102). By this he meant that there is a tendency within the discipline to hold onto established ways of doing things irrespective of whether the position is supported by research findings. Taris gives a number of examples of research topics that continue to attract academic interest despite limited evidence to support their viability or practical relevance, such as worksite physical fitness programmes and presumed links between human resource management practices on the one hand and employee well-being, skills, motivation, and productivity on the other. If professional practice in OHP is to gain the respect of employers, and its practitioners are to become an essential element within occupational health provision, it is essential that practitioners do not make the mistake of advancing particular notions and approaches to the protection and promotion of employee well-being that run counter to the empirical evidence. This potential pitfall could be minimized if practitioners were required to undergo continuing professional development (CPD) activities. These might include, among other things, attendance at conferences where state of the art research is presented and discussed. CPD governance structures do not, at present, exist for OHP practitioners and, indeed, could not do so in the absence of a professional OHP career structure. The development of a professional career structure ought therefore to be considered a priority activity for the discipline's representative bodies.

It is, of course, possible that EAOHP and SOHP could facilitate practitioner CPD activity outside of formal regulatory provision. This might be achieved with relative ease through the introduction of practitioner-oriented activity streams within the biennial conference of each body, attendance at which could be linked to unofficial CPD credits. Such activity streams would provide an arena for presentations by practitioners for practitioners, as well as presentations by academics with a focus on the translation of scientific findings for a practitioner audience.

## Regulation of professional practice

Upon conclusion of professional OHP training, in whatever form it might ultimately manifest, it is reasonable to expect that practitioners will be required to sign up to a code of conduct and ethics. It is difficult to forecast how OHP professional practice might be regulated across national borders upon the introduction of professional training pathways, but it might be speculated that adherence to a code could feasibly be monitored by discipline-specific representative groups, perhaps under the authority of national, regional, or international regulatory bodies. Such an arrangement would serve to empower the OHP representative bodies with responsibility for an important role in the governance of OHP professional practice. As the EAOHP and the SOHP work towards the professionalization of OHP practice it is likely that the merits and demerits of numerous regulatory mechanisms will have to be considered; how practice might best be governed in the future remains uncertain, but what is certain is that care needs to be taken to ensure that it is presided over in a way that protects the hard-won reputation of the discipline and its practitioners.

## Summary

The imperative to formalize OHP professional practice suggests an enhanced role for the discipline's representative bodies in the development of recognized training pathways and the regulation of practitioner activities. It is incumbent upon these bodies to actively engage with national, regional, and international psychological regulatory bodies to discern how OHP practice might be formalized and professionalized.

## SUMMARY AND CONCLUSIONS

- In a period of two decades OHP has established itself as self-sustaining applied scientific discipline.
- Future trends in OHP research will be determined by external forces related to developments in work organization, and forces internal to the discipline associated with the evolution of science.
- There exist a number of barriers to the publication of OHP research generated by and of use to practitioners. OHP is an applied branch of science; the international community needs to ensure that appropriate publication opportunities exist for the dissemination of practice-oriented research.
- Education and training is recognized by the discipline's representative bodies as key to the long-term sustainability of research and professional practice. Researchers have begun to investigate the possible constitution of a core educational curriculum; an important first step in the creation of programme accreditation procedures that are likely to exist as a key component within future professional training pathways.
- OHP is an applied discipline: the establishment of professional practice as a career of choice is important to its longevity.

- EAOHP and SOHP have an important role to play in the formalization and professionalization of OHP practice.

In the conclusion to his 1913 tract on the freshly defined specialty of 'economic psychology', Münsterberg noted that:

> What is needed to-day is not to distribute the results so far reached as if they were parts of a definite knowledge, but only to emphasize that the little which has been accomplished should encourage continuous effort. To stimulate such further work is the only purpose of this sketch. ('The future development of economic psychology' section, para. 1)

The same holds true for this textbook. The aim herein has not been to offer a comprehensive account of OHP activity; rather, the goal was to introduce some of the key issues that the discipline has addressed, to outline theoretical concepts that facilitate an understanding of mechanisms that operate in the dynamic transaction between work and health, and to consider some of the methodological approaches used to help us understand these transactions. Moreover, it is hoped that the chapters within this book have inspired you, the reader, to consider a rewarding career in OHP.

## Suggestions for Further Reading

Schaufeli, W. (2004). The future of occupational health psychology. *Applied Psychology: An International Review, 53,* 502–517.

Sauter, S., Brightwell, W., Colligan, M., Hurrell, J., Katz, T., LeGrande, D., et al. (2002). *The changing organization of work and the safety and health of working people: Knowledge gaps and research directions.* (DHHS [NIOSH] Publication No. 2002-116). Cincinnati, OH: National Institute for Occupational Safety and Health.

Sinclair, R. (2009). The future of OHP: The experts speak (Part II). *Society for Occupational Health Psychology Newsletter, 6,* 14–16 (May).

Taris, T. (2006). Bricks without clay: On urban myths in occupational health psychology. *Work & Stress, 20,* 99–104.

Theorell, T. (2006). New directions for psychosocial work environment research. *Scandinavian Journal of Public Health, 34,* 113–115.

## References

Adkins, J. A. (1999). Promoting organizational health: The evolving practice of occupational health psychology. *Professional Psychology: Research and Practice, 30,* 129–137.

Anderson, N., Herriot, P., & Hodgkinson, G. (2001). The practitioner-researcher divide in industrial, work and organizational (IWO) psychology: Where are we now and where do we go from here? *Journal of Occupational and Organizational Psychology, 80,* 175–184.

Barling, J. (2005). Editorial: And now, the time has come. *Journal of Occupational Health Psychology, 10,* 307–309.

Barnes-Farrell, J. (2006). History of OHP and education of OHP professionals in the United States. In S. McIntyre & J. Houdmont (Eds.), *Occupational health psychology: Key papers of the European Academy of Occupational Health Psychology: Vol. 7* (pp. 425–426). Maia, Portugal: ISMAI Publishers.

Cooper, C. L., & Dewe, P. (2004). *Stress: A brief history,* Chichester: Wiley-Blackwell.

European Academy of Occupational Health Psychology (2002). *The promotion of education in occupational health psychology in Europe.* Nottingham: European Academy of Occupational Health Psychology.

European Federation of Psychologists' Associations (2006). *EuroPsy – The European Certificate in Psychology.* Retrieved April 23 2008, from www.efpa.be/doc/EuroPsyJune%202006.pdf

Fullagar, C., & Hatfield, J. (2005). Occupational health psychology: Charting the field. Paper presented at the 20th annual conference of the Society for Industrial and Organizational Psychology, Los Angeles, CA (April).

González-Romá, V. (2009). Editorial: Changes in EJWOP and plans for the future. *European Journal of Work and Organizational Psychology, 18,* 1–7.

Houdmont, J., & Leka. S. (Eds.) (2010). *Contemporary occupational health psychology: Global perspectives on research and practice, Vol. 1.* Chichester: Wiley-Blackwell.

Houdmont, J., Leka, S., & Bulger, C. (2008). The definition of curriculum areas in occupational health psychology. *European Academy of Occupational Health Psychology Newsletter, 7,* 3–5 (February).

Houdmont, J., Leka, S., & Cox, T. (2007). Education in occupational health psychology in Europe: Where have we been, where are we now and where are we going? In J. Houdmont & S. McIntyre (Eds.), *Occupational health psychology: European perspectives on research, education and practice, Vol. 2* (pp. 93–114). Maia, Portugal: ISMAI Publishers.

Kang, S., Staniford, A., Dollard, M., & Kompier, M. (2008). Knowledge development and content in occupational health psychology: A systematic analysis of the *Journal of Occupational Health Psychology,* and *Work & Stress,* 1996–2006. In J. Houdmont & S. Leka (Eds.), *Occupational health psychology: European perspectives on research, education and practice, Vol. 3* (pp. 27–62). Nottingham: Nottingham University Press.

Leka, S., Khan, S., & Griffiths, A. (2008). *Exploring health and safety practitioners' training needs in workplace health issues.* Wigston, UK: Institution of Occupational Safety and Health.

Macik-Frey, M., Quick, J., & Nelson, D. (2007). Advances in occupational health: From a stressful beginning to a positive future. *Journal of Management, 33,* 809–840.

Münsterberg, H. (1913). *Psychology and industrial efficiency.* Boston: Houghton Mifflin.

Nielsen, K., Randall, R., & Christensen, K. B. (2010). Developing new ways of evaluating organizational-level interventions. In J. Houdmont, & S. Leka (Eds.), *Contemporary occupational health psychology: Global perspectives on research and practice, Vol. 1,* (pp. 21–45). Chichester: Wiley-Blackwell.

Norcross, J., Kohout, J., & Wicherski, M. (2005). Graduate study in psychology: 1971–2004. *American Psychologist, 60,* 959–975.

Raymond, J., Wood, D., & Patrick, W. (1990). Psychology training in work and health. *American Psychologist, 45,* 1159–1161.

Schaufeli, W. (2004). The future of occupational health psychology. *Applied Psychology: An International Review, 53*, 502–517.

Schneider, D., Camara, W., Tetrick, T., & Sternberg, C. (1999). Training in occupational health psychology: Initial efforts and alternative models. *Professional Psychology, 30*, 138–142.

Sinclair, R. (2006). Decisions and dilemmas in constructing an OHP training programme. In S. McIntyre & J. Houdmont (Eds.). *Occupational health psychology: Key papers of the European Academy of Occupational Health Psychology, Vol. 7* (pp. 431–432). Maia, Portugal: ISMAI Publishers.

Sinclair, R., Hammer, L., Oeldorf Hirsch, A., & Brubaker, T. (2006). Do academics and practitioners agree on perceived occupational health priorities? Paper presented at the *APA/NIOSH Work Stress and Health Conference*, Miami, FL (March).

Smith, A. (2001). Perceptions of stress at work. *Human Resource Management Journal, 11*, 74–86.

Smith, A., Johal, S., Wadsworth, E., Davey Smith, G., & Peters, T. (2000). *The scale of perceived stress at work: The Bristol stress and health at work study.* Sudbury, UK: HSE Books.

Smith, A., Wadsworth, E., Moss, S., & Simpson, S. (2004). *The scale and impact of drug use by workers.* Sudbury, UK: HSE Books.

Taris, T. (2006). Bricks without clay: On urban myths in occupational health psychology. *Work & Stress, 20*, 99–104.

Tetrick, L. (2006). Editorial. *Journal of Occupational Health Psychology, 11*, 1–2.

Tetrick, L., & Ellis, B. (2002). Developing an OHP curriculum that addresses the needs of organizations and labor unions in the USA. In C. Weikert, E. Torkelson, & J. Pryce (Eds.), *Occupational health psychology: Empowerment, participation and health at work.* (pp. 158–161). Nottingham: I-WHO Publications.

Wadsworth, E., Dhillon, K., Shaw, C., Bhui, K., Stansfeld, S., & Smith, A. (2007). Racial discrimination, ethnicity and work stress. *Occupational Medicine, 57*, 18–24.

Wallis, A., & Dollard, M. (2008). Local and global factors in work stress: The Australian dairy farmer exemplar. *Scandinavian Journal of Work, Environment and Health Supplements, 6*, 66–74.

# Author Index

Adkins, J. A. 6, 7, 316
Agut, S. 204
Ajzen, I. 258
Akalin-Baskaya, A. 237, 241
Albertsen, K. 115, 117–18, 175
Allen, J. 167, 169
Allen, T. 26
Allen, T. D. 71
Allen, T. J. 237
Amaranto, E. 77
Andersen, A. 41
Anderson, N. 304
Arkkelin, D. 228
Armenakis, A. 176
Arneson, H. 178
Arnold, J. 104
Arvey, R. D. 78
Aust, B. 141, 143, 173, 175
Avey, J. B. 209, 215, 216
Avolio, B. J. 196, 199, 208–9, 215, 216

Baade, E. 18
Babbie, E. 280
Bachiochi, P. D. 277–8, 279
Baker, D. 44
Baker, E. A. 281
Bakker, A. B. 44, 67, 72, 196, 199, 201,
    203–7, 209–10, 211–12
Bal, P. M. 212
Baldursson, E. 5, 12, 14, 225

Bambra, C. 95, 117
Bandura, A. 215, 258
Barham, L. 72
Baric, L. 169
Barker, M. 75
Barling, J. 9–10, 15, 23, 201, 303
Barlow, C. 126
Barnes-Farrell, J. 8, 307
Barnett, R. C. 214
Baron, R. A. 74–5
Baron, R. M. 237
Baruch, Y. 289
Bate, R. 126
Bauer, G. 147, 149
Beale, D. 42, 225, 243
Beck, J. S. 98
Beckers, D. G. J. 288
Beehr, T. A. 42, 62, 70–1, 107
Beerman, B. 143
Belkic, K. 44
Bell, C. 180
Ben-Avi, I. 61
Benedict, J. O. 238, 239
Berlyne, D. E. 229
Bernstein, I. H. 292
Bhagat, R. S. 104, 105
Bhui, K. 305
Biggs, A. 72, 77, 78
Biner, P. M. 240–1
Black, C. 255

Blewett, V. 168
Block, J. 209
Blonk, R. W. B. 113
Bohle, P. 117
Bolger, N. 288
Bond, F. W. 91, 93, 96, 98, 108, 113–14,
    172, 283–4
Bongers, P. M. 66, 286
Bonnes, M. 245
Bordeaux, C. 71
Bosma, H. 44
Boswell, W. R. 67
Boubekri, M. 241
Bowditch, J. 181
Boyer, L. L. 241
Branch, S. 75–6
Brand, J. L. 237, 240
Brandenburg, U. 141
Branigan, C. 197–8
Brehm, J. W. 233
Brehm, S. S. 233
Brewerton, P. 277
Brill, M. 238, 243
Briner, R. 90
Brinley, A. 71
Broersen, S. 44
Bronzaft, A. L. 242
Brooks, M. J. 237
Brough, P. 68, 69, 71–2, 74, 75–8
Brown, J. M. 78
Brown, S. L. 207
Brubaker, T. 11, 308
Bruck, C. S. 71
Bulger, C. 12, 309–10, 314
Bunce, D. 90, 96, 98, 108–9, 114–16,
    283
Buono, A. 181
Burke, R. 70, 183, 184
Burns, R. L. 241
Büssing, A. 23, 24
Butler, A. B. 78
Butler, D. L. 240–1
Butler, R. J. 78
Bybee, R. 169

Caillard, J.-F. 263
Camara, W. 10, 308

Cameron, K. S. 200
Campagna, A. F. 96
Campbell, D. T. 107, 283, 285
Campbell, E. A. 78
Campion, M. A. 245
Candy, B. 39, 44
Cannon, W. B. 36
Canter, D. V. 227
Caplan, R. D. 38
Carlopio, J. R. 237–8
Carrere, S. 244
Carroll, J. M. 203
Cartwright, S. 58, 80, 169
Casper, W. J. 71
Castellano, C. 77
Caulfield, N. 159
Caza, A. 200
Cecil, M. A. 98
Celebi, M. 237, 241, 242
Chan, D. K. 73, 77
Chang, D. 159
Chen, P. Y. 6, 8, 19, 64, 71
Chen, S. 72
Cheng, G. H. 73
Choudry, R. M. 258
Christensen, K. B. 115, 175, 304
Christensen, L. B. 270
Chu, C. 166, 167, 169
Coffey, K. 216
Cohen, A. 19
Cohen, S. 42, 69, 230, 234
Cohn, M. A. 216
Combs, G. M. 215
Conner, M. 63
Cook, T. D. 107, 115, 283, 285
Cook, T. J. 116
Cooper, C. L. 23, 38, 47, 58–60, 63, 65, 68,
    80–1, 95, 101, 105, 140, 159, 169, 172,
    179, 199, 258, 299
Cordray, D. 117, 183
Corneil, D. 168
Cornoni-Huntley, J. 162
Cottrell, R. 169
Cousins, R. 46, 169
Cox, S. 36, 46
Cox, T. 3, 5, 7, 12, 14, 21–3, 25, 31–2, 34,
    36–7, 41–2, 45–7, 57, 89, 100, 104–5,

Cox, T. (*Cont'd*)
109, 115, 116, 125–7, 129–34, 136, 139, 152, 225, 234, 306
Craik, K. H. 227
Crosby, F. 214
Csikszentmihalyi, M. 195, 199

Dahl-Jørgensen, C. 117, 183
Dahlgren, G. 162, 163
Danon, E. 74
Darr, W. 102, 104, 113
Davey Smith, G. 305
David, S. 77
Davis, A. 288
Davis, L. 169
Davy, J. 69
Daykin, N. 168
de Cuyper, N. 25
De Geus, A. 253
de Jonge, J. 44, 59, 212
de Lange, A. H. 25, 40, 66, 68, 286
DeArmond, S. 6, 8, 19
Deci, W. L. 206
Deelstra, J. T. 274
Degioanni, S. 77
DeJoy, D. M. 217
Demerouti, E. 44, 67, 72, 204–5, 206–7, 209–10, 211, 212, 258
Demmer, H. 162, 177, 178, 180, 184
Dempster-McClain, D. 214
Dewe, P. 37, 47, 65, 95, 101, 299
Dhillon, K. 305
Dhondt, S. 40
Diener, E. 79
Ditman, D. 95
Dobson, L. D. 116
Dodson, J. D. 36
Doherty, L. 179
Dollard, M. F. 10, 159, 300, 302, 313
Donaldson-Fielder, E. 99
Dormann, C. 44, 59, 113
Driscoll, T. 166
Dryden, W. 98
Ducki, A. 143, 173, 175
Dutton, J. 200, 201, 208, 211
Duvall-Early, K. 238, 239
Dwyer, D. 65
Dwyer, S. 166, 169

Eakin, J. M. 162
Eby, L. T. 71
Eden, D. 61, 212
Edington, D. M. A. 167
Edwards, J. R. 38
Egan, M. 95, 117
Einarsen, S. 75
Einhorn, H. J. 127
Ekberg, K. 178
Ekman, P. 196
Elacqua, T. C. 62
Elfering, A. 66, 288
Ellis, A. 98
Ellis, B. 11, 308
Ellis, N. 168
Ellsworth, P. 196
Elo, A. L. 92, 93, 96, 116
Elshaugh, C. 159
Emery, F. 18
Ervasti, J. 92, 96, 116
Etzioni, D. 72, 74, 212
Euwema, M. C. 205
Evans, G. W. 225, 234–5, 237, 240, 242, 243, 244–5

Faragher, B. 81, 95, 105, 159
Feild, H. 176
Feldman, D. C. 63, 73
Feldman, J. 162
Fenlason, K. 70–1
Ferguson, E. 37, 63
Fife-Schaw, C. 78
Fiksenbaum, L. 70
Fineman, S. 201
Finkel, S. M. 216
Finnegan, M. C. 241
Fishbein, M. 258
Fiske, D. 285
Fiske, S. T. 244
Flaxman, P. E. 91, 93, 96, 108, 113–14, 283
Floderus-Myrhed, B. 17
Folkman, S. 37, 45, 47, 67, 235
Forman, S. G. 98, 100
Fox, H. 15
Fox, M. 65
Frame, R. 78
Frankenhaeuser, M. 17
Fredrickson, B. L. 196, 197–8, 201, 208, 216

Fredslund, H.  115, 175
French, J. R. P.  38
French, W.  180
Frese, M.  113
Frick, K.  136, 254
Fried, Y.  63
Friesen, W. V.  196
Fullagar, C.  8, 14–15, 307, 315–16
Furnham, A.  228, 239

Gadeyne, S.  73
Ganster, D. C.  65, 95, 177, 182
Gardell, B.  17
Gardner, D.  237–8
Gareis, K. C.  214
Gelfand, M. J.  75
Gerstberger, P. G.  237
Geurts, S.  94, 172, 179
Giga, S. I.  95, 105, 137, 139, 159, 184
Gini, A.  166
Glanz, K.  163
Glasner, T.  286
Glazer, S.  62
Glencross, P. M.  244
Goetzel, R.  163, 258
Golaszewski, T.  167, 258
Golden-Biddle, K.  281
Goldenhar, L.  178, 182, 183, 184–5, 281
González-Romá, V.  203, 304
Gottlieb, B. H.  72
Gotts, C.  36
Grant, A. M.  207–8
Grebner, S.  288
Green, K.  162
Green, M.  61
Greenberg, C.  178
Greenglass, E.  70
Greenleaf, R.  253
Griffin, R. W.  74
Griffin-Blake, C. S.  217
Griffiths, A.  3, 11, 15, 31–2, 45, 47, 57, 89, 100, 104–5, 109, 115, 125–6, 129–34, 139, 175, 182, 185, 235, 309
Grundemann, R.  94
Gutzwiller, F.  147

Hakanen, J. J.  206–7, 211
Halbesleben, J. R. B.  204

Haldorsen, T.  41
Hale, A. R.  258
Hall, E. M.  41, 42, 61, 69
Hallqvist, J.  44
Hamilton, P.  162
Hammer, L.  11, 308
Hanisch, K.  74
Harden, A.  159, 166–8, 175, 179, 183
Harris, S.  176
Hasle, P.  258
Hatfield, J.  8, 14–15, 307, 315–16
Heaney, C.  95, 163, 169, 178, 281
Heerwagen, J. H.  241
Heimstra, N. W.  226
Heiskanen, M.  77
Herold, J.  214
Herriot, P.  304
Herst, D. E. L.  71
Heuven, E.  210
Hiramitsu, K.  242
Hobfoll, S. E.  206
Hochschild, A.  213
Hodgkinson, G.  304
Hoel, H.  75
Hogarth, R. M.  127
Hollon, S. D.  240
Holmes, T. H.  73
Holt, D.  176
Holtom, B. C.  289
Hovden, J.  258
Houdmont, J.  12, 32, 47, 105, 306, 309–10, 314
Houtman, I. L. D.  66, 286
Hox, J. J.  281
Huang, Y. H.  6, 8, 19
Hudson, P.  258
Hughes, E. L.  63
Hull, R. B.  241
Hulme, A.  173
Hurrell, J. J.  2, 15, 20, 182
Hurst, N. W.  126

Iddekinge, C. H.  245
Inness, M.  9–10
Israel, B. A.  281
Ito, A.  242

Jackson, P. 67
Jackson, S. 293
Jackson, S. E. 108, 110, 202
Jacobshagen, N. 66
Jamal, M. 60
Janssen, P. P. M. 212
Jex, S. M. 62
Jick, T. 184
Johal, S. 305
Johansson, G. 17, 244
Johns, G. 102, 104, 113, 115
Johnson, D. 225, 237, 242, 243
Johnson, J. V. 17, 41, 42, 61, 69
Johnson, S. 59, 81
Jones, F. 63, 66, 70

Kahn, R. 18, 38, 61
Kahn, W. A. 212
Kalliath, T. 68, 71, 72, 76
Kang, S. Y. 10, 300, 302, 312–13
Kaplan, A. 237
Karanika-Murray, M. 32, 46, 105
Karasek, R. 17, 32–3, 39–44, 52, 60, 63,
    65–6, 68, 91, 104, 144, 241, 258, 301
Katz, T. 178
Kaufmann, G. 70
Kawakami, N. 44
Keegel, T. 89, 159, 166
Kelloway, E. K. 72, 74
Kelly, P. J. 46, 169
Kenny, D. A. 237, 285
Kerlinger, F. N. 270, 271, 272
Kerr, A. 184
Kessler, R. C. 214
Keyton, J. 281
Khan, S. 11, 46, 309
Kim, J. S. 96
King, L. 199
Kinicki, A. 69
Kinnunen, U. 74
Kirchmeyer, C. 213
Kissling, D. 147
Kittel, F. 173
Kivimaki, M. 44
Kjaerheim, K. 41
Kleinman, J. 162
Kogan, M. 71

Kohlbacher, M. 149
Kohler, J. 173, 175, 177, 178, 182
Kohout, J. 312
Kolt, G. S. 36
Kompier, M. 3, 10, 23, 66, 94, 103, 109, 111,
    113, 117, 143, 172, 175, 177, 179,
    181–2, 274, 286, 300, 302, 313
Kornhauser, A. 18
Kotter, J. 177, 181, 184
Kouvonen, A. 44, 258
Kramer, D. M. 166, 179, 181
Kremen, A. M. 209
Kristensen, T. S. 23–4, 103, 109, 113, 143–4,
    258, 274
Kuendig, S. 147
Kuhn, K. 143

Laboute, R. 163–4, 165
LaMontagne, A. D. 89, 140, 159, 166–7,
    169, 173, 175–6, 177, 178–9
Landsbergis, P. A. 44, 61, 89, 117, 178
Lapierre, L. M. 72
Larson, M. 208
Lawler, E. 19
Lawrence, C. 42, 225
Lazarus, R. S. 37, 41, 45, 47, 67, 235
Le Blanc, P. M. 42, 281
Le Fevre, M. 36, 38
Leana, C. R. 73
Leather, P. J. 42, 225, 241, 243, 244
LeBlanc, M. M. 74
Lee, H. B. 270, 271
Lee, K. 75
Lee, L. 225
Lee, S. 46, 169
Lee, Y. 237, 240
Lehmann, K. 147, 149
Leiter, M. P. 37, 202, 204, 215
Leka, S. 11, 12, 45–6, 125–6, 130–1, 133,
    138, 152, 306, 309–10, 314
LePine, J. A. 59, 60
LePine, M. A. 59, 60, 67
Lepore, S. J. 242
Levecque, K. 73
Levi, I. 49
Levi, L. 17, 49
Levine, S. 18

Levy-Leboyer, C. 228
Lewin, K. 32, 50, 244, 281
Lewis, R. 99, 101
Liao, H. 78
Linan, L. 167
Lindstrom, K. 23
Lipsey, M. 117, 183
Liu, C. 280
Llorens, C. 143–4
Lloret, S. 203
Locke, K. 281
Lockwood, A. 71
Loivette, S. 91, 93, 108, 113
Lopez, S. 199
Louckx, F. 73
Louie, A. M. 89, 159
Lovegrove, T. E. 241
Luthans, F. 196, 199, 200, 208, 209–10, 214, 215–16
Luz, J. 61
Lyubomirsky, S. 207

McCaig, R. H. 46, 169
McCauley, C. 211
McCoy, J. M. 225, 226, 229, 239, 244–5
McFarling, L. H. 226
McGrath-Higgins, A. L. 217
Macik-Frey, M. 8, 9, 10, 299, 300, 302, 307
Mackay, C. J. 36, 46, 169
McMillan, B. 63
McWilliams, J. 41, 177
Maes, S. 40, 173
Maher, A. 230, 237, 238, 239–40
Makuc, D. 162
Mancuso, R. A. 197–8
Manfredi, S. 179
Manimala, M. 76
Margolis, B. 19
Marmot, M. 40, 44, 162
Marshall, J. 58
Martin, C. 184
Maslach, C. 202, 215, 293
Maslow, A. H. 65
Matheny, J. 36
Mattila, P. 92, 96, 116
Mauno, S. 74
Mauthner, M. 159

Mehrabian, A. 239–40
Meier, L. L. 66
Meijman, T. F. 206
Melamed, S. 61
Menard, S. 286
Menon, S. 62
Merritt, D. 68
Michie, S. 172
Miechenbaum, D. 98
Mikkelsen, A. 61, 68, 117, 183
Milgram, S. 231
Millward, L. 277
Milton, D. K. 244
Mitchell, R. 77
Moen, P. 214
Moghadam, L. Z. 42
Moncada, S. 143–4
Moodie, R. 173
Moore, E. O. 241
Moors, G. 73
Morgeson, F. P. 245
Moss, S. 305
Moyles, P. 70
Mulder, G. 206
Mullarkey, S. 67
Mumford, T. V. 246
Münsterberg, H. 13, 18, 303, 319
Munz, D. 173, 175, 177, 178, 182
Murphy, C. 166, 171
Murphy, L. R. 20, 90, 93–4, 97, 107, 109, 113, 117, 177, 182
Murta, S. G. 106, 159, 175, 185

Naidoo, J. 161, 181
Nakasone, T. 242
Narayanan, L. 62
Neenan, M. 98
Nelson, D. 8, 9, 199, 299
Ncssc, R. M. 207
Neuman, J. H. 74–5
Newsham, G. R. 244
Ng, T. W. 63
Niedhammer, I. 77
Nielsen, K. 115, 117–18, 175, 183, 185, 304
Nielsen, N. 90
Nilsson, I. 240–1
Noack, H. 160

Noblet, A. J.  41, 95, 105, 159, 166, 169, 171,
    175–6, 177, 179
Norcross, J.  312
Norman, S. M.  209, 215, 216
Nowack, K.  172
Nunnally, J. C.  292
Nutbeam, D.  162, 179, 185
Nutting, S. M.  78
Nytrø, K.  117, 183

Oakley, A.  159
O'Brien, G.  178
O'Connell, B.  64
O'Connor, D. B.  63
O'Connor, M.  149
O'Donnell, M.  167
O'Driscoll, M. P.  47, 62, 65, 68, 71–2, 76,
    78, 95, 101
Oeji, P.  40
Oeldorf Hirsch, A.  11, 308
Ogaard, T.  61
O'Hara, K.  107
Ohly, S.  210
Oksanen, T.  258
Oldenburg, B.  106, 159
Oldham, G.  230
O'Learly-Kelly, A. M.  74
Oliver, S.  159
Olson-Buchanan, J. B.  67
Orians, G. H.  241
Ornstein, S.  236
Osborn, D. P.  243
Ostry, A.  89, 159
O'Toole, J.  19

Parker, D.  258
Parker, S.  67, 210
Parkes, K. R.  63, 70, 94, 95, 103–4, 113
Passchier, W. F.  242
Passchier-Vermeer, W.  242
Patera, J. L.  215
Patrick, W.  2, 6, 21, 298, 303
Paul, G.  99
Peersman, G.  159
Peeters, M. C.  42, 281
Peiro, J. M.  23, 204
Pek, J.  216

Pelletier, K.  169
Perhoniemi, R.  211
Peter, R.  44
Peters, T.  305
Peterson, C.  199
Peterson, M.  258
Petticrew, M.  95, 117
Plomp, H. N.  94, 109, 112, 115
Podsakoff, N. P.  59, 60
Poelmans, S. A.  68
Polanyi, M. F. D.  162, 166, 167, 170–1, 177,
    178, 179
Pollard, T. M.  73
Popovich, M.  71
Probst, T. M.  73
Pyrgas, M.  225

Quick, J. C.  2, 7, 8, 9, 21, 299
Quinlan, M.  117
Quinn, R.  19, 61, 200

Rafaeli, E.  288
Rahe, R. H.  73
Ramsay, S.  75
Randall, R.  89, 99–101, 104, 109, 115–18,
    126, 129–31, 134, 139, 304
Raphael, D.  163
Rasband, G.  163
Raver, J. L.  75
Raymond, J.  2, 6, 21, 298, 303
Reuterwall, C.  44
Reynolds, S.  90, 175, 185
Rial González, E.  3, 5, 12, 14, 31, 46, 89,
    126, 130, 132, 225
Rice, R. W.  243
Richardson, K. M.  89, 95, 100, 104,
    112–14
Richman, J. A.  75
Rimer, B.  163
Rodwell, J.  41, 177
Rose, G.  162
Rosen, L. N.  42
Rospenda, K. M.  75
Rothstein, H. R.  89, 95, 100, 104, 112–14
Rozin, P.  211
Russell, J. A.  203
Ryan, R. M.  206

Saksvik, P. 117, 183
Salanova, M. 203, 204, 217–18
Satzer, R. 130
Sanderson, K. 106, 159
Santos, A. 225
Sauter, S. L. 2, 15, 20, 23, 90, 93–4, 97, 109, 113, 117, 300–1
Schaubroeck, J. 68, 95
Schaufeli, W. B. 44, 196, 199–201, 203–4, 206, 210–12, 217–18, 281, 299, 302
Scheck, C. 69
Schein, E. 252
Schene, A. H. 113
Scheurs, P. J. G. 44, 289
Schkade, D. 207
Schmid, M. 147
Schnall, P. L. 44
Schneider, D. 10, 308
Scholten, H. 173
Shulte, P. 183, 185
Schwartz, B. 211
Sears, L. E. 73
Secchiaroli, G. 245
Seligman, M. E. P. 79, 195, 199, 209, 233
Selye, H. 35, 36
Semmer, N. K. 66, 94, 111, 115, 117, 288
Sepmeijer, K. J. 289
Shadish, W. R. 115, 283
Shain, M. 166, 179, 181
Shannon, D. 99
Shapiro, D. 175, 185
Sharp, J. J. 100
Shaw, A. 159, 168
Shaw, C. 305
Sheldon, K. M. 199, 207
Shepard, L. 19
Shipley, M. 162
Shirom, A. 63, 206
Siegrist, J. 23, 32, 33, 39, 43, 44, 52, 91, 258, 301
Sime, W. E. 95
Simpson, S. 305
Sinclair, R. 7, 11, 73, 307, 308–9, 315
Siu, O. L. 76
Skattebo, A. 78
Slesina, W. 141
Smith, A. 305

Smith, A. P. 59
Smith, B. 169
Smith, D. M. 207
Smith, W. 169
Smulders, P. 94
Snoek, J. 61
Snyder, C. R. 199, 209, 215
Solomon, L. Z. 241
Sonnenfeld, J. 232
Sonnentag, S. 212, 288
Sorensen, G. 172
Sparks, K. 63, 81, 94–5, 103–4, 113
Spector, P. E. 26, 62, 64, 68, 272, 280, 288
Staines, G. 19
Stajkovic, A. D. 209
Staniford, A. K. 10, 300, 302, 313
Stanks, J. 126
Stansfeld, S. 39, 40, 44, 305
Starren, A. 256
Steel, P. 75
Steinberg, J. 77
Stephenson, K. 109
Stern, R. M. 127
Sternberg, C. 10, 308
Stokhols, D. 258
Stone-Romero, E. F. 283
Stroem, S. 74
Strümpfer, D. J. W. 208
Sullivan, L. 225, 243
Sullivan, S. E. 104, 105
Sundstrom, E. 238, 241, 243
Sutherland, V. J. 140
Sutton, M. 71
Symonds, C. 34

Taira, K. 242
Tait, R. 126, 127
Tan, G. Y. 73
Taris, T. W. 40, 44, 66, 204, 281, 286, 287, 289–90, 299, 317
ten Brummelhuis, L. 25
Terra, N. 95
Tetrick, L. 10–11, 15, 23, 201, 303, 308
Theorell, T. 17, 23, 39, 44, 91, 104, 258, 301, 304, 305
Thirlaway, M. 36, 46
Thoits, P. A. 258

Thompson, S. 169
Thomson, L. 126
Thosrud, E. 18
Toivanen, H. 98
Tomas, J. 46
Toppinen-Tanner, S. 211
Town, J. P. 243
Trenberth, L. 47
Troup, C. 47
Tsutsumi, A. 44
Tucker, J. S. 61, 68
Tugade, M. M. 197–8
Turner, N. 201
Tvedt, S. 90, 115, 117–18

Uhmann, S. 44
Ulrich, R. S. 225, 235, 241, 245
Ursin, H. 18

Vallance, D. A. 166
van der Heijden, K. A. 127
van der Hek, H. 94, 109, 112, 115
van der Klink, J. J. L. 113
Van der Vaart, W. 286
Van Dijk, F. J. H. 113
Van Harrison, R. 38
Van Rhenen, W. 204
Van Scheppingen, A. 259
van Vegchel, N. 44
van Veldhoven, M. 44
Vandenberg, R. J. 217
Vanroelen, C. 73
Vartia, M. 75
Vedung, E. 117
Veitch, R. 228, 244
Verbrugge, L. M. 214
Verhoeven, C. 173
Vink, P. 94
Vinokur, A. D. 207
Vischer, J. 225, 234, 236, 237, 240
von Hippel, C. 230, 237, 238, 239–40

Wadsworth, E. 305
Waldron, I. 214
Wall, T. 67
Wallis, A. 302
Walters, M. D. 244

Warr, P. B. 66, 68
Watts, J. 225
Weiner, S. P. 277–8, 279
Wellens, B. T. 59
Wells, M. 244
West, M. J. 241
Westman, M. 61, 72, 74, 212
Wethington, E. 214
Whatmore, L. 169
Wheeler, A. R. 204
Whitehead, M. 95, 117, 162, 163
Whitelaw, S. 184
Wicherski, M. 312
Wiezer, N. 40
Williams, R. M. 214
Williams, S. 172
Willis, T. A. 42
Willness, C. R. 75
Wills, T. 69
Wilson, J. F. 258
Wilson, M. G. 217
Wimbush, E. 184
Wohlwill, J. F. 232
Wolfe, D. 61
Wood, D. 2, 6, 21, 298, 303
Wright, T. A. 199
Wrzesniewski, A. 210–11
Wyon, D. 240–1

Xanthopoulou, D. 204–5, 207, 210, 211

Yamamoto, T. 242
Yassi, A. 168
Yerkes, R. M. 36
Yildirim, K. 237, 241, 242
Yin, R. K. 281
Youssef, C. M. 196, 197, 208

Zachartos, A. 201
Zahn, L. G. 237
Zajack, M. 73
Zapf, D. 75, 113
Zavela, K. 169
Zawacki, R. 180
Zickar, M. 18
Zimring, C. 228
Zwetsloot, G. 136, 252, 254, 256–7, 259

# Subject Index

ABCDE approach 209
'absence of disease' 160, 162, 166
absenteeism 51, 261
    health and 57, 71, 75, 81
    intervention and 96, 102, 104, 111, 113
    risk management 141, 142
absorption (work engagement) 203–4
Acceptance and Commitment Therapy 98
accreditation 5, 310, 317
action plan 217
    Istas21 method 144, 145–6
    risk management 129–30, 132, 134–5
    SME-vital 147–8
    workplace health promotion 175, 176,
        181–3
action research 281–2
    participative 94, 95, 96, 108
actions (environmental psychology) 227
active interventions 97
'active jobs' 39–40, 65
acute stress response 36
adaptation
    diseases of 36
    General Adaptation Syndrome 35–6
    level theory 232, 233, 238–9
added-value 257, 259
advertisement (job specification) 13–15
aggression 74–5, 77
alarm stage (GAS model) 35
altruism 167, 195, 207

Amalgamated Engineering Union 17
*American Journal of Public Health* 42
American Psychological Association 18, 20,
        26, 199, 314
André Büssing Memorial Prize 24–5
anti-social behaviour 59, 74–6
anxiety 11, 19, 38, 47
    health and 61–2, 64, 65, 66, 67
apathy 205
applied psychology 23, 64, 110, 212, 312
appraisal 89, 94, 117, 237
    cognitive 37, 45, 46, 97
arousal level 229–30, 231, 233
artefacts 252
ASSET model 81
attention process 239
audit 14, 133–4
    stress 80–1, 149–50
    wellness 217–18
automatic thoughts 99
autonomy 63, 64, 205, 206

Brabantia Project 172–3
basic assumptions 252
behaviour
    anti-social 59, 74–6
    -constraint approach 232–3
    –environment relationships 226–34
    physical work environment and 236–43
    positive organizational 199–204

behaviour (*Cont'd*)
  responsible 257–9
  *see also* cognitive behavioural therapy
    (CBT)
behavioural outcome measures 104
behavioural risk factors 163–5
Best Paper Prize 24
'big questions' (societal needs) 51
biofeedback 99–100
body mass index 44
boredom 205
British Psychology Society 316
broaden-and-build theory 197, 216–17
buffering effects 61, 66, 67–8, 69–71
bullying 74–6, 77–8, 129
burnout 35, 42, 74, 77
  research methods 270–2, 275, 281, 293
  work engagement and 202–4, 205–6,
    215
business network for CSR 259–60
BUSINESSEUROPE 153

capabilities (psychosocial risk
    management) 135, 140
capacity building 182, 217
capital
  human 254, 255, 264
  psychological 208–10, 211, 215, 216
  social 254, 255, 258
cardiovascular health/disease 17, 24, 39,
    41–2, 162, 198–9
career development 125
case studies 280–1
causal inferences 275, 276
CEEP 153
challenge stressors 59–60, 67
Chartership 316
chronic fatigue syndrome 35
classical measurement theory 291
closed-ended questions 278
code of conduct 317–18
cognition 37, 89, 94
cognitive appraisal 37, 45, 46, 97
cognitive behavioural models 258
cognitive behavioural therapy (CBT) 91,
    97–8, 99, 112, 113
cognitive mediation 233–4
cognitive performance 103

cognitive stressors 59
commitment 62, 204
Committee on Cardiology in Occupational
    Health 24
common method variance problem 305
communication (internal/external) 184
compensation hypothesis 241
complete panel design 286–7
concepts (research design) 274–5
concurrent validity 293
confidentiality 101, 143, 285–6
conservation of resources theory 206–7
constraint (behaviour) 232–3
construct validity 292, 293
contemporary theory (stress) 34–6
  interactional 37–44
  transactional 44–8
content analysis 280
content validity 293
context/contextualization 137–8, 278
contingency planning 184
continuing professional development 316,
    317
continuous improvement, risk and
    135–6
continuous learning 264
control 44–5, 271
  health promotion and 161–2
  locus of 66, 68
  perceived 240, 242–3
  perceived loss of 232–3
  personal 9, 58, 65, 67, 68
  procedures (research) 275–6
control group 106–11, 116, 276
convergence of education 311–12
convergent validity 293
cooperation (in education) 312–14
coordinating group 175–8, 184
Copenhagen Burnout Inventory 24
Copenhagen Psychosocial Questionnaire
    (CoPsoQ) 24, 143–6
coping
  interactional theories 37, 41, 45, 48
  strategies 67, 97, 100, 231, 234–5,
    242
  transactional theories 37, 47, 48
core curriculum 12, 306–10
coronary heart disease 40

corporate culture 136, 250–66
  business case for well-being 261–5
  corporate social responsibility and 256–7,
    259–60
  health management and 257–9
  key issues/definitions 251–3
  partnership-based 262–3
  workplace health promotion 253–5
corporate social responsibility (CSR) 252,
    255–60
corporate values 250–1, 257–9
criterion-related validity 293–4
Cronbach's alpha 291–2
Cross-sectional research 286–90
crossover theory 72, 73, 74
CSR Europe 259–60, 261
CSR Laboratory 259, 261
cue controlled relaxation 98–9
culture
  corporate see corporate culture
  learning 264
  organizational 78, 117, 125, 134, 250–66
culture–work–health model 258
curriculum 10–11
  core 12, 306–10
  existing (scrutiny of) 8–9
cynicism (in burnout) 202, 203, 205

damage (four Ds) 196, 200–1, 302
Danish Society of Psychosocial Medicine 24
data analysis 145
data collection 145
  data richness/depth 278
  qualitative approach 277–82
  quantitative approach 277–9, 283–90
death (in GAS model) 35
decision authority 65, 68
dedication (work engagement) 203, 204
deductive approach 271
Delphi study 3, 11, 309
Demand–Control–Support model 41, 42,
    69–70, 91
Demand–Control theory 32, 39–44, 60–1,
    63, 65–6, 68–9, 144, 301
Demand-Induced Strain Compensation 44
Demand–Skill–Support model 44
Demands–Resources model 44, 67, 205–6
dependent variables 35, 275, 283, 304–5

depersonalization 42
depression 35, 61, 64, 68, 113, 216
design
  concepts and variables 274–5
  research 270, 273–7
  workspace 234–6
design interventions
  evaluating 105–12
  promotion of well-being 88–90,
    93–100
  workplace health promotion
    programmes 175, 176, 181–3
designing jobs (to do good) 207–8
DG Employment, Equal Opportunities &
    Social Affairs 152
DG Health & Consumers 152
diary studies 210, 212–13, 282, 287–8
disease
  absence of 160, 162, 166
  four Ds approach 196, 200–1, 302
  prevention strategies 169
disorder (four Ds) 196, 200–1, 302
distributive justice 43
divergent validity 293, 294
doctorate in OHP (DOHPsy) 312
downsizing 73, 74
dysfunction (four Ds) 196, 200–1, 302

early response-based theories 34–6, 43
early stimulus-based theories 34–5, 43
economic factors 79
economic psychology 13, 18, 303
economic stressors 73–4
education 10–11
  core curriculum 12, 306–10
  future directions 299, 306–14
  see also curriculum; training
effect evaluation 102–14
efficacy (engagement) 202, 216
Effort–Reward Imbalance (ERI) theory 32,
    39, 43–4, 49, 91, 301
EfH Group 253, 262–5
emergency response (GAS model) 35
emerging psychosocial risks 3–4
emotion 37
  negativity bias 195–9
  positive 196, 197–9, 216–17
emotional distress 43, 214

emotional exhaustion  67
emotional intelligence  46
emotional labour  77
emotional strain  110
emotional stressors  59
emotional support  69–70
Employee Assistance Programmes  101
employee development agreement  217
employees
    needs assessment  175, 176, 178–80
    perception of intervention  118
    primary intervention by  93
    in risk management process  138–9
    turnover  57, 72–3, 75, 78, 110, 113, 141
    *see also* workers
energy (engagement)  202, 203–4
engagement *see* work engagement
'engineering' models  34–5
Enterprise for Health (EfH) network  253,
    262–5
environmental conditions  125
environmental load  230–2, 233
environmental psychology (of workplace)
    definitions  226–9, 233
    environment–behaviour relationships
        226–34
    stress perspective  234–6
    well-being and  236–43
equipment (psychosocial hazards)  125
equity theory  39, 43
errors (in measurement)  291
espoused core values  252
ethics  140, 252, 257–8, 317–18
ETUC  153
ETUI  153
ETUI–REHS  153
EuroFound  261
Europe  126–7
    education (development)  314
    OHP (defined)  5–6
    OHP (emergence)  16–18
    PRIMA–EF  46, 124, 152–3
European Academy of OHP (EAOHP)  5–6,
    20, 21–5, 303–4, 306–7, 309–11, 314, 317
European Agency for Safety and Health at
    Work (EU-OSHA)  3–4, 31, 46, 124,
    152, 168, 256

European Certificate in Psychology
    (EuroPsy)  311–12
European Commission's 6th Framework
    Programme  152
European Council's Framework Directive
    89/391/EEC  126, 128–9
European Federation of Psychologists'
    Associations  311
European Foundation for the Improvement
    of Living and Working Conditions
    152–3
European Framework for Psychosocial Risk
    Management  46, 124, 152–3
*European Journal of Work and
    Organizational Psychology*  179, 304
European Network for Workplace Health
    Promotion (ENWHP)  147, 169, 171
eustress  36
evaluation
    action plans  132
    health circles  143
    settings-based approach  174–5, 185–6
    SME-vital  148–9
    Work Positive  149–52
    workplace health promotion  185–7
evaluation of interventions
    criteria  102–5
    effect  102–14
    process  114–18
    research designs  105–12
evidence-informed practice  137
exhaustion
    in burnout  202, 203, 205
    stage (GAS model)  35
experiences  227
experimental research  273–4, 275, 276
expert surveys  10–12
expertise  46, 182
explanation goal (research)  270–1
expression of hostility  74, 75
external communication  184
external expertise  182
external factors (research)  300–1
external policies (corporate social
    responsibility)  256
externalization, ethics and  140
extraversion  239

face validity 292, 293
facial expressions 196, 197
family–work conflict 59, 63, 71–2, 77, 78, 125
family–work satisfaction 63
fatigue 16, 35, 287
Federal Association of Company Health Insurance Funds (Germany) 141–3
Federal Institute for Occupational Safety and Health (Germany) 152
feedback 45, 49, 127
    health circles 141, 142
feedforward 45, 49
female workers 77–8
field experiment 216–17
field setting 273, 276
fight-or-flight response 36
financial returns/turnover 210, 211
Finnish Institute of Occupational Health (FIOH) 152
first-line monitoring 179
fit for purpose 47, 139, 227–8
flexible working hours 96
focus groups 151, 153, 179, 279–80
fortigenesis 208
Foundations of behavioural research (Kerlinger) 272
four Ds approach 196, 200–1, 302
framing (micro interventions) 215

'gain spiral' 206
gender differences
    bullying 76
    crossover theory 72
    stress 77–8
    working hours 63
General Adaptation Syndrome (GAS) 35–6
Germany 152
    health circles 141–3
Global Plan of Action for Workers' Health 129
globalization 10
goal setting 175–6, 180–1, 209, 215–16

harassment 74, 75
    see also sexual harassment
harm 35, 125, 126, 128–30

Hawthorne effect 107
hazards
    psychosocial 2–4, 19, 45, 124–53
    work-related stressors 58–76
health
    care (costs) 166–7
    corporate 250–3
    definitions 160–6, 253
    determinants 162–3, 173
    issues 175, 176, 178–80
    role (in workplace) 263–4
    work organization and 57–81
health circles 141–3, 147, 148
health management
    corporate culture and 254–5, 257–9
    implementation of processes 257
    integrated approach 254–5
Health of Munition Workers Committee 16
health promotion, workplace (WHP) 141
    case example 157–9
    corporate culture and 253–5
    corporate social responsibility 256–7
    definitions 160–5
    individual-based approach 165–9, 173
    settings-based approach 165–6, 169–86
Health Promotion Switzerland 146–9
health psychology 5, 6
Health and Safety Authority 149–52
Health and Safety Executive 46, 47, 129, 256
    Management Standards 149–52
Health and Safety at Work Act (1974) 17
Health Scotland 149–50
Health and Welfare Canada 178
healthy organization 264
Healthy Work (Karasek and Theorell) 17
high-risk occupations 76–7
'high strain job' 39–40, 65
hindrance stressors 59, 60, 67
history (quantitative research) 283–4
hope 208–9, 210, 215, 216
horizontal bullying 75
horizontal control 68
human capital 254, 255, 264
    see also employees
human resource management 10, 11, 13, 75, 255, 308
hypotheses/hypothesis-testing 271–2, 281

identification
    of key factors (risk management) 139
    work engagement and 203–4
impact evaluation 185–6
implementation
    health circles 142–3
    health management initiatives 257
    interventions 88–90, 93–101
    Istas21 145–6
    SME-vital 147–8
    well-being strategy 260
    Work Positive 150–1
    workplace health promotion 174–6,
        183–4
independent variables 275, 283, 304
individual-based approach (workplace
    health promotion) 165–9, 173
individual ability 46
individual interventions 116, 119
individual lifestyle factors 159, 162–3,
    165–9, 170, 172, 173
inductive approach 271
Industrial Fatigue Research Board 16
Industrial Health Education Society 17
Industrial Health Research Board 16
industrial psychology 1
ineffectiveness (in burnout) 202
influence 10, 110
information acquisition 127
informational support 68
inhibition 239, 240
Institute of Occupational Medicine
    146, 149
Institute of Social and Preventive
    Medicine 146
Institute of Work, Health and Organisations
    (IWHO) 21–3, 152, 225
instrumental support 68
instrumentation (quantitative
    research) 284
integrated health management
    approach 254–5
inter-personal conflict 64
interactional theories/models 34, 35,
    37–44, 45
internal communication 184
internal consistency 291

internal factors (research trends) 300
internal policies (CSR) 256
internal validity 276
internalization of values 257–9
International Commission on Occupational
    Health (ICOH) 24, 152
International Congress of Applied
    Psychology 312
International Coordinating Group for
    Occupational Health Psychology 26,
    311, 314
*International Journal of Workplace Health
    Management* 304
International Labour Organization
    (ILO) 124–5, 127–9, 152, 258–9
International Society of Behavioral
    Medicine 24
interpersonal relationships 125
intervention
    different levels 139–40
    future research 300–1, 302
    group 106, 108, 110, 116
    implementation 175, 176, 183–4
    positive 214–18
    risk reduction and 131–2, 134–5
interventions (promoting well-being)
    design 88–90, 93–100
    evaluation 102–18
    implementation 88–90, 93–101
    levels of 90–3
    primary 91–7, 101, 107, 110, 112–19
    role of theory 88–90
    secondary 92, 97–101, 112–16, 119
    tertiary 92, 100–1, 119
interviews 279–80
intrinsic motivation 302
introversion 239
involvement (engagement) 202
Iso-Strain model 41–2, 63
Istas21 method 143–6
Italian Institute for Occupational Safety and
    Prevention (ISPESL) 152

Jakarta Declaration 161
job(s)
    active 39–40, 65
    advertisement/specification 13–15

content 125
control 59, 63, 65–8, 108, 118–19,
    125, 144
crafting 210–13
designed (to do good) 207–8
insecurity 73, 74, 81
passive 39, 65
re-design intervention 92, 95, 101
-related skills training 100
resources 205–7, 209–12, 258
strain 39–40, 44, 65, 110, 241–2, 258
Job Demand–Control–Support model 41,
    42, 61, 69–70, 91
Job Demand–Control theory 32, 39–44,
    60–1, 63, 65–6, 68–9, 144, 301
Job Demands–Resources model 44, 67,
    205–6, 209, 258
job satisfaction 19, 141, 209, 302
    health and 61, 68, 71, 72
    physical workspace and 238, 240–3
    stress and 39, 51, 102, 104–5, 113
    well-being and 102, 104–5, 113
*Journal of Applied Psychology* 64, 110,
    212–13
*Journal of Occupational Health Psychology*
    2, 9, 10, 20, 26, 50, 108, 298–300, 302,
    307–8, 312–13, 315
*Journal of Occupational and Organizational
    Psychology* 81, 116
*Journal of Organizational Behavior* 62
journals (publication challenges) 303–5

key groups (in studies) 280
knowledge creation 281, 282
knowledgeable experts 46

laboratory setting 273, 274
leadership 258
    socially responsible 264–5
    style 252–3, 279
learned helplessness 232–3, 242
learning
    culture 264
    lifelong 264
    *see also* education; training
Life Events instrument 73
life satisfaction 216

lifelong learning 264
lifestyle factors (health promotion) 159,
    162–3, 165–9, 170, 172, 173
'living company' 253
living conditions 162, 164
locus of control 66, 68
longitudinal designs 286–90, 300
'loss spiral' 206
loving-kindness meditation (LKM) 216
'low strain job' 39–40, 65
Luxembourg Declaration 147, 169

McKinsey's 7-S model 251
macro interventions 215, 217–18
management
    science 50
    support 175–7
Management of Health and Safety at Work
    Regulations (1999) 126
Management Standards (HSE) 149–52
manipulation check 106, 110, 117
Maslach Burnout Inventory 202
matching hypothesis 42, 67
maturation (quantitative research) 284
measurement (research methods) 290–4
meditation training 216
mental health 11, 18, 66, 79, 216, 261
meta-analysis 60, 63, 75, 112
micro interventions 214–17
Mitsubishi 281
moderating effects 61, 66, 67–8, 69–71
moderator–mediator variable 237
monitoring resources 184
motivation 10, 19, 60, 215, 302
    intervention and 103, 111, 117
    risk management 137, 141, 147, 148
    stress and 39, 43
movement, adaptation and 232
multi-method approach (needs
    assessment) 179
multidisciplinary perspective 6–7, 14
multimodal stress management
    training 100
multitrait-multimethod approach 207
musculo-skeletal disorders 40, 66
music (environmental load model) 231–2
myocardial infarction 44

National Advisory Environmental Health
    Committee 19
National Health Service 149–52
National Institute of Occupational Health
    (Copenhagen) 24
National Institute for Occupational Safety
    and Health (NIOSH) 19, 20, 200, 300,
    307, 314
natural science paradigm 105–6
nature themes (in offices) 241
needs, changing (identifying) 184
needs assessment 175, 176, 178–80
negative affectivity 64
negativity bias 195–9
noise (in workplace) 235, 240, 242–3
non-auditory effects of noise 242–3
non-equivalent pre-test–post-test control
    group 283
non-experimental research 273–5, 285–6
non-intervention (research) 302
non-response 289
non-screeners (stimulation) 239
North America
    education (development) 314
    OHP (definition) 5, 6–7
    OHP (emergence) 18–21

observational methods 274, 279
obstructionism 74
obtrusive observations 279
occupational groups (high risk) 76–8
occupational health psychologists 13–15
occupational health psychology
    accreditation of programmes 310
    achievements/developments 298–9
    definitions 2–8
    education (future directions) 306–14
    emergence (as discipline) 15–21
    environmental psychology and 234–6
    future directions 298–319
    positive 194–219, 302–3
    professional practice (future) 314–18
    representation of 21–6
    research methods 269–95
occupational safety and health 172
    corporate social responsibility
        and 256–7, 258

risk management approach 126–7
Occupational Safety and Health Act
    (1970) 19
Occupational Safety and Health
    Administration (US) 11, 308
offices/office work 226, 230–2, 236–40, 242
online intervention 215–16
open-ended questions 280
open-plan office 230–2, 236–40, 242
optimism 161, 200, 208–9, 210, 211, 215,
    216
organization of work (hierarchical
    model) 300–1
organizational-level interventions 92, 104,
    105, 113–14, 115, 119
organizational commitment 62, 204
organizational constraints 64
organizational culture 78, 117, 125, 134,
    250–66
organizational health 253
organizational outcome measures 104–5,
    113–14, 115, 119
organizational psychology 48, 50
organizational social capital 258
organizational stress health audit 149–50
organizational values 250–3
organizational well-being 177, 178
Ottawa Charter 162–6, 168, 169–72
outcome evaluation 185–6
    interventions 102–5, 113–17
outcomes
    risk management process 136
    work–family conflict 71–2
outliers 289
outsourcing 74, 137
overload 234
overt aggression 74
overtime (diary study) 288
ownership, risk management and 135, 137

participants 273–4, 278
participative action research 94, 95, 96, 108
participative approach 135, 138–9
partnership 262–3
'passive jobs' 39, 65
passive secondary interventions 97
pathogenesis 208

perceived control 240, 242–3
perceived loss of control 232–3
perception 37, 45, 94, 118, 237
performance 208–10, 229–30, 231
Person–Environment Fit theory 37–9,
    100, 228
person–environment relationship 226–34
person–job fit 211
personal control 9, 58, 65, 67, 68
physical stressors 59
physical workspace *see* environmental
    psychology (of workplace)
physiological measures 103–4
physiological models 35–6
physiological risk factors 163–5
placebo effect 106, 116
planned behaviour, theory of 258
planning (settings-based WHP) 174–83
police work 77
policy, risk management and 127–9, 136–7
Polish Central Institute for Labour
    Protection (CIOP-PIB) 152
positive emotions 196, 197–9, 216–17
positive interventions 214–18
positive occupational health pyschology
    (POHP) 160, 194–219
  examples of 202–14
  future research 302–3
  negativity bias 195–9
  positive interventions 103, 214–18
  positive psychology 199–202
positive organizational behaviour
    (POB) 199–200
Positive Organizational Scholarship
    movement 200
positive psychology 199–202
positive spillover 213–14
post-test scores 107–9, 215, 284
pre-test–post-test control group 283
pre-test scores 107–9, 215, 284–5
prediction goal (research) 271
predictive validity 293
PRIMA-EF 46, 124, 152–3
primary interventions 7, 91–2, 101, 134
  effectiveness 112, 113–14, 119
  evaluation 107, 110, 115, 117, 118–19
  implementing 93–6, 97

primary prevention 7
priorities (WHP programme) 175–6, 180–1
prioritization 4, 145, 239
privacy (in offices) 237, 238–40, 242
proactive behaviour 212–13
problem-solving 142, 147, 217
  interventions 97, 108
  strategy 126, 127
problem analysis 92
process based theories 34, 35, 37, 45
process evaluation 114–18, 183, 184, 186
productivity 16, 18, 19, 57, 75, 254, 255,
    261, 263–4
professional practice (future) 314–18
professional training 306–7, 316–17
programme evaluation (WHP) 185–6
*Promotion of Education in OHP in Europe*
    (EAOHP) 306
*Psychological Bulletin* 285
psychological capital 208–10, 211, 215–16
psychological contract 43–4
psychological outcomes (interventions)
    103, 105, 113
psychological reactance 232–3
*Psychological Science in the Public*
    *Interest* 79
psychological strain 61, 63, 65–7, 69, 71–3
psychological well-being 69, 71, 73, 102,
    105, 240
psychology
  negativity bias in 195–9
  positive 199–202
  *see also* positive occupational health
    psychology (POHP)
*Psychology and Industrial Efficiency*
    (Münsterberg) 13
psychometrics 290–4, 305
psychosocial hazards 2–4, 19, 45, 124–53
psychosocial interventions 92, 94
psychosocial questionnaire 24, 143–6
psychosocial risk 3–4, 17–18, 163–4
psychosocial risk management 32, 46
  best practice 136–40
  international examples 140–53
  key aspects/stages 132–6
  model 130–2
  workplace level 124–53

psychosocial stressors 58–76
psychosocial work environment 24
PsyD programmes 312
publication challenges (future) 303–6
publicity 145
published research themes 9–10

qualitative research 47, 117, 277–82
quality circles 142
Quality of Employment Survey series 19
quantitative research 277–9, 281, 283–90
quasi-experiments 106–7, 110, 117, 274,
    275, 276, 281, 283–5
questions (research) 270, 271–2, 278

random assignment 283
randomized control trials 106, 111, 139
Rational Emotive Behavioural Therapy 98
reactance 232–3
recall bias 288
recovery 35, 212–13
redundancy 73
regional cooperation (education) 312–13
regression to the mean 284–5
regulation of professional practice 317–18
relaxation training 98–9, 100, 112–13
reliability
    of interventions 102–4, 107, 119
    risk management process 137, 139
    of variables 290, 291–2, 305
research
    design 105–12, 270, 273–7
    emergence of OHP 15–21
    exploratory 278
    future directions 299–306, 312–13
    process 270–3
    published themes 9–10
    qualitative 47, 117, 277–82
    quantitative 277–9, 281, 283–90
    work-related stress 49–52
research methods 269–95
    data collection 277–90
    designing a study 270, 273–7
    measurement and psychometrics 290–4
    research process 270–3
resilience 46, 50, 208–9, 210, 215–16
resistance stage 35

resources 184, 205–7, 209, 258
response based theories 34, 35–6, 43
response rates (surveys) 288–90
responsible behaviour 257–9
    see also corporate social responsibility
restriction-of-range effects 289
reverse buffering 70
rewards 258
    effort and 32, 39, 43–4, 49, 91, 301
risk
    conditions 163–4
    definitions 128–30
    occupational groups 76–8
    reduction 127, 132, 134–5, 141
    see also psychosocial risk management
risk assessment 46
    interventions 92, 105, 119
    risk management 127–8, 130–4, 141,
        144, 146, 150–1
risk management
    in occupational safety and health 126–7
    policy and 127–9
    process 46, 136
    see also psychosocial risk management
role ambiguity 61, 62, 64, 69, 95–6, 110,
    125, 181
role changes (at work) 59, 73–4
role conflict 61–3, 64, 69, 110, 125
role overload 61, 62, 69
role stressors 61–2

safety culture 258
salutogenesis 208
Scandinavian Journal of Work, Environment
    and Health 24
schemas (in interventions) 98
Scientific Committee on Psychosocial
    Factors (ICOH) 24
scientific journals 303–5
scientific method 270–1
screeners (stimulation) 239
script (of sessions/interviews) 280
secondary interventions 7, 92, 101, 134, 139
    effectiveness 112–13, 114, 119
    evaluation 115, 116
    implementing 97–100
selection (quantitative research) 284–5

selectivity, response rates and 289
self-actualization 65
self-efficacy 66, 68, 116, 195, 208–9, 210, 211, 215
self-esteem 69, 210, 211, 302
self-fulfilment 65
self-managed teams (SMTs) 182
self-regulation 234
self-report questionnaires 103–5, 113
self-report surveys 207, 242
sensitivity, intervention 102, 104, 119
sensory stimulation 232
servant leadership 253
setting (research study) 273–4
settings-based approach 165–6, 169–73
    evaluation 174–5, 185–6
    implementing 174–5, 183–4
    planning 174–83
sexual harassment 75, 78, 281
shared values 250–1, 263, 264, 265
Shell 258
single-item approach 305
situational analysis 180
skill discretion 65
small and medium-sized enterprises
    (SMEs) 109, 139, 146–9, 256
SME-vital 146–9
social capital 254, 255, 258
social density 227
social dialogue 138–9
social ecological models 258
social and environmental psychology 5–6
social epidemiology 43
social learning theory 258
social psychology 32, 43, 48, 50
social reciprocity 43–4
social stimulation 232
social support 110, 234, 258, 274, 275
    health and 59, 61, 68–71
    POPS 205–6, 209
    stress and 41–2, 44–5, 51
societal needs (stress research) 51
Society for Occupational Health Psychology
    (SOHP) 6, 18, 20–1, 23, 25–6, 303–4,
    309–10, 311, 314, 317–18
Society of Psychosocial Medicine 24
socio-environmental approach 163–4, 165

sociology of work 50
sociotechnical intervention 94
Solomon four-group design 107, 110
Spain (Istas21 method) 143–6
staff see employees
stakeholder interviews 135
starter workshops (SME–vital) 147
steering committee (health circles) 142
steering groups 96, 151
stimulation 232, 239
stimulus-based theories 34–5, 43
stimulus screening 239–40
strain 62, 64
    crossover theory 72
    emotional 110
    hypothesis 39–40, 41, 42, 65
    job-related 44, 110, 241–2, 258
    psychological 61, 63, 65–7, 69, 71–3
stress 274
    audit 80–1, 149–50
    -buffering hypothesis 69–70
    environmental psychology 234–6, 239
    process 45
    resistance 46
    threshold 34
Stress (Cox) 23
Stress Inoculation Training (SIT) 98
stress management 58
    interventions 88–119
    multimodal training 100
    relaxation training 98–9
    training (SMT) 97
stressors 35, 92, 280
    challenge 59–60, 67
    cognitive 59
    economic 73–4
    emotional 59
    hindrance 59, 60, 67
    physical 59
    role 61–2
    traumatic operational 77
    workplace psychosocial 58–76
Stroop test 240
structural based theories 34, 35, 37–45
structural equation modelling 110, 207
study design 286–7
sub-goaling strategy 215, 216

sunlight penetration (in offices) 241–2
supportive climate 209, 210
surveys/survey design 285–6
Switzerland (SME-vital) 146–9

tertiary interventions 92, 134, 139
  effectiveness 119
  implementing 100–1
test–retest reliability 292
testing (quantitative research) 284
theoretical saturation 280
theory development 271
thought–action repertoire 196, 197
threats 34–6, 45, 49, 67, 73
TNO Quality of Working Life – Work and
  Employment (Netherlands) 152
trade unions 11, 17, 143–6, 168, 308
training 6, 8, 10, 20, 97
  future directions 299, 306–14
  pathways (professional) 5, 316–17
  relaxation 98–9, 100, 112–13
transactional theories/models 34, 35, 37,
  41, 44–8, 67
transactions 227
translation phase 130–1, 134–5
'traumatic operational stressors' 77
true experiments 283–5
true score 291
Type III errors 116–17

UEAPME 153
uncertainty 41, 61–2, 73, 74, 80
underemployment 73
underload 234
undoing hypothesis 197–9
unemployment 51, 73, 79, 204
UNIZO 153
unobtrusive observation 279
upwards bullying 75
US Department of Health, Education and
  Welfare 19
Utrecht Work Engagement Scale
  (UWES) 204

validity
  internal 276
  interventions 102–4, 106, 107, 119

risk management process 137
  threats to 106
  variables 290, 292–4, 305
values
  corporate 250–1, 257–9
  internalization of 257–9
  leadership 264–5
variables 274–6, 286–7, 290–2, 304–5
vertical control 68
victimization (at work) 129
vigour (work engagement) 203, 204
violence (at work) 74, 75
vitamin model (mental health) 66

'waiting list' group 106
well-being 3, 13, 14, 20, 50, 79, 81, 205, 212,
  274
  business case for 261–5
  corporate culture and 250–66
  corporate social responsibility 256–7,
    258, 259–60, 261
  environmental psychology 234, 236–43
  interventions to promote 88–119
  psychological 69, 71, 73, 102, 105, 240
  psychosocial stressors 57–61, 63–4,
    66–71
  subjective 66
*Well-being and Performance* 99
wellness audit 146, 148, 217–18
windows (in workplace) 240–2
*Women in Management Review* 179
work
  conferences 96
  demand 59, 60–3
  environment (interventions) 92
  –family conflict 59, 63, 71–2, 77, 78, 125
  –family interface 213–14
  intensification 264
  –life balance 64, 179
  –non-work interface 96
  plan preparation 145
  schedule 125
work-related stress 8, 19, 23, 31–52, 301
  research agenda (future) 49–52
  theories (observations) 48–9
  theories (overview) 32–3
  theories (taxonomy) 34–48

Work, Stress and Health conference
    series 20, 26
*Work in America* 19
work engagement 202–4, 206–7, 210–13,
    215, 217
Work Environment and Cardiovascular
    Diseases conference 24
*Work and Health* (Kahn) 18
Work Organisation Assessment
    Questionnaire (WORQ) 46
work organization and health 57–81
    psychosocial stressors 58–76
    special groups of workers 76–8
Work Positive – Prioritizing Organizational
    Stress Resource 150
Work Positive pack 149–52
*Work and Stress* 2, 10, 23, 24, 25, 50, 299,
    300, 302, 312–13
workers
    health (determinants) 170–1
    special groups 76–8
    *see also* employees
working conditions 205, 262–3
    health promotion 159, 162, 164, 168,
        172, 180

job crafting 210–13
    risk management and 130, 143, 147
    stress and 40, 43
    well-being and 96, 104, 110, 113–14
working group (Istas21 method)
    145
working hours 59, 63–4, 81, 96
workload 64, 125, 206, 275, 286
workplace
    environmental psychology of 225–45
    fit for purpose 228–9
    health promotion 141, 157–88, 253–5
    noise 235, 240, 242–3
    psychosocial risk management 124–53
    psychosocial stressors 58–76
    role of health in 263–4
    violence 74, 75
    windows in 240–2
workshops 24, 147, 153, 218
World Health Organization (WHO) 129,
    152, 159, 160, 161, 253
    Ottawa Charter 162–6, 168, 169–72

Yerkes-Dodson model/law 36, 229–30,
    231

Printed in Great Britain
by Amazon